The Eighteenth Century
The Intellectual and Cultural Context
of English Literature, 1700–1789

Longman Literature in English Series

General Editors: David Carroll and Michael Wheeler
University of Lancaster

For a complete list of titles see pages x and xi

The Eighteenth Century

The Intellectual and Cultural Context of English Literature, 1700 – 1789

James Sambrook

Longman

London and New York

LONGMAN GROUP LIMITED
Longman House, Burnt Mill, Harlow
Essex CM20 2JE, England
Associated companies throughout the world

Published in the United States of America
by Longman Inc., New York

First published 1986

BRITISH LIBRARY CATALOGUING PUBLICATION DATA
Sambrook, James
   The eighteenth century—The Intellectual and cultural context of
   English literature, 1700–1789—(Longman literature in English series)
   1. England—Intellectual life—18th century
   I. Title
   942.07   DA485

ISBN 0-582-49306-4 csd
ISBN 0-582-49305-6 ppr

LIBRARY OF CONGRESS CATALOGUING IN PUBLICATION DATA
Sambrook James.
   The eighteenth century —the intellectual and cultural context of English literature,
1700–1789.

   (Longman literature in English series)
Bibliography: p.
   Includes index.
   1. English literature— 18th century—History and criticism. 2. Great Britain—
Intellectual life—18th century. 3. Great Britain—Civilization—18th century.
I. Title. II. Series.
PR441.S33 1986   820'.9'005   84–29705
ISBN 0–582–49306–4
ISBN 0–582–49305–6 (pbk)

Set in 9/10pt Bembo (Linotron 202)
Produced by Longman Singapore Publishers (Pte) Ltd.
Printed in Singapore

Contents

List of Plates

Acknowledgements

We are grateful to the following for permission to reproduce illustrations: BBC Hutton Picture Library (Plate 2); the trustees of the British Museum (Pls 1, 2, 11, 16 & 18); Derby Art Gallery (Pl. 13); *Country Life Magazine* (Pls 5 & 20); C. Cottrell-Dormes esq., Rousham (photo: Courtauld Institute of Art) (Pl. 17); The National Maritime Museum, London (Pl. 14); Tate Gallery (Pl. 9); Warburg Institute (Pls 6,7 & 8); the Marquess of Tavistock & trustees of the Bedford estates (Pl. 10); and Kenneth Woodbridge (Pl. 19).

Editors' Preface

The multi-volume Longman Literature in English Series provides students of literature with a critical introduction to the major genres in their historical and cultural context. Each volume gives a coherent account of a clearly defined area, and the series, when complete, will offer a practical and comprehensive guide to literature written in English from Anglo-Saxon times to the present. The aim of the series as a whole is to show that the most valuable and stimulating approach to literature is that based upon an awareness of the relations between literary forms and their historical context. Thus the areas covered by most of the separate volumes are defined by period and genre. Each volume offers new informed ways of reading literary works, and provides guidance to further reading in an extensive reference section.

As well as studies on all periods of English and American literature, the series includes books on criticism and literary theory, and on the intellectual and cultural context. A comprehensive series of this kind must of course include other literature written in English, and therefore a group of volumes deals with Irish and Scottish literature, and the literatures of India, Africa, the Caribbean, Australia, and Canada. The forty-six volumes of the series cover the following areas: pre-Renaissance English Literature, English Poetry, English Drama, English Fiction, English Prose, Criticism and Literary Theory, Intellectual and Cultural Context, American Literature, Other Literatures in English.

David Carroll
Michael Wheeler

Longman Literature in English Series

General Editors: David Carroll and Michael Wheeler
University of Lancaster

Pre-Renaissance English Literature

English Literature before Chaucer
English Literature in the Age of Chaucer
English Medieval Romance

English Poetry

English Poetry of the Sixteenth Century
* English Poetry of the Seventeenth Century *George Parfitt*
English Poetry of the Eighteenth Century, 1700 –1789
* English Poetry of the Romantic Period, 1789 –1830 *J. R. Watson*
English Poetry of the Victorian Period, 1830 –1890
English Poetry of the Early Modern Period, 1890 –1940
English Poetry since 1940

English Drama

English Drama before Shakespeare
English Drama: Shakespeare to the Restoration, 1590 –1660
English Drama: Restoration and the Eighteenth Century, 1660 –1789
English Drama: Romantic and Victorian, 1789 –1890
English Drama of the Early Modern Period, 1890 –1940
English Drama since 1940

English Fiction

English Fiction of the Eighteenth Century, 1700 –1789
English Fiction of the Romantic Period, 1789 –1830
* English Fiction of the Victorian Period, 1830 –1890 *Michael Wheeler*
English Fiction of the Early Modern Period, 1890 –1940

English Prose

English Prose of the Renaissance, 1550 –1700
English Prose of the Eighteenth Century
English Prose of the Nineteenth Century

Criticism and Literary Theory

Criticism and Literary Theory from Sidney to Johnson
Criticism and Literary Theory from Wordsworth to Arnold
Criticism and Literary Theory from 1890 to the Present

The Intellectual and Cultural Context

The Sixteenth Century
The Seventeenth Century
* The Eighteenth Century, 1700 –1789 *James Sambrook*
The Romantic Period, 1789 –1830
The Victorian Period, 1830 –1890
The Twentieth Century: 1890 to the Present

American Literature

American Literature before 1865
American Poetry of the Twentieth Century
American Drama of the Twentieth Century
American Fiction, 1865 –1940
American Fiction since 1940
Twentieth-century America

Other Literatures

Irish Literature since 1800
Scottish Literature since 1700

Indian Literature in English
African Literature in English
Caribbean Literature in English
Australian Literature in English
* Canadian Literature in English *W.J. Keith*

* *Already published*

Author's Preface

The chronological limits of this volume have been determined by the overall plan of the series to which it belongs. One terminal date has proved easy to observe, and so I rarely find it necessary to continue discussion of any topic beyond 1789: the other date, 1700, has necessarily been disregarded to the extent of allowing for a discussion of Newton and Locke because a study of eighteenth-century intellectual life which omitted these two men would be like *Hamlet* without either the Prince or the ghost of his father.

The arrangement of material in my first five chapters under broad topical headings (Science, Religious Ideas, Philosophy, Politics and History, and Aesthetics) may appear to have some logic, as indicating five distinct realms of ideas or objects of study (external nature, God, the mind, society, and art), but the reader will soon discover that these divisions are to a very considerable degree arbitrary. That the most important writers, for instance, Newton, Locke, Shaftesbury, Addison, Hume, Priestley, Burke, and Adam Smith, each appear in more than one chapter is evidence not so much of the survival of many-sided 'Renaissance men' into the eighteenth century as of the close interrelations of all forms of intellectual enquiry in that period. There was no boundary between ethics, economics, and history, or between ethics and aesthetics, or between science and religion; there was not even a terminology to define those particular boundaries if they could have been drawn: the word 'aesthetics' was not used at all, and 'science' and 'economics' were not used in their modern sense during our period. Although what we call science (then still called natural philosophy) was beginning to become more specialized towards the end of the century, a philosopher was still able to look upon all those fields of knowledge as his proper province, and, as the pages of the *Spectator* and the *Gentleman's Magazine* show all too clearly, an educated man could still take an interest in them all. To a student of the eighteenth century it seems at times almost as if every path of thought communicates with every other: astronomy provides aids to navigation and proofs of the existence of God, current political and economic thought influences the interpretation of ancient Roman history, the empirical and mathematical methods of science are applied to aesthetics and moral philosophy; such instances, large and small, could be multiplied almost indefinitely. It follows that much of my material could be transposed from one of the following chapters to another without damage to the general plan.

Chapters 1 to 5, taken as a whole, are intended to give some sense of the intellectual climate in which eighteenth-century imaginative literature grew and flourished. Chapter 6, 'Visual Arts', is concerned with parallel imaginative works in the four arts, architecture, sculpture, painting, and gardening, which, according to Sir Joshua Reynolds, 'address themselves primarily and principally to the imagination'. Chapter 7, 'Models', is intended to give some notion of the wide eclecticism of eighteenth-century culture: the 'intellectual climate' to which I have referred produced effects as varied as the English weather, because the winds of cultural influence in this period blew from remote areas in the north, east, and west, as well as from their old prevailing quarter, the Mediterranean south. Chapter 8 is a 'Conclusion' in which perhaps nothing is concluded, for I make no attempt to impose a factitious unity upon the intellectual life of the eighteenth century: I merely indicate some of the connections between the material of the earlier chapters, giving most attention to the idea of the imagination because this is likely to be of most interest to students of literature; finally, I question some of the labels that have been attached to the eighteenth century by critics and historians. The plates are not intended to constitute a epitome of eighteenth-century art, but to illustrate phases and varieties of taste; they are as pertinent to Chapter 7 as to Chapter 6.

It is a pleasure to acknowledge the vigilant assistance of Norma Martin and John Swannell (not for the first time), and of Jill Bennett, Sheila James, and Tony Palmer.

James Sambrook

Chapter 1
Science

The last edition of Johnson's *Dictionary* published in our period defines the word 'science' as 'knowledge', 'certainty grounded on demonstration', 'art attained by precepts, or built on principles', 'any art or species of knowledge', and 'one of the seven liberal arts'. Though the old liberal arts included arithmetic, geometry, and astronomy, and though the second of Johnson's definitions points towards later semantic developments, it was not until long after the great lexicographer's death that 'science' became synonymous with what he would have referred to as 'natural philosophy'. Nevertheless, the process by which science (in the modern sense) came to be regarded as the truest form of knowledge and its system became the model for other systems of knowledge was well under way in the eighteenth century. It was then that most educated men incorporated the most accessible discoveries of the previous century, the age of Galileo, Kepler, and Newton, into their ordinary view of the physical world.

The realization that the earth was a lesser planet of one relatively unimportant star among millions proved to be less chastening than one might expect; its most widespread effect was to encourage confidence in the sublime capacity of the human mind and in the power of scientific method. If men were excited by the vastness and order of the universe they were no less excited by the fact that human intelligence could formulate the laws which governed the motions, relations, and physical properties of that universe. Science gave new freedom and new hope, as if mental and stellar horizons were expanding together: the sudden and huge growth of ordered and apparently certain knowledge seemed greatly to enlarge the possibilities of intellectual, moral, and practical improvements. Increasing knowledge of the heavenly system provided demonstrations of the power and wisdom of God, and supplied practical aids to navigation; increasing knowledge of the physical and chemical properties of matter provided further demonstrations of the power and wisdom of God, and brought about improvements in manufacturing industry: the Steam Age dawned. At the same time, increasing knowledge of the physical world made the hypothesis of a God unnecessary for some men. Encouraged by the successes of experimental science in general, and supported by increasing knowledge of optics and physiology, philosophers for a while came to believe that they, too, might be able to discover natural laws which would make their conclusions and predictions as reliable as those of the scientists.

Though philosophy was not transformed into the hoped-for science of mind, the investigations of eighteenth-century philosophers into perception, sensibility, and imagination were of incalculable value to poets, novelists, and critics.

For poets, philosophers, and theologians, as well as for other scientists, the great intellectual hero of the eighteenth century was Sir Isaac Newton (1642–1727), 'the Miracle of the present Age' as Addison called him (*Spectator*, no. 543). Of course the modern scientific revolution was under way before Newton was born; scientific enquiry was organized in the Royal Society before he was heard of; his great synthesis was based in considerable part upon the researches of Boyle, Barrow, Hooke, Flamsteed, and Wallis, as well as upon those of Continental natural philosophers such as Descartes, Galileo, Kepler, and Huyghens; but for eighteenth-century Englishmen scientific advance was to a remarkable extent identified with the single name of Newton. The triumph of mind represented by his work had an awe-inspiring, elemental, universal quality which seemed comparable with Nature itself. As Pope's famous couplet makes clear, Newton personified enlightenment:

> Nature and Nature's Laws lay hid in Night;
> God said Let Newton be! and all was Light.

(Pope's compliment was particularly apt in view of Newton's discovery that all the colours are contained in white light, a discovery that delighted several generations of poets.)[1]

The blaze of new scientific knowledge which glorified Newton's name was generated by a union of empirical observation with mathematical method. The title of his great book is *Philosophiae Naturalis Principia Mathematica*, the mathematical principles of natural philosophy (i.e. science); in its Preface, dated 8 May 1686, Newton writes: 'I have in this treatise cultivated mathematics as far as it relates to philosophy.' His method is to deduce mathematical formulae from the observed motions of bodies in the heavens and on earth, and then from these formulae to deduce other motions which could be checked against further observations: 'for the whole burden of philosophy seems to consist in this – from the phenomena of motions to investigate the forces of nature, and then from these forces to demonstrate the other phenomena'.[2] Thus Newton applied his principles of motion to account for many hitherto unexplained natural phenomena, such as perturbations in the moon's orbit, the rise and fall of tides, and the behaviour of light. He was able to show by his calculations, for instance, that comets were not mysterious, haphazard, or new-created phenomena, but subject to the same law of gravitation as the planets; thus enabling Edmund Halley to plot, in 1682, the orbit of the comet that bears his name, and to prophesy its return in 1758.

In one aspect Newton's achievement was the consolidation of that seventeenth-century intellectual revolution, begun by Bacon, which almost banished metaphysics and mystery from the natural sciences; in another it was prophetic of continuing revolutions as inevitable as the return of a comet. Instead of deducing knowledge of particular phenomena from general a priori assumptions about whole systems, scientists and, increasingly after Newton, other thinkers followed the practice of ascending gradually from observation and experiment, by way of analysis, towards general theories. The process of analysis was unending. general principles, even Newton's principle of gravitation, could never be other than provisional. Indeed, Newton himself was aware of certain irregularities in the movements of celestial bodies which could not be accounted for by his laws of motion, and believed that the cumulative effect of such irregularities would be to destroy the equilibrium of the solar system if God did not intervene at long intervals to set the system to rights. Later generations of astronomers and mathematicians, down to Pierre Simon Laplace (1749–1827), were able to offer naturalistic explanations of these irregularities, and so confirm the accuracy of Newtonian principles in their non-metaphysical aspect, with the result that no large-scale revision was called for until the Einstein era.

Though Newton's principles were rapidly accepted in Britain, they were resisted in some quarters on the Continent, particularly in France, where the system of Descartes set out in *Principia Philosophiae* (1644) was accepted by most philosophers until almost the middle of the eighteenth century. The concept of gravitation, a force acting at a distance across apparently empty space, seemed absurd to mechanical philosophers who believed that bodies could move only when pushed. In the opinion of Descartes, for instance, the planets were moved by the pressure of ether in a solar vortex. Newton was able to demonstrate conclusively that such a hypothesis could not account for the motions actually observed, whereas his own principle of gravitation could.

He was cautious in ascribing a mechanism to universal gravitation. In the *General Scholium* which he added to the second edition of his *Principia* in 1713 he wrote:

I have not been able to discover the cause of those properties of
gravity from phenomena, and I [feign] no hypotheses; for
whatever is not deduced from the phenomena is to be called an
hypothesis; and hypotheses, whether metaphysical or physical,
whether of occult qualities or mechanical, have no place in
experimental philosophy. . . . And to us it is enough that
gravity does really exist, and acts according to laws which we
have explained, and abundantly serves to account for all the
motions of the celestial bodies, and of our sea.

Nevertheless, in the concluding paragraph of the *General Scholium* he speculated that pressure in the ether, 'a most subtle spirit', accounted both for gravitation and for the structure and some physical properties of matter:

We might add something concerning a most subtle spirit which
pervades and lies hid in all gross bodies; by the force and action
of which spirit the particles of bodies attract one another at near

4 THE EIGHTEENTH CENTURY

distances, and cohere, if contiguous; and electric bodies operate
to greater distances . . .; and light is emitted, reflected,
inflected, and heats bodies; and all sensation is excited, and the
members of animal bodies move at the command of the will.[3]

Independent of such speculation, gravitation worked. The investigations of
astronomers, physicists, and mathematicians in England and Europe
throughout the eighteenth century all bore witness that the principle of
gravitation, that every body attracts every other body with a force proportional to its mass and inversely proportional to the square of the distance
between them, is as comprehensive as it is simple. Newton himself declares
that Nature 'will be very conformable to her self and very simple'[4]; so a
single formula can account at once for the fall of a pebble and the movements
of the stars. The principle of gravitation, a particularly cogent expression of
unity in variety, seized the imagination of men as fully as it satisfied their
understanding.

Newton's second great success, the development of a calculus method,
was of great value to the evolution of mathematics and therefore to
science in general; it was applauded by Englishmen in the eighteenth
century, if only because of the nationalistic passions aroused by the
shameful priority dispute between Newton and Leibniz[5]; but it did not
influence the wider intellectual life of eighteenth-century Britain nearly as
obviously as did his theory of celestial mechanics, or his third great
achievement, the theories concerning light which were eventually
published in Opticks (1704).

The figure of 'Newton with his prism' caught the imagination of Englishmen some generations before Wordsworth. In a paper read to the Royal
Society early in 1672 Newton described the first of a series of famous
experiments in his makeshift camera obscura:

having darkened my chamber, and made a small hole in my
window-slits, to let in a convenient quantity of the Sun's light, I
placed my Prisme at his entrance, that it might be thereby
refracted to the opposite wall. It was at first a very pleasing
divertisement, to view the vivid and intense colours produced
thereby; but after a while applying my self to consider them
more circumspectly, I became surprised to see them in an oblong
form; which, according to the received laws of Refraction I
expected should have been circular.[6]

This oblong form was the effect of light of different colours being refracted
through different angles, for, as Newton's further experiments demonstrated, white light was a mixture of many colours. Men accepted so
revolutionary a notion rather slowly, but when they did it seemed that a new
world of Nature was revealed. James Thomson conveys the excitement of
this discovery in A Poem sacred to the Memory of Sir Isaac Newton (1727), when
he praises the great scientist for untwisting 'all the shining Robe of Day', and
exclaims:

Did ever Poet image aught so fair,
Dreaming in whispering Groves, by the hoarse Brook!
Or Prophet, to whose Rapture Heaven descends!

Newton does not claim to know more about the mechanism of colour than
he does of gravitation. Both are known by their effects:

> if at any time I speak of Light and Rays as coloured or endued
> with Colours, I would be understood to speak not
> philosophically and properly, but grossly, and accordingly to
> such Conceptions as vulgar People in seeing all these
> Experiments would be apt to frame. For the Rays to speak
> properly are not coloured. In them there is nothing else than a
> certain Power and Disposition to stir up a Sensation of this or
> that Colour. For as Sound in a Bell or musical String, or other
> sounding Body, is nothing but a trembling Motion, and in the
> Air nothing but that Motion propagated from the Object, and
> in the Sensorium 'tis a Sense of that Motion under the Form of
> Sound; so Colours in the Object are nothing but a Disposition
> to reflect this or that sort of Rays more copiously than the rest;
> in the Rays they are nothing but their Dispositions to propagate
> this or that Motion into the Sensorium, and in the Sensorium
> they are Sensations of those Motions under the Forms of
> Colours.[7]

The sensorium is that part of the brain where nerves terminate. Just as
Newton's celestial mechanics rests upon the presuppositions that time and
space are absolute and that matter is particulate, his science of optics rests
upon certain assumptions concerning the physiology of perception,
assumptions made explicit in Locke's distinction between primary and secondary qualities (see Ch. 3 below) and which the joint authority of Newton
and Locke was to make highly influential throughout the eighteenth
century. Such assumptions are made clearer in the speculative queries added
by Newton to successive editions of the *Opticks* between 1704 and 1718 –
those queries which, after the *General Scholium* of the *Principia*, proved to be
the writings of his most accessible to the understanding of non-scientists.

The queries as expanded and revised in 1718 constituted Newton's last
notable publication. Though they were put forward ostensibly as a programme of possible future research by other natural philosophers, they were
accepted, not unreasonably, by most of his readers as statements of his
considered convictions about the ultimate nature of things. In their final
form they reintroduce and elaborate Newton's concept of the ether as it
appeared in the *General Scholium* to the *Principia*. This expanded, tenuous
fluid medium which extends throughout the entire universe, and which in a
more subtle and rarefied state pervades the pores of bodies, accounts for
gravity and for magnetism and (static) electricity: 'If any one would ask how
a Medium can be so rare, let him tell me how . . . the Effluvia of a Magnet
can be so rare and subtile, as to pass through a Plate of Glass without any

Resistance or Diminution of their Force, and yet so potent as to turn a magnetick Needle beyong the Glass?' Taking up the theory of the Dutch philosopher Christian Huyghens that light is a pulse or 'pression' in the ether, Newton suggests that his hypothetical ethereal medium also accounts for the mechanics of vision, and perhaps for hearing and the other senses:

> Is not Vision perform'd chiefly by the Vibrations of this
> Medium, excited in the bottom of the Eye by the Rays of Light,
> and propagated through the solid, pellucid and uniform
> Capillamenta of the optick Nerves into the place of Sensation?
> And is not Hearing perform'd by the Vibrations either of this or
> some other Medium, excited in the auditory Nerves by the
> Tremors of the Air, and propagated through the solid, pellucid
> and uniform Capillamenta of those Nerves into the place of
> Sensation? And so of the other Senses.

The ethereal medium accounts also for bodily motions: 'Is not Animal Motion perform'd by the Vibrations of this Medium, excited in the Brain by the power of the Will, and propagated from thence through the solid, pellucid and uniform Capillamenta of the Nerves into the Muscles, for contracting and dilating them?'[8]

There is no significance in the fact that a First Cause is not introduced to account for those mechanical causes discussed in the queries about ether which Newton added to the 1718 edition. Those queries which he allowed to stand from earlier editions state his often-repeated opinion that 'the main Business of natural Philosophy is to argue from Phaenomena without feigning Hypotheses, and to deduce Causes from Effects, till we come to the very first Cause, which certainly is not mechanical'. The important questions to be answered are modern restatements of those put by God to Job: 'Whence is it that Nature doth nothing in vain; and whence arises all that Order and Beauty which we see in the World? To what end are Comets. . . .? . . . How came the Bodies of Animals to be contrived with so much Art, and for what ends were their several Parts?'[9]

Newton's discoveries and conjectures were most highly valued by his contemporaries because they satisfied feelings of religious awe and devotion, and seemed to offer rational grounds for a belief in God. They were repeatedly employed by scientists, divines, essayists, and poets to reinforce a traditional physico-theological argument which was intended to demonstrate the existence and benevolent attributes of God on the evidence of the created universe: see pp.27–30 below. Newton shared the religious certainty of most of his contemporaries. The famous passage from the *General Scholium* to the *Principia* (quoted above), where Newton repudiates hypotheses, follows some very unequivocal hypotheses:

> This most beautiful system of the sun, planets, and comets,
> could only proceed from the counsel and dominion of an
> intelligent and powerful Being. . . . Since every particle of
> space is *always*, and every indivisible moment of duration is

everywhere, certainly the Maker and Lord of all things cannot be
never and *nowhere*. . . . He is omnipresent not *virtually* only, but
also *substantially*; for virtue cannot subsist without substance. In
him are all things contained and moved; yet neither affects the
other: God suffers nothing from the motion of bodies; bodies
find no resistance from the omnipresence of God. It is allowed
by all that the Supreme God exists necessarily; and by the same
necessity he exists *always* and *everywhere*.[10]

Like most of his contemporaries, Newton accepts the old Stoic conception
of the universe as a finite world surrounded by infinite space: 'we cannot
imagine any limit anywhere without at the same time imagining that there is
space beyond it'. Though we cannot imagine infinity we can understand it,
because we can understand 'that there exists a greater extension than any we
can imagine'.[11]

According to the *General Scholium*, God is omnipresent in space not
figuratively but literally: infinite space is an attribute of God. There is a
bolder hypothesis in some of the queries added to the 1706 Latin edition of
the *Opticks*, and retained as the climax and conclusion to that treatise as
Newton left it in 1718. In query 28 he writes: 'Is not infinite Space the
Sensorium of a Being incorporeal, living, and intelligent, who sees the
things themselves intimately, and thoroughly perceives them, and compre-
hends them wholly by their immediate presence to himself: Of which things
the Images only carried through the Organs of Sense into our little
Sensoriums, are there seen and beheld by that which in us perceives and
thinks?' That Newton may have had some misgivings over this conjecture
appears from a correction in the 1718 edition, first printed as a cancel in some
copies of 1706, whereby the literal sensorium of God is transformed into a
figurative one: 'does it not appear from Phaenomena that there is a Being
incorporeal, living, intelligent, omnipresent, who in infinite Space, as it
were in his Sensory, sees the things themselves', etc. The literal divine
sensorium remains, however, in query 31 of the 1718 edition, where
Newton asks whether the system of Nature can be other than the effect of
'the Wisdom and Skill of a powerful ever-living Agent, who being in all
Places, is more able by his Will to move the Bodies within his boundless
uniform Sensorium . . . than we are by our Will to move the Parts of our
own Bodies'.[12]

Newtons speculations on interstellar space and on human vision come to
rest in the notion of the infinite divine sensorium and its bounded human
analogue, the point of interaction between mind and matter, object and
subject. His business finally is with the problem of perception, which so
exercised the minds of eighteenth-century philosophers. However for-
bidding the mathematics, his vision of a universe in which every act of
human perception and every motion of countless suns and planets is a
vibration in the ether, his revelation of a maze of colour hidden within the
light of common day, and his heroic binding of the suns and planets to their
orbits created wonder and excitement among his non-scientist readers.
Whatever Blake and Keats might think, Newton's achievements and

speculations were, for most of the eighteenth century, the stuff of religion and poetry.

In the *Spectator*, no. 565 (9 July 1714) Addison looks up to the infinite host of stars, 'or, to speak more Philosophically, of Suns', remembers that Huyghens had speculated on the likelihood that 'there may be Stars whose Light is not yet travelled down to us, since their first Creation', refers to Job and the Psalmist on the insignificance of man, and is reduced to a state of 'secret Horror'. The horror is duly dispelled, though, when he recollects Newton's 'noblest and most exalted' conception of infinite space as God's sensorium; there could be no doubt that God had cognizance of Joseph Addison. Many in the nineteenth century were dismayed by what they saw as the cold emptiness of interstellar space, but throughout the eighteenth century most thinking Englishmen were comforted and exalted, much as Addison was.

Addison was only one of the more influential popularizers of Newton; others of equal or greater importance included the Boyle lecturers (see Ch. 2 below) and, following rather a different direction, Voltaire. A less philosophical influence was exercised by a work such as *Il Newtonianismo per le Dame* (1737), which was Newton's *Opticks* simplified for the understanding of ladies by Francesco Algarotti, a not altogether respectable ladies' man. More representative perhaps is the contribution of John Theophilus Desaguliers (1683–1744), one of a group of Newton's devoted disciples in the Royal Society who broadcast their master's principles in a shower of popular textbooks and learned papers. Desaguliers lectured on the Newtonian system of optics and mechanics at his house in Westminster from 1712 and later at a coffee-house in Covent Garden, being the first of many distinguished learned men in that century to give lectures on scientific topics to the general, non-academic public. His allegorical poem, *The Newtonian System of the World, the best Model of Government* (1728), was an early example of the many attempts in that century to apply Newtonian principles to non-scientific fields of intellectual endeavour. At this period most scientific research was still well within the comprehension of most educated men: from its early years the Royal Society (founded 1662) had included literary figures and men of affairs among its members; throughout the eighteenth century the most widely-read periodicals regularly contained news of scientific discoveries and discussion of their effects upon general intellectual life. Museums were established: most notably the Ashmolean at Oxford in 1683 and the British Museum in 1759. Popular interest in science was satisfied too by lectures and demonstrations. The first complicated scientific instrument intended as a teaching aid rather than a research tool was designed about 1700 by George Graham: it was a portable planetarium, a machine for exhibiting the motions of the planets in their orbits around the sun by means of globes, slender rods, and wheels. The copy of the machine made by John Rowley was called an 'orrery' in honour of Rowley's patron, Charles Boyle, fourth Earl of Orrery; it was under this name that Steele described the machine in the *Englishman* no. 11 (29 October 1713). According to Steele, 'it is like receiving a new Sense to admit into one's Imagination all that this Invention presents to it. . . . It administers the

Pleasure of Science to any one.' Steele's essay brings out something of the wonder and delight aroused in ordinary people by demonstrations of science; but a far more vivid effect is achieved in the masterly painting of Joseph Wright of Derby, *A Philosopher giving that Lecture on the Orrery in which a Lamp is put in the place of the Sun* (1766): see Plate 13. In this painting the philosopher is a dominating figure, casting a huge shadow; he pauses as the young man on the left takes notes; all the others, including the painter himself on the right, are raptly attentive. The elliptical metal bands of the orrery and the faces of the onlookers catch the light which emanates from the lamp, thus dramatizing not only the power of the sun to bring into view and, as it were, 'create' a planet or a coat-button, but the power of Newtonian science to enlighten men.

Though science was greatly popularized in the eighteenth century, the rapidly growing scale of scientific investigation initiated an inevitable drift towards specialization. Significantly, the earliest recorded use of the word 'physics' in its modern specialized sense (i.e. excluding chemistry) is in an English translation in 1715 of the first general textbook to expound the principle of gravitation, *Astronomiae physicae et geometricae elementa* (1702), by Newton's friend David Gregory (1661–1708), who was responsible for introducing Newtonian philosophy to the universities of Edinburgh and Oxford. Among his successors at Edinburgh was Colin Maclaurin (1698–1746), author of the widely-admired *Account of Sir Isaac Newton's Philosophy*, first drafted in 1728 but not published until 1748. At Oxford the principles of Newton were taught also by John Freind (1675–1728), who in a series of lectures published in 1709 took up the suggestion in query 31 of Newton's *Opticks* and argued that chemical reactions are attributable to a universal law of attraction, and by John Keill (1671–1721), whose challengingly-titled *Introductio ad veram physicam* (1701) was long regarded as the best introduction to the *Principia*.

There was a natural home for Newtoniansim at the college of John Ray, Isaac Barrow, and Newton himself. Richard Bentley (1662–1742), the greatest classical scholar of his age, made it his business during a long and stormy career as Master of Trinity (1700–42) to consolidate the college's position as a centre of scientific excellence. To this end he erected an observatory in the college, the only observatory in Cambridge at that time, and he advanced the careers of younger Newtonians such as Roger Cotes (1682–1716), editor of the second edition of the *Principia*, and Robert Smith (1689–1768), who in his *Complete System of Opticks* (1738) expounded and developed Newton's work in that field. Appropriately, when Newton was knighted by Queen Anne in 1705, the first Englishman to be so honoured for scientific achievement, the ceremony took place in the Master's lodge at Trinity, with Bentley as host.

The Newtonian movement advanced too in much humbler seminaries: for instance at Watts's Academy in Little-Tower Street, London, where mathematics, astronomy, and experimental philosphy were taught in the 1720s by Newton's friend James Stirling, and where, with significant consequences for the development of mid-century poetry, Newtonianism was imbibed by Stirling's fellow tutor, James Thomson. Before the date of

Newton's death the principles of his natural philosophy were firmly established in British universities as well as in the Royal Society, of which he was
President from 1703 to his death.

For the most part, this first generation of Newtonians expounded, illustrated, and consolidated their master's work in his own fields, but striking
advances were also made. James Bradley (1693–1762) in 1728 discovered and
calculated the aberration of light (i.e. the difference between the true and the
observed positions of heavenly bodies caused by a combination of the earth's
motion and the time taken by light to reach the observer), and in 1731
discovered that a nutation (i.e. a slight oscillation) in the earth's axis
hypothesized by Newton was in fact due to the moon's orbit. These discoveries, in which Newton's fields of mathematics, astronomy, mechanics,
and optics were united, had a 'Newtonian' quality inasmuch as they were
simple explanations of highly complex phenomena. They confirmed the
truth of Newton's mechanical principles while, to the extent that they
explained away some of those irregularities in the apparent movements of
celestial bodies which Newton had found inexplicable, they made Newton's
hypothesis regarding God's direct intervention in the workings of the solar
system to the same extent less needful.

Of these Newtonian disciples, Gregory, Keill, Cotes, Smith, and Bradley
all occupied chairs of astronomy at Oxford or Cambridge in the first half of
the eighteenth century. Bradley was appointed Astronomer-Royal in 1742,
following Flamsteed and Halley in that office. The study of astronomy and
mathematics attracted at this period more Englishmen of genius than did the
other sciences; while then, as nowadays, astronomy received a great deal of
attention from the informed general public. Astronomy was the most generally accessible of all the scientific fields embraced by the greatest intellectual
achievement of the age, Newton's *Principia*. Astronomy testified to the
glory of God just as comfortingly as it did to the power of man's intellect.
Astronomy had an obvious practical value, too, in furthering one of the
most cherished national aspirations of the eighteenth century, the expansion
of trade through the improvement of navigation. The post of
Astronomer-Royal was created in 1675 for the stated purpose of 'rectifying
the tables of the motions of the heavens, and the places of the fixed stars, so
as to find out the so much desired longitude of places for the perfecting the
art of navigation'.[13] The career of the second Astronomer-Royal, Edmund
Halley (1656–1742), dramatically illustrates the required blend of the
theoretical and the practical in what might fairly be regarded as a heroic age
of science. He compiled the earliest meteorological chart ever published; he
discovered that the 'fixed stars' move; he speculated on gravitational
attraction without being able to provide mathematical proof, but his observations complemented Newton's calculations in the *Principia*, as well as in
his own most celebrated work, the *Astronomiae Cometicae Synopsis* (1705). In
one sense, his greatest achievement was to persuade Newton to complete
and publish the *Principia*, the printing costs of which were met from Halley's
own slender resources. His prefatory ode to the *Principia* set the tone for
praise of Newton over the next 100 years: 'Nec fas est proprius mortali
attingere divos' (Nearer the Gods no mortal may approach). A decade before

publication of the *Principia* Halley was on the island of St Helena, using a sextant of his own improved design in the compilation of a catalogue of stars of the Southern Hemisphere; a decade after the *Principia* he was carrying on his researches into compass variation as captain of a sloop-of-war, sailing to the extremities of the South Atlantic on one voyage and contending with mutiny on another. His ascent of Snowdon in order to test his method of determining height by the barometer and his experimental descents in a diving bell of his own invention were uneventful by comparison.

In the first year of the eighteenth century, when the ship commanded by Captain Halley, F.R.S., encountered icebergs of incredible size at latitude 52° south, the reformed pirate William Dampier (1652–1715) was in command of a ship making hydrographic surveys of the coasts of Australia and New Guinea; both men were searching for the great southern continent. It is no coincidence that the well-known explorer Lemuel Gulliver claims Dampier for cousin and reports with gravity and respect upon the researches of an academy thought to resemble the Royal Society; for Swift was alive to the spirit of his times. Though the advance of knowledge took its ironic revenge upon Swift's backward-looking satire of experimental science in Book III of *Gulliver's Travels* (for instance, men learned how to 'condense the air' and extract nitrogen from it, and thereby manufacture synthetic nitrogenous fertilizers which have made rather more than two ears of corn and two blades of grass to grow where only one grew before), and though the Lagado Academy researchers, like the prototype Gulliver Martinus Scriblerus, are throwbacks to outdated, seventeenth-century characterizations of the proud and foolish virtuosi, Gulliver's kinship with Dampier makes him very much a man of his age. It was a century of adventurous scientific expeditions, of which some of the most notable were undertaken to seek confirmation of the Newtonian world system.

For instance, in the 1730s the Académie des Sciences in Paris sent out two scientific expeditions, one to Lapland, the other to Peru, to measure a one-degree arc of the earth's meridian. This measurement showed that a degree of latitude at the Arctic Circle is nearly two-thirds of a degree greater than one at the equator, and so proved the truth of Newton's hypothesis that the earth is an ellipsoid flattened at the poles. Voltaire's poem celebrating the expeditions represents the spirit of Newton from the empyrean encouraging his disciples to produce empirical proof of his mathematical model. A first-hand account of the northern expedition by Pierre-Louis Maupertuis (1698–1759), translated as *The Figure of the Earth determined from Observation at the Polar Circle* (1738), received widespread attention in England. The romantic poetry of Thomson, and through him of Coleridge, was indebted to descriptions by Maupertuis of dancing meteors, rose-fringed streams, lakes, and mountains which gave the northern landscape the air of 'an enchanted Island in a Romance . . . a Place of Resort for *Fairies* and *Genii*'.[14]

Thirty years after Maupertuis returned from Lapland, expeditions were sent by Catherine II of Russia to Siberia and by the Royal Society to Tahiti with the purpose of observing the transit of Venus across the sun's disc, and thereby, it was hoped, determining the distance of the sun from the earth. This experiment had first been recommended by Halley in 1679, two years after he himself had made from St Helena the first complete observation of the transit of Mercury. The transit of Venus occurred on 3 June 1769; it would not occur again until 1874. Command of the expedition to Tahiti was entrusted to James Cook (1728–79), who now made the first of his three great explorations of the Pacific, the fruits of which were almost as significant for moral philosophy and romantic literature as they were for hydrography and natural history: see Chapters 7 and 8.

The method adopted by the French expeditions to determine the shape of the earth was to observe the meridian altitude of a star, to travel north or south until its altitude had changed by one degree, and to measure the distance travelled. The field-work lasted for over a year and was possible only because the instruments used for observation and timing had been made to a very high degree of precision by George Graham (1675–1751) of London, one of the first of a new breed of instrument-makers who sprang up to serve science in the eighteenth century. Graham provided Halley and Bradley with astronomical instruments more accurate than any seen before, and he also made the most complex and exact planetarium, or 'orrery', of that age. On his voyages of exploration Cook used a copy of the chronometer with which the clock-maker John Harrison (1693–1776) had in 1764 won the cash prize offered by Parliament from 1713 for a method of accurately determining longitude. Harrison's mechanical ingenuity solved a long-standing problem which had tasked the wits of astronomers, including Halley, as well as instrument-makers.

The demands of navigation and of experimental science went together; but what is perhaps surprising is that the need for accurate measurement was so late to develop among scientists. Though the thermometer was invented by Galileo in about 1590, experimental scientists for the next 100 years or more were content simply to note the fact of a change in temperature without feeling the need to quantify that change; then, in the third and fourth decades of the eighteenth century, were devised the three systems of calibration still associated with the names of their inventors, Réaumur, Fahrenheit, and Celsius. Following the triumph of Newton's 'mathematical way', scientists everywhere had become convinced of the need for mathematical rigour. As always, advances in one field showed the way forward in others: for instance, astronomical methods of navigation were made far more exact as a result of Bradley's discoveries of the aberration of light and the nutation of the earth's axis. The French scientists returning from Lapland and Peru had the philosophic satisfaction of proving a theory; Maupertuis staked his claim to be France's Newton with his bold attempt to devise a complete system of formulae for motions in his *Essai de Cosmologie* (1751); on a more practical level, the determination of the length of a degree of latitude marked a great step forward in map-making and navigation. In 1781, using a great reflecting telescope, an enlarged version of the device invented by Newton, William Herschel (1738–1822) discovered Uranus, the first planet to be found since antiquity. Within less than a year the formulae of its motion had been calculated by Laplace, using Newton's principles as refined by the discoveries of Bradley and others. Some years later, in his *Mécanique Céleste*, Laplace added the last refinements to Newton's system, ridding it of all irregularities. It is said that when Napoleon asked him about the place of God in his system, Laplace replied that he had no need of that hypothesis.

Astronomy, mathematics, mechanics, and optics developed throughout the eighteenth century along lines indicated by Newton, generally yielding full confirmation of his principles. Other sciences during the same period did not always benefit to the same degree from Newton's legacy; for though the Newtonian 'mathematical way' was always highly serviceable, Newton's principles, and still more his hypotheses, were sometimes a hindrance in the formulation of theory. For instance, the pioneer plant physiologist Stephen Hales (1677–1761), author of *Vegetable Staticks* (1727), measured the quantities of water absorbed by plant roots and transpired by their leaves, and made the important discovery that something from the atmosphere enters through the leaves into the composition of plants; but, since he accepted Newton's corpuscular theory of light, he supposed that light itself, the substance, was a food.

Hales held to the ether theory, as did many English Newtonians, some of whom identified the ether with an electrical fluid or element. Research in accordance with this hypothesis proved unfruitful, whether its findings were couched in the sober terms of *An Essay towards an Explication of Electricity deduced from the Aether of Sir Isaac Newton* (1746), by the respectable chemist and portrait-painter Benjamin Wilson (1721–88), or in the more ambitious assertions of *The Subtile Medium proved . . . the Qualities of Aether or Elementary Fire of the Ancient Philosophers to be found in Electrical Fire* (1756), by Richard Lovett (1692–1780), who also claimed to be able to cure sore throats by the use of electricity. There was useful experimental work along other lines: advances were made in the investigation of insulators and conductors by Stephen Gray (d. 1736); storage of electricity became possible with the invention of the Leyden jar in 1745; and there was a shock of excited wonder through Europe after Benjamin Franklin (1706–90) flew his kite in a thunderstorm in 1752 and demonstrated that lightning is electricity.

It was with Franklin's encouragement that Joseph Priestley (1733–1804) wrote his *History and Present State of Electricity* (1767), which records many of his own ingenious experiments. At the end of this work he adds a set of queries, thus imitating the example of Newton's *Opticks*, though without achieving anything remotely comparable to the widespread effect of Newton's queries. Searching for a kind of Newtonian synthesis, Priestley speculates that chemistry and electricity, the two sciences which deal with the latent properties of matter, will eventually be united in a single theory, and he agrees with Newton that light will prove to be the key to electrical phenomena, 'and other, at present, occult properties of bodies'. In the following year it seemed that his speculations might be confirmed, when he observed that electrical discharges upon metal plates formed concentric areas, each having all the colours of the spectrum, and somewhat resembling 'Newton's rings' (the circles of colour between a lens and a flat piece of glass). If eighteenth-century poets were fascinated by Newton's rainbow it is hardly surprising that scientists were too; but the crock of gold still evaded the electricians' grasp. At the end of the century the science of electricity was still too young to yield any satisfactory unifying theory: no Newton was in sight.

Most practical applications of electrical science lay in the future also, though Franklin invented the lightning rod, and it is said that when a woman in Priestley's Nonconformist congregation complained of being possessed he exorcized the devil by means of an electric shock machine, thus becoming the pioneer of electroconvulsive therapy. By contrast, what might be called practical chemistry was well advanced, inasmuch as refiners of metals, soap-boilers, and other tradesmen had over the years developed a considerable empirical understanding of chemical processes. Chemistry attained a high degree of intellectual respectability in England after the publication in 1661 of *The Sceptical Chymist* by Robert Boyle (1627–91), though Newton was almost as devoted an alchemist as he was a theologian, which is saying a great deal. From its inception the Royal Society compiled and published histories of chemical craft technologies, but scientists and technicians in this field remained far more widely separated than they were, for instance, in astronomy and navigation. As Bernard Mandeville (see Ch. 3 below) justly noted in 1729:

> Soap-boyling, Grain-dying, and other Trades and Mysteries,
> are from mean Beginnings brought to great Perfection; but the
> many Improvements, that can be remembered to have been
> made in them, have for the Generality been owing to Persons,
> who either were brought up to, or had long practis'd and been
> conversant in those Trades, and not to great Proficients in
> Chymistry or other Parts of Philosophy, whom one would
> naturally expect those Things from. [15]

The great proficients in chemistry did eventually bring forth many improvements; but at the time that Mandeville was writing, their efforts were still impeded by some residues of Aristotelian science, in particular the belief that fire, air, and water must be, in some sense, elements. Beside these residues were modern, wholly mechanical, explanations of chemical phenomena. The combination of old and new is nicely represented in some conjectures associated with that permanently valuable scientific achievement, Boyle's Law. The law by which Boyle's name is immortalized among schoolboys refers to what its formulator called 'the Spring of the Air', for Boyle conjectured that the elasticity and compressibility of air might be mechanically explained by regarding its particles as tiny coiled springs. He realized, of course, that the ordinary atmosphere contained a mixture of effluvia, but it appears that he believed that the air itself was homogeneous, just as white light was thought to be before Newton's researches.

It was Priestley who added a new dimension to chemical thought in a series of brilliant experiments by which he discovered between 1767 and 1775 no fewer than nine kinds of 'air'. His work on the 'air' that would later be called hydrogen earned him notice as Mr Inflammable Gas, alongside Newton as Mr Obtuse Angle, in Blake's *An Island in the Moon*, written in 1787, but more significant was his isolation of oxygen in 1774. The name of this gas, as indeed the use of the word 'gas' in its modern scientific sense, came later; Priestley thought of his newly-discovered substance as 'dephlogisticated air', in keeping with the phlogiston theory which was formulated in Germany in the early years of the eighteenth century and had come to dominate chemistry completely by the time Priestley came to manhood. According to this theory, combustion depended upon a hypothetical sulphureous element or inflammable principle called phlogiston: when a substance was heated its phlogiston was given off into the air. The theory neatly explains a great deal in the phenomena of combustion, but does so backwards. It was phlogistic thinking that led Priestley to conceive and carry out fertile experiments, but eventually such thinking prevented any further advance.

Among Priestley's notable British contemporaries were Joseph Black (1728–99), who isolated 'fixed air', later called carbon dioxide, and Henry Cavendish (1731–1810), who discovered that water, once thought to be a pure element, is a compound of two gases. The wonderful effect of Black's discovery that a gas can be 'fixed in', that is combined with, a solid appears in the Preface by one of his colleagues to the printed text of Black's lectures on chemistry in 1803:

> He had discovered that a cubic inch of marble consisted of about
> half its weight of pure lime and as much air as would fill a vessel
> holding six wine gallons. . . . What could be more singular
> than to find so subtile a substance as air existing in the form of a
> hard stone, and its presence accompanied by such a change in
> the properties of the stone?[16]

The tone is like that of Addison writing nearly a century earlier about new worlds revealed by the telescope and microscope. The new world of chemical combinations could not be so easily visualized as those worlds, but its discovery brought the same kind of imaginative enlargement and enhanced awareness of the mystery of nature. Black's researches into latent heat (i.e. heat taken up without change in temperature), and particularly his discovery of the very high latent heat of steam, had a more tangible effect: it gave James Watt the idea of the condenser, which was patented in 1769. This meant that a really efficient steam-engine was at last a possibility, and the Industrial Revolution, with all its effects upon social and intellectual life, was greatly accelerated. Priestley, Black, and Cavendish were notable experimenters, well known and widely admired in their day, but it was left to a Frenchman, Antoine Laurent Lavoisier (1743–94), to interpret their experiments correctly, discard phlogiston for good, and in his *Traité élémentaire de Chimie* (1789) unite fact and theory into a synthesis that provided a secure foundation for later constructions.

Before the end of the eighteenth century, general intellectual life was not greatly influenced by the researches of chemists. Electricity was seen by most people as little more than the provider of drawing-room tricks and games with shock-machines. Physiology, to which chemistry was often seen as an adjunct, was quite another matter. In this science, particularly as it was studied at the University of Leyden, Newtonian principles were incorporated into a widely influential view of human nature.

The key figure was the Dutchman Hermann Boerhaave (1668–1738), who incorporated Newton's empirical and mathematical methods into his teaching of medicine, chemistry, and botany at Leyden. An English historian of medicine, writing in 1780, testifies to his influence: 'The age of Boerhaave forms a memorable epoch in the history of physic. Theory, which before had been entirely conjectural, now assumed a more plausible and scientific appearance.'[17] La Mettrie, the leading French materialist, was one of Boerhaave's pupils; so was Albrecht von Haller (1708–77), the Swiss statesman who, as a poet in Die Alpen (1732), made the Alps fashionable, and, as a scientist in countless writings, established the groundwork of systematic physiology, a science which he described as 'the exposition of the motions by which the living machine is agitated'.[18] Voltaire attended Boerhaave's lectures. Linnaeus was for a while Boerhaave's botanical curator. Among Boerhaave's many British pupils were William Cullen (1710–90), the teacher of Joseph Black, and Henry Pemberton (1694–1771), who was employed by Newton to superintend the third edition of the Principia (1726), and wrote an admired popularization, A View of Sir I. Newton's Philosophy (1728). Through Leyden there was a rich two-way traffic in ideas between Britain and the Continent.

In his lectures and in the standard textbook Elementa chymia (1732) Boerhaave, following Boyle and Newton, taught an essentially mechanical chemistry. Thus he believed that air performs a mechanical, not a chemical, function in combustion, and that fire and heat, like light, are a material substance composed of very fine particles that can push their way between the particles of other substances and alter the gravitation-like forces of attraction that hold them together. Boerhaave's physiological theories are equally mechanical; he explains sense-perception and muscular motion in terms of wholly mechanical laws, and regards physiological and pathological processes as the result of mechanical rather than chemical forces. He could have received such notions from the Scottish mathematician and physician Archibald Pitcairne (1652–1713), who taught for a short while at Leyden, but the concept of the body as a machine was generally accepted as a corollary of Cartesian philosophy. Boerhaave, like most of his contemporaries, including Newton, was a dualist; he believed that mechanical laws cannot account for thought, which belongs wholly to the soul. Nevertheless it was Boerhaave's experimental work on the mechanism of the nervous system which opened the way for La Mettrie's denial of dualism and assertion of the materiality of the soul. Referring to Boerhaave, La Mettrie writes in L'homme machine (1748): 'He explains by virtue of mechanism alone all the faculties of the rational soul. The most metaphysical of thoughts, the most intellectual and eternally true, are all reduced by the famous theoretician to the laws of motion.'[19] Mechanical notions of physiology were not associated with any particular condition of religious belief: Pitcairne, Voltaire, and La Mettrie were all freethinkers of one sort or another; Boerhaave, Linnaeus, and Haller were Christians.

In England some of the more doctrinaire applications of mechanical principles appeared in the writings of Richard Mead (1673–1754), a friend of Newton, Bentley, and Boerhaave. For instance, in *A Mechanical Account of Poisons* (1702), after noting that snake poison is effective only when the skin is punctured and is harmless when swallowed, he concludes that hard particles transferred from the venom to the bloodstream bring about death by mechanical, not chemical means. In a bizarre combination of astrology and pathology, *De imperio solis ac lunae in corpora humana* (1704), he argues that the gravitational force of heavenly bodies acts directly upon human bodies to affect their health. His later work, as an advocate of vaccination and of the isolation of sufferers from contagious diseases, is more in keeping with modern orthodoxy.

George Cheyne (1671–1743), like Mead, was a pupil of Pitcairne, and, like Mead, eventually built up a fashionable and influential medical practice in London. As one of the most xenophobic supporters of Newton's primacy in the invention of the calculus,[20] he was, if anything, an even more ardent Newtonian than Mead; but for the causes of ill health he looked to diet rather than gravitation. In his *Observations on Gout and on the Bath Waters* (1720) and *Essay on Health and Long Life* (1724), both based upon observation and experiment, he recommended to the carnivorous and scurvied English gentry a far more vegetarian diet than the one they were accustomed to, and was ridiculed for his pains. He was the most widely known of the many serious eighteenth-century medical writers who turned their attention to that range of neuroses and psychoses known as 'the Hypochondriack and Hysterick Passions, vulgarly call'd the Hypo in Men, and Vapours in Women' (to quote from the title-page of a treatise written in 1711 by the physician Bernard Mandeville, see Ch. 3 below), or known more simply and more chillingly as 'the English Malady' which is the title of Cheyne's major treatise.[21] Cheyne, like other writers, was led from his clinical observations of such bodily-cum-mental disorders to speculate upon the relationship between mind and body. The propositions of his physiology are dualistic and Newtonian: he claims 'That the Intelligent Principle, or *Soul*, resides somewhere in the Brain, where all the Nerves, or Instruments of Sensation terminate, like a *Musician* in a finely fram'd and well-tun'd Organ-Case; that these Nerves are like keys, which, being struck on or touch'd, convey the Sound and Harmony to this sentient Principle, or *Musician*.'[22] Such propositions are more speculative than the definitions and queries from Newton's *Opticks* quoted earlier in this chapter: Cheyne sees identity where Newton merely suggests analogy.

Cheyne returns to the relationship between body and soul in five discourses on 'the Principles and Theory of Philosophical Medicine' which he added to his treatise on diet, *An Essay on Regimen* (1740). In one of these discourses, 'Philosophical Conjectures of Spiritual Nature, and the human Spirit in particular', Cheyne considers it probable that only God is pure and immaterial spirit, and that all created spirits, including creatures such as angels, have bodies. Contrariwise, created living things have souls; so that 'wherever there is any degree of life, vegetative, sensitive, or rational, there is probably some degree of a soul, or spirit, immaterial, immortal, and progressive'. All life, except God himself, has a dual nature; for 'we may be certain, that spiritual substance is in most, if not in all its qualities, contradictory, at least contrary, to body, or material substance, and *vice versa*. Cheyne concludes: 'The best notion, idea, or perception, we can frame of created life, is that of a nice, delicate, finely contrived machine, of a vast variety of organs set in motion by the first cause, and continued by an internal self-motive spring, which spring is this spiritual substance.'[23] The internal, mechanical–spiritual, self-motive spring enabled religion and science to go on ticking reassuringly in time with one another, as they generally did in eighteenth-century England.

Though Cheyne suggests that man is very far from being the only creature placed on this isthmus of a middle state, this suggestion is in accordance with the same general notion which runs through Pope's great lines in the *Essay on Man* (II. 1–18). This notion is that all creation constitutes a great chain of being composed of 'an immense, or . . . infinite, number of links ranging in hierarchical order from the meagerest kind of existents, which barely escape non-existence, through "every possible" grade up to the *ens perfectissimum* – or . . . to the highest possible kind of creature, between which and the Absolute Being the disparity was assumed to be infinite – every one of them differing from that immediately above and that immediately below it by the "least possible" degree of difference.'[24] The notion of the great chain of being was conceived by Plato and developed in the Middle Ages. Until well into the eighteenth century it provided a traditional and well-used framework of ideas not only for theology, moral philosophy, politics, and social thought, but for several fields of science, of which natural history is of particular importance.

The efforts of collectors and classifiers throughout the eighteenth century identified a prodigious number of hypothetical links in that section of the great chain of being which extended below man. Scientific expeditions sent to every corner of the globe by the learned societies and governments of a dozen European states returned with countless hitherto unknown specimens. For example, the two naturalists Daniel Carl Solander (1736–82), a pupil of Linnaeus, and Joseph Banks (1743–1820), who travelled with Cook to observe the transit of Venus, returned with 1,000 new species of plants, pressed or preserved in spirits, 500 fish, 500 skins of birds, 'insects innumerable', and hundreds of drawings of less portable objects of curiosity. The rapid organization of such discoveries into a system was made possible by the taxonomy of Carl Linnaeus (1707–78), which by the third quarter of the century was almost universally accepted among naturalists. The enlargement of his *Systema Natura* from 12 pages in its first edition (1735) to 824 in its tenth edition (1758) testifies as much to the growth of the subject as to Linnaeus's wider grasp of it.

Though Linnaeus's taxonomy eventually proved an indispensable tool for most working naturalists, it was sometimes rejected because it did not fairly reflect the finest gradations of the great chain of being. Buffon, for instance, in the opening discourse of his *Histoire naturelle* (1753), declares that the vastness and multiplicity of nature cannot be reduced to arbitrary systems such as Linnaeus's, formed within the mind of man and not intrinsic to nature herself. In this he is following Locke, who asserts that genera and species are not 'Things regularly and constantly made by Nature . . . but an Artifice of the Understanding'.[25] Locke's *Essay* (see Ch. 3 below) includes one of the best-known and widely-influential restatements of the idea of the chain of being:

> in all the visible corporeal World, we see no Chasms, or Gaps. All quite down from us, the descent is by easy steps. . . . There are Fishes that have Wings. . . . Porpoises have the warm Blood and Entrails of a Hog, not to mention what is confidently reported of Mermaids, or Sea-men . . . and so on till we come to the lowest and the most inorganical parts of Matter, we shall find every-where, that the several *Species* are linked together, and differ but in almost insensible degrees.[26]

Some differences were less insensible and some links less obvious than others. Philosophers and naturalists had particular difficulty in determining the link between man and the beasts closest to him on the chain of being. From the early years of the century, however, there was general agreement that if a link had been found it was the orang-outang or the chimpanzee, two animals that were frequently confused with one another. In 1699 the anatomist Edward Tyson (1650–1708) published his dissection of a chimpanzee under the title *Orang Outang, sive Homo Sylvestris, or the Anatomy of a Pigmy*. Tyson pointed to structural resemblances between monkey and man, and suggested (in an act of wild rationalization characteristic of this age) that the pygmies and satyrs of ancient legend were apes. Other writers of the period argued that the orang-outang resembled man not only in the shape of his body but in the configuration of his sensibility, 'his ready Apprehension, and his gentle and tender Passions'. We are assured that if the orang-outang could but speak he 'might perhaps as justly claim the Rank and Dignity of the human Race, as the savage *Hotentot*, or stupid native of Nova Zembla'.[27] The French physiologist Julien Offroy de la Mettrie (1709–51) claimed, in his notorious treatise *L'homme machine* (1748), that man differs from other animals only in the complexity of his machinery; the superiority of his thinking matter over that of other creatures is attributable only to his fortunate invention of language and numbers. If the orang-outang were educated by means of the newly-invented deaf-and-dumb alphabet he would rapidly acquire human characteristics. La Mettrie's fellow-countryman Charles Bonnet (1720–93), author of *Palingenesie philosophique* (1770), went so far as to claim that the amiable orang-outang could be educated to serve as a polite *valet de chambre*. In Britain such simian speculations were best known through the writings of Rousseau's Scottish disciple James Burnett, Lord Monboddo (1714–99), who in his *Origin and Progress of Language* (1773–92) gave a pleasing account of an orang-outang who could play the flute but never learned to speak; the creature was a modern representative of the infantine state of our own species as it must have been in the remote past. The theories of Monboddo were ridiculed by satirists until well into the following century (see, for instance, Peacock's *Melincourt, or Sir Oran Haut-ton* (1817)), though they eventually came to appear less absurd in the light of later developments in anthropology.

Far, far below the anthropoid apes on the great chain of being were the zoophytes, classified by Aristotle as intermediate between plants and animals, and fair quarry for eighteenth-century naturalists hunting for more missing links. It was widely believed that the missing link had been secured when the French naturalist Abraham Trembley (1700–84) published in his *Mémoire pour servir à l'histoire d'un genre de polypes d'eau douce* (1744), the results of a series of experiments on the genus of polyp later named by Linnaeus 'hydra', on account of its capacity for regrowing severed limbs. Trembley suggested that the creature must be both plant and animal, for it has the shape of a plant and has a plant-like capacity for regeneration and multiplication by means of cuttings, but it is sensitive, mobile, and carnivorous like an animal. Other apparently plant-like animals of very low organization, such as sea-anemones and corals, were proposed as missing links, but their animal nature, and that of the freshwater polyp, was established by John Ellis (1710–76), the man whom Linnaeus looked upon as 'the main support of natural history in England'. Ellis's *Essay towards the Natural History of Corallines* was published in 1755, but he greatly extended his researches later, using the collection of rare corals brought back by his friend Solander from Cook's first Pacific voyage. Ellis also studied the 'sensitive plant' and insectivorous plants, and concluded that they are vegetables.

Ellis's discoveries represent but a few of the many triumphs of microscopy in that century. Though some satirists ridiculed the virtuosi with their 'flea-glasses', most thinking men, like Addison in the *Spectator*, no. 420, were 'not a little pleased to find every green Leaf swarm with Millions of Animals'. The microscope's range of natural observations revealed the chain of being extending down and down to ever smaller and simpler units of life. By the end of the seventeenth century it was well known that a single drop of water teemed with countless tiny organisms, and it was reasonable to suppose that better microscopes would reveal yet smaller particles of life. Partly on the basis of this supposition, the universal philosopher Gottfried Wilhelm Leibniz (1646–1716) revived and developed Giordano Bruno's conception of the monad, the atom that is at once material and spiritual. From this conception grew Leibniz's theology and moral philosophy (see Ch. 3 below) as well as a startling scientific synthesis totally opposed to Newton's.

In his *Monadologie* (1720) Leibniz argues that the particles which constitute what appears to our senses as matter are not hard, dead atoms, but minute packets of energy without extension or shape; they are spiritual entities with powers of perception and sensation; they move themselves according to the pre-existent law of nature laid down by God; each monad is a concentration of the universe, a world in something less than a grain of sand. Each monad, as a primordial principle of existence, is indestructible. The number of monads is constant; from the moment of creation 'the same force and vigour remains always in the world, and only passes from one part of matter to another, agreeably to the laws of nature, and the beautiful pre-established order'. That being so, Leibniz makes merry with the belief of Newton and the Newtonians that God intervenes from time to time to set the machinery of the solar system to rights: 'According to their doctrine, God Almighty wants to wind up his watch from time to time: otherwise it would cease to move. He had not, it seems, sufficient foresight to make it a perpetual motion.'[28] Leibniz subscribed to a biological doctrine widely held until the end of the eighteenth century, that every present and future organism existed at the beginning of time within a Chinese box of germs inside a primeval ancestor. This belief was in accordance with the biblical text (Ecclesiastes 1.9): 'The thing that hath been, it is that which shall be . . . and there is no new thing under the sun.' Nevertheless, as we have seen, Leibniz allowed that force and vigour could pass from one part of nature to another, so that evolution is not ruled out. In his *Protogaea* (1693) he points to fossil evidence that species have become extinct in the past, and that other species now alive apparently did not exist in the past. The great chain of being might still be in the process of completion in time, as the ever-living monads regroup themselves according to God's pre-ordained plan.

There was certainly ample geological evidence that the shape and composition of the earth had changed in the course of time. Leibniz, like Descartes before him and like his English contemporaries Thomas Burnet and William Whiston (see Ch. 2 below), believed that the earth first came into being as a liquid vortex at great heat, slowly became cool and solid at its circumference, and at some stage was covered by a great sea. All serious geologists in the opening years of the eighteenth century attributed existing features of the earth to a succession of physical catastrophes in the past, but they agreed that this past could be no more remote than the 6,000 years allowed by biblical tradition, perhaps adding some years for whatever allegorical interpretation one was prepared to attach to the six days of creation. Something of the intellectual background to geological science at that time may be learned from the correspondence between Newton and Thomas Burnet in 1680. Burnet argued that the days of creation in Moses' account were not to be taken literally; Newton in reply suggested that each day of creation would be much longer than our days if one assumed that the earth was accelerated from rest by divine force until it reached its present rate of rotation.[29] During the course of the following century the biblical tradition was quietly discarded. In his *Époques de la nature* (1779) George Louis Leclerc, Comte de Buffon (1707–88), substituted for the six days of creation a scheme of evolution extending over six vast ages: when the planets were formed, when the earth was cooled and consolidated, when waters covered the earth, when tropical animals such as elephants inhabited the Northern Hemisphere, when the continents drifted apart, and finally when man appeared. In print Buffon asserted that the age of the earth must be about 75,000 years, but privately he allowed that to account for the facts of geology its true age must be very much greater.

Newton, as we have seen, was content to accept the biblical account of creation; his system required God to organize matter and set it in motion. By Buffon's time some French philosophers who had turned from Newtonian physico-mathematical science to the more exciting, expanding, speculative field of biology thought they had found evidence to show that matter ordered itself. For a while the strongest evidence was in a series of experiments described in *Observations microscopiques* (1747) by Buffon's English friend John Turberville Needham (1713–81). Needham found that boiled gravy, sealed (as he thought) from the air, swarmed with microscopic life, thus apparently proving that spontaneous generation is possible. Needham's experimental findings were disproved in 1768 as a result of more precise experiments by Lazzaro Spallanzani (1729–99), but the general theory of spontaneous generation continued to be upheld by some influential thinkers, not least of whom was that bright luminary in the French Enlightenment, Denis Diderot (1712–84). In his widely-discussed and controversial *Lettre sur les aveugles* (1749) he argued that if spontaneous generation was possible then belief in God was no longer necessary to account for the creation of organized matter and life; God is a useless hypothesis employed to 'explain' what cannot yet be comprehended by human reason and natural laws. Furthermore, as life can form itself under our eyes, it is reasonable to suppose that there have been many worlds which have dissolved, reformed themselves, and dissolved again; the present organization of natural forms is nothing more than trial and error, a rough-and-ready process of natural selection. In *De l'interpretation de la nature* (1754) Diderot drily puts his theories of evolution into the mouth of an imagined atheistical philosopher who suggests that the elements of life have existed from eternity and have combined themselves by chance into different forms at different periods, so that entire species have evolved, decayed, and died, to be replaced by others; he suggests that millions of years may have passed between each of these developments, and believes it probable that more developments will occur. Diderot concludes ironically that religion spares us these errors. The fullest development of Diderot's notions of evolution occurs in his brilliant *Rêve de d'Alembert*, written in 1769; but as that dangerous work was not printed until 1830 it had no influence on eighteenth-century thought.

Buffon's *Époques de la nature* provide a time-scale for environmental changes which result in transformations of whole species of plants and animals. His massive, heroic *Histoire naturelle*, begun in 1749 and still un-completed at his death in 1788, offers a full account of the entire natural world with remarkably little reference to a creator or to a distinct, historical act of creation. In the introductory sections of the *Histoire naturelle* Buffon refers to Needham's spontaneously-generated infusoria, Trembley's reg-enerated polyp tissue, and other experimental evidence, to prove that life is a potentiality of matter itself. Influenced by Leibniz's theory of monads, he postulates an indeterminate quantity of *molécules organiques* dispersed in nature, which by joining together according to regular and intelligible mechanical laws are responsible for producing all living things.

Within its own terms Newton's beautifully accurate mathematical model accounted for the state of nature; but as the eighteenth century advanced, men were more and more inclined to see nature as a process rather than a state. Creation is continuous, as Immanuel Kant (1724–1804) asserts, com-bining hints from Newton and from Leibniz, in his ambitious *Allgemeine Naturgeschichte und Theorie des Himmels (General History of Nature and Theory of the Heavens*, 1755): 'The future succession of time, by which eternity is unexhausted, will entirely animate the whole range of space to which God is present, and will gradually put it into that order which is comfortable to the excellence of His plan. . . . The Creation is never finished or complete. It did indeed once have a beginning, but it will never cease.'[30] Scientific theories to account adequately for evolution did not begin to appear until after 1789, but before that date evolutionary notions begin to appear in theology, philosophy, and historiography, as we shall see in the following chapters.

Notes

Place of publication is London unless otherwise stated.

1. See Marjorie Hope Nicolson, *Newton demands the Muse: Newton's 'Opticks' and the Eighteenth Century Poets* (Princeton, NJ, 1946).

2. *Mathematical Principles of Natural Philosophy*, translated by Andrew Motte, 1729, edited by Florian Cajori (Berkeley, Calif., 1934), pp. xvii–xviii.

3. Ibid., p. 547. For 'feign' Cajori has 'frame': the original Latin reads 'hypotheses non fingo'.

4. *Opticks*, reprinted from the fourth edition, edited by E. T. Whittaker (1931), p. 397, query 31.

5. See A. Rupert Hall, *Philosophers at War: The Quarrel between Newton and Leibniz* (Cambridge, 1980).

6. *Philosophical Transactions*, 6 (19 February 1672), 3075.

7. *Opticks*, pp. 124–25; Book i, Part ii, Definition.

8. Ibid., pp. 353–54; queries 22, 23, 24.

9. Ibid., p. 369; query 28.

10. *Mathematical Principles*, pp. 544–45.

11. *Unpublished Scientific Papers of Isaac Newton*, edited by A. R. Hall and M. B. Hall (Cambridge, 1962), pp. 133–34.

12. *Opticks*, pp. 370, 403. Variants of the Latin edition of 1706 are taken from Richard S. Westfall, *Never at Rest: A Biography of Isaac Newton* (Cambridge, 1980), p. 647.

13. 'Flamsteed', in *Dictionary of National Biography* (1889), xix 243.

14. Thomson, *Winter* (1744), ll. 860–77; Coleridge 'The Destiny of Nations'; see James Thomson, *The Seasons*, edited by J. Sambrook (Oxford, 1981) pp. 243–44, 393; J. L. Lowes, *The Road to Xanadu* (Boston, 1964), pp. 34, 93–94.

15. *The Fable of the Bees*, edited by F. B. Kaye (Oxford, 1924), ii, 144–45.

16. Quoted in John Read, *Humour and Humanism in Chemistry* (1947), p. 185.

17. Henry Manning, *Modern Improvements in the Practice of Physic*, quoted in Peter Gay, *The Enlightenment* (1969), ii, 18.

18. Quoted in Preserved Smith, *The Enlightenment, 1687–1776* (1934), p. 108.

19. La Mettrie, *Œuvres philosophiques*, (1774), i, 265, translated by A. Vartanian, in *Diderot and Descartes* (Princeton, NJ, 1953), pp. 233–34.

20. See Hall, pp. 131–36.

21. See Cecil A. Moore, 'The English Malady', in *Backgrounds of English Literature 1700–1760* (Minneapolis, 1953), pp. 179–235.

22. George Cheyne, *The English Malady: or, A Treatise of Nervous Diseases of all Kinds* (1733), pp. 4–5, quoted in John A. Dussinger, 'The Sensorium in the World of "A Sentimental Journey"', *Ariel*, 13 (1982), 6.

23. *Essay on Regimen* (1740), pp. 122–24.

24. A. O. Lovejoy, *The Great Chain of Being* (Cambridge, Mass., 1936), p. 59.

25. *An Essay concerning Human Understanding*, edited by Peter H. Nidditch (Oxford, 1975), pp. 433–34; Book iii, Chapter v, section 9.

26. Ibid., pp. 446–47; iii, vi, 12.

27. Richard Blackmore and John Hughes, *The Lay-Monastery* (1714), p. 28, quoted in Lovejoy, pp. 234–35.

28. Leibniz to Caroline, Princess of Wales, November 1715, in *The Leibniz–Clarke Correspondence*, edited by H. G. Alexander (1956), pp. 11–12.

29. Westfall, p. 391.

30. Quoted in Stephen Toulmin and June Goodfield, *The Discovery of Time* (New York, 1966), p. 130.

Chapter 2
Religious Ideas

Eighteenth-century England was a Christian country. Most educated laymen were greatly concerned about religion. The greatest volume of printed book production still consisted of sermons and other devotional works. Church- and chapel-going was habitual, except in some of those areas where the poorest among the masses of new industrial workers were huddled. Modern critics have made much (too much) of the so-called unspirituality, even paganism, of eighteenth-century church buildings in the classical style, but it is worth remembering that most Anglican churches were still wholly or mostly medieval Gothic buildings, duly provided with Gray's 'long-drawn isle and fretted vault'. It was the Nonconformists who were more accustomed to plain, Doric-columned square rooms for their places of worship; but such surroundings do not appear to have damped their religious enthusiasm. The generality of Anglican clergy were not the venal and torpid time-servers of legend; nevertheless, reform of their ecclesiastical organization was very slow: in particular, the age-old pattern of dioceses and parishes bore little relation to population growth, so that the new industrial villages and the suburban slums of the larger manufacturing towns were left in spiritual darkness until they were penetrated by Methodism.

As will be seen from the following pages, the Church of England encompassed a broad range of belief, but the Act of Uniformity of 1662 excluded from the Church a still broader range of doctrine and a considerable variety of church organization, represented by Presbyterians, Independents, Baptists, Quakers, Unitarians, and many less significant old Dissenting bodies. The greatest Nonconformist movement of the eighteenth century, Methodism, began within the Church of England, and the Evangelical spirit which it fostered was well at work among Anglicans and Dissenters by the end of our period. Despite the sectarian polemics of Swift and some of his contemporaries, the Anglican and Dissenting churches, which had been literally at war with one another under Charles I, were now easily able to accommodate to one another's existence. Both were very active in establishing charity schools, and they were associated together in the two most important societies for the furtherance of religious education, the Society for Promoting Christian Knowledge (1696) and the Society for the Propagation of the Gospel in Foreign Parts (1701), as well as in the many local societies for the reformation of manners set up from 1695 onwards. English Roman

Catholics remained a tiny, inoffensive, and ineffective minority, though they provided a convenient bogey for politicians as sane as Sir Robert Walpole and as mad as Lord George Gordon.

The early stages of the Gordon Riots in 1780, where English Papists were identified with our traditional enemies across the Channel, and the burning of Joseph Priestley's house in 1791, where English Unitarians were identified with new enemies in Revolutionary France, alike illustrate that an English mob, even in the later years of the century, could be roused to physical violence by allegations that 'Church and King' were in danger; but the intellectual climate in which educated men carried on religious debate is better exemplified in four *Letters concerning Toleration* (1689, 1690, 1692, and 1706) by John Locke (1632–1700). Locke had lived through the Civil War and his primary concern now is to argue that religion cannot be maintained by force of arms, so the *Letters concerning Toleration* perhaps belong more to politics than to theology: Locke's own grounds for religious belief are more fully revealed in *An Essay concerning Human Understanding* (1690), the work which, according to his many eighteenth-century admirers, made him the Newton of the human mind.

According to Locke, we arrive at the idea of a God by a chain of reasoning. By our own processes of mental reflection, working upon ideas derived from sensation (see Ch. 3 below), we acquire 'the *Ideas* of Existence and Duration; of Knowledge and Power; of Pleasure and Happiness; and of several other Qualities and Powers, which it is better to have, than to be without'; then 'we enlarge every one of these [ideas] with our *Idea* of Infinity; and so putting them together, make our complex *Idea of God*'.[1] By further reasoning we discover that this supreme Being is the First Cause, so his existence becomes undeniable. Locke denies the whole doctrine of innate ('inborn') ideas, in particular the traditional belief that God has imprinted an idea of himself in the minds of all men. He asks rhetorically, 'hath not Navigation discovered, in these latter Ages, whole Nations, at the Bay of *Soldania*, in *Brasil*, in *Boranday*, and the *Caribee* Islands, *etc.*, amongst whom there was to be found no Notion of a God, no Religion?'[2]

Once reasonable men choose to apply their understanding to the matter they may come to a knowledge of a God by demonstration, which offers a degree of certainty second only to intuition. The proof of God's existence follows from man's knowledge of his own existence and the logical necessity of a First Cause to account for such existence: the evidence which we carry about with us is 'equal to mathematical Certainty'.[3] Equal certainty is attainable in the science of ethics: '*Morality is capable of Demonstration*, as well as Mathematicks.'[4] Christians, furthermore, find religious and moral certainty in revelation, as Locke concedes in *The Reasonableness of Christianity* (1695). Christ came to reveal to all a divine moral law which some wise men, such as Solon, Plato, and Cicero, had partly apprehended earlier; his performance of miracles in fulfilment of Old Testament prophecies validated the moral law thus revealed; but the moral law is primarily acceptable because it conforms to reason. New Testament revelation, uncorrupted by Popish accretions of course, is itself acceptable to reason because it rests upon what Locke accepts as empirical evidence, in the form of dependable records of external, sensible signs.

Though there is no reason to doubt that Locke was a sincere Christian, his admission of reason and external evidence as the arbiters of theological truth opened the way to freethinking, as too did his suggestion that revelation was intended chiefly for the unreasoning multitude:

> Though the works of nature, in every part of them, sufficiently evidence a Deity; yet the world made so little use of their reason, that they saw him not. . . . Reason, speaking ever so clearly to the wise and virtuous, had never authority enough to prevail on the multitude. . . . The greater part of mankind want leisure or capacity for demonstration. . . . And you may as soon hope to have all the day-labourers and tradesmen, the spinsters and dairy-maids, perfect mathematicians, as to have them perfect in ethics this way.[5]

It was especially for such people that God sent a Saviour to preach 'such a Gospel as the poor could understand: plain and intelligible'. Locke sums up mere revelation, unsupported by rational demonstration, as 'a religion suited to vulgar capacities; and the state of mankind in this world, destined to labour'.[6] The social implications of such statements are almost as interesting as the theological.

Few men would have disagreed with Locke that the works of nature evidence a deity; and though many might still have questioned the sufficiency of that evidence, their number was diminishing in his day. It was a commonplace well before the eighteenth century that Christianity rested upon two books, the Bible and the Book of Nature. The material universe is, in the words of Sir Thomas Browne, 'that universal and publick Manuscript that lies expans'd into the Eyes of all', a manuscript whose mystical letters are better read by heathens than by Christians, who 'disdain to suck Divinity from the flowers of Nature'.[7] Christians, though, were beginning to take theological nourishment at Nature's breast. Browne wrote these words in the 1630s, only a few years before the father of English natural history, John Ray (1627–1705), composed his college exercise, *The Wisdom of God manifested in the Works of the Creation*. Ray's book, printed in 1691, remained a standard work of science and theology throughout the eighteenth century, reaching its twelfth edition in 1759, and enjoyed a new lease of life when much of its material was incorporated into another standard work, William Paley's *Natural Theology* (1802). Ray employs his own pioneering understanding of plant and animal anatomy to show the artfulness with which every object in the natural world is contrived, and concludes that such art can be accounted for only by the existence of an intelligent creator. How else, he asks, could matter 'run itself into such a curious Machine, as the Body of Man is'?[8] The argument was put in more general terms in a frequently reprinted sermon by Ray's contemporary, Archbishop Tillotson (1630–94): 'As any curious Work, or rare Engine doth argue the Wit of the Artificer; so the variety, and order, and regularity, and fitness of the Works of God, argue the infinite wisdom of him who made them.'[9] The machine that eighteenth-century theologians and others brought most readily to mind when they made this analogy was a clock or watch. The comparison is found in John Ray's *Wisdom of God* and is used by philosophers as different as Bolingbroke and Joseph Butler; its use goes back at least as far as Cicero, in *De natura deorum*, II, 34, though Cicero, of course, compares the divine intelligence which contrived the world with a human intelligence which can contrive a sundial or a water-clock.

As always, Addison speaks most clearly for his generation. He claims in the *Spectator*, no. 465 that 'The Supream Being has made the best Arguments for his own Existence, in the Formation of the Heavens and the Earth', quoting in support the opening verses of Psalm 19, and concluding with his own hymn of natural religion, 'The spacious Firmament on high', in which he elaborates the Book of Nature metaphor, declaring that the sun publishes, the moon repeats, and the planets confirm the same glad tidings: 'In Reason's Ear they all rejoice.' Perhaps the Platonic music of the spheres is at the back of Addison's mind, but by his day reason's ear had been considerably sharpened by the effects of the seventeenth-century scientific revolution. Implicitly here, as explicitly in the *Spectator*, nos. 565 and 393, where Addison similarly mingles the Old Testament and the new natural philosophy, scientific discoveries are used in a manner highly typical of the age to strengthen the old argument for the existence of God from the design of the material universe.

In the *Spectator* no. 543, Addison speaks of Newton, 'the Miracle of the Present Age', as having drawn from the order of nature 'Demonstrations of infinite Power and Wisdom'. Newton himself declared roundly that the world could not have arisen 'out of a Chaos by the mere Laws of Nature. . . . Such a wonderful Uniformity in the Planetary System must be allowed the Effect of Choice' by an intelligent agent.[10] In the *Spectator, no.* 387, the physico-theological argument is proved by immediate aesthetic experience rather than by the operations of the understanding. Addison claims that 'the whole Universe is a kind of Theatre filled with Objects that either raise in us Pleasure, Amusement, or Admiration . . . and fill the Mind with a perpetual Succession of beautiful and pleasing Images'; so, for instance, 'Fountains, Lakes and Rivers, are as refreshing to the Imagination, as to the Soil through which they pass'. Nevertheless, rational evidence is also drawn from Newton: God has arranged that nature's predominant colour is green, and Newton's *Opticks* provides the physiological theory explaining why, as Addison says, 'the Rays that produce in us the Idea of Green' comfort and strengthen the eye and 'excite a very pleasing and agreeable Sensation'. The notion of green as an 'idea' is from Locke (see Ch. 3 below); here, as in the regular series of papers on the pleasures of the imagination, the philosophies of Locke and Newton are employed in the analysis of experiences that are equally aesthetic, rational, and devotional. In the *Spectator*, no. 489 we are told that a storm at sea arouses in the man who sails upon it an 'agreeable Horror', giving 'his Imagination one of the highest Kinds of Pleasure. . . . The Imagination prompts the Understanding, and by the Greatness of the sensible Object, produces in it the Idea of a Being who is neither circumscribed by Time nor Space.' Similarly, in the *Spectator*, no. 393: 'The Creation is a perpetual Feast to the Mind of a good Man. . . . Natural Philosophy quickens this Taste of the Creation, and renders it not only pleasing to the Imagination, but to the Understanding.' Many of these *Spectator* papers were avowedly 'lay sermons', but Newton's teaching was heard from the regular pulpit some twenty years earlier in the mouths of those lecturers who, under the terms of the will of the great scientist Robert Boyle (1627–91), sought to prove the Christian religion against infidels.

The first Boyle lectures, preached from the pulpit of old St Martins-in-the-Fields in 1692 by Richard Bentley, the future Master of Trinity College, Cambridge, were written in consultation with Newton, and draw heavily upon his work; they draw also upon Locke's argument that the idea of God is not innate. According to Bentley, the activity of matter depends ultimately upon a non-mechanical principle or force implanted by the Creator; gravitation is miraculous, and God intervenes, as Newton claimed, to maintain a universal order (see Ch. 1 above). Samuel Clarke (1675–1729), like Bentley a disciple of Newton in close communication with his master, followed suit in the Boyle lectures of 1704, where he speaks of gravitation as the will of God expressed in the universe. Like Newton, Clarke sternly follows the mathematical way of reasoning; by a process of a priori agrument as nearly logical as the subject will allow, he proves that there is a chain of causation leading back to a first cause whose essence is inconceivable but whose being and some of whose attributes are demonstrable. In dealings with men God obeys his own laws of equity and goodness out of necessity, according to the natural, necessary relations, fitness, and proportions of the things he has created, precisely 'as the Addition of certain Numbers, necessarily produces a certain Sum, and certain Geometrical or Mechanical Operations, give a constant and unalterable Solution of certain Problems or Propositions'.[11] Though Clarke's Boyle lectures were widely admired and had run into eight editions by 1717, it appeared to some readers that such mathematical demonstrations exposed the weakness of Christianity. Anthony Collins, the freethinker, drily remarked that until Dr Clarke undertook to demonstrate the existence of God nobody had ever entertained any doubts upon that point. As the most celebrated traveller of his age along 'the high *Priori* Road', Clarke was later ridiculed in Pope's *Dunciad*, iv. 455–72, and in Warburton's note to iv. 647, 'See *Mystery* to *Mathematics* fly!' Against the a priori method, which depends upon knowledge independent of experience, Pope sets the a posteriori arguments of natural religion: 'to *Nature's* Cause by *Nature* led'. These conventional arguments of natural religion were greatly elaborated by William Derham (1657–1735) in the Boyle lectures of 1711 and 1712, *Physico-Theology, or a Demonstration of the Being and Attributes of God from his Works of Creation*, which ran into at least twelve English editions between 1713 and 1760.

The best-known of the Boyle lecturers preached natural religion, but they believed its findings to be entirely congruent with revelation. Clarke's second series of Boyle lectures in 1705, for instance, offers the usual arguments for the truth of Christian revelation, based upon external evidence of prophecy and miraculous confirmation of prophecy. This is the line taken by the Newtonian scientist, William Whiston (1667–1752), in his 1707 Boyle lectures, printed as *The Accomplishment of Scripture Prophecies* (1708). Physico-theological writers in this period commonly made a point of tracing agreements between the Book of Nature and the Bible; among such writers, devout geologists inevitably took a particular interest in Genesis and Revelations. Thomas Burnet (1635–1715), whose *Telluris Sacra Theoria* (1680–89, English translation 1684–89) was praised by Steele and Addison in the *Spectator*, and was a major source for Thomson's *Seasons*, reconciles geology and revelation by adopting an allegorical interpretation of the Bible that allows him to disregard all references to calendar time in the Old Testament; but the literal accuracy of the Bible is reaffirmed by Whiston in *A New Theory of the Earth* (1696), 'wherein the creation of the world in six days, the universal deluge, and the general conflagration, as laid down in Holy Scripture, are shown to be perfectly agreeable to reason and philosophy'. Geological stratification and marine fossils on land were, of course, powerful evidence for the biblical Deluge, as was demonstrated in John Woodward's pioneering *Essay toward a Natural History of the Earth* (1695).

Newtonian Boyle lecturers and other physico-theologians defended religion so ably and seemingly so comprehensively by the appeal to nature that it began to appear that supernatural revelation was at best irrelevant and at worst false. The concept of God as mathematician and mechanic, based upon scientific study of his works, made miracles appear incredible, or at least unworthy of so rational and prescient a God. Newton's new philosophy, at first a defence of Christianity, as Newton intended, became a means of attack upon it: Locke's new philosophy suffered a similar fate.

In 1696, a year after Locke's *The Reasonableness of Christianity*, appeared a work with the apparently complementary title, *Christianity not Mysterious, or a Treatise showing, that there is nothing in the Gospel contrary to Reason, nor above it*, written by a down-at-heels Irishman John Toland (1670–1722). In the pragmatic way of Locke's *Essay concerning Human Understanding*, Toland argues that assent to religious belief can be secured only by rational demonstration, and that Scriptural assertions concerning matters of historical fact must therefore be subjected to the closest rational scrutiny. He allows, perhaps without complete sincerity, that there is nothing 'above reason' in the New Testament, but in his (by no means original) view the primitive truth and simplicity of the Christian gospel had been sophisticated by 'mysteries', in the shape of rites and doctrines, imported by the early Fathers from various pagan religious communities which supplied all the early converts to Christianity. Toland refers to the Fathers' injunction 'to adore what we cannot comprehend', and adds: 'This famous and admirable Doctrine is the undoubted Source of all the *Absurdities* that ever were seriously vented among *Christians*. Without the Pretence of it, we should never hear of the *Transubstantiation*, and other ridiculous Fables of the Church of *Rome*; nor of any of the *Eastern Ordures*, almost all receiv'd into this *Western Sink*.'[12] The argument, though not the tone, of Toland's disproof of transubstantiation is derived from *The Rule of Faith* (1666) by John Tillotson, later Archbishop of Canterbury, and Toland's attack on the corruptions of Christianity is directed ostensibly against the Roman Church, but his fierce anticlericalism was hardly less damaging to other Christian sects; so, not surprisingly, his book was condemned by the Irish House of Commons and burned by the common hangman in 1697.

In his later writings Toland continued to rationalize the Scriptures: he argued for instance in his *Tetradymus* (1720) that the pillar of a cloud and the pillar of fire in Exodus 13 were not miraculous, but merely the effects of a signal fire contained in an iron pot hoisted to the top of a pole in the Israelite vanguard. When he writes on the history of religions, his theme is always priestly deceit: he retells the story of Hypatia (1720) in order to illustrate the wickedness of priests, just as Charles Kingsley would do over 100 years later; in the *History of the Druids* (1726) he remarks that these Celtic priests were adept in juggling and sophistry, and adds: 'to be masters of both, and withal to learn the art of managing the mob, which is vulgarly called *leading the people by the nose*, demands abundant study and exercise'.[13]

Toland believed that in all ages there have been two forms of religion: one, the established, public religion, was devised by priests for the benefit of the credulous, superstitious rabble who would obey a moral code (and, more importantly, defer to their rulers) only out of fear of divine punishment; the other, the esoteric religion of the enlightened few, was always some variety of pantheism. The word 'pantheist' first appears in English in the title of Toland's tract *Socinianism . . . recommended by a Pantheist to an Orthodox Friend* (1705). By his restatement of the doctrine of Socinus, who denied the pre-existence as well as the divinity of Christ, Toland places himself somewhat further away from Christian orthodoxy than those Arians, such as Newton, Clarke, and Whiston, who went no further than denying Christ's full divinity; but in his pantheism he sets himself in opposition to the Newtonians. Newton separated matter and motion; matter in its natural state is inert; only force gives it motion, and force derives ultimately from the will of God in action. Reviving some of the notions of Giordano Bruno and Spinoza, Toland argues that matter and motion are one, and that nature contains within itself an explanation of all its phenomena. God is not transcendent, or a personality; God and nature are one. These views are expressed in *Letters to Serena* (1704), where the writings of Locke and Newton are surprisingly forced into agreement with Toland's materialist thesis. His *Pantheisticon* (1720) describes a religious service for philosophers, the climax of which is the chanting of a hymn 'Praise to the All'; but, in accordance with Toland's principle that there were two religions, such a service was to be celebrated only when the servants had left the room.

Toland received a pension from the good-hearted Earl of Shaftesbury, but repaid this generosity by surreptitiously publishing in 1699, from an incomplete and uncorrected draft, his patron's *Inquiry concerning Virtue*. This treatise, later acknowledged by its author and printed in full in Shaftesbury's *Characteristicks of Men, Manners, Opinions, Times* (1711), has a freethinking tendency inasmuch as it offers a system of ethics quite free from divine sanctions of any kind. In Shaftesbury's opinion, man has a moral sense antecedent to and independent of any belief in God :(see Ch. 3 below). Men first shape their gods according to their moral ideas, but then their religious beliefs serve to confirm their virtues or vices; so a religion based upon unenlightened morality is more harmful than atheism. To illustrate his point Shaftesbury disingenuously postulates the case of a certain hypothetical religion which his readers could hardly have failed to recognize as Judaism:

> If there be a Religion which teaches the Adoration and Love of a
> GOD, whose Character it is to be captious, and of high
> resentment, subject to Wrath and Anger, furious, revengeful;
> and revenging himself, when offended, on others than those
> who gave the Offence: and if there be added to the Character of
> this GOD, a fraudulent Disposition, encouraging Deceit and
> Treachery amongst Men; favourable to a few, tho for slight
> causes, and cruel to the rest: 'tis evident that such a Religion as
> this being strongly enforc'd, must of necessity raise even an
> Approbation and Respect towards the Vices of this kind, and
> breed a suitable Disposition, a capricious, partial, revengeful,
> and deceitful Temper.[14]

Shaftesbury's own religion is of a very different temper; he describes himself as a theist, or one who believes 'that every thing is govern'd, order'd, or regulated *for the best*, by a designing Principle, or Mind, necessarily good and permanent'.[15] The italicized phrase is now perhaps best known through Voltaire's frequent reiteration of it in his satire upon Leibniz's optimism in *Candide*. Leibniz, though, admitted that most of the ideas in his *Théodicée* (1710) were anticipated in Shaftesbury's *The Moralists*, published a year earlier.

Freedom of thought and the absurdity of fanaticism are Shaftesbury's topics in his plea for religious toleration, *A Letter concerning Enthusiasm* (1708). If men reason ill in matters of religious truth, he declares, reason, not the magistracy, should teach them to do better: 'Let but the Search go freely on, and the right Measure of every thing will soon be found.'[16] Religious enthusiasm, however erroneous, should not be repressed by violence; fanaticism should be opposed, not by equal fanaticism, but by ridicule. In his *Essay on the Freedom of Wit and Humour* (1709) Shaftesbury develops his arguments into a general doctrine that ridicule is the most effective test of truth; but, however comforting this doctrine may have been to the satirists, it was regarded by orthodox theologians as a threat to Christianity. Berkeley's *Alciphron, or the Minute Philosopher* (1732) contains one of many contemporary attacks upon Shaftesbury as a freethinking scoffer against religion.

Anthony Collins (1676–1729), like Toland, was a follower of Locke, but, unlike Toland, proved to be an acceptable disciple to their master. In his *Essay concerning the Use of Reason* (1707) Collins attacks the distinction between things 'contrary to' and things 'above' reason, a distinction of great importance to theologians who sought to defend mysteries against critics such as Toland. In *A Discourse of Free-Thinking, occasion'd by the Rise and Growth of a Sect call'd Free-Thinkers* (1713), which owes as much to

Shaftesbury as to Locke, Collins defines freethinking as 'the Use of the Understanding, in endeavouring to find out the meaning of any Proposition whatsoever, in considering the nature of the Evidence for or against it, and in judging of it according to the seeming Force or Weakness of the Evidence'.[17] On this basis he claims that free use of the understanding will banish superstition, which at certain points in his *Discourse* he appears to equate with supernaturalism. Like Toland, he mischievously cites Tillotson in support of his own views, hailing the good archbishop as one 'whom all English Free-Thinkers own as their Head'.[18] Collins puts the case for natural against revealed religion, pointing out that believers in the latter, 'neglecting what God speaks plainly to the whole World, take up what they suppose he had communicated to a few'[19]; but goes on to show that, in any case, the Bible, the basis of revealed religion, is textually so obscure and corrupt and has so many inaccuracies and absurdities that it cannot possibly be a sure foundation of belief.

Like Toland and Collins, Henry St John, Viscount Bolingbroke (1678–1751), was a professed follower of Locke, 'my master, for such I am proud to own him'.[20] Bolingbroke was also the last of the early-eighteenth-century freethinkers to appear in print: the essays and fragments on ethics and religion which did so much to shape Pope's *Essay on Man* in the 1730s were first published in 1754 by David Mallet, his legatee. Johnson's judgement on author and editor is well known but will bear repetition: 'Sir, he was a scoundrel, and a coward: a scoundrel, for charging a blunderbuss against religion and morality; a coward, because he had not resolution to fire it off himself, but left half a crown to a beggarly Scotchman, to draw the trigger after his death.'[21]

Bolingbroke rejects divine revelation, either individual or corporate, except nature herself; he reiterates the argument from design, taking proofs from Ray, Derham, and their like, but insists that God does not interpose himself into the workings of his great machine. The universe continues distinct from the workman, like any human work, and 'infinitely better fitted up by the contrivance and disposition of it to answer all the purposes of the divine architect, without his immediate and continual interposition'. At this point in his discourse Bolingbroke abruptly introduces a clock, knowing that his readers will immediately recognize its metaphorical significance:

> Carry a clock to the wild inhabitants of the Cape of Good
> Hope. They will soon be convinced that intelligence made it:
> and none but the most stupid will imagine that this intelligence
> is in the hand that they see move, and in the wheels that they see
> turn. Those among them, who pretend to greater sagacity than
> the rest, may perhaps suspect that the workman is concealed in
> the clock, and there conducts invisibly all the motions of it.[22]

Bolingbroke is ridiculing the notion of God's immanence: he is saying, in effect, that to argue, as Newton did, that God continues to operate within his piece of workmanship is to be an over-ingenious Hottentot.

Bolingbroke's faith, such as it is, rests easily upon nature: 'The religion of nature, and therefore of the God of nature, is simple and plain; it tells us nothing which our reason is unable to comprehend, and much less anything which is repugnant to it. Natural religion and reason are always agreed, they are always the same.'[23] He agrees with Leibniz that 'infinite wisdom' has established 'the best of all possible systems',[24] and duly passes on this belief to Pope.

In England freethinkers were denounced from pulpit and press, were ostracized if they were not of high social rank, and in a few, rare cases were imprisoned or pilloried for blasphemy.[25] In France blasphemers were dreadfully tortured, and decapitated. Voltaire, the self-proclaimed literary heir of Bolingbroke, accordingly denounces Christianity more bitterly than any English freethinker does. In his *Examen important de milord Bolingbroke* (1767), purportedly written by Bolingbroke, Voltaire finds that every episode of Old Testament history is 'une hyperbole ridicule, une mensonge grossier, une fable absurde',[26] that Jesus was a mere human, a fanatic, ashamed of his bastardy, who preached firebrand sermons to a malcontent rabble and was duly hanged for his pains, that stories of his resurrection and other miracles and the invention of post-gospel doctrines such as the Trinity were the work of crafty men who intended to deceive and defraud the credulous, and that the later history of Christianity is a tale of persecution, tyranny, bloodshed, and misery. Voltaire's conclusion is that 'tout homme sensé, tout homme de bien, doit avoir la secte chrétienne en horreur'.[27] The remote God of natural religion worshipped by reasonable men has no connection with such bloody nonsense as Christianity.

Natural religion of a very different temper is expounded in the 'profession de foi du vicaire savoyard' in Rousseau's *Emile* (1762). Rousseau agrees with Voltaire and the English freethinkers that the gospel proofs of revealed religion are inadequate and that religious dogma makes men proud, intolerant, and cruel; but he claims that the beauty and holiness of the gospels testify that these books are not fraudulent. Rousseau believes that before our reason adduces the argument from design, we feel in our hearts the innate, God-given principle of justice and virtue which we call conscience. For all his acknowledgements to Locke and Clarke, Rousseau advances much further than Voltaire from the standpoint of early eighteenth-century English natural religion. An advance beyond Voltaire in a different direction, towards avowed atheism, is made at this time by the French materialists, Holbach, who translated Toland, and Helvétius. The influence of all four Frenchmen upon English freethinkers of Tom Paine's Jacobin generation was considerable, but it lies for the most part outside the chronological boundaries of the present volume.

By the time that Bolingbroke's posthumous blunderbuss was discharged, much of the heat had gone from the freethinking controversy in England, partly because 'free' opinions, duly moderated, were widely diffused among men who regarded themselves as tolerably orthodox Christians. Of the three best-known religious poems of the century, the *Essay on Man* (1733–34), the *Seasons* (1726–44), and *Night Thoughts* (1742–46), the first is a systematic treatise on, and the second is largely a rhapsody of, natural religion; only Young's poem, consciously intended to supply a significant deficiency of Pope's, is at all concerned with revealed religion.

The physico-theology preached by Boyle lecturers and other Anglican clergymen is natural religion, behind which lies the unspoken and perhaps unconscious assumption that if God has a prophet he is not Moses but Newton. Within the Church of England and the dissenting sects there was growing embarrassment in the face of those parts of the Old Testament least capable of being reconciled with enlightened notions of morality or the latest findings of science and history, and even where the New Testament was accepted *in toto* doubts were cast over the Fathers' interpretation of Scripture. In particular, the central Christian doctrine of the Trinity appeared to be unscriptural, probably a late importation from Greek philosophy; so that in the eyes of some Anglicans the Athanasian Creed now became as much of an embarrassment for its doctrine as for its, to say the least, uncharitable tenor. In *The Reasonableness of Christianity* Locke found the only essential article of the Christian faith to be a belief that Jesus is the Messiah; the additional doctrines taught by Apostles and Fathers alike are inessential. Samuel Clarke, widely regarded at the time as the inheritor of Locke's place as Britain's leading philosopher, propounded anti-Trinitarian views in *The Scripture Doctrine of the Trinity* (1712), and advanced a controversial proposal to revise the Book of Common Prayer so as to remove or rephrase all Trinitarian formulae.[28] Locke was denounced by some clerics as a Socinian, and Clarke by others as an Arian; the technical difference being that Arians denied Christ's divinity, whereas Socinians (later called Unitarians) also denied his pre-existence.

Clarke, like that other Arian, Whiston, was a disciple of Newton, and Newton believed that a massive fraud had been perpetrated in the fourth and fifth centuries to corrupt Christianity by fraudulently inserting Trinitarian sentiments into the New Testament, particularly at 1 John 5. 7 and 1 Timothy 3. 16. He set out his arguments in 1690 in two letters to Locke, under the title *An Historical Account of Two Notable Corruptions of Scriptures*, but the work was not printed until 1754 – in time to influence Priestley (who was as much devoted to Newtonian theology as to Newtonian science, see Ch. 1 above) and impel him some considerable distance along his path from Calvinism to Unitarianism.

In taking this path Priestley, in Basil Willey's words, 'merely illustrates in epitome what was going on widely amongst the dissenting congregations in the eighteenth century'[29]; by the 1760s freethinking had spread and been institutionalized as a growing Unitarian sect. Priestley shaped and was shaped by the famous Warrington Academy, the cradle of Unitarianism and a centre of radical politics, scientific progress, and academic excellence, which for its brief life from 1757 to 1786 challenged the intellectual leadership of Oxford and Cambridge. In his theological writings Priestley always describes himself as a Christian and sees himself as a defender of Christianity against sceptics, but, except for the pious tone, his arguments read just like those of the freethinkers two generations earlier. The corruptions discussed in his *History of the Corruptions of Christianity* (1782), for instance, include the Trinity, the Virgin Birth, the doctrines of Original

Sin, the Atonement and Predestination, and the plenary inspiration of Scripture. Unitarianism, he argues, was the faith of Christians in the Apostolic age.

What Priestley calls corruptions were all essential articles of faith in the Church of England, but the Latitudinarian clergy who dominated the Church down to the Evangelical revival in the late eighteenth century tended to concern themselves more with ethics than with points of doctrine. There was a general feeling that the religious life was to be lived in the ordinary world, and that the prime duty of man was to lead a life of good works in accordance with the precepts of St James. Archbishop Tillotson's sermons, which were greatly admired and widely imitated, concentrate upon good works and the need for men to imitate the divine benevolence in so far as it lay within their power. Such preaching had its tangible fruit in the growth of organized charity, evidenced particularly by the foundation of many new hospitals. The doctrine of justification by faith was less in evidence, despite the paradox that the much-admired Lockeian philosophy and Newtonian science, in so far as they proved the rule of inexorable law, lent support to the Pauline, Calvinist, and for that matter Anglican doctrine of election and its awful corollary, reprobation. If all things happen by necessity there can be no free will; God fixes the conditions of man's choice and determines from eternity the proportion of souls who will be saved (commonly reckoned as one in twenty), leaving the rest to be damned. This doctrine was preached in all its rigour by some Anglican divines, notably by the Methodist George Whitefield (1714–70), by A. M. Toplady (1740–78), author of 'Rock of ages', and, not without effect upon the poet Cowper, by John Newton (1725–1807); but probably most Anglicans were Arminians, that is believers in free will, because they felt that the doctrine of election was unreasonable and was not consistent with the enlightened belief that benevolence is the chief attribute of God. The theology of the Church of England was fairly summed up by William Pitt, Earl of Chatham, in 1773 as 'a Calvinistic Creed, a Popish Liturgy and Arminian Clergy'.[30]

We have seen how Christian apologeticists deploy against the attacks of freethinkers a range of rational defences, such as the argument from design, quasi-mathematical proofs, and the historical 'evidences' of revelation, all of which sought to defeat freethinking with its own weapons; the most comprehensive of such defences is *The Analogy of Religion Natural and Revealed to the Constitution and Course of Nature* (1736) by Joseph Butler (1692–1752), which was for nearly a century the classic Anglican argument for the truth of revelation. What is perhaps most remarkable about this work is its defensive tone. In his Preface Butler declares that although many people now look upon Christian revelation as fictitious and ridiculous he proposes to argue that the evidence, taken as a whole, tends to favour its probable truth; with reasonable beings 'probability is the very guide of life'. He claims that the argument from design is not as clear-cut as hitherto assumed, and that the difficulties in that argument are of precisely the same sort as those found in biblical revelation; the analogies between revelation and nature make it likely that they both proceed from the same author. Moral government by God, evident in our own consciences (see Ch. 3 below) as well as in external nature, should suffice to engage us 'to live in the general practice of all virtue and piety; under the serious apprehension, though it should be mixed with some doubt, of a righteous administration established in nature, and a future judgement in consequence of it'.[31] Butler offers in addition an orthodox defence of miracles as a necessary part of God's revelation in early, relatively barbarous periods, when man was unable to reason out his religion as he is now able to do. Throughout, Butler takes for granted the existence of an intelligent author of nature, and the immortality of the soul.

It is a striking testimony to the power and pervasiveness of both the argument from design and the appeal to ordinary reason in judging historical 'evidences' that the most authoritative defence of Christianity in the eighteenth century has to demonstrate the truth of revelation on the basis of its analogy with natural religion and its reasonable probability. When the freethinkers express doubts concerning revelation, Butler retorts, in effect, by showing that the same doubts might be expressed about natural religion. He rests his argument on the belief that no one among his opponents or his supporters could question the truth of natural religion, so he asks his readers to infer that revealed and natural religion are equally true. The response could be that they are equally false.

The most urbane and perhaps most effective critic of orthodox Christian apologetics during this period was David Hume (see Ch. 3 below). His notorious essay on miracles was first intended to form part of his *Treatise of Human Nature* (1739–40), but was withheld from that work on account of concern for the feelings of Joseph Butler, the only contemporary Christian apologeticist Hume respected. In December 1737 Hume wrote to Henry Home: 'I am at present castrating my work, that is cutting off its nobler parts; that is, endeavouring it shall give as little offence as possible, before which, I could not pretend to put it into the Doctor's hands.'[32] The essay was, however, published before Butler's death; it was incorporated into a recast version of Book One of the *Treatise*, published as *Philosophical Essays concerning Human Understanding* (1748), and later as *An Enquiry concerning Human Understanding* (1758).

Hume begins his essay 'Of Miracles' with a gracious acknowledgement to Archbishop Tillotson's concise, elegant, and strong argument against trans-ubstantiation, which, Hume alleges, has suggested the main lines of his own argument against all supernatural prodigies; here he follows Toland and Collins. All wise men proportion their belief in anything according to the evidence for it: the more inherently unlikely a fact, the more evidence is required to prove it; but testimony in favour of a miracle cannot conceivably outweigh testimony in favour of the 'natural law' which the miracle is said to violate. This argument holds even if, with Hume in the *Treatise*, we accept that the 'laws of nature' are known to us only as uniform, customary connections in our imaginations (see Ch. 3 below). There is not in all recorded history a single miracle attested by a sufficient number of men of such unquestioned good sense, education, and learning, as to secure them from the possibility of delusion, and of such integrity as to place them beyond the suspicion of deceit. With high good humour Hume exposes the absurdity of miracles and prophecies recounted in the Bible, and counts

himself well satisfied to have confounded 'those dangerous friends or disguised enemies to the *Christian Religion*, who have undertaken to defend it
by the principles of human reason'. Mere reason is insufficient to convince
us of the veracity of Christianity: 'And whoever is moved by *Faith* to assent
to it, is conscious of a continued miracle in his own person, which subverts
all the principles of his understanding, and gives him a determination to
believe what is most contrary to custom and experience.'[33] In his *Treatise*,
though, Hume shows that mere reason is insufficient to convince us of the
veracity of anything. Though his ironic tone and insistent scepticism in the
essay 'Of Miracles' was probably intended to vex the orthodox, his concluding reference to the continuing miracle of faith pointed out the best
refuge for Christianity, as the advancement of knowledge in this and the
following century made traditional arguments from revelation and from
design increasingly untenable.

In his *Natural History of Religion*, first published in *Four Dissertations*
(1757), Hume drily reviews many of the bizarre variant forms assumed by
religion down the ages. He finds that the earliest religions were polytheistic;
they personified man's hopes and fears, and arose in response to the innumerable, otherwise inexplicable accidents and chances of primitive life.
Agitated by hope and even more by fear, men 'examine the various and
contrary events of human life. And in this disordered scene, with eyes still
more disordered and astonished, they see the first obscure traces of divinity.'
In a footnote Hume reminds his readers that as early as Hesiod's time there
were 30,000 deities, but these were hardly enough for the tasks to be
performed by them: 'there was even a God of Sneezing', and the 'province of
copulation, suitable to the importance and dignity of it, was divided
amongst several deities'.[34] Men were first led to monotheism by the spirit of
adulation and flattery to which the superstitious are prone; here Hume offers
strange instances of superstitious adulation on the part of Zoroastrians,
Mahometans, and Roman Catholics. Polytheism is marked by toleration,
and brings in its train 'activity, spirit, courage, magnanimity, love of liberty,
and all the virtues, which aggrandize a people'; monotheism is intolerant and
entails 'the monkish virtues of mortification, pennance, humility and passive
suffering', so giving rise to the observation of Machiavelli, that Christianity
'had subdued the spirit of mankind, and had fitted them for slavery and
subjection'.[35] Polytheism is favoured by ignorant barbarians; monotheism is
now favoured by the learned because it rests upon the reasonable argument
from design. This argument is drawn from effects (the phenomena of
nature) to their hypothetical cause (God); but in the *Treatise* Hume had
thrown considerable doubt upon whether a cause could be known only from
its effect, and had argued that reason is no ground for belief. The last words
of Hume's *Natural History of Religion* are similar in temper to the conclusion
of his *Treatise* (p.60 below), though by a nicely-judged irony he now retreats
into, rather than escapes from, the philosopher's study:

> Doubt, uncertainty, suspence of judgment appear the only
> result of our most accurate scrutiny, concerning this subject.
> But such is the frailty of human reason, and such the irresistible

contagion of opinion, that even this deliberate doubt could
scarce be upheld; did we not enlarge our view, and opposing
one species of superstition to another, set them a quarreling;
while we ourselves, during their fury and contention, happily
make our escape, into the calm, tho' obscure, regions of
philosophy.[36]

Hume's last arguments for religious scepticism are placed in the mouth of
Philo, one of the speakers in *Dialogues concerning Natural Religion*, published
posthumously in 1779. The *Dialogues* is a loose imitation of Cicero's *De
natura deorum*, like that work a three-way dialogue, but unlike it in that all
three speakers are given excellent speeches. The weakest case is given to
Demea, representing 'rigid inflexible Orthodoxy', who first attempts to
prove the existence of God by the a priori reasoning of a Samuel Clarke, but
finally rests his case upon the individual man's awareness of ignorance and
feeling of misery:

> each Man feels, in a manner, the Truth of Religion within his
> own Breast; and from a Consciousness of his Imbecility and
> Misery, rather than from any Reasoning, is led to seek
> Protection from that Being, on whom he and all Nature is
> dependent. So anxious or so tedious are even the best Scenes of
> Life, that Futurity is still the Object of all our Hopes and Fears.
> We incessantly look forward, and endeavour, by Prayers,
> Adoration, and Sacrifice, to appease those unknown Powers,
> whom we find, by Experience, so able to afflict and oppress
> us.[37]

The second interlocutor, Cleanthes, described as a man of 'accurate
philosophical Turn', quotes with approval Locke's assertion that faith is
nothing but a species of reason, and puts forward the a posteriori argument
from design. To his use of the customary clock and clock-maker analogy the
third speaker, Philo, mischievously retorts that, as the world 'plainly resembles more an Animal or a Vegetable than it does a Watch, or a Knitting
Loom',[38] the creator could just as well be a vegetable as a mechanic. Demea
agrees with Philo that the argument from design is unsound, but is shocked
by the echo of his own reflections on human misery in Philo's description of
the plenitude of nature, so often adduced as a proof of God's goodness:

> Look round this Universe. What an immense Profusion of
> Beings, animated and organiz'd, sensible and active! You
> admire this prodigious Variety and Fecundity. But inspect a
> little more narrowly these living Existences, the only Beings
> worth regarding. How hostile and destructive to each other!
> How insufficient all of them for their own Happiness! How
> contemptible or odious to the Spectator! The whole presents
> nothing but the Idea of a blind Nature, impregnated by a great
> vivifying Principle, and pouring forth from her Lap, without

Discernment or parental Care, her maim'd and abortive
Children.[39]

Philo concludes that the first cause or causes of order in the universe have
neither goodness nor malice, and that nothing can be known for certain of
their being or their attributes. Finally, he asks in mock-plaintive tones for a
revelation, evidently not thinking the Christian revelation worth mentioning.

With his sharper intelligence and more urbane manner than Bolingbroke,
Voltaire, or any of the other freethinkers, Hume was regarded as a deadly foe
of Christianity: Johnson frequently inveighed against him; in Reynolds's
allegorical painting *The Triumph of Truth* Hume and Voltaire are represented
as demons being driven down to Hell by angels under the approving gaze of
James Beattie (see Ch. 3 below); but however harmful to Christianity,
Hume's attack was just as damaging to that theistic natural religion favoured
by the freethinkers. In showing that religion arises from passion and imagination, fear and desire, Hume challenged the notion of 'natural reason',
and disproved the existence of any single, universal natural religion. The
claim in his *Natural History* that polytheism predated monotheism challenged
the widespread assumptions that the idea of one God is innate in man or at
least is to be easily apprehended from the workings of nature, that the religion
of nature, and therefore the God of nature, is simple and plain, and that
Christianity is therefore as old as the creation. Hume showed that, on the
contrary, religions evolve slowly in the course of time, as the product of
various cultures. Though he does not believe that their evolution is necessarily
progressive, Hume thus shares the eighteenth-century tendency to see history
in evolutionary terms. Finally, whether intended ironically or not, his allusion
in the essay 'Of Miracles' to a continuing miracle of faith and the words he puts
into Demea's mouth concerning the felt truth of religion within a man's own
breast, pointed to a defence of Christianity independent of external evidences
or reason.

In the eighteenth, as in earlier centuries, many Christians affirmed with
Pascal that the heart has its reasons which the reason knows nothing of. This
certainly was the belief of the most admired devotional writer of the century,
William Law (1686–1761). In Law's view, to trust in mere reason is to be a
'nominal Christian', a 'historical Christian', or a 'liberal Christian', and to
indulge in the same kind of gross idolatry as the freethinkers. The evidence is
within the believer's own heart in the witness of his spirit to the inward desire
for holiness. The proof of the faith is the faith itself, the turning to God. Thus
he writes in *The Way to Divine Knowledge* (1752): 'This is Christian Redemption; on the one side, it is the *Heavenly Divine Life offering itself again to the
inward Man, that has lost it.* On the other side, it is the *Hope, the Faith, and Desire
of this inward Man, hungering, and thirsting, stretching after, and calling upon this
Divine and Heavenly Life.*'[40] Religious faith rests upon the unshakable
subjective ground of man's will, desire, and creative imagination:

Our own Will and desirous Imagination . . . resemble in some
Degree the Creating Power of God, which makes things out of
itself or its own working Desire. . . . We are apt to think that our

RELIGIOUS IDEAS 41

> *Imaginations* and *Desires* may be played with, that they rise and
> fall away as nothing, because they do not always bring forth
> outward and visible Effects. But indeed they are the greatest
> reality we have, and are the true *Formers* and *Raisers* of all that is
> real and solid in us. All outward Power that we exercise in the
> Things about us, is but a *Shadow* in Comparison of that *inward
> Power*, that resides in our *Will, Imagination* and *Desires*.[41]

Though eventually he came to detest Law's quietism and mysticism, John
Wesley (1703–91) was thoroughly overwhelmed, as Johnson was, by Law's
Serious Call to a Devout and Holy Life (1729). Wesley's aversion to reason was
markedly more intense than Law's, for he broke off his study of
mathematics because he feared it would lead to atheism, and he rejected
Newtonian astronomy as dangerous to faith. He believed that sin is the
moral cause of earthquakes, whatever their natural cause may be, and he
looked upon every accident in his life as proof of the direct and immediate
intervention of God or the Devil. He stubbornly believed in witchcraft,
lamenting in 1768 that infidels have hooted it out of the world: 'They well
know (whether Christians know it or not) that the giving up of witchcraft is
in effect giving up the Bible.'[42]

Infidelity had made fewer encroachments upon Christian faith on the
Continent at this time, to judge by the fact that witches were still being
burned by Protestants as late as 1782 in Switzerland, and by Roman
Catholics as late as 1793 in Poland. The last witch to be judicially convicted
in England was Jane Wenham,[43] who in 1712 was found guilty by a
Hertfordshire jury after three clergymen had testified that she had conversed
with the Devil in the shape of a cat, but she was respited by the sceptical
judge until a pardon was obtained. At one point in the trial, when it was
alleged that the prisoner could fly, the judge observed that flying was not
contrary to English law. The English and Scotch laws against witchcraft
were repealed in 1736, but mob law, as usual, lagged behind; in1751, again
in Hertfordshire, an old woman was ducked as a witch by her neighbours,
and so done to death.[44]

In his superstitions, though perhaps in nothing else, Wesley was very
close to the common people, Locke's 'unreasoning multitude', to whom his
preaching so powerfully appealed. It is said that he travelled 250,000 miles
and preached 40,000 sermons; certainly he reached the lowest classes of
society, those scarcely touched by the Anglican Church or even by the old
Dissenting churches. It was an extraordinary achievement to establish a new
and very extensive Christian church in the course of a single lifetime; the
spread of Methodism belongs, however, more to social history than to the
history of ideas.

Wesley's theology was hopefully Arminian. Bitterly opposed to
Whitefield's Calvinism, he preached the doctrine of good works and the
gospel that salvation is free for all who believe. His authority is always
Scripture confirmed by personal experience, the testimony of the believer's
own spirit: 'The testimony of the Spirit is an inward impression of the soul,
whereby the Spirit of God directly witnesses to my Spirit, that I am a child

of God; that Jesus Christ hath loved me, and gives himself for me; and that all my sins are blotted out, and I, even I, am reconciled to God.'[45] The orthodox view of such subjectivism is contained in Bishop Joseph Butler's well-known reproof to Wesley in 1739: 'Sir, the pretending to extraordinary revelations and gifts of the Holy Ghost is a horrid thing, a very horrid thing.'[46]

Despite the triumph of Methodism, the old Dissenting churches continued strong. The leading figures in eighteenth-century Nonconformity, Isaac Watts (1674–1748) and Philip Doddridge (1702–51), both professed, in so far as such a belief is possible, a 'moderate Calvinism'; their faith was evangelical but not unreasonable. Watts, characteristically, is both orthodox and liberal in his *Psalms of David imitated in the Language of the New Testament* (1719), when he enlightens the jealous God of the Old Testament with the assistance of the New. In his Preface he claims that his imitations do more honour to Christ than would be done by 'going back again to the Jewish forms of worship, and the language of types and figures'. So,

> Where the Psalmist uses sharp invectives against his personal
> enemies, I have endeavoured to turn the edge of them against
> our spiritual adversaries, Sin, Satan, Temptation. . . . Where
> the Psalmist describes religion by the fear of God, I have often
> joined faith and love to it. . . . Where he talks of sacrificing
> goats or bullocks, I rather choose to mention the sacrifice of
> Christ, the Lamb of God.[47]

Watt's metrical psalms, such as 'Jesus shall Reign where'er the Sun' and 'O God our Help in Ages Past', and his other well-known hymns inaugurate the great age of English hymnody, to which Doddridge, the Wesleys, Smart, Cowper, and John Newton made such notable contributions, but his most remarkable evangelical production is perhaps the *Divine Songs attempted in easy Language for the Use of Children* (1715). This work, which was enlarged in many editions to Watts's death and reprinted in countless more (probably well over seven hundred by the end of the nineteenth century), earned the respect of Johnson, at whose insistence Watts was included in the *English Poets*: Johnson wrote, 'Every man, acquainted with the common principles of human action, will look with veneration on the writer who is at one time combating Locke, and at another making a catechism for children in their fourth year. A voluntary descent from the dignity of science is perhaps the hardest lesson that humility can teach.'[48]

It is difficult to overestimate the importance of hymns in the eighteenth century. At a time when nearly everybody engaged in some act of corporate worship, whether in church or chapel or at an open-air Methodist prayer meeting, hymns were the common man's poetry and theology. Donald Davie hardly overstates the case when he writes:

> There is quite clearly *prima facie* quantitative evidence for
> supposing that Watts's *Hymns and Psalms* ('Watts Entire', as it
> came to be called) has been more influential than any of the

works of its century that we think of as most popular – more than Johnson's *Dictionary*, more than *Robinson Crusoe* or *Gulliver's Travels*, more even than *The Seasons* or 'Ossian'.[49]

The same can be said of the most widely used of the 6,000 hymns written by Charles Wesley (1707–88), such as 'Lo! He comes with clouds descending', 'Rejoice, the Lord is King', 'Soldiers of Christ arise', 'Hark! the herald-angels sing', 'Jesu, Lover of my soul', and 'Love Divine, all loves excelling', and of many other hymns written in the eighteenth century and still part of our common culture. Such hymns include 'Christians, awake, salute the happy morn' by John Byrom (1692–1763), 'Hark the glad sound! the Saviour comes' and 'Ye servants of the Lord' by Philip Doddridge, 'Guide me, O Thou great Jehovah', from the Welsh of William Williams (1717–91), 'All hail the power of Jesu's name' by Edward Perronet (1721–92), and 'Rock of ages cleft for me' by Augustus Montague Toplady (1740–78). The collection of *Olney Hymns* (1779) by John Newton and William Cowper contains Newton's 'How sweet the name of Jesus sounds', his 'Glorious things of thee are spoken', and Cowper's 'God moves in a mysterious way.'

Though the freethinkers caused some fluttering in holy dovecotes, the intellectual, moral, and social life of Britain was overwhelmingly Christian: 'Indeed, the age of Wesley, Cowper, and Dr Johnson was perhaps as "religious" as the seventeenth century itself, though it had ceased to fight with the sword about rival doctrines of Christianity, and was, therefore, somewhat tolerant of still wider differences of opinion.'[50] To the names of Wesley, Cowper, and Johnson could be added the great majority of the writers, thinkers, and men of action of the eighteenth century. Our period opens with the work that first made Steele famous, his *Christian Hero* (1701), described on its title-page as 'an Argument proving that no Principles but those of Religion are sufficient to make a great Man'; in 1789, at the end of our period, we find Lieutenant William Bligh (not the ogre of legend, but one of the most notable English navigators in a great age of navigation) composing prayers for his dying companions on their heroic open-boat voyage across more than half the Pacific after the famous mutiny on HMS *Bounty*.

Notes

1. *An Essay concerning Human Understanding*, edited Peter H. Nidditch (Oxford, 1975), p. 314; Book II, Chapter xxiii, Section 33. This passage is quoted in Addison, *Spectator*, no. 531 (8 November 1712).

2. *Essay concerning Human Understanding*, pp. 87–88; I, iv, 8.

3. Ibid., p. 619; IV, x, 1.

4. Ibid., p. 516; III, xi, 16.

5. *The Reasonableness of Christianity*, in *Works* (1801), vii, 135, 146.

6. Ibid., 157–58.

7. *Religio Medici* (1643), Part i, Section xvi, in *Works of Sir Thomas Browne*, edited by C. Sayle (Edinburgh, 1912), i, 25.

8. Quoted in Basil Willey, *The Eighteenth-Century Background* (1940), p. 38.

9. Sermon lxxxiii, 'The Wisdom of God in the Creation of the World', in John Tillotson, *Works* (1712), i, 623.

10. *Opticks*, edited by E. T. Whittaker (1931), p. 402; query 31.

11. *British Moralists*, edited by L. A. Selby-Bigge (Oxford, 1897), ii, 31.

12. *Christianity not Mysterious* (1696), section ii, introduction.

13. Quoted in Stuart Piggott, *The Druids* (Harmondsworth, 1974), p. 120.

14. *Characteristicks*, second edition (1714), ii, 48.

15. Ibid., ii, 11.

16. Ibid., i,10.

17. *Discourse of Free-Thinking* (1713), p. 5.

18. Ibid., p. 171.

19. Ibid., p. 39.

20. Bolingbroke, *Philosophical Works* (1754), iii, 355.

21. Boswell's *Life of Johnson*, edited by G. B. Hill, revised by L. F. Powell (Oxford, 1934), i, 268.

22. Bolingbroke, ii, 59.

23. Bolingbroke, iv, 259–60.

24. Bolingbroke, v, 332.

25. See 'Annet, Peter (1693–1769)', and 'Woolston, Thomas (1670–1733)' in *Dictionary of National Biography*, ii, 9–10; lxii, 437–9.

26. *Œuvres complètes*, edited by L. Moland (Paris, 1877–85), xxvi, 201.

27. Ibid., p. 298.

28. See Norman Sykes, *Church and State in England in the XVIIIth Century* (Cambridge, 1934), pp. 386–88.

29. Willey, p. 181.

30. Quoted in Donald Davie, *A Gathered Church* (1978), p. 8.

31. *Analogy*, Part i, Conclusion, in *Works of Butler* (Edinburgh, 1810), i, 173.

32. *The Letters of David Hume*, edited by J. Y. T. Greig (Oxford, 1932), i, 25.

33. *Enquiries*, edited by L. A. Selby-Bigge, second edition (Oxford, 1902), paras. 100, 101, pp. 130–31.

34. *Natural History of Religion and Dialogues concerning Natural Religion*, edited by A. W. Colver and J. V. Price (Oxford, 1976), p. 32.

35. Ibid., pp. 62–63.

36. Ibid., p. 95.

37. Ibid., pp. 219–20.

38. Ibid., p. 202.

39. Ibid., p. 241.

40. *The Works of the Reverend William Law* (1762, reprinted 1892–93), vii, 190.

41. *An Appeal to all that Doubt, or Disbelieve the Truths of the Gospels, whether they be Deists, Arians, Socinians, or Nominal Christians . . . to which are added. Some Animadversions upon Dr. Trapp's Late Reply* (1740), in *Works* (1762, reprinted 1892–93), vi, 72.

42. *Journals of John Wesley*, edited by Nehemiah Curnock (1983), v, 375.

43. See *Dictionary of National Biography*, (1899) i x, 253.

44. 'Osborne, Ruth (1680–1751)', in ibid. (1895), xlii, 293–94.

45. *Standard Sermons*, edited by E. H. Sugden (1921), i, 208.

46. A. Duncan-Jones, *Butler's Moral Philosophy* (Harmondsworth, 1952), p. 21.

47. Quoted in David Fountain, *Isaac Watts Remembered* (Worthing, 1974), p. 58.

48. *Lives of the Poets* (1784), iv, 286–7.

49. *A Gathered Church: The Literature of the English Dissenting Interest, 1700–1930* (1978), pp. 33–34.

50. G. M. Trevelyan, *English Social History* (1942), p. 353.

Chapter 3
Philosophy

Philosophy, 'something intermediate between theology and science',[1] was more accessible to the well-informed reading public in the eighteenth century than at any period before or since. The *Spectator*, fairly reflecting the interests of thoughtful, literate men in the reign of Queen Anne, brought modern science within the comprehension of its readers, it satisfied their great appetite for theological discourse, and it provided them with modern philosophy. Addison, who could gauge the temper and taste of his age perhaps better than anyone else, announced in the *Spectator*, no. 10 (1711), with justifiable pride and only a touch of self-mockery: 'It was said of Socrates that he brought Philosophy down from Heaven, to inhabit among Men; and I shall be ambitious to have it said of me, that I have brought Philosophy out of Closets and Libraries, Schools and Colleges, to dwell in Clubs and Assemblies, at Tea-Tables and in Coffee-Houses.'

Philosophy retained some of its heavenly, or at least its theological nature for Addison, whose most characteristic literary form was the lay-sermon, but the general tendency of eighteenth-century philosophy was away from theology, towards science. Philosophers were greatly impressed by the successes of contemporary scientists in the acquisition of what appeared to be certain knowledge and they were eager to gain an equal degree of certainty in their own investigations. So they were inclined to give structures of a mathematical kind to their speculations; they were stimulated by current theories in optics and physiology to make fresh approaches to the question of the relationship between mind and matter (an old problem posed in a particularly acute form by Descartes in the previous century); and they undertook a search into the means of knowledge that was intended to be as far-reaching as the scientists' search into the physical objects of knowledge. The larger aim of most eighteenth-century philosophers was to establish secure foundations for morality, now that morality was no longer, in Leslie Stephen's phrase, 'the handmaid of theology'.[2] The theories of 'moral sentiments' and the notions of 'social love' and 'sympathy' which they developed in pursuit of this aim were of great importance for poets, novelists, and literary critics of the day; but even more important for imaginative literature and criticism were the overall subjective tendencies of early eighteenth-century philosophy and its validation of the creative imagination. These literary-critical developments are traced in Chapter 5, but they are implicit in the present chapter, where the starting-point is, again, John Locke.

When eighteenth-century Englishmen celebrated, as they often did, their native intellectual giants, the name most commonly linked with Newton was Locke; he is the one philosopher referred to in Addison's *Spectator* papers even more frequently than Newton himself. In *An Essay concerning Human Understanding* (first published 1690, fourth, revised, edition, 1700) Locke modestly refers to himself as an under-labourer, clearing the ground of rubbish a little to assist master-builders such as Newton. He does not aspire to systemize the world of mind as Newton systemized the world of matter, but, in his way, he is no less bold an explorer in carrying out his declared purpose 'to enquire into the Original, Certainty, and Extent of humane knowledge; together, with the Grounds and Degrees of Belief, Opinion, and Assent'. From the outset he makes it clear that he will not 'meddle with the Physical Consideration of the Mind' or be concerned 'to examine, wherein its Essence consists, or by what Motions of our Spirits, or Alterations of our Bodies, we come to have any Sensation by our Organs, or any *Ideas* in our Understandings; and whether those *Ideas* do in their Formation, any, or all of them, depend on Matter or no'. Materialist implications would, however, be explored by some of his successors, particularly in France. Locke defines 'Idea' as 'whatsoever is the Object of the Understanding when a Man thinks': that is, an idea is an intermediate object between the knowing mind and some ultimate object of perception. Such ideas include sense-data, memories, and more abstract conceptions; but Locke habitually refers to them all, whether sensory or conjectural, as 'pictures'. At one point he takes the camera obscura (so valuable to Newton) as a model for the way in which such pictures are painted in the mind: 'methinks the *Understanding* is not much unlike a Closet wholly shut from light, with only some little openings left, to let in external visible Resemblances, or *Ideas* of things without'.[3] The dominant metaphor of ideas as pictures reinforces Locke's demonstration that our simple ideas are principally derived from sight, the most comprehensive of our senses and the chief intermediary between matter and mind. This metaphor is Addison's starting-point when he develops his theory of the imagination on the basis of Locke's psychology; Addison also alludes to the camera obscura.

Clearing the ground of rubbish, Locke begins his *Essay* by refuting the hypothesis, shared by ancient Stoics and modern Cartesians, that certain notions are innate in the mind. In its place he puts forward the theory advanced earlier by Aristotle and Bacon[4] (those least mystical of philosophers), that the mind is a *tabula rasa* at birth, and acquires all ideas by experience:

> Let us then suppose the Mind to be, as we say, white Paper,
> void of all Characters, without any *Ideas*; How comes it to be
> furnished? Whence comes it by that vast store, which the busy
> and boundless Fancy of Man has painted on it, with an almost
> endless variety? Whence has it all the materials of Reason and
> Knowledge? To this I answer, in one word, From *Experience*: In
> that, all our Knowledge is founded; and from that it ultimately
> derives it self. Our Observation employ'd either about *external*,

*sensible Objects; or about the internal Operations of our Minds,
perceived and reflected on by our selves, is that, which supplies our
Understandings with all the materials of thinking.*

Though 'Reflection', that is our own perception of the internal operations of
our minds, is 'not Sense, as having nothing to do with external Objects; yet
it is very like it, and might properly enough be call'd internal Sense'.[5] The
notion of 'internal sense' was developed by Hutcheson and others, but it was
the vivid conception of the mind as white paper that seized the imagination
of generations of reformers, inspiring them with the hope of being able to
transform the operations of human nature through a reshaping of environment. If the mind at birth truly is a *tabula rasa*, then moral and
intellectual differences between individual men as well as differences of
manners and customs between societies are occasioned only by relatively
easily removable differences in education. During our period this argument
was pushed to its greatest lengths in France, notably by Claude Adrien
Helvétius (1715–71), and duly played its part in the ferment of ideas which
gave rise to the French Revolution; the neologism 'perfectibilité', to denote a
wholly secular notion of individual or social improvement, first appears in
France towards the end of Helvétius's life, some twenty years before it
crosses the Channel and adopts an English spelling. Locke himself, of
course, did not go far along the revolutionary road, but in *Some Thoughts
Concerning Education* (1693) he explores less ambitiously many of the
practical pedagogic consequences of his denial of innate ideas. This work,
which reached its fourteenth edition by 1772, was not without its influence
on educators, both real and fictional: Mr B. gave a copy of it to Pamela, and
Lord Chesterfield gave one to his son; its precepts also shaped Walter
Shandy's programme for the education of young Tristram.

Despite his initial unwillingness to meddle with the physical consideration
of the mind or to speculate upon whether ideas depend upon matter, it
appears that Locke assumes with Newton that physical objects do exist, and
that perception is brought about causally by the action of physical objects on
the mind through the senses and the brain. He raises the possibility to be
explored by Berkeley, that the existence of ideas in the mind is no proof of
the existence of external objects: 'whether there be any thing more than
barely that *Idea* in our Minds, whether we can thence certainly infer the
existence of any thing without us, which corresponds to that *Idea*, is that,
whereof some Men think there may be a question made'; but his common
sense will not allow him to believe that the external world is not real. He
points to the difference between dreaming of being in the fire and actually
being in it: 'we certainly finding, that Pleasure or Pain follows upon the
application of certain Objects to us, whose Existence we perceive, or dream
that we perceive, by our Senses, this certainty is as great as our Happiness,
or Misery, beyond which, we have no concernment to know, or to be'.[6]
This utilitarian conclusion is highly characteristic of Locke.

The powers by which external objects produce ideas in the mind are called
by Locke qualities; of these he distinguishes two kinds, primary and secondary. Primary qualities are 'Solidity, Extension, Figure, Motion or Rest,

and Number'. Secondary qualities 'in truth are nothing in the Objects themselves, but Powers to produce various Sensations in us by their *primary Qualities* . . . as Colours, Sounds, Tasts, etc.'[7] Locke's primary qualities are exactly those presupposed by Newton in the *Principia*; their distinction from secondary qualities is implied by Newton's speculations concerning colour in the *Opticks*. Primary qualities would exist if no one perceived them; secondary qualities are inconceivable without perception. Even though our ideas of secondary qualities, unlike our ideas of primary qualities, are not exact resemblances of 'the thing in itself', Locke does not regard secondary qualities as subjective. Some of his popularizers, however, seem to allow this possibility: there is a particularly suggestive passage in Addison's papers on the imagination, quoted in Chapter 5 below.

Though Locke refers to the mind metaphorically as a camera obscura, he speaks also of ideas being admitted through the senses and the nerves, 'which are the Conduits, to convey them from without to their Audience in the Brain, the mind's Presence-room'.[8] This presence-room metaphor implies that the understanding has the active role of a ruler or judge. In Locke's view the mind is both passive and active. It is passive like a camera obscura when it receives simple ideas from sensation and reflection (this passiveness, coupled with the notion of the *tabula rasa*, is a warrant for the reality of the external world); but the mind is active when exerting its power over simple ideas in order to combine them into complex ideas, or to relate them to one another, or to abstract from them. Such activity is not always deliberate: as Locke shows in his influential chapter on the association of ideas (Book III, Ch. xxxiii), the Mind may combine ideas just as powerfully by chance as by volition. This was Mrs Shandy's case, as Sterne indicates with his reference to 'the sagacious Locke, who certainly understood the nature of these things better than most men'.[9]

Though the number of complex ideas is infinite, they may all be categorized as substances, modes, or relations. Ideas of substances are such natural combinations of simple ideas as are taken to represent distinct particular kinds of things: for instance, the idea of a swan is 'white Colour, long Neck, red Beak, black Legs, and whole Feet, and all these of a certain size, with a power of swimming in the Water, and making a certain kind of Noise, and, perhaps, to a Man, who has long observed those kind of Birds, some other Properties'. Nevertheless, the abstract idea of pure substance, the 'Substratum' in which duly united simple ideas subsist, remains a problem: 'all our *Ideas* of the several sorts of Substances, are nothing but Collections of simple *Ideas*, with a Supposition of something, to which they belong, and in which they subsist; though of this supposed something, we have no clear distinct *Idea* at all'.[10] Whereas substances, by definition, subsist by themselves, modes do not. Modes are attributes of substances, such as the complex ideas signified by the words 'piety', 'triangle', 'gratitude', 'beauty', 'justice', 'theft', and so on. Relation 'consists in the consideration and comparing one *Idea* with another'.

I have dwelt at length upon Locke's theory of a causal connection between sensation and knowledge because it particularly influenced creative writers and critics in the eighteenth century. Knowledge of objects by sensation was, however, placed by Locke in the lowest of three degrees of certainty. In the second degree he placed 'demonstration', by which we know 'the Existence of a GOD' (the indefinite article is revealing). In the highest degree, following Descartes, he placed 'intuition', by which we know our own existence: 'In every Act of Sensation, Reasoning, or Thinking, we are conscious to our selves of our own Being; and in this Matter, come not short of the highest degree of *Certainty*.'[11] For Locke, though, 'our selves' are no more, or less, substantial than our states of consciousness: '*Socrates* waking and sleeping is not the same Person . . . *Self* is that conscious thinking thing, (whatever Substance, made up of whether Spiritual, or Material, Simple, or Compounded, it matters not) which is sensible, or conscious of Pleasure and Pain, capable of Happiness or Misery, and so is concern'd for it *self*, as far as that consciousness extends.'[12] The parenthesis might disconcert orthodox Christians, but the notion of the self constantly being remade as it becomes conscious of new sensations was to become one of the intellectual foundations of the eighteenth-century sentimental novel.

The emphasis here upon pleasure and pain, happiness and misery, is in keeping with Locke's somewhat Hobbesian viewpoint on morals, from which pleasure, happiness, and good are one and the same. Locke from time to time claims that moral philosophy is as capable of real certainty as mathematics, because the ideas involved in a moral system, like those involved in mathematics, are modes; but his own moral system is essentially that it is reasonable to obey God's will as revealed in the Scriptures, because to do so will bring reward and happiness, and to fail to do so will entail punishment and misery. Locke, like Newton, is a professing Christian; he does not consider the possibility that 'God' might be merely 'a God', but in his argument to demonstrate that what are taken by some philosophers to be universal innate moral principles, such as justice, piety, gratitude, equity, and chastity, are actually no more than the effects upon individual persons of shared cultural environment and common experience, he notes that morality differs greatly in different times and places:

> He that will carefully peruse the History of Mankind, and look
> abroad into the several Tribes of Men, and with indifferency
> survey their Actions, will be able to satisfy himself, That there
> is scarce that Principle of Morality to be named, or *Rule* of
> *Vertue* to be thought on . . . which is not, somewhere or other,
> *slighted* and condemned by the general Fashion of *whole Societies*
> of Men, governed by practical Opinions, and Rules of living
> quite opposite to others.[13]

The single reference to 'Sin' in Locke's compendious index to *An Essay Concerning Human Understanding* is not to original sin: it reads 'Sin with different Men stands for different actions'. If Newton's work eventually opened the way to relativity, Locke's more rapidly opened the way to relativism.

Though Locke is over-modest in calling himself nothing more than Newton's under-labourer, his psychology is consistent with and rests upon the assumptions of Newtonian physics; in his theology too he is close to Newton. Their great German contemporary Leibniz challenged Newtonian physics and theology (see Ch. 1 above), and partly on that account proved far less influential in eighteenth-century England than Locke was. The implication of Leibniz's theory of monads is that God in the act of creation has preformed every shape of life that the monads are ever destined to assume and has ordained everything that is ever going to happen. As Leibniz argues in his *Essais de Theodicée sur la bonté de Dieu, la liberté de l'homme, et l'origine du mal* (1710), God has the power to create any world that is logically possible and necessarily chose to create the best of all possible worlds. The world contains evil of course, but we can be logically certain that a world without evil would not be as good as the world containing precisely the quantity of evil that we find in this one. This optimistic doctrine is stated most memorably in Pope's *Essay on Man*:

> Of Systems possible, if 'tis confest
> That Wisdom infinite must form the best. . . .
> One truth is clear, 'Whatever IS, is RIGHT.'
>
> (I. 43–44, 294)

It is satirized most fiercely in Voltaire's *Candide*, where, after his involvement in the natural calamity of the Lisbon earthquake of 1755 and the human cruelty of an *auto da fé*, the hero asks: 'si c'est ici le meilleur des mondes possibles, que sont donc les autres?' Voltaire was a major champion of Newton and Locke in Europe; he shared with them a pragmatic temper that was outraged by Leibniz's fatalistic acceptance of 'necessary' evil and he was highly unsympathetic to any kind of metaphysical system-building devoid of experimental basis.

Eighteenth-century Englishmen were hardly more sympathetic towards questions raised against Newtonian physics and Lockeian psychology by George Berkeley (1685–1753) who, in *A Treatise concerning the Principles of Human Knowledge* (1710) seeks to show that the commonly received 'scientific' notion of the existence of matter is false, and that what are called material objects of sense exist only in the mind, and are the impressions made upon our minds by the immediate act of God. Berkeley accepts that there are ideas and that there is something which perceives them and exercises such operations as imagining and remembering upon them, a something which Berkeley calls indifferently '*mind, spirit, soul*, or *my self*': these words 'do not denote any one of my ideas, but a thing entirely distinct from them, wherein they exist, or, which is the same thing, whereby they are perceived; for the existence of an idea consists in being perceived'. The notion of objects existing without relation to their being perceived is unintelligible: 'Their *esse* is *percipi*, nor is it possible they should have any existence, out of the minds or thinking things which perceive them.'[14] The whole universe is mind-dependent:

> Some truths there are, so near and obvious to the mind that a
> man need only open his eyes to see them. Such I take this

important one to be, viz. that all the choir of heaven and
furniture of the earth, in a word all those bodies which compose
the mighty frame of the world, have not any subsistence
without a mind; that their *being* is to be perceived or known.[15]

Locke claimed that ideas in the mind are caused by 'powers' in the external
natural object: Berkeley denies that unthinking matter can be the cause of
ideas; he denies Locke's distinction between primary and secondary qualities, and cuts at one stroke through the difficulties experienced by Locke in
his efforts to conceive of the relationship between ideas which are in our
minds and external objects which are not. Matter, if it exists, is unknowable
to us; Newtonian time, space, and motion are inconceivable. Berkeley
recognizes that physical objects are really more permanent than they would
be if they depended for their existence upon being perceived by some human
mind; but he asserts that they all exist as ideas in the infinite mind of God; so,
in effect, the physical world does exist independently of the mind of the
human perceiver. Indeed, the world of appearances is a manifestation of the
spiritual presence of God, so it follows that, directly and immediately
through our senses, we are able to maintain continuous communication with
the divine spirit.

Berkeley's theory of immaterialism is restated in the more elegant,
popular, and Platonic form of *Three Dialogues between Hylas and Philonous*
(1713). In them Hylas puts the 'scientific' point of view: for instance in the
first dialogue he explains colour in only slightly parodied Newtonian terms
as 'nothing but a thin fluid substance, whose minute particles being agitated
with a brisk motion, and in various manners reflected from the different
surfaces of outward objects to the eyes, communicate different motions to
the optic nerves; which being propagated to the brain, cause therein various
impressions: and these are attended with the sensations of red, blue, yellow,
&c'. Philonous, representing Berkeley's point of view, is able to persuade
Hylas that such 'motions' are quite unknown, and to force him eventually
into a position of complete scepticism concerning the 'real existence' of
objects of sense. In the second dialogue Philonous launches into a rhapsodic
survey of natural beauties somewhat in the enthusiastic vein of Theocles in
Shaftesbury's *The Moralists*:

> Look! are not the fields covered with a delightful verdure? Is
> there not something in the woods and groves, in the rivers and
> clear springs that soothes, that delights, that transports the soul?
> At the prospect of the wide and deep ocean, or some huge
> mountain whose top is lost in the clouds, or of an old gloomy
> forest, are not our minds filled with a pleasing horror? Even in
> rocks and deserts, is there not an agreeable wildness?

He continues to enthuse over the sublimity, beauty, and glory of natural
objects, and concludes by asking Hylas how he can believe that such things
are not real: 'How should those principles be entertained, that lead us to
think all the visible beauty of the creation a false imaginary glare?'[16] He

might well have asked the same question of Addison (see Ch. 5 below). Paradoxically, these noble and delightful scenes *are* real, for though they do not depend upon the mind of the human perceiver they depend upon the mind of God.

For all its importance in the developments of nineteenth-century and twentieth-century philosophy, Berkeley's theory of immaterialism did not exercise much influence upon its author's contemporaries. The reaction of most readers appears to have been one of polite incredulity, but Johnson's refutation has a certain brutal directness. Boswell reports: 'I observed, that though we are satisfied Berkeley's doctrine is not true, it is impossible to refute it. I never shall forget the alacrity with which Johnson answered, striking his foot with mighty force against a large stone, till he rebounded from it, "I refute it *thus*".'[17]

The only criticism of Newton and Locke at all widely accepted in early eighteenth-century England is in the Platonism and sentimental ethics of the writings by Anthony Ashley Cooper, third Earl of Shaftesbury (1671–1713), collected in 1711 as *Characteristicks of Men, Manners, Opinions, Times*. Shaftesbury's method, like Locke's, is self-examination. Locke had made the understanding its own object and had sought to let in some light upon his own mind: Shaftesbury more ambitiously exhorts his reader and himself to 'make a formal Descent on the Territorys of *the Heart*'.[18] Locke had attempted to devise by the empirical method a science of morals as exact as mathematics: Shaftesbury uses the term '*Moral Arithmetick*' to describe his own moral philosophy in *An Inquiry concerning Virtue and Merit* (first published in 1699), because, he claims, 'the Subject treated may be said to have an Evidence as great as that which is found in Numbers or Mathematicks'. This evidence is found in our own feelings; to be exact, in the feelings of that remarkably amiable noble moral-arithmetician who is writing. Shaftesbury takes Locke's image of the understanding as a ruler or judge giving audience to ideas as they are ushered into his presence chamber, but for Shaftesbury the key figure (whether advocate or judge) is the heart, because the heart's business is with values, not things: 'In these vagrant Chambers or Pictures of *Manners*, which the Mind of necessity figures to itself, and carrys still about with it, the Heart cannot possibly remain neutral; but constantly takes part one way or other.' So 'in all disinterested Cases' it 'must approve in some measure of what is natural and honest, and disapprove what is dishonest and corrupt'.[19]

Though Shaftesbury does not argue that there are ideas which are literally innate (for 'connatural' is his term), he claims that man is endowed with a moral sense or natural faculty which, when developed and cultivated by reflection, enables him to distinguish right from wrong as immediately, spontaneously, and intuitively as (Shaftesbury claims) the eye distinguishes beauty from ugliness, or the ear distinguishes harmony from discord. This moral sense is antecedent to and independent of any belief in God; the basis of morality is not the arbitrary will of God, and men do not act virtuously only out of a fear of hell or hope of heaven. To follow virtue out of desire for reward or fear of punishment is not to be virtuous: 'There is no more of *Rectitude*, *Piety*, or *Sanctity* in a Creature thus reform'd, than there is

Meekness or *Gentleness* in a Tyger strongly chain'd.' Virtue lies in following our natural affections, 'such as are founded in Love, Complacency, Good-will, and in a Sympathy with the Kind or Species'. To do so happens also to be in every man's interest, for 'the Wisdom of what rules, and is FIRST and CHIEF *in Nature*, has made it to be according to the *private Interest* and *Good* of every-one, to work towards the *general Good*'[20]; but self-interest should of course not be his motive. Pope sums it up in the concluding lines of the *Essay on Man*:

> That REASON, PASSION, answer one great aim;
> That true SELF-LOVE and SOCIAL are the same;
> That VIRTUE only makes our Bliss below;
> And all our Knowledge is, OURSELVES TO KNOW.

Shaftesbury was not the first to claim that virtue is benevolence and that benevolent feelings are natural to man, and the term 'moral sense' was not of his coining, for the Cambridge Platonist Henry More had used it in his *Divine Dialogues* (1668), Dialogue II, Section xviii; but it was from Shaftesbury's writings that two or three generations of poets, novelists, and other moralists imbibed their notions of natural virtue, until, towards the end of our period, the headier brew of Rousseau became available.[21]

Shaftesbury's Platonic belief that physical objects are merely shadows of the ideal world beyond themselves emerges most clearly in *The Moralists, a Philosophical Rhapsody* (1709), a work of which Leibniz wrote: 'I found in it almost all of my *Theodicy* before it saw the light of day. The universe all of a piece, its beauty, its universal harmony, the disappearance of real evil.' *The Moralists* is a series of dialogues on 'Natural and Moral Subjects' between four characters, the most important of whom are the sceptic Philocles (the narrator) and the freethinker Theocles, who represents Shaftesbury's own viewpoint and who often assumes 'the boldest poetic manner of Plato'[22] when he contemplates the beautiful objects of nature and recognizes in them a supreme beauty to which they all belong. In the last of the dialogues, particularly, he employs the 'loose Numbers' of poetic prose as he apostrophizes 'mighty Nature! Wise Substitute of Providence', and sings of 'Nature's Order.' Pope, who borrows freely from Shaftesbury in his *Essay on Man*, ridicules 'Theocles' raptur'd Vision' in *Dunciad*, IV, 488–90, but the rapture is essential to the philosophy; the rhapsodic manner of proceeding is itself a recognition of the inadequacy of discursive reasoning. Nature's order is recognized intuitively in the rush of delight which accompanies aesthetic appreciation rather than by anything resembling that process of scientific reasoning which revealed to many of Shaftesbury's contemporaries an ordered but mechanical world. The order revealed is organic, not mechanical: 'All things in this World are *united* . . . as the *Branch* is united with the *Tree*.' The vegetable metaphor here is of course a significant corrective to the Newtonian clock metaphor and other current machine metaphors. In such moments of recognition, inspired with 'Harmony of Thought', the mind of man is immediately conscious of the universal mind from which it is derived, and is not in any way dependent upon sensation for this consciousness:

Thought we own pre-eminent, and confess the reallest of
Beings; the only Existence of which we are made sure, by being
conscious. All else may be only Dream and Shadow. All which
even *Sense* suggests may be deceitful. . . . Thus we are in a
manner conscious of that *original* and *eternally existent* THOUGHT
whence we derive *our own*.

Thus the '*Original* SOUL, diffusive, vital in all, inspiring *the Whole*', communicates with us 'so as in some manner *to inhabit* within our Souls'.[23] At some points such assertions tend towards Berkeley's immaterialism, which is also Platonic in inspiration, but Shaftesbury does not argue the philosophical question out, as Berkeley does, for this work is a rhapsody, not a treatise, a discourse, or even an essay; furthermore his God is not Berkeley's, but the deity of natural religion, crossed with hints from the neo-Platonic system of Plotinus, who postulated three ascending grades of reality: nature (of which the physical world is a projected dream), the world soul, and the world mind.

Towards the end of *The Moralists* Theocles launches himself into an imaginary journey through the sublime and beautiful wonders of the natural world, in which he is accompanied for a while by Philocles, who then checks himself, wondering why he is so 'deep in this *romantick* way', and asking what it was possessed him, when he was passionately struck with objects of this kind. 'No wonder, reply'd [Theocles], if we are at a loss when we pursue the *Shadow* for the *Substance*. For if we may trust to what our Reasoning has taught us; whatever in Nature is beautiful or charming, is only the faint Shadow of that *First Beauty*.' When contemplating beautiful objects and recognizing in them the shadow of transcendent intellectual beauty, the mind, which is man's divine part, apprehends itself in its truest nature:

there is nothing so divine as BEAUTY: which belonging not to
Body, nor having any Principle or Existence except in MIND and
REASON, is alone discover'd and acquir'd by this diviner Part,
when it inspects *It-self*. . . . 'Tis thus the *improving* MIND,
slightly surveying other Objects, and passing over Bodys, and
the common Forms, (where only a Shadow of Beauty rests)
ambitiously presses onward to Its *Source*, and views *the Original*
of Form and Order in that which is intelligent.

In his 'Miscellaneous Reflections' of 1714 Shaftesbury sums up: 'What is BEAUTIFUL is *Harmonious* and *Proportionable*; what is Harmonious and Proportionable, is TRUE; and what is at once both *Beautiful* and *True*, is, of consequence, *Agreeable* and GOOD.'[24] His repudiation of the mechanistic account of external nature and his exposition of a version of Platonism rest upon an understanding of his own nature.

Shaftesbury's notion of natural virtue suited the tastes and sensibilities of many, but it did not go unchallenged. A particularly forthright attack upon it and its author was made by Bernard Mandeville (1670–1733) in *A Search into the Nature of Society*, added in 1723 to the second edition of his *Fable of the Bees: or Private Vices, Public Benefits*. Mandeville, arguing *ad hominem*, sarcastically observes that Shaftesbury must have inferred his flimsy, socially useless moral philosophy from the circumstances of his own sheltered, affluent, indolent life: 'That boasted middle way, and the calm Virtues recommended in the Characteristicks, are good for nothing but to breed Drones, and might qualify a Man for the stupid Enjoyment of a Monastick Life, or at best a Country Justice of the Peace.' Mandeville's scornful confounding of the Aristotelian doctrine of the golden mean with Popish asceticism and modern rusticity was particularly unkind. He speculates that had Shaftesbury 'been of a Warlike Genius or a Boisterous Temper, he would have chose another Part in the Drama of Life, and preach'd a quite contrary Doctrine: For we are ever pushing our Reason which way soever we feel Passion to draw it, and Self-love pleads to all human Creatures for their different Views, still furnishing every individual with Arguments to justify their Inclinations.'[25]

In his own inimitable rough-humoured tone Mandeville repeats the arguments of Hobbes and Locke to show that all moral standards are relative and that there are no innate moral principles. Ideas of virtue are wholly conventional; they originate in the artifice of politicians who wish to make men useful to one another in social organizations. Shaftesbury's moral system is visionary: 'the hunting after this *Pulchrum & Honestum* is not much better than a Wild-Goose-Chase'[26]; but the peril of this foolish pursuit is that it encourages hypocrisy by concealing man's true selfish nature from himself. Man's individual selfishness and pride are the basis of commercial prosperity, and therefore the foundation of social good and of consequent individual happiness. This is in accordance with Mandeville's belief that private vices are public benefits (see Ch. 4 below).

Mandeville trailed his coat in the face of many cherished eighteenth-century beliefs other than the prevalent belief in natural virtue; consequently *The Fable of the Bees* attracted well over a hundred refutations or detailed condemnations before the end of the century. His detractors included Dennis, Law, Berkeley, Hume, Adam Smith, Fielding, Gibbon, Montesquieu, Diderot, and Rousseau, to name but a few.[27] One of the first and fullest responses came from Francis Hutcheson (1694–1747), the intention of whose *Inquiry* (1725) is evident enough from its full title: *An Inquiry into the Original of Our Ideas of Beauty and Virtue; in Two Treatises. In Which the Principles of the Late Earl of Shaftesbury Are Explain'd and Defended, against the Author of the 'Fable of the Bees' and the Ideas of Moral Good and Evil Are Establish'd, According to the Sentiments of the Antient Moralists. With an Attempt to Introduce a Mathematical Calculation in Subjects of Morality.*

As appears from his division of the work into two distinct treatises, the first 'Concerning Beauty, Order, Harmony, Design', the second 'Concerning Moral Good and Evil', Hutcheson does not mingle ethics and aesthetics quite as intimately as Shaftesbury does. He is altogether less of a Platonist. His starting-point is Locke's distinction between sensation and reflection or 'internal sense'. According to Hutcheson there are distinct, immediate impressions of internal senses, such as a 'sense of beauty' or a 'moral sense', just as there are of the outer, five senses: just as God 'has determin'd us to receive, by our *external Senses*, pleasant or disagreeable Ideas of Objects, according as they are useful or hurtful to our Bodys . . . in the same manner he has given us a MORAL SENSE, to direct our Actions, and to give us still *nobler Pleasures*'.[28] The existence of the moral sense ensures that in the presence of a good action we experience a pleasurable feeling of approval, the converse in the case of a bad action. Such feelings are quite independent of any feelings associated with any rational calculations concerning our own advantage. The moral sense is both passive and active in that it both recognizes good actions and motivates us to act well. As we might expect, the 'nobler Pleasures' given by the moral sense are in the exercise of benevolence, which for Hutcheson, as for many other moralists of his century, effectively embraces all the other virtues. Hutcheson's definition of the best action as the one 'which procures the *greatest Happiness* for the *greatest Numbers*'[29] was popularized by Jeremy Bentham (1748–1832) in his *Introduction to the Principles of Morals and Legislation* (1789); but the history of Benthamite utilitarianism lies outside the chronological limits of this volume. Despite his apparently utilitarian formula, Hutcheson insists that moral approval arises from a God-given moral sense, not from man's calculation of utility. Typical of his age, Hutcheson assigns the leading role in his moral philosophy to God, but this role is as contriver of some newly-recognized natural phenomenon (in this case the internal senses), not the traditional office of judge.

The belief that God wishes to make men happy and that he has bestowed upon them a moral sense, called conscience, moral reason, or divine reason, is central to the moral philosophy expounded by Joseph Butler in his *Fifteen Sermons* (1726) and the dissertation 'Of the Nature of Virtue' appended to his *Analogy of Religion* (1736, see Ch. 2 above). Heart and understanding, intuition and reason, are united in the conscience, which is the highest principle in human nature. Lower principles, such as hunger, fear, or love of fame, have greater strength at some times in some men, but the principle of conscience has supreme authority over all the others, and invariably in all men at all times it approves 'justice, veracity, and regard to common good'.[30] Butler insists that the separate principles, considered separately, no more give us the idea of man's whole nature than the separate parts of a watch taken to pieces give us the idea of a watch. The constitution of man is formed by the relations that parts have to one another, the chief relation of which is the authority of conscience over the other parts. The whole constitution, from its very nature, is adapted for virtue, just as a watch is constituted to measure time. This is true whether or not individual moral constitutions, like individual watches, may be found to be out of order. Here again is the pervasive notion of God the clock-maker. Addressing himself to the central question of eighteenth-century ethics, the relationship between 'self-love and social', Butler argues that if men understand their true happiness and bear in mind the life to come as well as the present, they will discover that self-love and conscience, though principles quite distinct from one another, will invariably lead the same way.

In his dissertation 'Of Personal Identity' appended to the *Analogy*, Butler asserts that self is determined by identity of substance, that is, soul. His is one of several attempts by eighteenth-century thinkers to deal with the strange perplexities raised by Locke's argument that personal identity consists only in consciousness, that '*Socrates* waking and sleeping is not the same person'. Berkeley and Shaftesbury also wrestled with the great question of personal identity; but David Hume, in his *Treatise of Human Nature: An Attempt to introduce the experimental method of reasoning into Moral Subjects* (1739–40), overthrew the notion of a substantial self altogether: 'sameness of person is nowhere to be found; the identity which we ascribe to the mind of man, is only a fictitious one'.[31]

Hume's abolition of personal identity (and the identities we ascribe to anything else) is one of his later steps in an argument which takes Locke's theory of ideas to an elegant and fruitful sceptical conclusion. He begins his *Treatise* with the assertion that 'all the perceptions of the human mind resolve themselves into two distinct kinds, which I shall call IMPRESSIONS and IDEAS'. Perceptions which enter into the mind with 'most force and violence' are impressions: 'under this name I comprehend all our sensations, passions, and emotions, as they make their first appearance in the soul'. 'By *ideas* I mean the faint images of these [impressions] in thinking and reasoning.' Hume thus makes a distinction not observed by Locke, who referred to all perceptions as 'ideas'. Depending upon their degree of faintness, ideas may belong either to the memory, where the idea 'retains a considerable degree of its first vivacity, and is somewhat intermediate betwixt an impression and an idea', or the imagination, where 'it intirely loses that vivacity, and is a perfect idea'.[32]

As poems and romances embarrassingly testify, with their 'winged horses, fiery dragons, and monstrous giants', the imagination has the power to transpose simple ideas and unite them in what form it pleases; but customarily the same simple ideas in the imagination regularly fall together into complex ideas by the uniting principle of association. The gentle force of association arises from three qualities: resemblance, contiguity in time or place, and cause and effect: 'Here is a kind of ATTRACTION, which in the mental world will be found to have as extraordinary effects as in the natural.'[33] The metaphor from Newtonian physics is perhaps intended to underline the reference to 'experimental method' on Hume's title-page; but the analogy is faulty, inasmuch as gravitation is uniform, whereas every mind's association of ideas is different – a fact to which the Shandy household would testify a little later in the century

The complex ideas derived by this gentle, natural agency of association may be categorized in Locke's terminology, 'Substances, Modes, and Relations', though Hume will have no truck with Locke's notion of substance as a 'supposed something, or substratum'. For Hume, any idea of substance (e.g. 'swan') or of mode (e.g. 'beauty') 'is nothing but a collection of simple ideas, that are united by the imagination'.[34] Hume follows Berkeley in rejecting Locke's doctrine of abstract, general ideas. He argues, against Locke, that there are no distinct ideas of absolute space and time; according to Hume, such ideas, derived of course from impressions, are merely of the manner or order in which objects may be conceived to exist. As for the idea of external existence itself:

> Let us fix our attention out of ourselves as much as possible: let
> us chace our imagination to the heavens, or to the utmost limits
> of the universe, we never really advance a step beyond
> ourselves, nor can conceive any kind of existence, but those
> perceptions, which have appear'd in that narrow compass. This
> is the universe of the imagination, nor have we any idea but
> what is there produc'd.[35]

The origin of the impressions which produce our ideas is inexplicable. We
cannot say, with Locke, that ideas arise immediately from the object, or,
with Berkeley, that they are derived from God; nor can we say that they are
produced by some creative power in the mind. Even the idea of our own
existence is no more than 'the idea of what we conceive to be existent'.
Personal identity, the 'soul', can be known only as an inconceivably rapid
succession of perceptions. Sydney Smith wittily simplified the situation:
'Bishop Berkeley destroyed this world in one volume octavo; and nothing
remained, after his time, but mind; which experienced a similar fate from the
hand of Mr Hume in 1739.'[36]

Hume concludes that there can be no such thing as rational belief. The
'experimental method of reasoning' promised on his title-page leads to the
discovery that belief can only be a matter of feeling and habit. We believe
that some of our ideas are more true to 'Nature' than others because we feel
them differently: 'An idea assented to *feels* different from a fictitious idea,
that the fancy alone presents to us: and this different feeling I endeavour to
explain by calling it a superior *force*, or *vivacity*, or *solidity*, or *firmness*, or
steadiness.' Hume continues:

> 'Tis not solely in poetry and music we must follow our taste
> and sentiment, but likewise in philosophy. When I am
> convinc'd of any principle, 'tis only an idea, which strikes more
> strongly upon me. . . . Objects have no discoverable
> connexion together; nor is it from any other principle but
> custom operating upon the imagination, that we can draw any
> inference from the appearance of one to the existence of
> another.[37]

The distinction between 'fancy' in the first extract and 'imagination' in the
second extract just quoted does not anticipate Coleridge; like Addison,[38] Hume
uses the two terms indiscriminately. For him imagination, as we have seen, is
the 'faculty by which we form our fainter ideas' and unite them through the
natural process of customary association; but, since he argues that belief is
founded upon the vivacity of ideas, he has to take account of 'fictitious ideas' in
the lively imaginations of madmen, liars, and poets. He accepts that a poetical
description may have a sensible effect; but 'the ideas it presents are different to
the *feeling* from those which arise from the memory and the judgement. There
is something weak and imperfect amidst all that seeming vehemence of thought
and sentiment which attends the fictions of poetry'[39]: no Shaftesburian 'just
Prometheus under Jove' here (see Ch. 5 below).

By the end of the first book Hume is convinced that scepticism is logically irrefutable; nevertheless, he is convinced also that scepticism is psychologically untenable. In a disarming triumph of happy-tempered sobriety he admits that 'nature . . . cures me of this philosophical melancholy and delirium, either by relaxing this bent of mind, or by some avocation, and lively impression of my senses, which obliterate all these chimeras. I dine, I play a game of backgammon, I converse, and am merry with my friends.' The same remedy, 'carelessness and inattention', is available to others; so Hume takes it for granted, 'whatever may be the reader's opinion at this present moment, that an hour hence he will be persuaded there is both an external and an internal world'.[40] Thus, after reasoning away reason, Hume turns his irony upon himself. Nevertheless, he fulfils a very serious purpose in the first book of the *Treatise*: that is, to clear the ground for the later books on the passions and on morals, by showing that the assumptions on which we conduct our lives cannot be supported by rational argument, and that the basis for our moral behaviour must lie in something other than reason.

Locke writes an essay on the human understanding and Berkeley a treatise on human knowledge, but Hume, the system-builder, takes the more comprehensive topic of human nature; his study of the understanding in Book I of his *Treatise* is therefore complemented by an enquiry into the passions in Book II. Having demonstrated that belief is a matter of feeling or habit, not reason, he considers the old moral philosophical commonplace that reason should be superior to passion. His conclusion is that 'reason is, and ought only to be the slave of the passions, and can never pretend to any other office than to serve and obey them'. Thus he prepares the ground for Book III, 'Of Morals', which opens with the declaration that moral judgements are based upon feelings, not reason: 'Reason is wholly inactive, and can never be the source of so active a principle as conscience, or a sense of morals.' Furthermore, goodness and badness are not matters of external fact, that is to say intrinsic properties of men or actions: 'The vice entirely escapes you, as long as you consider the object. You never can find it, till you turn your reflexion into your own breast, and find a sentiment of disapprobation, which arises in you, towards this action. Here is a matter of fact; but 'tis the object of feeling, not of reason. It lies in yourself, not in the object.' Hume continues with a dry reference to Newton's physics and Locke's distinction between primary and secondary qualities: 'Vice and virtue, therefore, may be compar'd to sounds, colours, heat and cold, which, according to modern philosophy, are not qualities in objects, but perceptions in the mind: And this discovery in morals, like that other in physics, is to be regarded as a considerable advancement of the speculative sciences; tho', like that too, it has little or no influence on practice.'[41]

In Hume's view the motive for moral judgements lies not in supernatural or metaphysical sanctions, nor in any intrinsic quality of the object of judgement, nor even in a specific organ of 'moral sense', such as that postulated by Shaftesbury, Hutcheson, and others, but in the whole peculiar emotional nature of man. He finds a telling simile for the nature and force of that primal sympathy which he claims is shared by all men: 'The minds of all men are similar in their feelings and operations, nor can any one be actuated by any affection, of which all others are not, in some degree, susceptible. As in strings equally wound up, the motion of one communicates itself to the rest; so all the affections readily pass from one person to another, and beget correspondent movements in every human creature.'[42] In all men the same feelings spring out of the spectacle of human suffering and joy; thus the human violins naturally respond to one another.

Hume is a man of his enlightened age in placing a much higher value upon the social virtues than upon piety. 'Celibacy, fasting, penance, mortification, self-denial, humility, silence, solitude, and the whole train of monkish virtues' are in Hume's view really vices which 'stupify the understanding and harden the heart, obscure the fancy and sour the temper. . . . A gloomy, hair-brained enthusiast, after his death, may have a place in the calendar; but will scarcely ever be admitted, when alive, into intimacy and society, except by those who are as delirious and dismal as himself.'[43] The natural virtues of individual men are good for society: 'Meekness, beneficence, charity, generosity, clemency, moderation, equity, bear the greatest figure among the moral qualities, and are commonly denominated the *social* virtues, to mark their tendency to the good of society.' Thus it has come about that 'some philosophers', notably Hobbes and Mandeville, though Hume refers to neither by name, 'have represented all moral distinctions as the effect of artifice and education, when skilful politicians endeavour'd to restrain the turbulent passions of men, and make them operate to the public good, by the notions of honour and shame'. Hume, however, refutes such an artificial system of morality by an appeal to experience, claiming, first, that there are virtues other than the social ones, and, second, that 'had not men a natural sentiment of approbation and blame, it cou'd never be excited by politicians'. It is true that individual moral judgements tend to be made according to the interests of society, but this is because we have a concern for society arising from natural sympathy: it is the principle of sympathy 'which takes us so far out of ourselves, as to give us the same pleasure or uneasiness in the characters of others, as if they had a tendency to our own advantage or loss'.[44]

Though Hume effectively dethroned reason as the arbiter of truth, his scepticism was challenged by a group of Scottish philosophers, including Thomas Reid (1710–96) and James Beattie (1735–1803), who appealed to common sense, that is, to what Shaftesbury on the title-page of his *Essay on Freedom of Wit and Humour* (1709) referred to as 'Sensus Communis'. For Shaftesbury common sense is the natural, instinctive, and instantaneous knowledge of certain moral and philosophical truths which is shared by the great majority of mankind. Beattie, Reid, and their school claim that the essential feature of common-sense beliefs is that we are constitutionally unable to abandon them even when we cannot refute objections to them. Beattie's meretricious *Essay on the Nature and Immutability of Truth* (1770) aroused a great stir; it was thought by Johnson to have 'confuted' Hume, and was immortalized in an allegorical painting by Reynolds; but Reid's *Inquiry into the Human Mind on Principles of Common Sense* (1764) goes deeper into the problems that Hume had shown to be implicit in Locke's and Berkeley's doctrines of ideas. Reid claims that the idea of an object is an unnecessary hypothesis; mind and sensation are not separate realities, the second 'furnishing' the first with 'ideas', as in Locke's metaphor. Every operation of the senses implies immediate belief: 'When I perceive a tree before me, my faculty of seeing gives me not only a notion or simple apprehension of the tree, but a belief of its existence, and of its figure, distance, and magnitude; and this judgement or belief is not got by comparing ideas, it is included in the very nature of the perception.'[45] Common sense divides the world into mind and matter; Reid cannot believe that the mind is what Hume's *Treatise* makes it, 'an enchanted castle' where men are 'imposed upon by spectres and apparitions'[46]; his *Inquiry* is intended to head off what he fears will be philosophy's flight into subjectivism. In showing that rationalism was a blind alley, Hume offered a challenging alternative route to knowledge of the world and of ourselves. This challenge, refused by Reid and his school, was taken up by Kant, awakened from his dogmatic slumbers, as he said, by Hume's criticism of the concept of causality; but Kant's influence on English thought lies in the nineteenth century.

Back in Scotland, Hume's ethics proved to be more acceptable than his epistemology. Adam Smith (1723–90), the pupil of Hutcheson, is, like Hume, much concerned with the part played by the imagination in framing moral judgements. In his *Theory of Moral Sentiments* (1759) Smith argues that sympathy, 'a power which has always been taken notice of, and with which the mind is manifestly endowed',[47] is sufficient to account for all the effects attributed by Shaftesbury, Hutcheson, and others to the operation of a hypothetical 'moral sense'. Sympathy is not simply pity or benevolence, but is 'our fellow-feeling with any passion whatsoever'. It is an activity of the imagination, not an impression of the senses: 'our senses will never inform us' of another man's suffering. 'They never did, and never can, carry us beyond our own person, and it is by the imagination only that we can form any conception of what are his sensations.'[48] Such natural sympathy operates smoothly through four channels: first, we sympathize with the motives of the agent; secondly, we enter into the gratitude of those who receive the benefit of his actions; thirdly, we observe that his conduct has been agreeable to the general rules by which those two sympathies generally act; and, last of all, when we consider such actions as making a part of a system of behaviour which tends to promote the happiness either of the individual or of the society, they appear to derive a beauty from this utility, not unlike that which we ascribe to any well-contrived machine. Like Shaftesbury, Hutcheson, and Hume, Smith unites ethics and aesthetics; he is no less representative of his age in linking beauty with utility and in regarding society as a moral machine. Smith is perhaps unusual only in the degree to which he elaborates upon the machine metaphor: for instance, virtue is 'the fine polish to the wheels of society', while vice is 'the vile rust, which makes them jar and grate upon one another'.[49]

The moral machine is of course contrived by God, who thus acts through the constitution of human nature to ensure a pre-ordained result which is as happy as it is beautiful and useful: 'The happiness of mankind, as well as of all other rational creatures, seems to have been the original purpose intended by the Author of nature, when he brought them into existence.'[50] Smith's confidence in God's intention to promote human happiness was shared by many of his contemporaries. Not every one would have gone quite so far as William Wollaston in his *Religion of Nature Delineated* (1722) when, reversing Gwendolen Fairfax's dictum, he declares: 'To make itself happy is a duty, which every Being, in proportion to its capacity, owes to itself'[51]; but, in an odd illustration of the principle that duties and rights can be interchangeable, the pursuit of happiness was duly enshrined in the United States' Declaration of Independence (1776) as one of only three inalienable rights given to man by his Creator.

Hume's undermining of reason in his 'Newtonian' experimental investigation of the passions, the imagination, and, above all, sympathy opened the way not only for Adam Smith but for the more powerful sentimental philosophers of France. D'Alembert appealed to 'vérité de sentiment' which is based upon 'évidence du cœur'; Rousseau believed that to exist is to feel, and began his *Confessions* (1782) with the words 'Je sens mon cœur, et je connois les hommes'. When the sentimental philosophy returned to Britain from France towards the end of the eighteenth century it did so, however, with a temper very different from Hume's and with a new political force (see Ch. 4 below).

Though Hume questions the assumptions of Newton and Locke, he adopts from them his central notions that human nature is uniform, that the world of ideas is held together by the gravitational force of customary association, and that vice and virtue are perceptions in the mind. No eighteenth-century philosopher could avoid some dependence upon Newton and Locke, but the most complete synthesis of their ideas into a system of psychology is found in the *Observations on Man, his Frame, his Duty, and his Expectations* (1749) by David Hartley (1705–57). As he explains at the beginning of volume I, Hartley elaborates his theory of vibration 'from the hints concerning the performance of sensation and motion, which Sir Isaac Newton has given at the end of his *Principia*, and in the Questions annexed to his *Optics*', and his theory of association 'from what Mr Locke, and other ingenious persons since his time, have delivered'. Throughout, he intends to apply 'the method of analysis and synthesis recommended and followed by Sir Isaac Newton'.[52]

Hartley first considers what Locke had determined not to meddle with, the physical processes by which we have sensations and ideas. The immediate instrument of sensation, he claims, is a white medullary substance in the brain, the spinal marrow, and the nerves, consisting of tiny particles which respond to all motions of the ether, that subtle and elastic fluid which, according to Newton, is expanded through space and diffused through the pores of matter, and by which light is transmitted. External objects have the power to propagate motions in the ether, which are then communicated, in the form of minute vibrations of the medullary particles, along the fibres of the nerves into the brain. Though these vibrations are 'of the same kind with the oscillations of pendulums, and the tremblings of the particles of sounding bodies', they are too small to move whole nerves: 'For that the nerves themselves should vibrate like musical strings, is highly absurd; nor was it ever asserted by Sir Isaac Newton.' So much for Dr Cheyne (see Ch. 1

above). When vibrations are moderate they give sensations of pleasure; when they are so violent as to break the continuity of the nerves they cause pain. Sensory vibrations, thus communicated to the brain, soon fade, but if repeated they 'beget, in the medullary Substance of the Brain, a disposition to diminutive Vibrations, which may also be called Vibratiuncles'. These vibratiuncles, being the 'Vestiges, Types, or Images' of our sensations, constitute our ideas.[53] If several sensory vibrations are associated together in a series often enough, they attain a power over their corresponding series of ideal vibratiuncles, so that any one sensory vibration of the series will immediately, mechanically, and necessarily excite the entire series of vibratiuncles, that is to say, ideas. Hartley thus offers a physiological theory of the association of ideas, where Locke and Hume had concerned themselves only with psychology.

On this physiological basis Hartley erects an elaborate system in which the power of association accounts for the growth of our moral character from the animal stage of infancy, where we know the pleasures and pains of sensation only, to the fully adult state, where we have acquired the moral sense which compels us to benevolence. This moral sense is to be understood not as a distinct faculty but as the fully realized combination of all other faculties in the man who has grown to full moral stature by way of childhood discipline, experience of the world's rewards and punishments, religious hopes and fears, love of God, and so on. Through these stages of moral education the power of association works always towards the eventual happiness that God intends for us. Education is of vital importance of course, but the natural tendency of each individual mental system, and therefore of the great system of the world, is towards virtue and happiness, which, for Hartley as for Hutcheson and all other believers in the moral sense, were closely allied: 'And since the Course of the World and the Frame of our Natures, are so ordered, and so adapted to each other, as to enforce Benevolence upon us, this is a farther Argument of the kind Intentions of an overruling Providence. It follows hence, that Malevolence and consequently Misery, must ever decrease.' Indeed, 'Association . . . has a Tendency to reduce the State of those who have eaten of the Tree of the Knowledge of Good and Evil, back again to a paradisiacal one.'[54]

Despite the comfort of such a conclusion, Hartley was troubled by some of the implications of his theory, particularly 'in respect of the doctrine of *necessity*; for I was not at all aware, that it followed from that of association, for several years after I had begun my inquiries; nor did I admit it at last, without the greatest reluctance.'[55] In the second part of the book he attempts to reconcile his system with the Christian doctrine of free will, the immateriality of the soul, and Christian ethics. Such a union of science and religion impressed Coleridge so much that he christened his eldest child, born in 1796, with the names David Hartley; Wordsworth's notions of the role of nature and the mechanism of association in a child's mental and moral development owe much to Hartley; but the philosopher's disciples in France, and a few, such as Bentham, in England, found it easy to take his materialism and necessitarianism without the Christianity.

Joseph Priestley (see Chs 1 and 2 above) venerated Hartley's *Observations* next only to the Bible, and wrote an abridgement, *Hartley's Theory of the Human Mind on the Principles of the Association of Ideas* (1775), which, as so often with abridgements, became more widely known than the original itself. Hartley's opening sentence reads 'Man consists of Two Parts, Body and Mind', and he asserts that mind is an immaterial principle; but Priestley in the preface to his abridgement abolishes all distinction between mind and matter. In his *Disquisitions concerning Matter and Spirit* (1777) Priestley develops the theory, based partly upon his researches into electricity, that matter consists not of solid particles but of centres of force endowed with the powers of attraction and repulsion. The apparent solidity of matter is only our sensation of resistance to force; the whole universe is a manifestation of one force, in Priestley's view divine force. All so-called matter is energy; it is therefore capable of sensation and thought: mind and matter are one. As his most influential disciple Coleridge observed, Priestley 'stript matter of all its material properties; substituted spiritual powers'.[56]

Priestley's materialism, like other aspects of his theology, placed him securely in the intellectual company of the early-eighteenth-century freethinkers, particularly the pantheist Toland (see Ch. 2 above); like Toland, he claimed that the physics of Newton and the psychology of Locke were alike consistent with materialism. What Toland and Priestley had particularly in mind was one controversial and much discussed paragraph of the *Essay concerning Human Understanding* where Locke admits the possibility that matter can think, and concedes that 'All the great Ends of Morality and Religion, are well enough secured, without philosophical Proofs of the Soul's Immateriality'.[57] This paragraph was made much of by Voltaire in his discussion of Locke in the *Letters concerning the English Nation* (1733), but Voltaire's materialism appears tentative and almost as religious as Priestley's when compared with that of the physiologist La Mettrie (1709–51, see Ch. 1 above) in his *Histoire naturelle de l'âme* (1745) and *L'homme machine* (1748).

La Mettrie's starting-point is Descartes's proof that all the lower animals are merely machines. He pretends to believe that Descartes asserted that man has a dual nature, body and mind, matter and spirit, only as a ruse 'to make the theologians swallow a poison concealed behind an analogy'. Somewhat in Lemuel Gulliver's vexing vein, La Mettrie concludes that 'it is just this strong analogy which compels all scientists and competent judges to confess that those proud and vain beings distinguished more by their pride than by the name of men . . . are, at bottom, only animals and perpendicularly crawling machines'.[58] Like many other thinkers, La Mettrie was fascinated by the regenerative power of Trembley's polyp (see Ch. 1 above), which appeared to prove that whatever moves and directs matter is within matter, not outside it. The vastly more complex organization of his matter gives man a capacity for symbolic reasoning, but still he is a machine formed of one substance, in which various springs (thoughts) are put into motion by other springs (sensations) and give rise to other self-movements of matter. In La Mettrie's godless and soulless moral scheme, virtue is the avoidance of pain and achievement of pleasure; as men share common sensations they have the same capacity for happiness.

Other mid-century French thinkers, among them Diderot in *Lettre sur les aveugles* (1749, see Ch. 1 above) and *Pensées sur l'interprétation de la nature* (1754), Condillac in *Traité des sensations* (1754), and Helvétius in *De l'esprit* (1758), elaborated the materialist psychology and explored its moral consequences; driving Locke's theories to their logical conclusion, they claimed that morality depends upon sensations. The atheistical implications of such thought are most fully worked out in the *Système de la nature* (1770) written by the German-born Baron d'Holbach (1723–89), with the assistance of Diderot. In this treatise, the atheism of which shocked even Voltaire, Holbach incorporated whole sections from Toland's pantheistic *Letters to Serena* (see Ch. 2 above). As La Mettrie drew upon Trembley, so Holbach drew upon the recent, somewhat unsound, experimental results of Needham in the matter of spontaneous generation (see Ch. 1 above): 'In moistening flour with water and sealing up this mixture, it is found after a while, with the aid of the microscope, that organized beings have thereby been produced that enjoy a life of which flour and water were considered incapable. It is thus that inanimate matter is able to pass to life, which is itself only an assemblage of movements.' As so often, the sharpest debating point is in the supplementary question slipped into a footnote, where Holbach asks if 'the production of a man, independently of the ordinary means, would be more marvelous than that of an insect with flour and water?'[59] Holbach of course rejects all spiritual causes: what men call 'God' is merely the sum of material nature.

The corollary of materialism is determinism; for every motion of mind, like every movement of the planets, must be determined by some natural law. What Hartley feared might be the case was welcomed by French thinkers such as Diderot, who proclaimed 'tout est nécessaire', and D'Alembert, who, perhaps more ambiguously, said 'tout est comme il faut'. The doctrine of necessity came into vogue in the French Revolution, and was imported into England from Holbach by way of Godwin; but in our period a variety of determinist-materialism more typically English (because it compromises with the metaphysical notion of God) appears in Priestley's *The Doctrine of Philosophic Necessity Illustrated* (1777). Priestley argues that, like everything else in the constitution of nature, the will obeys a fixed law of nature, 'so that every volition or choice is constantly regulated and determined by what precedes it'. Consequently, 'there will be a necessary connection between all things past, present, and to come, in the way of proper cause and effect, as much in the intellectual as in the natural world'; it follows that 'all things past, present, and to come are precisely what the Author of nature really intended them to be, and has made provision for'.[60] Though they drew on quite different evidences, Priestley and Leibniz stood close together here, sharing an optimistic scientific world view which starts from God and accordingly returns to God. Atheistic French materialists, on the other hand, proclaimed the triumph of an uncompromisingly non-metaphysical view of man-in-nature, a view which they could claim, with some justice, to have derived ultimately from Newton and Locke; they substituted nature for God, but they contrived to be just about as optimistic, and on that account perhaps just about as scientific, as Leibniz and Priestley.

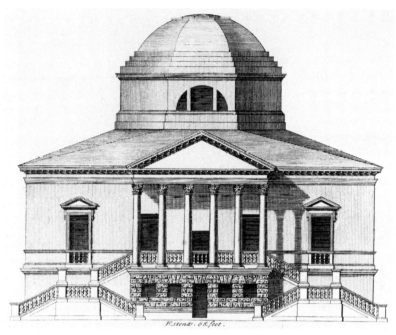

1 Lord Burlington, *Chiswick House*.

2 Nicholas Hawksmoor, *Mausoleum at Castle Howard*.

3 Sir John Vanbrugh, *Blenheim Palace*.

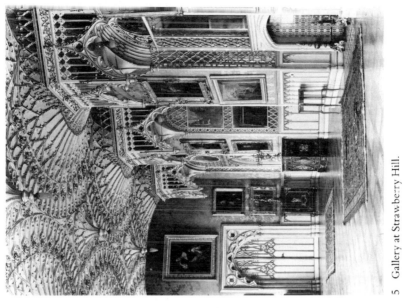

5 Gallery at Strawberry Hill.

4 James Gibbs, *St Martin-in-the-Fields*.

7 Peter Scheemakers, *Monument to Shakespeare.*

6 Louis François Roubiliac,
Monument to Lady Elizabeth Nightingale.

8   Michael Rysbrack, *Monument to Newton*.

9 Richard Wilson, *Cader Idris: Llyn-y-cau.*

10   Thomas Gainsborough,
Woodcutter courting a Milkmaid.

11   William Hogarth, *Gin Lane*.

Notes

1. Bertrand Russell, *History of Western Philosophy* (1946), p. 10.

2. *History of English Thought in the Eighteenth Century* (repr. 1962), II, 1.

3. *An Essay concerning Human Understanding*, edited by Peter H. Nidditch (Oxford, 1975), pp. 43, 47, 163: Book I, Chapter i, Section 2; I, i, 8; II, xi, 17.

4. Aristotle, *De Anima*, Book III; Bacon, *Novum Organum*, aph. 1.

5. *Essay concerning Human Understanding*, pp. 104–5; II, 1, 2, 4.

6. Ibid., p. 537; IV, ii, 14.

7. Ibid., p. 135; II, viii, 9, 10.

8. Ibid., p. 121; II, iii, 1.

9. *Tristram Shandy*, Volume I, Chapter iv.

10. *Essay concerning Human Understanding*, pp. 305, 316; II, xxiii, 14, 37.

11. Ibid., p. 619; IV, ix, 3.

12. Ibid., pp. 342, 341; II, xxvii, 19, 17.

13. Ibid., p. 72; I, iii, 10.

14. *Works of George Berkeley*, edited by A. A. Luce and T. E. Jessop, (1949), II, 41–42; *Principles*, paras 1–3.

15. *Works of George Berkeley*, p. 43; *Principles*, para. 6.

16. *Works of George Berkeley*, pp. 186, 210.

17. *Boswell's Life of Johnson*, edited by G. B. Hill, revised by L. F. Powell (Oxford, 1934), I, 471: 6 August 1763.

18. *Characteristicks*, second edition (1714), I, 355.

19. Ibid., II, 173.

20. Ibid., II, 55, 99, 175.

21. On the Cambridge Platonists see E. Cassirer, *The Platonic Renaissance in England*, translated by J. P. Pettegrove (Edinburgh, 1953); on the intellectual background of the 'moral sense' theory see Ernest Tuveson, *The Imagination as a Means of Grace* (Berkeley and Los Angeles, 1960).

22. Thomas McFarland, *Coleridge and the Pantheist Tradition* (1969), pp. 337, 277.

23. *Characteristicks*, second edition (1714), II, 345, 287, 369–70.

24. Ibid., II, 395, 426–27; III, 182–83.

25. *The Fable of the Bees*, edited by F. B. Kaye (Oxford, 1924), I, 333.

26. Ibid., 331.

27. Ibid., 401–53.

28. *An Inquiry into the Original of our Ideas of Beauty and Virtue* (1725), pp. 128–29; Treatise II, Section I, viii.

29. Ibid., p. 181; Section 3, viii.

30. *Dissertation on Virtue*, para. 1, in *Works* (1810), ii, 12.

31. *A Treatise of Human Nature*, edited by L. A. Selby-Biggs, second edition, text revised by P. H. Nidditch (Oxford, 1978), p. 259; Book i, Part iv, Section 6.

32. Ibid., pp. 1, 8; i, i, 1, 3.

33. Ibid., pp. 10–11; i, i, 3, 4.

34. Ibid., p. 16; I.i.6.

35. Ibid., pp. 67–68; I, ii, 6.

36. *Elementary Sketches of Moral Philosophy* (1850, based on lectures delivered 1805–6), introduction.

37. *Treatise*, p. 103; i, iii, 7, 8.

38. *Spectator*, no. 411 (21 June 1712).

39. *Treatise*, p. 631; i, iii, 10.

40. Ibid., pp. 269, 218; i, iv, 7, 2.

41. Ibid., pp. 415, 458, 469; ii, iii, 3, iii, i, 1.

42. Ibid., pp. 575–76; iii, iii, 1.

43. *An Enquiry concerning the Principles of Morals*, Section ix, Part 1, in *Enquiries*, edited by L. A. Selby-Bigge, second edition (Oxford, 1902), p. 270.

44. *Treatise*, pp. 578–79; iii, iii, 1.

45. *An Inquiry into the Human Mind*, edited by T. Duggan (Chicago, 1970), p. 268.

46. Ibid., p. x, quoting Reid's *Essays on the Intellectual Powers* (1785).

47. *Theory of Moral Sentiments*, edited by D. D. Raphael and A. L. Macfie (Oxford, 1976), p. 321; Part vii, Section iii, Chapter 3.

48. Ibid., p. 9; i, i, 1.

49. Ibid., pp. 326, 316; vii, iii, 3, 1.

50. Ibid., p. 166; iii, 5.

51. Quoted in Charles Vereker, *Eighteenth-Century Optimism* (Liverpool, 1967), p. 54.

52. *Observations on Man, His Frame, His Duty, and His Expectations* (1749), i, 4, 5.

53. Ibid., i, 11, 56.

54. Ibid., ii, 17; i, 83.

55. Ibid., i, Preface, p. iv.

56. *Biographia Literaria*, edited by J. T. Shawcross (Oxford, 1907), i, 91.

57. *Essay*, p. 542; iv, iii, 6.

58. A. Vartarian, *Diderot and Descartes* (Princeton, NJ, 1953), p. 206.

59. Ibid., p. 262.

60. *Doctrine of Philosophical Necessity* (1777), pp. 7–8; Section i.

Chapter 4
Politics and History

The period which began with the Battle of Blenheim, the Act of Union with Scotland, and the trial of Dr Sacheverell, and ended with the loss of the thirteen American colonies, Pitt's India Act, and the first landing of convicts in Botany Bay was not devoid of exciting or pregnant political events. A nation of shopkeepers willingly engaged in repeated colonial and commercial wars against its natural enemy France, and was able regularly to applaud the exploits of its military and naval heroes: Marlborough, Clive, Wolfe, Eliott, Rooke, Anson, Vernon, Hawke, Hood, Howe, Rodney, and the rest. The official national anthem and the 'unofficial' one, 'Rule Britannia!', were both composed in the 1740s, an era which has as much claim as the late nineteenth century to be called 'jingoist'. National self-confidence was a reflection of a real economic strength which, in our period, was as much attributable to what has been called the 'financial revolution' as to the more famous agrarian and industrial revolutions which were eventually to transform the face of the landscape, the quality of everyday life, and the social and political structures of society. Despite the alarms of the '45 and the potentially more dangerous Jacobite rising of 1715, political and religious battles were generally fought without recourse to arms. During the eighteenth century men slowly came to recognize the constitutional value of a legitimate opposition to the King's government; Parliament and the press became the arena for political debate.

The subject of this chapter is not eighteenth-century political history, but political ideas, as they operated both in contemporary politics and in attitudes towards history. The single event that most profoundly influenced eighteenth-century political activity and thought was the bloodless revolution of 1688; among philosophers, the best-known apologist of the revolution settlement was John Locke; so, like my last two chapters, this one must begin with Locke. As religious freethinking, adumbrated in *The Reasonableness of Christianity*, led to speculation about the nature of and sanctions for moral judgements, and as such speculation was directed into areas of psychology first explored in the *Essay concerning Human Understanding*, so the lines of eighteenth-century political debate were to a considerable extent laid down by the anti-theological arguments of Locke's *Second Treatise of Government*.

It is now believed that Locke composed most of his *Two Treatises of Government* before 1682, in order to justify the Protestant insurrections against Charles II which were being plotted by Locke's patron the first Earl of Shaftesbury (Dryden's Achitophel) and by other Whigs; but Locke's Preface, added shortly before the work was published anonymously in 1689 (title-page dated 1690), expresses the hope that his arguments will be 'sufficient to establish the Throne of our Great Restorer', William III, and 'to make good his Title in the Consent of the People'.[1] Thus it was that eighteenth-century readers read the *Two Treatises* as a justification of the Glorious Revolution. One of Locke's immediate purposes is to reply to *Patriarcha, or the Natural Power of Kings asserted* (1680), the posthumously published work of Robert Filmer (d. 1653), in which it is argued that God gave Adam absolute sovereignty over Eve, their posterity, and the whole world, that modern kings derive their titles by indefeasible hereditary succession from Adam, and consequently exercise natural, paternal authority over their subjects by divine right (the case advanced by David at the conclusion of *Absalom and Achitophel*). Having in his *First Treatise* refuted Filmer's religious, absolutist doctrine, Locke offers in his *Second Treatise* an alternative secular, contractual doctrine.

According to Locke, the King's title is made good in the consent of the people; rulers are officers exercising a 'Trust, which is put into their hands by their Brethren', a trust originating in a contract, seemingly more notional than historical, by which any number of men agree to 'unite into a Community, for their comfortable, safe, and peaceable living one amongst another, in a secure Enjoyment of their Properties, and a greater Security against any that are not of it'.[2] These men, who are free, equal, and independent in the 'state of nature' before they make their contract, agree to yield some of their independence and to obey elected rulers who will safeguard and regulate the institution of private property by adjudging between conflicting claims. The subjects' contract of obedience does not bind posterity; if a ruler betrays his trust, for instance by the arbitrary seizure of private property, his subjects have the right to resist and even to elect a new ruler, as they did in the case of William III. Resistance is legitimate because the contract does not supersede an antecedent and superior law of nature; indeed, the State's laws 'are only so far right, as they are founded on the Law of Nature, by which they are to be regulated and interpreted'.[3]

The concept of natural law is found in Aristotle. As elaborated by Cicero for the Romans, by the early Fathers for Christians, by Richard Hooker for Anglicans, and by Hugo Grotius for lawyers, this law is believed to be a code implanted by God in the understandings of all right-thinking people. In Cicero's words,

> Right reason is indeed a true law which is in accordance with
> nature, applies to all men, and is unchangeable and eternal. By its
> commands this law summons men to the performance of their
> duties; by its prohibitions it restrains them from doing wrong. Its
> commands and prohibitions always influence good men, but are
> without effect upon the bad.

God 'is the author of this law, its interpreter, and its sponsor'.[4] Defoe's enormous verse satire *Jure Divino* (1706), an attack on divine right and a justification of Locke's contract theory, is dedicated to Reason, the source of legal authority. Though it was universally agreed that natural law accords with right reason, there was no general consensus of opinion as to what precisely were its formulations. It appears that in Locke's understanding the law of nature ensured an individual man's rights to life, liberty, and property, and required of him the duty to honour contracts. Locke avoids detailed discussion of the way in which our minds acquire an awareness of natural justice, though in his *Essay concerning Human Understanding* he asserts that it is not an innate idea. He does not attempt, either in the *Essay* or the *Two Treatises*, to square his concept of universal natural law with his knowledge that men's notions of justice, equity, etc. vary greatly from one society to another (see Ch.3 above).

We have seen that the original contract is entered into for the protection of property. Locke defines political power as the right of making laws 'for the Regulating and Preserving of Property, and of employing the force of the Community, in the Execution of such Laws, and in the defence of the Common-wealth from Foreign Injury, and all this only for the Publick Good', and he repeatedly reminds his readers that 'Government has no other end but the preservation of Property'.[5] To account for the origin of so important an institution, Locke postulates that private property comes into being when man mixes his labour with the stock originally given by God to men in common: 'Though the Water running in the Fountain be every ones, yet who can doubt but that in the Pitcher is his only who drew it out?'[6] With the invention of money, more complicated mixtures and exchanges of labour can take place, as Locke illustrates by his enumeration of the materials and operations which go into the making of a loaf of bread – a passage remembered by Robinson Crusoe. Defoe's novel indeed nicely illustrates Locke's theories of property and contract. Crusoe is reduced (almost) to the state of nature, then mingles his labour with the natural resources of the island so that by natural right 'the whole country was my own mere property'; before he will co-operate with the Spanish and Portuguese who land there he insists on drawing up a contract by which he is recognized as the legitimate chief magistrate of what is now a new-created political society. As Locke made clear, labour and commerce put the difference of value upon everything: though nature has furnished the Red Indians of America with rich material resources, their failure to improve nature by their labour means that 'a King of a large and fruitful Territory there feeds, lodges, and is clad worse than a day labourer in *England*'.[7]

Locke's labour-theory of property was later seen to have radical implications, as too was his notion of inalienable popular rights, but as a man of his time he saw no reason to question a political and economic system in which any voice in government or any substantial share of property was denied to most of the labouring populace. The form of government he favours is a blend of monarchy, oligarchy, and democracy, in other words the 'mixed constitution' or limited monarchy established by the Glorious Revolution. It is intended to be a balanced system, in which the executive power of the monarch, acting through his servants, is separated from the legislative power of the lords and commons represented in Parliament.

Locke chooses to justify the mixed constitution abstractedly in terms of natural law and the notional contract, but many of his contemporaries and successors preferred to justify it by reference to history. The classical world provided models: according to Polybius, the Greek historian of Rome, checks and balances were the secret of Lycurgus's system of government and of the Roman republican constitution. These, however, were not the origins of the English system.

Most eighteenth-century historians, whether Whig or Tory, agreed that Parliament was a Gothic institution, evolved among ancient Germanic tribes and brought to Britain by the Angles, Saxons, and Jutes. Received history would have it that in Anglo-Saxon England sovereign power resided in the Witenagemot, which appointed kings and prescribed their powers and duties under the law; William the Conqueror imposed his 'Norman yoke' upon the freeborn English, but they never willingly gave up their Gothic liberties; in their first counter-attack against arbitrary power they secured Magna Carta, then over the centuries they reasserted the power of Parliament; finally, by the Glorious Revolution of 1688 the ancient equal mixture of power between king, lords, and commons was re-created, and the constitution regained what Swift, Addison, and others referred to as the 'Gothick balance'.[8] In his Preface to the *Two Treatises* Locke significantly refers to William III as 'our Great Restorer', but for their generation the best-known history of England's Gothic constitution was to be found in the *Discourses concerning Government* (1698) by the great Whig martyr Algernon Sidney (1622–83). For literary students there is a more accessible brief history in Steele's *The Englishman*, no. 28 (1713).[9] As Blake was to discover in another context, this history was adopted by both parties; for the Tory Bolingbroke (like Sidney, a plotter against the government, but spared martyrdom now that times and tempers had altered) recounted the history of the Gothic constitution in his celebrated 'Remarks on the English History', published serially in *The Craftsman* in 1730 and 1731. Bolingbroke claims indeed, on the authority of Dio Cassius, that Gothic liberties were based upon antecedent British liberties, so that the spirit of the English constitution is over seventeen hundred years old (*Craftsman*, no. 222, 2 October 1730).

History endorsed what Thomson, in *Liberty* IV (1736), 813–15, called

> the full the perfect Plan . . .
> Of BRITAIN's matchless *Constitution*, mixt
> Of mutual checking and supporting Powers,

but so, apparently, did the ubiquitous Newtonian philosophy. Government should in its delicate balance imitate the balance of the natural-law-abiding universe interpreted by Newton. This case is argued out in an allegorical poem, *The Newtonian System of the World the best Model of Government* (1728), by John Theophilus Desaguliers (see Ch. 1 above).

Both Locke's contract theory and the Gothic notion of elective monarchy were advanced in the 1680s to refute divine right and to justify resistance to absolutism. Absolute monarchy had few supporters in England after 1688, but when Anne came to the throne the notion of divine right was revived by some Tories, encouraged perhaps by the Queen's revival of the Stuart ritual of touching sufferers from scrofula, 'the King's Evil', in order to cure them miraculously (a touch that proved ineffective in the case of young Samuel Johnson). Though such Tories found Anne more acceptable on principle than Dutch William, those who were not Jacobites were fully prepared to believe that William III was brought to the throne by a particular act of God, who, wishing to preserve the Protestant religion in England, duly wafted the Dutch fleet over the Channel on the anniversary of the Gunpowder Plot, thus ensuring that James II would abdicate and yield his realm to its *de facto* king. Once William was accepted for the sake of religion, it was possible for the same reason to accept the Hanoverian succession; so most Tories in Parliament voted for the Act of Settlement in 1701.

Whigs in general believed that the monarch's title was validated by a Bill of Rights, not a divine right; in theory they were all strong supporters of the right of resistance and were satisfied with the notion of an elective monarchy. The ministers of the Crown, however, whether they led Whig administrations threatened by Jacobite conspiracies or Tory administrations threatened by the Americans' call for independence or by the clamour for popular rights at home, did not wish to hear any philosophical justification of resistance, whatever lip-service they might pay to the Glorious Revolution; therefore they found it expedient to forget Locke's contract and to deny the historical truth of Gothic liberties. A typical statement of the ministerial attitude comes from Lord Hervey, Pope's 'Sporus', in *Ancient and Modern Liberty stated and compared* (1734), when he argues that Britons were slaves throughout their entire history before 1688. Both the Lockeian contract and the Gothic constitution thus became in the eighteenth century, as in the 1680s, the property of the parliamentary and extra-parliamentary opposition to the prerogative of the Crown, a prerogative now exercised more by the King's ministers than by the King in person.

Believers in the antiquity of mixed government agreed, on the authority of Polybius, that the Roman republican constitution enshrined the principle of liberty and embodied some of the checks and balances thought to characterize the ancient Gothic system; they agreed further that it was Augustus who finally unbalanced that constitution and destroyed liberty, so entailing what Swift, in a warning to modern politicians in 1701, called 'the vilest Tyranny that Heaven in its Anger ever inflicted on a Corrupt and Poison'd People'.[10] The Augustan tyranny was widely regarded as the prime model for those absolute monarchies still ruling in parts of Asia and Europe in the eighteenth century and abhorred in Britain by government and opposition alike. In the fierce political controversy during the years of Walpole's ascendancy it was the opposition writers, however, who were more savage in their attacks upon Augustus, if only because of the convenient accident that Walpole's master, the second Hanoverian king, was named George Augustus.[11]

The English concept of mixed government implied that political power was shared, but such sharing fell, of course, a long way short of democracy.

When there was widespread industrial unemployment or when food prices were unduly high, mobs might riot and force government action; in 1766, for instance, in many parts of England the poor were 'driven to desperation and madness, by the exorbitant prices of all manner of provisions' (the effect of a poor agricultural summer), and rioted until Chatham's administration was compelled to forbid the exporting of corn; the London mob could be called out in particular political causes, such as those of Wilkes or Gordon, but its influence on Parliament was only marginal and intermittent. The lower orders had no place of their own in politics; they existed to be ruled, and most of them were scarcely aware of any agent of government other than their local magistrates. The propertyless labourers were assumed to have interests identical with 'the general interest of society'; Adam Smith wrote in *The Wealth of Nations* (1776):

> Though the interest of the labourer is strictly connected with that of the society, he is incapable either of comprehending that interest, or of understanding its connexion with his own. His condition leaves him no time to receive the necessary information, and his education and habits are commonly such as to render him unfit to judge even though he was fully informed. In the public deliberations, therefore, his voice is little heard and less regarded.[12]

What was true in 1776 was no less true in 1700.

Few thinking men or politicians would have disagreed with Locke that the business of government is the preservation of property, and therefore should be left in the hands of men of property. As property for eighteenth-century Englishmen signified above all else landed property, the electoral system ensured that both Houses of Parliament were composed of landowners and that most of the Commons were elected by landowners. Even Defoe, the most consistent advocate of the 'trading interest' in politics at the beginning of the century, a supporter of radical views in many fields, and an early advocate of parliamentary reform, insisted that political rights did not belong to all inhabitants of a country, but only to freehold landowners: 'the Freeholders are the proper owners of the Country: It is their own, and the other inhabitants are but sojourners, like lodgers in a house, and ought to be subject to such laws as the Freeholders impose upon them, or else they must remove, because the Freeholders having a right to the land, the other have no right to live there but upon sufferance.'[13] *A fortiori*, Swift, Bolingbroke, and other Tories agreed.

The primacy of what was always called 'the landed interest' was in part a consequence of the evident fact that the land was still, as it always had been, obviously and overwhelmingly, the first source of England's economic wealth. Farming supplied not only nearly all the country's food (barring 'luxuries' and spices) but the bulk of its industrial raw materials. Most machines were built largely of wood; horses were the principal sources of industrial power, the others being wind and falling water. Husbandry was still, as Socrates had called it, 'the mother of arts'. Even that inveterate and vehement town-lover Samuel Johnson wrote in 1756 two essays elaborating the self-evident truth that agriculture was 'the most necessary and most indispensable of all professions' and that it alone was the support of society. He even went on, following a tradition stretching back beyond Virgil's *Georgics*, to praise the virtue of rural life:

> Luxury, avarice, injustice, violence, and ambition, take up their
> ordinary residence in populous cities; while the hard and
> laborious life of the husbandmen will not admit of these vices.
> The honest farmer lives in a wise and happy state, which
> inclines him to justice, temperance, sobriety, sincerity, and
> every virtue that can dignify human nature.[14]

As Johnson's words reveal, the value of the land was not merely economic. Many men attached their most cherished values to the countryside; consequently the writings of the century are full of representations of the joys, the virtues, and the usefulness of country life, and Varro's commonplace, translated by Cowper as 'God made the country, and man made the town' (*The Task*, I. 749), echoes through eighteenth-century literature.

It is hardly surprising that eighteenth-century poets should celebrate the ancient pieties of rural life; what is perhaps remarkable is that so many of them should also applaud the benefits of trade and commerce. The gratulatory and prophetic note sounded in Prior's *Carmen Seculare* (1700) sounds more nobly in the conclusion of Pope's *Windsor Forest*; it runs through Thomson's *Seasons* and *Liberty* (not to mention his 'Rule, Britannia!)', and much of the work of Glover, Young, and their like; and finally is heard at full volume in John Dyer's *The Fleece* (1767), a woollen epic, described by a modern critic as 'in many ways the greatest patriotic poem in the language'.[15] During the same period the merchant began to appear as a stock heroic type on the stage and in the novel; the prototype of this figure is doubtless Steele and Addison's Sir Andrew Freeport, that man of 'natural Eloquence, good Sense, and Probity of Mind', 'of indefatigable Industry, strong Reason, and great Experience', who is 'pleasanter Company than a general Scholar' (*Spectator*, no. 549, and 2). Such patriotic poetical excitement and such awareness of what theatre audiences and novel-readers wanted were responses to a huge growth of trade and manufacture as mercantile empire was expanded in a great surge of war and diplomacy down to the end of the Seven Years War in 1763, by which time Britain had gained possession of India and most of America and the West Indies.

Voltaire observes in the tenth of his *Lettres Philosophiques* (1734) that trade was held in such esteem in England that old landed families happily engaged in it. He notes that the head of a City business was brother to Viscount Townshend, the agriculturist and statesman, whose brother-in-law Sir Robert Walpole, in turn, had a brother who kept a warehouse in Aleppo. Mischievously, he adds for the benefit of French readers a somewhat exaggerated anecdote telling how a subsidy of fifty million pounds, raised in half an hour by English merchants, enabled Prince Eugene to defeat the armies of Louis XIV. Defoe's approval of the mingling of aristocratic and mercantile blood in the body politic is no less sincere and rather more rhapsodic: 'the Blood of Trade is mix'd and blended with the Blood of Gallantry, so that Trade is the Life of the Nation, the Soul of its Felicity, the Spring of its Wealth, the Support of its Greatness, and the Staff on which both King and People lean'.[16]

If merchants were rarely praised in terms quite as extravagant as those used by Defoe, they were widely respected. This respect was, however, rarely extended to West Indian slave-plantation owners and so-called 'nabobs' in the East India Company, the men who, as Cowper wrote in *The Task*, 'Build factories with blood, conducting trade/At the sword's point' (IV. 681–82). Nicholas Amhurst in *Craftsman* no. 11 (1727) complains about nabobs who return home after three or four years laden with immense wealth, buy great estates, and display 'the same *governing Spirit* here . . . which they found practicable in those *foreign* and *arbitrary Commands*'; Goldsmith in *The Traveller* (1764) writes of

> The wealth of climes, where savage nations roam,
> Pillag'd from slaves to purchase slaves at home.
>
> (ll. 387–88)

As the century wore on, disquiet over English commercial imperialism increased, particularly in the 1780s, when Warren Hastings was impeached and when national organizations were set up for the abolition of slavery.

Nabobs and planters were regarded as especially dangerous when they bought their way into the House of Commons. Poor Lord Chesterfield was aggrieved when he tried to buy a seat for his son in the 1768 election and his offer of £2,500 was contemptuously refused by a boroughmonger, who said 'that there was no such thing as a borough to be had now; for the rich East and West Indians had secured them all, at the rate of three thousand pounds at the least; but many at four thousand; and two or three, that he knew, at five thousand'.[17] Lord Chatham, whose foreign policy was largely responsible for the acquisition of India, nevertheless complained that

> The riches of Asia have been poured in upon us, and have
> brought with them not only Asiatic luxury, but, I fear, Asiatic
> principles of government. Without connections, without any
> natural interest in the soil, the importers of foreign gold have
> forced their way into Parliament by such a torrent of private
> corruption as no private hereditary fortune could resist.[18]

Berkshire seems to have been a regular hunting-ground for nabobs in search of country estates, local influence, and parliamentary seats; it had five Anglo-Indian sheriffs between 1772 and 1789, and was called 'the English Hindoostan'. In Samuel Foote's comedy *The Nabob* (1772) the title-character asks the boroughmonger, 'O Nathan, did you tell that man in Berkshire I would buy his estate?'

In effect, Chesterfield and Chatham are defending traditional, aristocratic, and hereditary corruption of elections, but they believed, as many others did, that it was vital for the public interest that government should not be invaded by men who had no 'natural interest in the soil'. Mere possession of a landed estate might not, *pace* Toland (p.78 below), be a sufficient pledge of good behaviour and of a proper sense of responsibility for the general welfare of society.

There was an equally serious objection to the invasion of government by the new breed of men who were making fortunes out of the banks, stock markets, and other elaborate financial institutions which had proliferated and grown after the foundation of the Bank of England in 1694. Government was no longer to be financed only by current revenue, but by loans from wealthy subjects to whom it would return perpetual interest on a perpetual and ever-growing National Debt. People of many kinds – trustees of charitable bodies, spinsters, widows, professional men, and foreigners (especially the Dutch) – lent money to the government by purchasing stock issued by the Bank of England and the great chartered companies. Locke was one of the holders of the first issue of Bank of England stock. The most prominent individual lenders, however, were City of London merchants and financiers, and it was these men, together with all who worked in the Stock Exchange as factors, jobbers, or brokers, and anyone else closely involved in the complicated new machinery of public credit, who constituted the new 'moneyed interest'. While financiers always formed only a tiny minority in Parliament itself, they exercised a disproportionately large influence, because any administration needed the confidence of the moneyed interest to maintain the system of public credit without which national finances would collapse. This dependence seemed to grow as the National Debt grew. Bolingbroke notes in his last-written work, *Some Reflections on the State of the Nation*, that the Debt rose from a third of a million pounds in 1688 to eighty million in 1749. By 1752 David Hume, one of the least hysterical of men, was convinced that the practice of mortgaging public revenues was 'ruinous beyond all controversy', and that 'either the nation must destroy public credit, or public credit will destroy the nation'.[19] He therefore advocated repudiation of the Debt. Other philosophers were full of projects for redeeming it: for instance, Richard Price (1723–91), the radical reformer, produced several such schemes in the 1770s and 1780s.

It was believed by many that the moneyed interest, working insidiously behind government, had devised a mysterious machine for enriching itself and impoverishing the rest of the nation. Swift's papers in the *Examiner* (1711) worked upon the widespread suspicion that 'through the contrivance and cunning of stock-jobbers there hath been brought in such a complication of knavery and cozenage, such a mystery of iniquity, and such an unintelligible jargon of terms to involve it in, as were never known in any other age or country of the world'[20]; Pope, in the *Epistle to Bathurst* (1733), created a frightening comic fantasy of the diabolical workings of 'blest paper-credit'. Men's worst suspicions about the iniquity of paper-credit were confirmed by the South Sea Bubble of 1720, but the Treasury and the City learned the lessons of that affair, so that for the rest of the eighteenth century English public finance was more honest and efficient than that of any other European country. Had it not been so, England could not have fought its many expensive wars so successfully. Voltaire's story about Prince Eugene and the merchants is a tribute to the strength of finance rather than merely of trade.

The growing power of the moneyed interest was thought to pervert the natural order of government. Swift wrote in 1721: 'I ever abominated that scheme of politics (now about thirty years old) of setting up a money'd interest in opposition to the landed. For, I conceived, there could not be a truer maxim in our government than this, that the possessors of the soil are the best judges of what is for the advantage of the kingdom.' Moneyed men whose property was liquid could have little real care for the kingdom, since no tangible part of it belonged to them. As John Toland declared in 1701, government should be in the hands only of men with considerable landed estate who 'have a firm pledge in England to answer for their behaviour'; moneyed men could 'remove their effects into another country in four-and-twenty hours, and follow themselves the next night'.[21] Also in 1701 Defoe published his plan to reform Parliament by transferring the representation of already notorious rotten boroughs, such as Old Sarum, Bramber, and Dunwich, to hitherto unrepresented commercial centres such as Manchester, Leeds, and Halifax; the title of his plan, significantly, is *The Freeholder's Plea against Stock-jobbing Elections of Parliament Men*.

In an attempt to check the invasion of government by the moneyed men, Parliament in 1711, on a motion introduced by Bolingbroke, passed the Landed Property Qualification Act, which was intended 'to preserve the constitution and freedom of Parliament' by excluding from the House of Commons all except substantial landed men. In so far as it was not a dead letter, this Act merely encouraged more men of wealth to buy country estates, in many cases displacing old landed families who truly represented the 'landed interest'. The King of Brobdingnag asked Gulliver whether the English Commons chose as their representatives strangers with fat purses of money, or landed men from the neighbourhood; in the election of 1768, John Almon cautioned voters against 'fund-mongers, stock-jobbers, directors of incorporated companies, government contractors, court-jobbers, and such other sorts of people as may be rather styled instruments of power and preyers upon the people'[22]; but moneyed men inside and outside Parliament continued to exercise their influence upon government.

The City of London was the home of what Chatham, in a speech to the House of Lords in 1770, called the 'miserable jobbers of Change Alley' and 'the lofty Asiatic plunderers of Leadenhall Street', and also what in the same speech he called 'the fair merchant, whose liberal commerce is the prime source of national wealth'.[23] One of the fruits of commerce most often remarked upon by poets, novelists, and moralists was the great increase in the size, splendour, and (some would say) sophistication of London, on account of its position as the world's greatest commercial centre. Pope and other poets applaud London's international trade and deplore its Stock Exchange; Defoe, notably in his *Tour through the Whole Island of Great Britain* (1724–26), never tires of expressing his delight and wonder at the pull of the London market on all other parts of the kingdom. As he seems to have been one of the first to realize, the growth of London was the crucial factor in

England's transformation from a regionally based agricultural economy, providing for little more than subsistence (like the economy of France), to a powerful, integrated exchange economy. The growth of London encouraged mobility of population as well as money: so much so that, according to a modern demographer's calculation, one adult in every six in mid eighteenth-century England was either living in London or had spent part of his or her life there; this calculation leaves out of account large numbers of fleeting visitors.[24] This revolutionary new feature of social life was certainly evident to Arthur Young (1741–1820), the agricultural writer, when he complained in 1767 that good roads and cheap coach travel had increased tenfold the number of country fellows who have seen London: 'and of course ten times the boasts are sounded in the ears of country fools to induce them to quit their healthy clean fields for a region of dirt, stink, and noise. And the number of young women that fly thither is almost incredible.'[25]

Such mobility became a powerful engine of social and moral change because it assisted the rapid spread of new attitudes and new motivations: for instance, it strengthened a tendency for the cash nexus to replace social relationships based upon tradition and custom, and it encouraged the rapid growth of consumer demand. In other words, the words indeed of many moralists of that day, the expansion of London represented the growth and spread of selfishness, luxury, and vice. The name for London which William Cobbett would later popularize, 'the Wen', was current at least as early as 1775 as a convenient shorthand for the kind of views expressed so vigorously by Matthew Bramble and heartily endorsed by Smollett: 'the capital is become an overgrown monster; which, like a dropsical head, will in time leave the body and extremities without nourishment and support' (*Humphry Clinker*, 29 May).

In the gloomier portions of *The Task* Cowper represents London as a new Sodom, drawing to itself all the wealth of a nation utterly debauched by commerce. Furthermore, 'The town has ting'd the country'; luxury

> Taints downward all the graduated scale
> Of order, from the chariot to the plough.
>
> (IV. 553, 585–86)

The new commercial spirit brought about changes in the countryside, just as it did in London, and evoked, similarly, a mixed response from writers. Pope complained in the *Epistle to Bathurst* about the hectic circulation of money in the City, but in the *Epistle to Burlington* he applauds his friends who put money into the land:

> Who then shall grace, or who improve the Soil?
> Who plants like BATHURST, or who builds like BOYLE.
>
> (177–78)

Over fifty years later, approaching the Norfolk estate of Thomas Coke the famous agricultural improver, Arthur Young saw with enthusiasm the trim farms and cottages:

This is the diffusion of happiness; an overflow of wealth that gilds the whole country, and tells the traveller, in a language too expressive to be misunderstood, *we approach the residence of a man, who feels for others as well as for himself.* . . . The fault of modern luxury is the selfish concentration of wealth: praise is, therefore, justly due when it flows in a liberal stream that connects the ease and comforts of the tenants with the taste and pleasure of his landlord.[26]

By this time many parts of Britain had been 'gilded' by intensive, advanced farming techniques, the reclamation and cultivation of waste land, and the creation of compact farms by the redistribution, consolidation, and enclosure of open-field strips. The lead in such improvements might come first from the landlord or from his tenants; the process usually benefited both because it could greatly increase both rent and profits, but as new methods required increased working capital there was a tendency for the very small farmer to be squeezed out and reduced to the level of a landless labourer. The political economist Nathaniel Forster wrote in 1767 about districts where small farms had been swallowed up by large: 'Instead of an hardy, free, and intrepid race of men, contentedly enjoying the sweets of labour and alternate ease, the state's most useful subjects in peace, and its best soldiers in war, we are presented with the horrible picture of a few tyrant planters amidst a crowd of wretched slaves.'[27] The alleged disappearance of small farms was seen by many moralists as part of a general problem of rural depopulation, where such of the 'hardy, free' peasants as did not become slaves (that is, day-labourers) were compelled to seek employment in sordid, unhealthy industrial towns, or, worse, to emigrate. Goldsmith's *Deserted Village* (1770) perfectly crystallizes in its pastoral vein the emotions underlying many politico-economic pamphlets of the 1760s, though it should be remembered that the poem is concerned less with enclosure and depopulation in general than with the special and particularly reprehensible case of agricultural land being enclosed to provide pleasure grounds.

In our period the social consequences of the Industrial Revolution aroused less comment than did the effects of those developments in finance and agriculture which made that revolution possible. Praise of the export trade by men such as Defoe or Dyer is linked with praise of manufacturing, and writers who comment on the advance of scientific enlightenment often point to the century's revolutionary improvements in industrial machinery. The effect of mechanization on traditional domestic industries does not go unnoticed: Defoe, for instance, passing through Wiltshire on his Tour, notes that the hand-knitting of woollen stockings, once a very significant by-employment for both men and women 'is now much decay'd by the increase of the Knitting-Stocking Engine, or Frame, which has destroyed the hand-Knitting Trade for fine stockings thro' the whole Kingdom'.[28] Long before Defoe's time there were large-scale, heavily capitalized industries such as shipbuilding, metallurgy, and, indeed, the production of woollen goods, but the eighteenth century saw new industrial enterprises of a quantity and scale never known before. For instance, by 1785 the iron-founding firm of Darby, under the control of the third Abraham Darby, owned 20 miles of railways, laid at the cost of £800 per mile, whichconnected coal-mines to works which included 10 blast-furnaces, 9 forges, and 16 steam-engines. The whole employed capital of £100,000. Nevertheless, the sublime aesthetic experience of Coalbrookdale seems to have impressed literate visitors more strikingly than any social effects of industrialization. Matthew Boulton laid out his great Soho Works in Birmingham in 1765, thereby accumulated from the sale of 'toys' (that is, gilt, plated, and brassware) more than enough capital to finance James Watt's development of the steam-engine, and thereby advanced the Industrial Revolution. When Boswell met Boulton in 1776 he 'was struck with the thought of a Smith being a Great Man . . . He had about 700 people at Work. He was a sort of iron Chieftain, and seemed to be Fatherly to his tribe.'[29] Boswell was paying tribute to the work-discipline imposed by the factory system and also pointing to a polarization between master and man quite as wide as the one that Forster thought existed in rural society.

The financial, agricultural, and industrial revolution by which Britain became the world's leading commercial nation by the end of the eighteenth century was the subject of constant, painful debate. The language of this debate was for the most part taken from moral philosophy, its key words being 'luxury' and 'avarice'. Ancient historians from Herodotus onward believed that luxury corrupted the virtue of nations. From *Cooper's Hill* to Cowper's *Task* English poetry followed the ancients in deploring the luxury of the city while celebrating the comparative innocence of the countryside. The claim in Goldsmith's *Deserted Village* that men decay where wealth accumulates was widely accepted as a truism. Berkeley, for instance, observed, 'Frugality of manners is the nourishment and strength of bodies politic. It is that by which they grow and subsist, until they are corrupted by luxury, the natural cause of their decay and ruin . . . all our riches are but a poor exchange for that simplicity of manners which we despise in our ancestors.'[30]

Such orthodox views were vigorously challenged by Mandeville's *Fable of the Bees, or Private Vices, Publick Benefits* (1714–29), the voluminous and notorious treatise which grew out of his poetical *jeu d'esprit*, *The Grumbling Hive* (1705): see Chapter 3 above. Mandeville states the traditional objections to luxury:

> It is a receiv'd Notion, that Luxury is as destructive to the
> Wealth of the whole Body Politic, as it is to that of every
> individual Person who is guilty of it, and that a National
> Frugality enriches a Country. . . . What is laid to the Charge of
> Luxury besides, is that it increases Avarice and Rapine: And
> where they are reigning Vices, Offices of the greatest Trust are
> bought and sold; the Ministers that should serve the Publick,
> both great and small, corrupted . . . and lastly, that it
> effeminates and enervates the People, by which the Nations
> become an easy Prey to the first Invaders.[31]

Then he goes on cheerfully to demonstrate that luxury, avarice, and the corruptions consequent upon them are inseparable from national prosperity. He takes the strictly utilitarian view that effects are more important than motives; so he shows that pride, gluttony, lechery, envy, and other sins motivate conspicuous consumption on the part of luxurious people, creating employment for the industrious and so generating and widely distributing wealth. In the original verse fable Mandeville wrote that luxury

> Employ'd a Million of the Poor,
> And odious Pride a Million more.
> Envy it self, and Vanity,
> Were Ministers of Industry.

In the long prose notes, added later, he discomforted his readers by unsavoury examples of commercial success:

> A Highwayman having met with a considerable Booty, gives a
> poor common Harlot he fancies, Ten Pounds, to new-rig her
> from Top to Toe; is there a spruce Mercer so conscientious that
> he will refuse to sell her a Thread Sattin, tho' he knew who she
> was? She must have Shoes and Stockings, Gloves, the Stay and
> Mantua-maker, the Sempstress, the Linen-Draper, all must get
> something by her, and a hundred different Tradesmen
> dependent on those she laid her Money out with, may touch
> Part of it before a month is at an end.

Similarly the gin trade, constantly under attack from moralists, bestowed wide public blessings in 'the Rents that are received, the Ground that is till'd, the Tools that are made, the Cattle that are employ'd, and above all, the Multitude of Poor that are maintain'd, by the Variety of Labour, required in Husbandry, in Malting, in Carriage and Distillation'.[32] Mandeville recognized the arrival of a complex modern cash economy, based upon ever-increasing consumer demand, but he chose to proclaim his discovery in morally provocative terms, asserting that commercial activity is inconsistent with virtue.

The value of the cash nexus is argued in a more acceptable form in Steele's *Spectator*, no. 174 (19 September 1711), the ostensible subject of which is the mutual dependence of the landed and the trading interests. This paper takes the form of a debate between Sir Roger de Coverley and Sir Andrew Freeport. Sir Roger disparages the narrow, selfish, mercenary character of the merchant, and asks rhetorically 'how much is his punctual Dealing below a Gentleman's Charity to the Poor, or Hospitality among his Neighbours?' Sir Andrew replies by asking 'whether so many Artificers at work ten Days together by my Appointment, or so many Peasants made merry on Sir ROGER'S Charge, are the more obliged?' He concludes, 'Sir ROGER gives to his Men, but I place mine above the Necessity or Obligation of my Bounty'. In this revealing exchange Sir Roger is allowed to embody the old ideal of 'hospitality' and 'housekeeping', the values praised in

Jonson's *To Penshurst* and other 'Country-House poems' of the seventeenth century; but Sir Andrew has the last word when he proposes and justifies the social relationships of a modern cash economy.

Sir Andrew Freeport's argument that giving alms is in effect less charitable than giving employment is heard throughout the eighteenth century. Mandeville puts the case in forthright terms in his *Essay on Charity, and Charity Schools* (1723), but Johnson too, on one of the several occasions in conversations of the 1770s when he declared that luxury is socially beneficial, claimed that money is much better spent on luxury which gives employment to the industrious poor than in almsgiving which keeps the idle poor in idleness.[33] (Such a distinction between the undeserving and the deserving poor is common in eighteenth-century thought; it is memorably, if paradoxically, expounded in Shaw's *Pygmalion*, and can hardly be said to have disappeared today.) In fairness it should be said that Johnson elsewhere advocated almsgiving, and wrote against luxury, avarice, and the vanity of wealth in his two great imitations of Juvenal and in the lines he added to Goldsmith's *Deserted Village*. Even when he apparently endorses Mandevillian doctrine he condemns the illogicality of Mandeville's defining vice and virtue from different bases: 'He takes the narrowest system of morality, monastick morality, which holds pleasure itself to be a vice . . . and he reckons wealth as a publick benefit, which is by no means always true.'[34]

Like Johnson, Pope theoretically disapproves of Mandeville's cynical realism, but both of his *Moral Essays* on the use of riches explore the paradox that avarice and prodigality may be socially beneficial. The description of Timon's luxury in the *Epistle to Burlington* (1731) ends with a wry Mandevillian moral:

> Yet hence the Poor are cloath'd, the Hungry fed;
> Health to himself, and to his Infants bread
> The Lab'rer bears: What his hard Heart denies,
> His charitable Vanity supplies.
> (ll. 169–72)

The lesson is driven home in Pope's own footnote: 'The *Moral* of the whole, where PROVIDENCE is justified in giving Wealth to those who squander it in this manner. A bad Taste employs more hands and diffuses Expence more than a good one.' In the poem taken as a whole, Pope of course condemns modern commercialism just as unequivocally as he does in the *Epistle to Bathurst* (1733), where 'Av'rice, creeping on,/Spread like a low-born Mist' (ll. 137–38). Pope stands alongside his friends Swift and Bolingbroke in a tradition which is continued in the next generation by Smollett, Goldsmith, and many others, despite assurances by David Hume that the new commercial spirit activated by avarice and luxury really improves manners and morals.

Hume puts this case in two linked essays, 'Of Commerce' and 'Of Luxury', in *Political Discourses* (1752); significantly, the second of these essays was retitled 'Of Refinement in the Arts' when it was republished in 1760. He takes the common-sense view that any degree of luxury 'may be innocent or blamable . . . indulgences are only vices, when they are pursued at the expense of some virtue'. He recognizes that disinterested public spirit is not a powerful motive in these times, so 'it is requisite to govern men by other passions, and animate them with a spirit of avarice and industry, art and luxury'.[35] The awakening of avarice arouses men from indolence and impels them to improve manufactures and trade. Because of these improvements, less labour is required in the production of food and other necessities, so that in times of war men can readily be diverted from manufacturing into the army, where they are supported by the farmers' surplus food and by taxes upon newly-created wealth. Thus, contrary to common belief, luxury strengthens rather than weakens the State. Rome fell because of 'an ill-modelled government, and the unlimited extent of conquests',[36] not on account of Asiatic luxury; this was also Gibbon's conclusion.

Furthermore, Hume argues, 'where luxury nourishes commerce and industry' authority and consideration are drawn to 'that middling rank of men, who are the best and firmest basis of public liberty'. These people 'covet equal laws, which may secure their property, and preserve them from monarchical, as well as aristocratical tyranny'.[37] Thus luxury, again contrary to common belief, preserves liberty, rather than threatening it. At the same time, a society that improves its industry and mechanical arts commonly produces some refinement in the liberal arts. Trade and manufacture encourage the growth of cities; in cities men receive and communicate knowledge and acquire sociability: 'it is impossible but they must feel an increase of humanity, from the very habit of conversing together. . . . Thus *industry, knowledge,* and *humanity,* are linked together, by an indissoluble chain, and are found, from experience as well as reason, to be peculiar to the more polished, and, what are commonly denominated, the more luxurious ages.'[38]

Hume claimed that politics could be reduced to a science; Adam Smith's *The Wealth of Nations* (1776) was the first classic treatise of the new science of political economy. Though in his *Theory of Moral Sentiments* (see Ch. 3 above) Smith condemns the pernicious implications of Mandeville's philosophy, when he writes upon economic affairs he is, like Hume, a more thoughtful, more humane Mandeville. He recognizes that in the nature of things economic relations cannot be based upon benevolence, or even upon the principle of sympathy extolled in his *Theory of Moral Sentiments*: 'It is not from the benevolence of the butcher, the brewer, or the baker, that we expect our dinner, but from their regard to their own interest. We address ourselves, not to their humanity but to their self-love.'[39]

Smith observed that the wealth of the nation as a whole had grown enormously during the century, and that this was in spite of, rather than because of, government regulation of trade and manufacture. Throughout his treatise he argues for the free movement of capital, labour, and goods, and points to the unreasonableness of restraints upon imports and exports:

> The natural effort of every individual to better his own
> condition, when suffered to exert itself with freedom and
> security, is so powerful a principle, that it is alone, and without

any assistance, not only capable of carrying on the society to wealth and prosperity, but of surmounting a hundred impertinent obstructions with which the folly of human laws too often incumbers its operations.[40]

Individual liberty and general prosperity go hand in hand. Smith compares high wages and comfortable conditions in North America with destitution and famine in fertile Bengal: 'The difference between the genius of the British constitution which protects and governs North America, and that of the mercantile company which oppresses and domineers in the East Indies, cannot perhaps be better illustrated than by the different state of those countries.'[41] While moralists deplored the spread of luxury among the lower orders and used this as an argument for the depression of wages, Smith easily proves that the liberal reward of labour is advantageous to the whole of society.

In *The Wealth of Nations* Smith devotes ten times as much space to the commercial as to the agricultural system of political economy. The commercial system, he rightly claims, 'is the modern system, and is best understood in our own country and in our own times'.[42] Like Hume, he intends to make his readers fully alive to the fact that they belong to 'a nation of shopkeepers'.[43] Nevertheless Smith accepts the old wisdom that the most permanent wealth lies in the land. 'The ordinary revolutions of war and government easily dry up the sources of that wealth which arises from commerce only. That which arises from the more solid improvements of agriculture, is much more durable.' Smith is also aware, as Toland was, that a merchant can carry on his trade in any place, 'and a very trifling disgust will make him remove his capital and together with it all the industry which it supports, from one country to another'.[44] That being so, government is best left in the hands of landed owners.

Political controversy, when not focused, as political controversy usually is, upon extremely short-term issues, was much concerned with the effects of the growth of governmental power accompanying growth of the commercial system. The government of a flourishing commercial empire depended upon large and complicated financial institutions in order to fund the National Debt, to support a standing army and navy, and to protect and extend commerce. For all the compelling nostalgia of politicians who praised ancient rural values, there was no possibility of a return to a simple peasant economy, even if such a return were desirable. Through the creation of the National Debt the government and the 'moneyed men' came to depend upon one another; the most stable administrations, whether Whig or Tory, whether led by Walpole or by the younger Pitt, were those that most fully recognized the new circumstances. With the growing complexity of making war, maintaining empire, and regulating trade, the number of publicly-funded posts in the government's gift increased greatly. Governments found it easier to gather and maintain support in Parliament by giving offices, pensions, and contracts to Members and their dependants. From time to time, independent country gentlemen and other 'patriots' cried out against the presence of such 'placemen'; there was even a clause in the

Act of Settlement (1701), enacting that after the Hanoverian succession 'no person who has an office or place of profit under the King, or receives a pension from the Crown shall be capable of serving as a member of the House of Commons'. This clause, though, was a dead letter.

One particularly eminent class of placemen, the bishops, had been part of the political establishment for centuries. Most consecrations were made primarily on political grounds in order to strengthen the existing government; so, by and large, Anne and George III appointed Tories to the bench of bishops in the House of Lords, George I and George II appointed Whigs. The importance of the episcopal vote was strikingly demonstrated when the fate of Walpole's administration hung in the balance in 1733: on two occasions twenty-four out of the twenty-five bishops who voted cast their votes in support of Walpole, thus enabling the government to win by just one vote.

Any administration that was to be stable had to gather to itself a well-disciplined 'Court and Treasury Party', consisting of such 'placemen and pensioners' as civil, judicial, military and naval officers, court officials, government contractors, bishops, and others who were obliged to it for their employments and seats. This was the jobbery and bribery much complained of by 'patriots'; but it never became a wholesale corruption of Parliament. Any successful administration had to obtain the confidence of a substantial body of relatively independent members who wished to see the King's government carried on effectively, but who sought the patronage of the Crown to only a small degree. Parliamentary opposition consisted of a less stable alliance between various groups of 'outs' who longed for the spoils of office and a core of country gentlemen who were truly 'independent' in that they desired no offices or pensions and maintained in all its purity the consitutional theory of spearated powers – under which the King chose his 'servants', or his ministers, and the House of Commons existed as a kind of watch-dog, guarding the 'public interest' and acting as a check and balance against the King's servants. These independent country gentlemen and their allies constituted, in effect, an old-fashioned, backward-looking 'Country Party'.

For nearly two-thirds of our period the government was Whig; the finest literary examples of opposition rhetoric came from Tory pens in the years of Walpole's ascendancy; but the opposition between Whig and Tory was perhaps never as significant as that between Court and Country. Hume demonstrates in his essay 'Of the Parties of Great Britain', in *Essays, Moral and Political* (1742), that the division between Court and Country arises quite inevitably, as a matter of principle as well as of interest, in a mixed constitution where monarchical and republican elements are delicately balanced against one another. As early as 1717 there was piquant evidence for Hume's conclusion, when Walpole resigned his post as Chancellor of the Exchequer and went for three years into opposition against the Stanhope–Sunderland administration. Walpole, now a virtuous, independent country gentleman, regularly found himself in the same division-lobby as that arch-Jacobite William Shippen, as the two of them denounced many of the very Court policies that Walpole was to advocate as soon as he returned to power, faced with the task of restoring public credit after the crash of the South Sea scheme.

This episode notwithstanding, Country Party attitudes, as revealed in the work of such writers as Swift, Pope, Gay, Johnson, Fielding, Thomson, Lyttleton, and Chesterfield, were brought into sharp focus mainly in the course of opposition to Walpole's administration. It was this period that saw the development of legitimate, organized parliamentary opposition to the King's ministers by the Tory Bolingbroke and the dissident Whig Pulteney in alliance. The leading figures in this opposition were the 'honest men', familiar to readers of Pope and Thomson. Though Bolingbroke readily cast himself into the role of a gentleman farmer, not all the leaders of the Country Party were country gentlemen or representative of the landed interest: one of their ablest spokesmen was the city merchant, one-time Lord Mayor of London, Sir John Barnard (1685–1764), who was, with Pope, the only living cultural hero honoured in the opposition shrine of British Worthies at Stowe (see Ch. 6 below). Something of the wide spread of Country Party attitudes is indicated by the fact that *The Craftsman*, the Tory Bolingbroke's chief mouthpiece in the late 1720s and early 1730s, frequently quotes approvingly from *Cato's Letters* (1720–23), an organ of the so-called 'real Whigs' or Commonwealthmen, who were ideologically the heirs of the mid-seventeenth-century republicans.

Country Party supporters, as one would expect, were generally opposed to the 'moneyed interest': this is true even of Sir John Barnard, who, like William Pitt the elder, distinguishes sharply between merchants and financiers. An extreme example of Country opposition to the City may be found in *Cato's Letters*, which were mostly written by the Commonwealthman John Trenchard (1662–1723), who, adopting the name of the ancient antagonist of Caesarism, opposes a modern despotism created by the sinister influence of the City over the Court:

> What Briton, blessed with any sense of virtue, or with common
> sense; what Englishman, animated with a public spirit, or with
> any spirit, but must burn with rage and shame, to behold the
> nobles and gentry of a great Kingdom, men of magnanimity,
> men of breeding, men of understanding, and of letters; to see
> such men bowing down, like Joseph's sheaves, before the face
> of a dirty stock-jobber, and receiving laws from men bred
> behind counters, and the decision of their fortunes from hands
> still dirty with sweeping shops![45]

Supporters of Country attitudes generally favoured sumptuary or agrarian laws. As power always follows property, great inequalities of power could be prevented by placing bounds upon the acquisition of property. Eighteenth-century writers frequently made reference to the so-called 'Licinian' law in republican Rome, which was intended to restrict the size of landed estates but was never adequately enforced. According to Walter Moyle (1672–1721), the Commonwealthman, this law 'established the great Ballance of the Commonwealth, and would have render'd it immortal, had the Law been effectually put in execution'[46]; to preserve its balanced constitution England needed a similar law. The moral philosopher Francis Hutcheson (see Ch. 3 above) also advocated a law to limit property.[47] 'Country Party' writers were particularly vocal in their objections to luxury. It is a constant theme of both *Cato's Letters* and *The Craftsman* that men of debauched, effeminated, and luxurious tastes are easily bribed by ill-designing ministers who are able to pay pensions and sinecures out of the public exchequer; Bolingbroke refers to Mandeville as the apologist of a corrupt age. It would appear that luxury made it easier for the administration to increase its influence over Parliament, so throwing the constitution off balance by compromising that principle of separation of the legislative and the executive powers which was thought to be the cornerstone of political liberty.

The Country Party wanted cheap and efficient government. It favoured a citizen militia, rather than a standing, mercenary army in time of peace. From the seventeenth century a standing army in time of peace was seen as a potential tool of tyranny; but even in wartime the Country Party maxim was to fight always at sea, and to avoid committing a large, expensive army to Continental campaigns, particularly if they were fought (as they usually were) in defence of Hanover. This was the defence policy of William Pitt the elder, who, in our period, achieved a greater degree of popular support than any other minister of the Crown. It was for sound political reasons as well as sentiment that the sailor was a greater hero than the soldier in eighteenth-century England.

The completest expression of these Country Party attitudes is found in the writings of Bolingbroke, the Tory zealot who was one of the first to propound what has become known as 'the Whig interpretation of history'.[48] For Bolingbroke, 'history is philosophy teaching by examples'[49]; in writings such as his tendentious *Remarks on the History of England*, first published in *The Craftsman* (1730–31), he takes the usable past with its heroes, such as Alfred, Henry V, and Queen Elizabeth, and its villains, such as James I, his 'Prime Minister' the Duke of Buckingham, and, as always, that 'infamous Tyrant', Augustus.[50] A more philosophical, or at least more idealistic, work is the *Idea of a Patriot King* (written 1738, published 1749), in which Bolingbroke argues that a degenerate political society can be renewed only by a general reform of public life prompted by the example of a wise and virtuous monarch. Ideally the monarch provides a focus for reverence and a necessary element of stability in the balanced constitution, but he can play such a part only if he rules with very wide popular support; if he draws all his ministers from one party he becomes the creature of that party, and so loses the power that he needs to wield if the constitution is to remain in balance. So, while denying divine right, and indeed drawing much from Whig history and political theory, Bolingbroke arrives at something not very far removed from Filmer's patriarchal high-Tory idea:

> The true image of a free people, governed by a PATRIOT KING, is that of a patriarchal family, where the head and the members are united by one common interest, and animated by one

common spirit: and where, if any are perverse enough to have
another, they will be soon borne down by the superiority of
those who have the same.[51]

In keeping with this patriarchal idea, Bolingbroke modifies Locke's contract
theory by arguing that natural society is familial, and that the original
contract is made between extended families or clans with existing habits of
deference. This notion antedates Locke's *Two Treatises*; it is put forward, for
instance, in Sir William Temple's *Essay upon the Origin and Nature of Government*.

In the middle of the eighteenth century Locke's contract theory was still
'the fashionable system', as Hume called it when it came under his sceptical
gaze in the essay 'Of the Original Contract' in *Three Essays* (1748). Against
Locke, Hume logically argues that any valid contract implies an antecedent
agreement to honour contracts, but this itself is a contract, so there is an
infinite regression. Moving to pragmatic arguments, he claims that any
'original contract' is now so ancient and obliterated by change that it cannot
be supposed to retain any authority. History affords no evidence for an
original contract; almost all existing and earlier recorded governments
obtained their power by force or fraud. Most people make no enquiry about
their obedience to an existing government, 'more than about the principle of
gravity, resistance, or the most universal laws of nature.'[52] Obedience is
grounded in habit and in a utilitarian recognition that without such
obedience society could not subsist.

Hume's refutation of Locke was adopted by conservative political thinkers
all the more readily because in the second half of the eighteenth century the
contract theory was being reinterpreted in such a way as to justify radical
reform. Potentially the most radical of these new interpretations was that of
Rousseau, who, for a brief period before persecution mania resumed its
grasp upon his mind, enjoyed a warm and unlikely friendship with Hume,
'le bon David' as he called him. In his *Discours sur l'origine de l'inégalité* (1755)
Rousseau reflects upon the state of nature and the original contract with even
less claim to historical veracity than Locke. Rousseau acknowledges that the
state of nature perhaps never existed, but believes that it is necessary to have
just ideas of it in order to assess fairly our present state. These just ideas can
most easily be arrived at by imaginatively stripping away from contemporary man all artificial elements derived from his life in society; having
thus acquired a conception of natural man, it is possible, by intuition as
much as by research, to construct a history of humankind.

In Rousseau's state of nature, as in Locke's, men were free and equal. The
discovery of metallurgy and agriculture led to division of labour and the
institution of property, with the result that men were put into conflict with
one another; thus social inequality began, and with it avarice, ambition, and
war. The rich therefore persuaded the poor to enter with them into a
contract which established a supreme power in each community for the
protection of property and defence against common enemies; so the poor
foolishly but willingly consented to their own relative poverty in a society
where property, and therefore power, was very unequally distributed.

Under the countenance of a contract the strong oppressed the weak. Rousseau's history is accompanied by much of the ubiquitous eighteenth-century rhetoric on modern physical and moral effeminacy arising from the growth of selfishness and luxury.

Du contrat social (1762) similarly owes more to hypothesis than to history. Though Rousseau's observation tells him that social man is fettered, his instinct tells him that natural man is free: hence the famous opening of Rousseau's treatise, 'L'homme est né libre, et partout il est dans les fers. . . . Comment ce changement s'est il fait? Je l'ignore.'[53] The social contract of his title belongs to the future, not to the past; for Rousseu's ideal is that existing systems of social, political, and religious tyrannies should be replaced by a new contract, a spontaneous act of mutual trust among free and politically equal persons which will create a collective body, 'une personne publique', whose general will has the force of natural law. Rousseau's concept of the general will of the sovereign people or 'the state' has had an electrifying effect upon modern history; but *Du contrat social* was little known in England before 1789.

The most important political writings of Rousseau's greatest antagonist, Edmund Burke (1729–97), also belong to the period of the French Revolution, though Burke's *Vindication of Natural Society* (1756), which satirizes Bolingbroke, also ridicules the *Discours sur l'origine de l'inégalité*. In this work of sustained irony Burke uses Bolingbroke's freethinking arguments against revealed religion to attack all law and order in the artificial society that has resulted from man's dissatisfaction with the brutish state of nature. Burke's broader target is the whole field of speculative reasoning in political philosophy; even so, one is slightly surprised to see Bolingbroke being viewed as a radical alongside Rousseau. Such impatience with theory characterizes Burke's later, more celebrated writings. His defence of the Americans in the speech *On Conciliation with the Colonies* (1775) is an appeal to pragmatism and custom. Even if the English Parliament had the legal right to tax the colonists, the exercise of this right ran counter to the Americans' habit of self-government and their tradition of freedom. They were rightly objecting to innovation. Burke neatly and unexpectedly reverses the moral significance of Adam Smith's 'rust' metaphor (p.62 above) when he points out that the language of his House of Commons resolution, asserting the principle and practice of no taxation without representation, is taken from ancient Acts of Parliament:

> It is the genuine produce of the ancient, rustic, manly,
> home-bred sense of this country. I did not dare to rub off a
> particle of the venerable rust that rather adorns and preserves
> than destroys the metal. It would be a profanation to touch with
> a tool the stones which construct the sacred altar of peace. I
> would not violate with modern polish the ingenuous and noble
> roughness of these truly constitutional materials. Above all
> things, I was resolved not to be guilty of tampering: the odious
> vice of restless and unstable minds. I put my foot in the tracks of
> our forefathers; where I can neither wander nor stumble.

Revealingly, when Burke generously acknowledges the spirit of liberty among the Americans, he does so by praising their eager energy in pursuit of commerce. Thus he writes of the New England whalers:

> Whilst we follow them among the tumbling mountains of ice, and behold them penetrating into the deepest frozen recesses of Hudson's Bay, and Davis's Streights, whilst we are looking for them beneath the arctic circle, we hear that they have pierced into the opposite region of polar cold, that they are at the antipodes, and engaged under the frozen serpent of the south. Falkland Island, which seemed too remote and romantic an object for the grasp of national ambition, is but a stage and a resting-place in the progress of their victorious industry. Nor is the equinoctial heat more discouraging to them, than the accumulated winter of both the poles. We know that whilst some of them draw the line and strike the harpoon on the coast of Africa, others run the longitude, and pursue their gigantic game along the coast of Brazil. No sea but what is vexed by their fisheries. No climate that is not witness to their toils.[54]

Burke, like Pope, Thomson, Dyer, and many other poets of the century, is imaginatively excited by trade and industry.

One of the immediate effects of the American Revolution was greatly to intensify that demand for English parliamentary reform which had been voiced intermittently from the early years of the century. As early as 1701, in *The Freeholder's Plea against Stock-jobbing Elections of Parliament Men*, Defoe called for a transfer of representation from the most notorious rotten boroughs to some of the large, hitherto unrepresented, manufacturing towns; Bolingbroke's *Craftsman*, no. 421 (1734) and Lyttelton's *Letters from a Persian in England*, no. 54 (1735) made similar appeals. It was well known that the power of even this limited electorate was being progressively reduced, as freeholders in small, closed corporations were bought out, and as contested elections became less frequent, on account more of local arrangements made by party managers than of the operations of the Septennial Act (1716). Between 1700 and 1715 there were 8 general elections; between 1754 and 1790 there were 6; furthermore, in the county constituencies at these 6 elections there were only 37 contests out of a possible 240.[55] Shrinkage of the electorate coincided with that growth of commerce and industry which brought about a great enlargement of the literate, prosperous, propertied, and politically-aware 'public'. This unrepresented public was of course still very far from being a mass with levelling aspirations: democracy was heard of only on the lunatic fringe, where, for instance, Thomas Spence proposed in *The Real Rights of Men* (1775) that the inhabitants of each parish should on an appointed day form themselves into a corporation, expropriate all private land, and form a unit of self-government; parishes could subsequently freely federate from below, so producing something analogous to what Spence thought was the original Anglo-Saxon form of representative government.

Like the American crisis, the repeated expulsions of the repeatedly re-elected John Wilkes from the House of Commons betrayed a deep division between Parliament and the political public outside. The government's treatment of Wilkes and of the American colonists formed a twofold attack upon traditional English liberties, and the government was able to act with impunity because Parliament was packed with bribable members 'representing' tiny, closed, bribable boroughs. Reform movements were therefore set afoot in the 1770s and 1780s by several groups of 'patriots' who wanted to reduce the influence in Parliament of the Crown and of certain aristocratic factions. Burke, as spokesman for the aristocratic Rockingham Whigs, introduced a parliamentary motion for 'economical reform' intended to eliminate certain sinecures in the gift of the Crown, while outside Westminster, the 'Yorkshire Association' of country gentlemen and freeholders began their county meetings and their petitions to Parliament calling for short (i.e. triennial) Parliaments, a redistribution of parliamentary seats to abolish rotten boroughs and provide more equal representation, and calling, too, for the reduction of corrupt influence and profligate expenditure by the government.

A history of the movement which culminated in the Reform Act of 1832 lies outside the scope of the present volume; however, most of the reformers' aims, and some far more ambitious objectives, had been proclaimed by the date of the American Declaration of Independence, and a brief glance at writings published in 1776 (leaving aside the epoch-making *Wealth of Nations*) reveals a fair range and variety of radical views.

The first important work by the father of Victorian liberalism, Jeremy Bentham (1748–1832), is the *Fragment on Government* (1776), in which the great constitutional jurist Sir William Blackstone (1723–80) is attacked on account of his reverence for precedent and tradition, and his 'ungenerous antipathy' towards legal reform. Bentham looks upon 'the law of nature' as a meaningless phrase, and he accepts that Hume has destroyed the 'chimera' of the original contract once and for all. Government is to be judged by its effects, according to the utilitarian criterion of 'the greatest happiness of the greatest number'; it was far from obvious that this criterion was satisfied by the ancient, mixed constitution which Blackstone and others praised so highly.

Major John Cartwright (1740–1824) was a reformer who equalled Bentham in the length of his years and the copiousness of his writings, and was more prompt to embrace democracy. Cartwright's *Take your Choice* (1776) advocates universal adult manhood suffrage, redistribution of parliamentary seats into equal electoral districts, annual elections, and the ballot. Unlike Bentham, he appeals to tradition; he praises the 'all-excellent Alfred', under whose beneficent reign the Gothic constitution flourished and there was, as Cartwright believed, democratic and representative government at every level from the parish to the (annual) Parliament.

Richard Price (1723–91), like Cartwright a strong supporter of American independence, expressed the hopes of English reformers when he preached a sermon in 1781 on the American victory, taking as his text II Peter 3. 13, 'Nevertheless we, according to his promise, look for new heavens and a new earth, wherein dwelleth righteousness.' In his *Observations on Civil Liberty, the Principles of Government, and the Justice and Policy of the War with America* (1776) he gives a radical reinterpretation of the original contract, and, claiming that the principles he advances are those of Locke, he justifies human equality, natural rights, the sovereignty of the people, and continuous participation in government by the governed.

Price's *Observations on Civil Liberty* ran into seven editions in 1776 and made its author one of the best-known men in England; even so, it did not approach the fame and popularity of *Common Sense*, by Tom Paine (1737–1809), first published in America in the same year. Like Price, Paine calls upon the colonists to declare their independence and sees the American struggle for liberty as the dawn of a new age: 'We have it in our power to begin the world over again. A situation, similar to the present, hath not happened since the days of Noah until now.' In his brusque treatment of constitutional history he reminds his readers that the Jews had no kings in their peaceful, happy patriarchal age; from the Old Testament it appears that monarchy is more of a curse than a blessing upon a nation. Discussing the title of the Kings of England, he writes: 'A French bastard landing with an armed banditti and establishing himself king of England against the consent of the natives, is in plain terms a very paltry rascally original. It certainly hath no divinity in it.'[56] This attack develops not into the old Whig argument against divine right and in favour of mixed government, but into a slashing indictment of the institution of hereditary monarchy itself. The indictment is then extended to embrace the hereditary peerage, which, like the monarchy, is a residue of ancient tyrannies. Our common sense tells us that a republic in which all inhabitants are equally represented is a far better form of government than the rule of 'crowned ruffians'. When Paine returned to England in 1787 he had the reputation of being the inspirer of American independence; his most influential work, *The Rights of Man* (1791), was still to come, but this work and its effect upon the growth of democracy in Britain and Europe lie outside the scope of the present volume.

It hardly needs to be said that all the political writers mentioned in this chapter, whether they reverenced ancient political institutions or despised them, made use of history. Locke, in his treatise *On Education* (1693), repeated the general wisdom of his own and earlier ages when he declared that the study of history is absolutely necessary for the well-educated man, because an insight into public affairs can be learned properly only through experience or through the historical record. Day-to-day political debates were full of references to the usable past, to the glories of Alfred's and Elizabeth's reigns, for instance, or to the extinction of Roman liberty by Augustus. As there was a general belief that history is cyclic, it was thought that lessons might be learned from it. Swift, for instance, voices these convictions in his letters as well as in his published work: 'liberty . . . in England . . . has continued longer than in any other monarchy, and must end as all others have done. . . . As to the lust of absolute power, I despair it can ever be cooled, unless Princes had capacity to read the history of the *Roman* Emperors.'[57] The 'gloom of the Tory satirists', from Swift, Pope, and Bolingbroke to Goldsmith, and the gloom of many Whigs too, was caused to a considerable extent by the fear that the insidious pressures of luxury, political corruption, and creeping tyranny would drive Britain down the road taken by Augustan Rome into irreversible decline and disaster. However absurd such fears may seem now, it is salutary to be reminded by a modern scholar that 'To American colonials of the late eighteenth century, George III was a tyrant as odious as Tiberius'.[58]

The men who founded the United States knew the familiar historical analogies; by a nice coincidence the American Declaration of Independence and the first volumes of Gibbon's *Decline and Fall of the Roman Empire* were published in the same year. Though Gibbon (like Milton) considered many subjects for his major work, it seems inevitable to the hindsight of his readers that the greatest historian should choose what was for his age the greatest object-lesson of history. Bolingbroke wrote that 'history is philosophy teaching by examples', but it can hardly be claimed that his partisan abridgement of Rapin's Whig chronicle of Gothic liberties down to 1688 belongs to the new method of philosophical history which produced its finest fruit in Gibbon's work. The new method originated in Europe. Possibly the first of the new breed of philosophical historians was the Italian Giambattista Vico (1668–1744), whose *Scienza Nuova* (1725) offers a 'new science' in which history is the study not of great men and discrete events but of the processes by which whole nations pass through a life-cycle; his work was, however, far less familiar to eighteenth-century Englishmen than were the broad studies in social evolution by Montesquieu (1689–1755), *Considérations sur les causes de la grandeur et de la décadence des Romains* (1734) and *De l'esprit des lois* (1748). It was primarily Montesquieu who taught English historians that history is not a parade of events but a process governed by large, environmental, social, and cultural forces that a historian-philosopher can analyse and describe almost as confidently as a natural philosopher can describe a natural law. Montesquieu believed that a system of cause and effect operated as inexorably in human society as in external nature. A people's history was determined first by geography, climate, and natural resources, then by gradually evolving institutions, customs, laws, religions, commerce, and other forms of social activity, all of which interacted and brought about further evolution. For all this sociology, the pages of Montesquieu are not empty of human characters: for instance, in the *Considérations* he sees the clue to Augustus's life and the nature of his government in the fact that he wore a shirt of mail under his toga in the Senate House.

The description of *De l'esprit des lois* as 'too witty' is not unjust, but is perhaps a strange accusation to come from Voltaire, the other great French philosophic (and witty) historian. Like his friend Bolingbroke, Voltaire looks upon the study of history as the best moral philosophy. On receiving from the author a copy of Voltaire's *Le siècle de Louis XIV* in 1752, Lord Chesterfield wrote to his son: 'It came at a very proper time; Lord Bolingbroke had just taught me how History should be read. Voltaire shows me how it should be written.'[59] Voltaire's earlier *Histoire de Charles XII* (1731), the prime source for the finest passage in Johnson's greatest poem, is a moral dissertation on the vanity of military glory, to which its author has imparted the emotional energy and something of the dramatic shape of a stage tragedy. In his vast universal history, which bears the mock-modest title *Essai sur les mœurs et l'esprit des nations et sur les principaux faits de l'histoire depuis Charlemagne jusqu'à Louis XIII* (1756) Voltaire looks upon the whole earth from China to Peru as 'un vaste théâtre où la même tragédie se joue sous des noms différents'.[60]

Voltaire intends to be a scientist as well as moralist and dramatist: in his *Nouvelle considérations sur l'histoire* (1744) he calls for historians to adopt the Newtonian method of reducing the mass of observed phenomena to simple laws. For the most part more interested in broad economic, cultural, and intellectual developments than in the particular events of diplomacy and war, Voltaire seeks in his *Essai sur les mœurs* to identify the 'spirit' of an age or the 'spirit' of a whole nation through its history. Nevertheless, he sees that social progress is achieved largely through the activities of enlightened leaders, among whom he picks out for special praise the patriot kings, Alfred the Great of England and Henri IV of France. Though the same tragedy is acted all over the vast theatre of the earth, though crimes, follies, and misfortunes are the most conspicuous facts of history, especially, Voltaire would have us think, in Christian countries, he concludes that mankind does, however erratically, achieve some progress. According to Voltaire's historical perspective, men had improved their conditions of life in the past and could hope to do so in the future; his objection to the 'optimistic' theology of Leibniz (see Ch. 3 above) was that the belief that 'all is for the best in the best of all possible worlds' inhibits men's efforts for improvement.

The new idea of progress to which Voltaire gives his qualified assent may be seen as the outcome of the seventeenth-century scientific revolution. When, early in the following century in France and England, the dust had settled from the noisy 'Battle of the Books' between supporters of the ancients and supporters of the moderns,[61] it was widely acknowledged that modern man was superior to the ancients in his understanding of external nature. It was seen that, as nature is still the same, natural science would continue to advance, if only on account of the simple accumulation of knowledge, and it was not unreasonable to suppose that a parallel advance was possible in other fields of study. As the eighteenth century advanced, the notion of evolution, whether by slow, organic process or by catastrophe, invaded the sciences of biology and geology (see Ch. 1 above); at the same time the historical method was extended and systematized in such fields of social study as religion (Hume's *Natural History of Religion*), economics (Smith's *Wealth of Nations*), and the arts (see Ch. 5 below). Out of the study of history came the idea of civilization as a process by which societies rise from barbarism to what in the eyes of most men is a more worthy condition; the word 'civilization' itself did not, however, appear in French early enough for Voltaire to employ it in his *Essai sur les mœurs,* and its novelty in English is revealed by the fact that it does not appear in its ordinary, modern, non-legal sense in Johnson's *Dictionary*, though Boswell in 1772 suggested, 'with great deference' needless to say, that it should be included.[62]

Both Montesquieu and Voltaire were friends and admirers of Bolingbroke, from whom they derived their conception of, and admiration for, the Gothic constitution; both were also friends and admirers of Hume, who looked upon the original contract and the Gothic constitution with equal scepticism. It is not surprising that Voltaire judged Hume's *History of England* (1754–61) to be perhaps the best history written in any language: Hume's work had much in common with his own, including wit, a sense of drama, an awareness that the key to history lies below the level of political events, and an all-pervading religious scepticism.

In his essay 'Of the Study of History', in *Essays, Moral and Political* (1742), Hume extols the aesthetic and imaginative delights of reviewing the great spectacle of progress: 'what more agreeable entertainment to the mind than to be transposed into the remotest ages of the world, and to observe human society, in its infancy, making the first faint essays toward the arts and sciences; to see the policy of government, and the civility of conversation refining by degrees, and every thing which is ornamental to human life advancing toward perfection'.[63] This is part of Hume's argument to persuade women to read history books instead of novels, an argument in the course of which he tells the delightful tale of his own attempts to woo with the aid of Plutarch's *Lives*, so we cannot discount a certain measure of irony; nevertheless, Hume's belief in the possibility of progress is at least as strong as Voltaire's. For Hume, progress is essentially the economic advance that brings improvements in the liberal as well as the mechanical arts, and strengthens the middling men who are 'the best and firmest basis of public liberty'. Economic growth, he declares in the *History*, 'not only creates healthy organs in society, not only improves tastes and manners: it also raises the level of morals: for virtue, which is nothing but a more enlarged and cultivated reason, never flourishes to any degree, nor is founded on steady principles of honour, except where a good education becomes general.'[64]

In the judgement of Edward Gibbon (1737–94), Hume was the 'Tacitus of Scotland', and Tacitus was 'the first of historians who applied the science of philosophy to the study of facts'. Gibbon acknowledges that he was enchanted by 'the calm philosophy, the careless inimitable beauties' of Hume, and used to close the volume 'with mingled sensations of delight and despair'; he was impressed too by 'the energy of style and boldness of hypothesis' in Montesquieu.[65] Gibbon is certainly not deficient in boldness and energy as he takes in the political, ecclesiastical, social, economic, intellectual, and cultural history of a millennium and a half for his narrative of the fall of the Roman Empire and the rise of Christianity, the transition from imperial Rome to papal Rome. His vast history expands from, but in a sense is contained in, a single impression in a particular place: 'It was at Rome, on the 15th of October 1764, as I sat musing amidst the ruins of the Capitol, while the barefooted friars were singing vespers in the temple of Jupiter, that the idea of writing the decline and fall of the city first started to my mind.'[66]

This famous passage makes an unforced but powerful contrast between past grandeur and present superstition. It hardly needs to be said that

Gibbon's history of the Christian religion, like Hume's, is a 'natural' or
secular history, animated by an aristocratic distaste for intolerance, zeal,
persecution, and tyranny; but his description of pagan Rome in its grandeur
also brings out his liberal detestation of tyranny. He makes much of the
paradox that, though Rome reached its highest peak of civilization under the
benevolent despotism of the Antonine emperors, the seeds of decay were
sown when the balanced, free constitution of the republic was extinguished,
and 'uniform government . . . introduced a slow and secret poison into the
vitals of the empire'. He presents the usual eighteenth-century view of
Augustus with more than usual acidity: 'A cool head, an unfeeling heart, and
a cowardly disposition, prompted him, at the age of nineteen, to assume the
mask of hypocrisy, which he never afterwards laid aside.' Augustus is the
'crafty tyrant, who disguised his absolute monarchy with the trappings of a
commonwealth and found that men would easily submit to slavery provided that they were respectfully assured that they were still free'.[67]
   In Chapter 38, at the point where he originally intended to conclude his
narrative, Gibbon reviews the fall of the Western Empire. He notes the 'deep
foundations of the greatness of Rome' in the civic virtue nourished by 'the
firm and equal balance of the constitution; which united the freedom of
popular assemblies, with the authority and wisdom of a senate, and the
executive powers of a regal magistrate'. Civic virtue was undermined by the
system of imperial government: 'The distinctions of personal merit and
influence, so conspicuous in a republic, so feeble and obscure under a
monarchy, were abolished by the despotism of the emperors, who substituted in their room a severe subordination of rank and office, from the
titled slaves, who were seated on the steps of the throne, to the meanest
instruments of arbitrary power.' It was undermined also by the rise of
Christianity: 'The clergy successfully preached the doctrines of patience and
pusillanimity; the active virtues of society were discouraged; and the last
remains of military spirit were buried in the cloister.' Above all, the very size
of the empire loosened the social bonds which originally held it together:

> the decline of Rome was the natural and inevitable effect of
> immoderate greatness. Prosperity ripened the principle of
> decay; the causes of destruction multiplied with the extent of
> conquest; and, as soon as time or accident had removed the
> artificial supports, the stupendous fabric yielded to the pressure
> of its own weight. The story of its ruin is simple and obvious;
> and, instead of inquiring why the Roman empire was
> destroyed, we should rather be surprised that it had subsisted so
> long.[68]

Nevertheless, though the fall of Rome may represent 'the triumph of
barbarism and religion', this triumph appears short-lived if one's view is
long enough: 'The experience of four thousand years should enlarge our
hopes, and diminish our apprehensions: we cannot determine to what height
the human species may aspire in their advances towards perfection; but it
may safely be presumed, that no people, unless the face of nature is changed,

will relapse into their original barbarism.' Chapter 38 ends, apparently without irony, 'We may therefore acquiesce in the pleasing conclusion, that every age of the world has increased, and still increases, the real wealth, the happiness, the knowledge, and perhaps the virtue, of the human race.'[69] Despite his sceptical temper, Gibbon had a tenacious and passionate belief in progress. Writing on the great comet in the time of Justinian, he observes that, though Seneca and the Chaldean astronomers rightly conjectured that comets are only planets of a longer period and more eccentric motion, the generality of men before the time of Newton and Halley chose to view them superstitiously. The same comet that was thought to have taken Julius Caesar's soul to heaven reappeared during the Crusades, allowing both Christians and Mahometans to 'surmise, with equal reason, that it portended the destruction of the infidels'; in 1680, though, it 'was presented to the eyes of an enlightened age'; on a future appearance the calculations of Newton and his fellows 'may perhaps be verified by the astronomers of some future capital in the Siberian or American wilderness'.[70]

By a nice coincidence, Smith's *Wealth of Nations*, Bentham's *Fragment on Government*, the last volume of Diderot's *Encyclopédie*, and the first volume of Gibbon's *Decline and Fall*, all informed by the spirit of liberty and progress, were all published in the same year, the year of the American Declaration of Independence: Gibbon's book, surprisingly, is in some respects as forward-looking as any of the others.

Notes

1. *Two Treatises of Government*, edited by P. Laslett (Cambridge, reprinted 1963), p. 155.

2. Ibid., pp. 437, 349; *Second Treatise*, paras 95, 231.

3. *Two Treatises*, p. 293; *Second Treatise*, para. 12.

4. *De republica*, iii, 22.

5. *Two Treatises*, pp. 286, 347; *Second Treatise*, paras 3, 94.

6. *Two Treatises*, p. 307; *Second Treatise*, para. 29.

7. *Two Treatises*, p. 315; *Second Treatise*, para. 41.

8. Swift, *Enquiry into the Behaviour of the Queen's Last Ministry* (1715), in *Prose Works* v, edited by H. Davis and I. Ehrenpreis (Oxford, 1953), 180; Addison, *The Freeholder*, edited by J. Leheny (Oxford, 1979), no. 53 (22 January 1716), p. 264.

9. Edited by Rae Blanchard (Oxford, 1955), pp. 113–16.

10. *Contests and Dissentions in Athens and Rome*, edited by F. H. Ellis (Oxford, 1967), p. 110.

11. On the reputation of Augustus in the eighteenth century see Howard D. Weinbrot, *Augustus Caesar in 'Augustan' England* (Princeton, NJ, 1978).

12. *Wealth of Nations*, edited by E. Cannan (1904, reprinted 1961), I, 277.

13. *The Original Power of the Collective Body of the People of England, Examined and Asserted* (1702), p. 18.

14. 'Some Thoughts on Agriculture, both Ancient and Modern; with an account of the Honour due to an English Farmer' and 'Further Thoughts on Agriculture' in *The Universal Visitor*, February and March 1756.

15. Bonamy Dobrée, *English Literature in the Early Eighteenth Century* (Oxford, 1959), p. 518.

16. *Defoe's Review* (New York, 1938), II, 9; 6 March 1705.

17. *Letters of Lord Chesterfield*, edited by B. Dobrée (1932), VI, 2832.

18. *Correspondence of the Earl of Chatham*, edited by W. S. Taylor and J. H. Pringle (1838–40), III, 405.

19. 'Of Public Credit' in *Essays, Moral, Political, and Literary* (Oxford, 1963), pp. 356, 366.

20. *Prose Works*, edited by H. Davis, (Oxford, 1940), III, 6–7.

21. *Art of Governing* (1701), pp. 165–66.

22. *Political Register*, (January 1768), II, 42.

23. Motto in *Cobbett's Political Register*, 25 January 1806.

24. See E. A. Wrigley, 'London and the Great Leap Forward', *The Listener*, 6 July 1967, pp. 7–8.

25. *The Farmer's Letters to the People of England* (1767), p. 354.

26. *Annals of Agriculture*, II (1784), 381–82.

27. *Enquiry into the Causes of the present high Price of Provisions* (1767), p. 115.

28. *A Tour thro' the whole Island of Great Britain*, edited by G. D. H. Cole (1927), I, 217–18.

29. *Private Papers of James Boswell* (privately printed, 1931), XI, 186.

30. *An Essay towards preventing the Ruin of Great Britain* (1721), in *Works*, edited by A. A. Luce and T. E. Jessop (1953), VI, 74, 75.

31. *Fable of the Bees*, edited by F. B. Kaye (Oxford, 1924), I, 108, 115.

32. Ibid., I, 88, 91–92.

33. *Boswell's Life of Johnson*, edited by G. B. Hill, revised by L. F. Powell (Oxford, 1934), III, 55–56; see also II, 170, 218.

34. Ibid., III, 291–92.

35. *Essays, Moral, Political, and Literary*, pp. 275, 269.

36. Ibid., p. 282.

37. Ibid., p. 284.

38. Ibid., p. 278.

39. *Wealth of Nations*, I, 18.

40. Ibid., II, 49–50.

41. Ibid., I, 82.

42. Ibid., I, 449.

43. Ibid., II, 129; the phrase that Napoleon would make famous was apparently coined by Smith.

44. Ibid., I, 445.

45. *Cato's Letters* (1724), IV, 297–98.

46. *Essay on the Constitution of the Roman Government*, in *Works* (1726), I, 91.

47. *System of Moral Philosophy* (1755), II, 248; Book III, Chapter vi.

48. Herbert Butterfield, *The Englishman and his History* (Cambridge, 1944), p. 2.

49. *Letters on the Study and Use of History*, in *Works* (1754), II, 266.

50. *Craftsman*, nos. 219, 220, 254 (12, 17 September 1730, 15 May 1731).

51. *Works* (1754), III, 83.

52. *Essays, Moral, Political, and Literary*, p. 456.

53. *Political Writings of Rousseau*, edited by C. E. Vaughan (Cambridge, 1915), II, 23.

54. *Works of Edmund Burke* (1826), III, 94, 45–46.

55. L. B. Namier and J. Brooke, *History of Parliament, 1754–90* (1964), I, 9.

56. *Complete Writings of Thomas Paine*, edited by P. S. Foner (1945), I, 45, 14.

57. *Correspondence of Jonathan Swift*, edited by H. Williams (Oxford, 1965), IV, 337.

58. J. W. Johnson, *The Formation of English Neo-Classical Thought* (Princeton, NJ, 1967), p. 62.

59. *Letters of Lord Chesterfield*, v, 1858.

60. *Essai sur les mœurs*, edited by R. Pomeau (Paris, 1963), II, 395.

61. See R. F. Jones, *Ancients and Moderns*, second edition (St Louis, 1961).

62. H. Mason, *Voltaire* (1975), p. 35; *Boswell's Life of Johnson*, II, 155.

63. *Essays, Moral, Political, and Literary*, p. 560.

64. *History of England* (1808–10), I, 222.

65. *Memoirs of the Life of Edward Gibbon*, edited by G. B. Hill (1900), pp. 96, 122; *Decline and Fall of the Roman Empire*, edited by J. B. Bury, revised edition, 1926–29), I, 230.

66. *Memoirs*, p. 167.

67. *Decline and Fall*, I, 56, 60–61, 70–72, 78, 103–4.

68. Ibid., IV, 160–63, II, 181.

69. Ibid., IV, 169.

70. Ibid., IV, 433–44.

Chapter 5
Aesthetics

The word 'aesthetics' was not used in eighteenth-century England, but it is employed in this chapter, for the sake of convenience, to cover a discussion of some significant writings on taste, on certain forms of perception, and on literary and artistic creativity. Eighteenth-century poets, artists, and critics developed their notions of the creative imagination alongside the philosophers discussed in Chapter 3: both groups of writers took Locke's theories of perception as a starting-point, so it is proper that this chapter should begin with Locke, even though his aesthetic theories need not detain us long.

Casting himself in the role of an under-labourer for Newton, he wishes to 'speak of things as they are', and must therefore accept that 'all the Arts of Rhetorick, besides Order and Clearness, all the artificial and figurative applications of Words Eloquence hath invented, are for nothing else but to insinuate wrong *Ideas*, move the Passions, and thereby mislead the Judgement, and so indeed are perfect cheat'. Locke pays tribute to the active power of the mind 'in varying and multiplying the Objects of its Thoughts, infinitely beyond what *Sensation* or *Reflection* furnished it with',[1] but does not allow that it possesses truly creative powers. His direction of philosophy towards psychological investigation and his constant appeal to experience rather than to reason bore fruit in the development of eighteenth-century aesthetics; his suggestive speculations on the association of ideas and his doctrine that all knowledge is ultimately derived from sensation were adopted by many critics and passed by way of Hartley to Wordsworth and Coleridge, but there is no evidence to suggest that he would have welcomed the conclusions that they drew from them.

Locke comes closest to a discussion of art in his famous distinction between wit and judgement. Wit is the facility for rapidly combining ideas which appear to have some congruity with one another, 'thereby to make up pleasant Pictures and agreeable Visions in the Fancy': judgement is the power to discriminate between ideas and to detect differences, so that one is not misled into mistaking one thing for another; the exercise of this power is the difficult and disciplined path to knowledge, 'a way of proceeding quite contrary to Metaphor and Allusion'.[2] Implicit here is the contrast between the false, misleading, uncertain, metaphorical language of poetry and the clear, positive, plain, literal language of science which had already been made by Thomas Sprat in his *History of the Royal Society* (1667). According to Locke, wit and judgement set out upon divergent courses, one away from, the other towards true knowledge, but literary critics of the next generation usually prefer to see them as potential partners. Pope, for instance, echoing Dryden, notes in *An Essay on Criticism* (1711),

> For *Wit* and *Judgment* often are at strife,
> Tho' meant each others' Aid, like *Man* and *Wife*
>
> *(ll. 82–83)*

and his editor, Warburton (1751), observes: '*Judgment* will learn where he should comply with the charms of Wit; and *Wit* how she ought to obey the sage directions of Judgment.'

We are told by Joseph Warton that Locke 'affected to despise poetry, and he depreciated the ancients; which circumstance . . . was the source of perpetual discontent and dispute betwixt him and his pupil, Lord *Shaftesbury*, who in many parts of the Characteristics, has ridiculed Locke's philosophy, and endeavoured to represent him as a disciple of *Hobbes*; from which writer, however, it is certain, that *Locke* borrowed frequently'.[3] Had Locke ever enunciated a theory of the poetic imagination of 'fancy' it is not inconceivable that it might have read rather like Hobbes's: 'Time and Education begets Experience; Experience begets Memory; Memory begets Judgement and Fancy; Judgement begets the Strength and Structure, and Fancy begets the Ornaments of a Poem.'[4] So starkly mechanical an account of the imagination, based upon an implicitly materialist view of nature, could hardly appeal to men of taste or to poets.

For the Earl of Shaftesbury there is no division between ethics and aesthetics (see Ch. 3 above); beauty and good, which 'are still *one and the same*', are recognized by the same faculty. This faculty is known as the 'moral sense' when it responds to human actions and discerns human affections and passions, but it is known as the sense of beauty when the eye opens upon shapes and the ear upon sounds. The source of beauty in all works of art is not matter but mind: '*the Beautiful, the Fair, the Comely*, were never in . . . *Body* it-self, but in the *Form* or *forming Power*, . . . What is it but *the Design* which strikes? What is it you admire but MIND, or the Effect of *Mind*?' The same is found to be true of all works of nature also; even (or perhaps particularly) when we contemplate less obvious beauties. In his imaginary journey through the universe at the climax of *The Moralists*, a journey followed soon by, amongst others, Addison in *Spectator*, no. 420, Mallet in *The Excursion*, and Thomson in *The Seasons*, Theocles finds that the deserts.

> want not their peculiar Beautys. The Wildness pleases . . . the
> scaly Serpents, the savage Beasts, and poisonous Insects, how
> terrible soever, or how contrary to human Nature, are
> beauteous in themselves, and fit to raise our Thoughts in
> Admiration of that *Divine Wisdom*, so far superiour to our short
> Views.

Those whom the wildness pleases, those who give way to their growing passion for 'Things of a *natural* kind', such as rude rocks, mossy caverns, unwrought grottoes, and waterfalls, are as deep in the *'romantick* way' as ordinary lovers are, because, whether they know it or not, they love ideal beauty. As the beauty of art is the expression of man's mind, so natural beauty is the expression of the universal, divine mind: 'Whatever in Nature is beautiful or charming, is only the faint Shadow of that *First Beauty*:[5]; and, as Shaftesbury repeatedly reminds us, all beauty is truth. Though his variety of Platonism had little effect on eighteenth-century metaphysics, it prompted the emergence of a new kind of nature-poetry in Thomson's *Seasons*, and influenced developments in this kind for over a century.

When he insists that 'the Beautifying, not the Beautify'd, is the really *Beautiful*',[6] Shaftesbury directs our attention from the work of art to the artist by a critical manœuvre just as decisive as, albeit less transparent than, the one by which Coleridge, near the end of Chapter 14 of *Biographia Literaria*, substitutes the question 'what is a poet?' for 'what is poetry?'. The poet then described by Coleridge bears more than a chance resemblance to 'the Man who truly and in a just sense deserves the Name of *Poet*' described 100 years earlier by Shaftesbury in *Soliloquy: or Advice to an Author* (1710)[7]: 'Such a *Poet* is indeed a second *Maker*: a just PROMETHEUS, under JOVE. Like that Sovereign Artist or universal Plastick Nature, he forms *a Whole*, coherent and proportion'd in it-self, with due Subjection and Subordinacy of constituent Parts.'

The mythical allusion is to a familiar fable in Plato's *Protagoras*, 320–22, and Ovid's *Metamorphoses*, I, 78, telling how the Titan Prometheus stole the fire of creative power from the gods and mixed it with human clay, so that man became a partaker in the divine condition. Though this appealing myth of Prometheus as the 'plastick Artist', or as the allegorical representation of 'plastick Nature',[8] is not as centrally important for Shaftesbury as it is for, say, the Shelleys, it plays a significant part elsewhere in his writings: for instance at the beginning of *The Moralists*, where it is used in the argument about whether a god is responsible for imperfections in nature.

The Promethean figure described in *Advice to an Author*, the 'Moral Artist, who can thus imitate the Creator', is very different from the 'insipid Race of Mortals . . . whom we Moderns are contented to call *Poets*, for having attain'd the chiming Faculty of a Language, with an injudicious random use of Wit and Fancy'. As Shaftesbury does not include much specific literary criticism in his writings on aesthetics, we cannot be certain as to which contemporary rhymers are attacked here, in what appears to be a minor skirmish in the battle of the books between ancients and moderns; but later he ridicules the admirers of Dryden: 'the young *Fry* which you may see busily surrounding the grown Poet, or chief Play-house *Author*, at a *Coffee-House*'.[9]

The moderns under attack are mere contrivers who imitate the outward forms or mere body of nature, whereas the poet described in ideal perfection imitates the inworking, organizing, creative principle in nature. Coleridge makes the same distinction: 'If the artist copies the mere nature, the *natura naturata*, what idle rivalry! . . . you must master the essence, the *natura naturans*, which presupposes a bond between nature in the higher sense and the soul of man.'[10] The creative principle, *natura naturans*, is what Shaftesbury calls 'the GREAT GENIUS' (see Ch. 6, Landscape gardening, below), and 'that Sovereign Artist or universal Plastick Nature', taking the term 'plastic nature' from the Cambridge Platonist Ralph Cudworth, for whom it signifies the organic principle, subordinate to God rather than God himself, which animates matter and accounts for growth and purposive behaviour. It is not without passing interest that Shaftesbury, the freethinker, should find the terminology of Plato's myth, 'Prometheus under Jove', more congenial than Cudworth's. As 'plastic Nature' animates, forms, and shapes phenomena into a harmonious whole, so does the artist by his analogous 'plastic' (in Coleridge, 'esemplastic') power.

Shaftesbury's notions concerning the creative imagination as analogous to 'the creatrix or sovereign plastic nature' reappear in a work entitled *Plastics, or the Original Progress and Power of Designing Art*, a treatise devoted largely to the visual arts and intended to be its author's crowning achievement, but left incomplete and fragmentary upon his early death and not published until the present century.[11] *Characteristicks*, though, was well known, frequently commented upon, and widely influential through the greater part of the eighteenth century. Shaftesbury's work made no claims to be a systematic philosophy; but it was important because it epitomized a unified sensibility, a harmony between the inner and the outer world at the point where the good, the true, and the beautiful are recognized to be one. His aesthetics confirmed poets in their traditional, instinctive beliefs in creative genius and an animated universe. In the first half of the century the direct, acknowledged debt of the 'new' poets Thomson and Akenside to Shaftesbury is obvious enough; but Pope, whether the debt is direct or not, stands in the same ancient intellectual tradition as Shaftesbury when, in the course of his account of the great chain of being at the opening of Book III of *An Essay on Man*, he writes about the activity of 'plastic Nature', and of a vital, not mechanical, harmony in which 'Parts relate to whole;/One all-extending, all-preserving Soul/Connects each being'.[12] Shaftesbury's work was well known on the Continent. Diderot admired him, and Montesquieu numbered him as one of the four great poets among philosophers (the others being Montaigne, Malebranche, and Plato). In the second half of the century Shaftesbury's influence was considerable in Germany, where Wincklemann, Lessing, Wieland, Herder, Kant, Schiller, and Goethe knew his work.[13] Though Coleridge makes no direct mention of him, it is, of course, much of Shaftesbury's doctrine that is reimported in a modified form from Germany by Coleridge.

Theocles' discovery that the wildness pleases marks an important stage in English theorizing about the sublime, but he was certainly not alone in his admiration for mountains and desert places. According to Thomas Burnet's 'sacred theory' of the earth (see Ch. 2 above), the mountains and the great oceans were the debris of a prelapsarian world, fractured, mangled, overturned, and flooded as the direct consequence of Adam's sin. Mountains 'are the ruins that show a certain magnificence in Nature; as from old Temples and broken Amphitheaters of the *Romans* we collect the greatness of that people', and yet they inspire the mind with 'great thoughts and passions; we do naturally upon such occasions think of God and his greatness, and whatsoever hath but the shadow and appearance of INFINITE, as all things have that are too big for our comprehension, they fill and overbear the mind with their Excess, and cast it into a pleasing kind of stupor and admiration'.[14] Though Burnet is a physico-theological writer, he goes beyond any rational argument from design in claiming that the terror and awe aroused in the beholder by sublime objects in nature are immediate and irrefutable evidence of the existence and power of the Creator. Burnet's influence in shaping the notions of the sublime advanced by Addison, Young, Thomson, and Burke is plain enough; he was quoted and praised by both Coleridge and Wordsworth; but the critic of his generation most fully identified by contemporaries with the idea of the sublime was John Dennis (1657–1734).

Dennis gives an early account of the aesthetic experience afforded by the sublime in nature with a description of crossing the Alps, first published in his *Miscellanies in Verse and Prose* (1693). He writes of 'the impending Rock that hung over us, the dreadful Depth of the Precipice, and the Torrent that roar'd at the bottom', and of the 'craggy Clifts, which we half-discern'd thro' the misty Gloom of the Clouds that surrounded them'. The scene produced in him 'a delightful Horrour, a terrible Joy, and at the same time, that I was infinitely pleas'd, I trembled'. He reflects:

> If these Hills were first made with the World, as has been a long
> time thought, and Nature design'd them only as a Mound to
> inclose her garden Italy; Then we may well say of her what
> some affirm of great Wits, that her careless, irregular and
> boldest Strokes are most admirable. For the Alps are works
> which she seems to have design'd, and executed too in a Fury.[15]

Though he concludes by accepting Burnet's explanation that mountains are not parts of the original creation but are the ruins of that creation, it is the parallel that Dennis draws between natural creation and bold, irregular, even furious artistic creation which remains most striking; effectively, he moves backwards and forwards between the relatively new application of the term 'sublime' to objects of nature and the old application of it to works of art, which originated in the anonymous Greek treatise of the first or second century A.D., *Longinus on the Sublime*. Longinus finds that the sublime in literature rests primarily upon grandeur of ideas and the capacity for strong emotion, supplemented by certain features of rhetoric; sublimity is the echo of a noble mind and a passionate heart. Both the sublime in nature and the sublime in art are known by their immediate, overwhelming effect upon the spectator.

In his ambitious *Advancement and Reformation of Modern Poetry* (1701) Dennis investigates the nature of artistic genius and uses the notions of Longinus to build up an aesthetic theory based entirely upon emotion. He argues that all art is the expression of passion and that the highest art, the sublime, is the expression of the most enthusiastic passion. As religious subjects give us more frequent and stronger enthusiasms than any other, the modern poet should turn to these, taking Milton as his grand example; furthermore, to the extent that Christianity is true and classical paganism is false, the modern will have the advantage of the ancients. In his no less ambitious, but unfinished, *Grounds of Criticism in Poetry* (1704) Dennis sets out to analyse the kinds of enthusiastic passion, which he believes are six in number: admiration, terror, horror, joy, sadness, and desire. Though his analysis was never completed, the importance Dennis ascribes to violent emotion as the source of aesthetic pleasure and his general psychological approach to criticism helped to lay down the lines upon which eighteenth-century aesthetics were to develop. Dennis was ridiculed by Pope, but he earned the respect of many other of his younger contemporaries (as well as that of Wordsworth and Coleridge later) and his programme of advancement and reformation of poetry was carried out, in a fashion, by Thomson and Young. Even so, both as Miltonist and as writer upon aesthetics in general, he was in his own day and for the rest of his century eclipsed by Addison.

Addison, whom we have already met as the popularizer of Newton, was so much the popularizer also of Locke that Hume ventured to prophesy that he would be read with pleasure when Locke was entirely forgotten.[16] In the *Spectator*, no. 291, one of the series of eighteen papers on *Paradise Lost* which for over a century constituted the best-known and most respected critical interpretation of Milton, Addison claims that knowledge of Locke's *Essay concerning Human Understanding* is necessary for the literary critic; the *Spectator*, no. 62 takes for its text Locke's 'admirable Reflection upon the difference of Wit and Judgement'; but the influence of Locke is most pervasive and most important in a series of eleven papers on the pleasures of the imagination (*Spectator*, nos. 411–21). These papers, drawn from a treatise which Addison probably wrote in the 1690s, examine the psychological basis of aesthetic experience; they constitute an enquiry into the imagination less systematic than, but nevertheless comparable with, Locke's enquiry into the understanding.

Addison's aesthetic notions are based upon the premises of Lockeian psychology. First, that all ideas are traceable to sense impressions, and that sight is the principal sense: 'It is this sense which furnishes the Imagination with its Ideas; so that by the Pleasures of the Imagination or Fancy (which I shall use promiscuously) I here mean such as arise from visible objects, either when we have them actually in our view, or when we call up their Ideas into our Minds'. Second, that the mind has the power to retain, alter, and compound these ideas, so that by his imagination 'a Man in a Dungeon', for instance, 'is capable of entertaining himself with Scenes and Landskips more beautiful than any that can be found in the whole Compass of Nature' (*Spectator*, no. 411). The mind is also able to associate one idea with another involuntarily; this capacity is regarded by Locke as dangerous but by Addison as beneficial:

> We may observe, that any single Circumstance of what we have formerly seen often raises up a whole Scene of Imagery, and

awakens numberless Ideas that before slept in the Imagination;
such a particular Smell or Colour is able to fill the Mind, on a
sudden, with the Picture of the Fields or Gardens where we first
met with it, and to bring up into View all the Variety of Images
that once attended it. Our Imagination takes the Hint, and leads
us unexpectedly into Cities or Theatres, Plains or Meadows
(*Spectator*, no. 417).

Out of deference to Locke, Addison concedes that the pleasures of the
understanding are more improving than those of the imagination. Yet,

A beautiful Prospect delights the Soul, as much as a
Demonstration; and a Description in *Homer* has charmed more
Readers than a Chapter in *Aristotle*. Besides, the Pleasures of the
Imagination have this Advantage, above those of the
Understanding, that they are more obvious, and more easie to
be acquired. It is but opening the Eye, and the Scene enters. The
Colours paint themselves on the Fancy (*Spectator*, no. 411).

When he writes of colours painting themselves or circumstances raising a
scene Addison seems to regard the imagination as a mirror or as a theatrical
stage for the representation of sense impressions; when he comes to a
discussion of metaphor and allegory in the *Spectator*, no. 421 he regards it in
complementary terms as a mirror of the understanding:

By these Allusions a Truth in the Understanding is as it were
reflected by the Imagination; we are able to see something like
Colour and Shape in a Notion, and to discover a Scheme of
Thoughts traced out upon Matter. And here the Mind receives a
great deal of Satisfaction, and has two of its Faculties gratified at
the same time, while the Fancy is busy in copying after the
Understanding and transcribing Ideas out of the Intellectual
World into the Material.

Either way, the imagination is a sort of amphibious faculty which links
together the worlds of intellect and of sensation; it occupies a position within
man analogous to man's own position on the Great Chain of Being (see Ch.
1 above).

The primary pleasures of the imagination arise from visible objects: the
secondary pleasures arise from 'the Ideas of visible Objects, when the
Objects are not actually before the Eye, but are called up into our Memories,
or formed into agreeable Visions of Things that are either absent or
Fictitious' (*Spectator*, no. 411). The terms of this distinction may well have
been suggested by Locke's notion of the primary and secondary qualities of
objects, also a very important concept for Addison; but essentially Addison's
distinction is only the old one between nature and the art which imitates
nature.

The natural objects which please the imagination are divided in the

Spectator, no. 412 into three categories: the great, the uncommon, and the beautiful. The great corresponds to what men would soon afterwards agree to refer to as the sublime; examples of great objects include 'a vast uncultivated Desart . . . high Rocks and Precipices, or a wide Expanse of Waters', where we are struck by a 'rude kind of Magnificence'. Such objects produce an effect of enlargement in the mind, for 'Our Imagination loves to be filled with an Object, or to grasp at any thing that is too big for its Capacity', and 'the Mind of Man naturally hates every thing that looks like a Restraint upon it'. That being so, 'wide and undetermined Prospects are as pleasing to the Fancy, as the Speculations of Eternity or Infinitude are to the Understanding'.

'Every thing that is *new* or *uncommon* raises a Pleasure in the Imagination, because it fills the Soul with an agreeable Surprise, gratifies its Curiosity, and gives it an Idea of which it was not before possest.' The new and the uncommon provide a form of mental refreshment which 'bestows Charms on a Monster' and 'recommends Variety'. The variety of some natural object in motion, such as a waterfall, is particularly pleasing:

> We are quickly tired with looking upon Hills and Valleys,
> where every thing continues fixt and settled in the same Place
> and Posture, but find our Thoughts a little agitated and relieved
> at the sight of such Objects as are ever in Motion, and sliding
> away from beneath the Eye of the Beholder.

'But', Addison continues, 'there's nothing that makes its way more directly to the Soul than *beauty*'; it instantly 'strikes the Mind with an inward Joy', giving immediate satisfaction to the imagination. We are so constituted as to find beauty in, for instance, 'Gaiety or Variety of Colours, in the Symmetry and Proportion of Parts', but it must be admitted that 'there is not perhaps any real Beauty or Deformity more in one piece of Matter than another'.

The great, the uncommon, and the beautiful are known by their effects, so Addison's three categories are as much subjective as objective; like Locke, his concern is with the operations of the mind. As he is unable however, to proceed any further than Locke in explaining the efficient causes of mental events, he moves directly, in the *Spectator*, no. 413, to the consideration of the final causes of the pleasures of the imagination. We have already seen, in *Spectator*, no. 387 (Ch. 2 above), that Addison believes that God has framed man so that he can act upon him through his imagination. In *Spectator*, no. 413, taking his categories in turn, Addison explains that God has made us naturally delight in what is great or unlimited in order to 'give our Souls a just Relish' of the contemplation of his divine being, and that God 'has annexed a secret Pleasure to the idea of any thing that is *new* or *uncommon*, that he might encourage us in the Pursuit after knowledge, and engage us to search into the Wonders of his Creation'; God's purpose in making us delight in beauty is explained in greatest detail, with an extraordinary application of Locke's 'great Discovery', confirmed by Newton, 'that Light and Colours, as apprehended by the Imagination, are only Ideas in the Mind, and not Qualities that have any Existence in Matter' (see Ch. 1 above, see also the *Spectator*, no. 387).

He has given almost every thing about us the Power of raising
an agreeable Idea in the Imagination: So that it is impossible for
us to behold his Works with Coldness or Indifference, and to
survey so many Beauties without a secret Satisfaction and
Complacency. Things would make but a poor Appearance to
the Eye, if we saw them only in their proper Figures and
Motions: And what Reason can we assign for their exciting in
us many of those Ideas which are different from any thing that
exists in the Objects themselves (for such are Light and
Colours), were it not to add Supernumerary Ornaments to the
Universe, and make it more agreeable to the Imagination? We
are every where entertained with pleasing Shows and
Apparitions, we discover imaginary Glories in the Heavens,
and in the Earth, and see some of this Visionary Beauty poured
out upon the whole Creation; but what a rough unsightly
Sketch of Nature should we be entertained with, did all her
Colouring disappear, and the several Distinctions of Light and
Shade vanish? In short, our Souls are at present delightfully lost
and bewildered in a pleasing Delusion, and we walk about like
the Enchanted Hero of a Romance, who sees beautiful Castles,
Woods and Meadows; and at the same time hears the warbling
of Birds, and the purling of Streams; but upon the finishing of
some secret Spell, the fantastick Scene breaks up, and the
disconsolate Knight finds himself on a barren Heath, or in a
solitary Desart.

The ordinary landscape, philosophically considered, thus becomes a landscape of romance.

What Addison makes of Locke's secondary qualities in his likening of the
ordinary man's perception of the ordinary external world to a state of
enchantment is not to be confused with his own concept of the secondary
pleasures of imagination, the pleasures derived from art. He accepts the
conventional view of his day that art imitates nature, but as he proceeds he
tends to shift his ground a little. Sometimes he insists that art cannot
compete with nature, even claiming at one point in the *Spectator*, no. 414 that
the most perfect art he ever saw was the moving images (the unfixed
photographs, as it were) of the river and park produced by the famous
camera obscura in Greenwich Observatory, because such an art bears the
closest possible resemblance to nature. On the other hand, by the *Spectator*,
no. 418 he is allowing that art may excel nature,

because the Imagination can fancy to it self Things more Great,
Strange, or Beautiful, than the Eye ever saw, and is still sensible
of some Defect in what it has seen; on this account it is the part
of a Poet to humour the Imagination in its own Notions, by
mending and perfecting Nature where he describes a Reality,
and by adding greater Beauties than are put together in Nature,
where he describes a Fiction.

Other critics might describe such art as an imitation of ideal nature; for instance, Dryden, a critic to whom Addison is generally much indebted, recommends that artists should 'endeavour to correct and amend the common nature, and to represent it as it was at first created, without fault'[17]; Reynolds writes in similar terms (see p.128–29 below), but not Addison.

The art 'wherein the Poet quite loses sight of Nature, and entertains his Reader's Imagination with the Characters and Actions of such Persons as have many of them no Existence, but what he bestows on them', what Dryden called 'the Fairy kind of writing', is Addison's subject in the *Spectator*, no. 419. In bringing to life imaginary beings, such as fairies, witches, demons, and personified abstractions, the poet 'must work altogether out of his own Invention', so 'the fairy way' is the most difficult way of writing. In such writing the imagination displays to the full its creative power; it 'makes new Worlds of its own', by it 'we are led, as it were, into a new Creation'. This only slightly qualified claim is repeated in *Spectator*, no. 421 with reference to all great poetry: the power of the poet's imagination 'has something in it like Creation; . . . it makes Additions to Nature, and gives a greater variety to God's Works'. The fantasy world which Locke so detests because it has no empirical foundation in nature is welcomed by Addison as a valid addition to the world created by God. It hardly needs saying that Shakespeare is the greatest master of the fairy way of writing, by virtue of his 'noble Extravagance of Fancy' which 'made him capable of succeeding where he had nothing to support him besides the Strength of his own Genius' (*Spectator*, no. 419). This genius is the natural genius, 'never disciplined and broken by Rules of Art', which Addison distinguishes in the *Spectator*, no. 160 from genius developed by study. With Addison, as with Dryden, Johnson, and most of their contemporaries, literary theory is determined to a great extent by the need to accommodate Shakespeare. When, in the *Rambler*, no. 125 (1751), Johnson claims that 'Imagination, a licentious and vagrant faculty, unsusceptible of limitations, and impatient of restraint, has always endeavoured to baffle the logician, to perplex the confines of distinction, and burst the enclosures of reality . . . every new genius produces some innovation', it is Shakespeare he has principally in view, as, of course, also in his more detailed testimony to the power of rich, inventive genius in the *Preface to Shakespeare* (1765).

Alongside Shakespeare stood Spenser, a more consistent exponent of the fairy way of writing, whose example led eighteenth–century critics to analyse personification and allegory. The trail of interpretation is blazed by John Hughes (1677–1720) in his edition of Spenser's *Works* (1715). 'Allegory', writes Hughes, 'is indeed the *Fairy Land* of Poetry, peopled by Imagination; its Inhabitants are so many Apparitions; its Woods, Caves, wild Beasts, Rivers, Mountains and Palaces, are produc'd by a kind of magical Power, and are all visionary and typical.' Being at once visionary and typical, allegory unites the particularity of one man's dream image with the generality of abstracted truth: 'Every Allegory has . . . two Senses, the Literal and the Mystical; the literal Sense is like a Dream or Vision, of which the mystical Sense is the true Meaning or Interpretation.'[18] The vehicle of meaning, then, is the vision; the poem at its literal, most immediately apprehended, level is a dream.

The poetry of the century is full of Spenserian imitations; the best of them, Thomson's *The Castle of Indolence* (1748), creates a landscape which seems to represent the half-perceiving, half-creating imagination:

> A pleasing Land of Drowsy-hed it was:
> Of Dreams that wave before the half-shut Eye
>
> (I. vi. 1–2)

Though not allegorical, Thomson's *Seasons* is what Geoffrey Hartman calls it, 'a visionary history',[19] rather than a simply descriptive poem. The images that make up the work 'Croud fast into the Mind's creative Eye' (*Autumn*, 1730, line 1016); what is portrayed is a 'Landskip, gliding swift/Athwart Imagination's vivid Eye', with the poet

> lost in lonely Musing, in a Dream,
> Confus'd of careless Solitude, where mix
> Ten thousand wandering Images of Things
>
> (*Spring*, 1744, ll. 458–59, 461–63)

In *Night Thoughts, Night the Sixth* (1744) Edward Young finds man's true wealth in his own senses, 'which inherit Earth and Heavens', and

> Take in, at once, the Landscape of the World,
> At a small Inlet, which a grain might close,
> And half create the wonderous World, they see.

But for the 'magic Organ' of the senses, 'Earth were a rude, uncolour'd Chaos still' (ll. 423, 428–30, 433). Thus before the middle of the century, stimulated by Addison's remarks on the fairy way of writing and by his application of Locke's theory of primary and secondary qualities, poets were moving rapidly towards the notions of perception and imagination which would be elaborated by Wordsworth and Coleridge.

The poets were, as usual, ahead of the philosophers. The first writer on aesthetics to achieve prominence after Addison was Shaftesbury's disciple Francis Hutcheson, whose moral philosophy we have already glanced at (Ch. 3 above). Like Addison, he is concerned primarily with aesthetic effects, but he is far more systematic and rather less interesting than Addison. His *Inquiry into the Original of our Ideas of Beauty and Virtue* (1725) opens with definitions: '*Beauty* is taken for *the Idea rais'd in us*, and a *Sense* of Beauty for *our Power of receiving this Idea*.' Though ideas of beauty are received through the external senses of seeing and hearing (as Addison says, 'It is but opening the Eye, and the Scene enters'), Hutcheson insists that the sense of beauty is a distinct internal sense: first, because many people have excellent vision and hearing, but apparently lack the capacity to derive much or any pleasure from music, painting, architecture, or natural landscape; second, because beauty may be seen in cases 'where our *External Senses* are not much concern'd'.[21] such as mathematical theorems and universal truths.

Hutcheson's stated purpose is to discover 'what is the immediate Occasion' of ideas of beauty 'or what real Quality in the Objects ordinarily excites them'. He allows that the sense of beauty will differ greatly in different men; he reminds his readers that beauty is not a quality supposed to be in the object, but rather it denotes the perception of some mind; nevertheless his conclusions are as far from relativism or solipsism as can be conceived. Believing that the great underlying principle of the entire natural creation is uniformity amidst variety, he deduces that the natural law determining beauty is the compound ratio between these two factors, 'so that where the *Uniformity* of Bodys is equal, the Beauty is as the *Variety*; and where the *Variety* is equal, the Beauty is as the *Uniformity*'. On a sliding scale of degrees of beauty Greek and Roman art stand highest, but Gothic and Oriental art have their place; there may be variety of taste though there is only one principle of beauty. So the Goths were mistaken in believing that their own architecture was superior to that of the Roman buildings which they destroyed, but it is still real beauty which pleased them: 'For the *Gothick Pillars* are *uniform* to each other, not only in their *Sections*, which are *Lozenge-form'd*; but also in their *Heights* and *Ornaments*: Their *Arches* are not one *uniform Curve*, but yet they are *Segments* of *similar Curves*, and generally equal in the same Ranges. The very *Indian Buildings* have some kind of Uniformity.'[22] In any case the Goths' aversion to Roman buildings was partly on account of their aversion to the Romans themselves, their enemies; this is one of those cases, of the sort which Locke deplored, where association of ideas hinders true perception. Hutcheson's remarks on Gothic architecture reveal that he, like most of his contemporaries, had not looked at medieval buildings at all carefully. He is more assured when he applies his compound-ratio law of beauty to such purposes as demonstrating that a square is more beautiful than a triangle, but there he moves into an arid region of aesthetic geometry whither we need not follow him. Such efforts make us aware of the pressure of Newton's example upon eighteenth-century philosophers, compelling them to seek universal, and if possible mathematical, laws in their own fields.

As we have already seen (Ch. 3 above), David Hume too is very much the heir of Newton when he describes his *Treatise of Human Nature* (1739–40) as 'An Attempt to introduce the experimental method of reasoning into Moral Subjects'. His remarks on aesthetics in the *Treatise* are quite subsidiary to his main topics, but they accord with the general tendency of eighteenth-century critics to judge works of art in terms of their subjective effects, as well, of course, as with the subjectivism of his own philosophy.

According to Hume, our belief that there is an external world is only the product of an act of imagination which unites a succession of distinct impressions (that is, sensations, passions, and emotions) into the appearance of continued reality. Our ideas arise from these impressions, though the origin of the impressions themselves remains inexplicable; our idea of beauty, which Hume also calls a 'sentiment' of beauty, is a collection of simple ideas united by the imagination. Beauty cannot be defined in objective terms as a system of proportions or relations; it is discerned only as a taste or sensation:

If we consider all the hypotheses, which have been form'd
either by philosophy or common reason, to explain the
difference betwixt beauty and deformity, we shall find that all
of them resolve into this, that beauty is such an order and
construction of parts, as either by the *primary constitution* of our
nature, by *custom*, or by *caprice*, is fitted to give a pleasure and
satisfaction to the soul.

Nevertheless, it is Hume's view that we can speak of beautiful objects;
furthermore, that, though custom and caprice hardly admit general
principles, the objects which we feel by the primary constitution of our
nature to be beautiful are those best fitted to our use and pleasure.
Effectively, Hume endorses the traditional Horatian formula of *utile dulci*:

Thus the conveniency of a house, the fertility of a field, the
strength of a horse, the capacity, security, and swift-sailing of a
vessel, form the principal beauty of these several objects. . . .
Most of the works of art are esteem'd beautiful, in proportion
to their fitness for the use of man, and even many of the
productions of nature derive their beauty from that source.

Objects are beautiful when they are fitted to the use of their possessors, but it
is of course not only their possessors who find them beautiful. Our sense of
beauty depends upon that general principle of sympathy which is the foundation of our whole moral life and is far stronger than cold judgement. This
principle of sympathy operates to arouse the sentiment of beauty and render
an object pleasing even when we have a more strongly founded feeling
which makes the same object displeasing: 'as when the fortifications of a city
belonging to an enemy are esteem'd beautiful upon account of their
strength, tho' we cou'd wish that they were entirely destroy'd. The imagination adheres to the *general* views of things, and distinguishes betwixt the
feelings they produce, and those which arise from our particular and
momentary situation.'[23] Hume neatly separates aesthetic feeling from other
feelings without having to postulate any special aesthetic 'sense'.

Hume does not make any categorical distinction between the beautiful and
the sublime in his *Treatise*, but he touches on sublimity (which, following
Addison, he calls 'greatness') in the course of a general discussion of distance
in space and time. He mentions the same kinds of great objects and ideas as
Addison, 'a wide plain, the ocean, eternity, a succession of several ages', but
his business is to analyse the psychological experience and to do so more
searchingly than Addison does. Explaining why, as Longinus had discovered, 'a very great distance encreases our esteem and admiration for an
object', he argues that it is in the constitution of our nature that both the
passions and the imagination exert their force by opposition to difficulty:

'Tis a quality very observable in human nature, that any
opposition, which does not entirely discourage and intimidate
us, has rather a contrary effect, and inspires us with a more than

ordinary grandeur and magnanimity. In collecting our force to overcome the opposition, we invigorate the soul, and give it an elevation with which otherwise it wou'd never have been acquainted. . . .

This is also true in the inverse. Opposition not only enlarges the soul; but the soul, when full of courage and magnanimity, in a manner seeks opposition. . . .

Whatever supports and fills the passions is agreeable to us; as on the contrary, what weakens and infeebles them is uneasy. As opposition has the first effect, and facility the second, no wonder the mind, in certain dispositions, desires the former, and is averse to the latter.[24]

Hume invokes this psychological principle of opposition in his essay 'Of Tragedy' (1757), where he attempts to explain the 'unaccountable pleasure which the spectators of a well-written tragedy receive from sorrow, terror, anxiety, and other passions that are in themselves disagreeable and uneasy'. Any strong emotion, says Hume, will tend to strengthen another emotion, even one of contrary tendency, provided that this contrary emotion is not strong enough to predominate. 'Nothing endears so much a friend as sorrow for his death. The pleasure of his company has not so powerful an influence.' When we are spectators of a stage tragedy, terror, sadness, and anxiety agitate the mind, but this agitation serves only to strengthen the feelings aroused by admiration of the author's and actors' skill and by the beauty of eloquence. It is not that eloquence counterbalances distress, but that it actually converts distress into pleasure by the infusion of a new feeling:

The impulse or vehemence arising from sorrow, compassion, indignation, receives a new direction from the sentiments of beauty. The latter, being the predominant emotion, seize the whole mind, and convert the former into themselves, at least tincture them so strongly as totally to alter their nature. And the soul being at the same time roused by passion and charmed by eloquence, feels on the whole a strong movement, which is altogether delightful.[25]

This delight is of course a pleasure of the imagination, an immediate emotion, not a rational calculation. Critical analysis of the eloquence may follow, and educated judgement may confirm feeling, but here, as elsewhere, reason is the slave of sentiment and of passion (see Ch. 3 above).

The fundamental difference between judgement and sentiment is set out clearly in Hume's essay 'Of the Standard of Taste' (1757), in which he addresses himself to one of the most frequently debated aesthetic questions of the century: whether it is possible to determine fixed standards of taste. Not all judgements are correct, but

a thousand different sentiments excited by the same object are all right: because no sentiment represents what is really in the

object. It only marks a certain conformity or relation between
the object and the organs or faculties of the mind; and if that
conformity did not exist, the sentiment could never possibly
have being. Beauty is no quality in things themselves: It exists
merely in the mind which contemplates them; and each mind
perceives a different beauty. One person may even perceive
deformity where another is sensible of beauty; and every
individual ought to acquiece in his own sentiment, without
pretending to regulate those of others.

Nevertheless, Hume claims, common sense suggests that there is a standard
of taste; for 'whoever would assert an equality of genius and elegance
between Ogilby and Milton, or Bunyan and Addison, would be thought to
defend no less an extravagance, than if he had maintained a mole-hill to be as
high as Teneriffe, or a pond as extensive as the ocean'.[26] (Hume's
common-sense proof, so far as it refers to Bunyan and Addison, perhaps
does not now have the effect he intended; a taste even for Ogilby is not
inconceivable perhaps in an age more relativist even than ours.)

Hume has no doubt that there are critical principles in which men of
educated taste broadly concur; these are 'general observations concerning
what has been universally found to please in all countries and in all ages';
they are founded, like the principles of the experimental sciences, upon
experience. According to the constitution of our nature, 'the original
structure of the internal fabric', there are particular forms or qualities that are
calculated to please and others to displease; 'and if they fail of their effect in
any particular instance, it is from some apparent defect or imperfection in
the organ'. Our perception of beauty is like our perception of colour:

If, in the sound of the organ, there be an entire or a considerable
uniformity of sentiment among men, we may thence derive an
idea of the perfect beauty; in like manner as the appearance of
objects in daylight, to the eye of a man in health, is
denominated their true and real colour, even while colour is
allowed to be merely a phantasm of the senses.

In the light of this analogy, aesthetics and ethics stand side by side: for, as
we have already seen in the *Treatise*, vice and virtue 'may be compar'd to
sounds, colours, heat and cold, which, according to modern philosophy, are
not qualities in objects, but perceptions in the mind' (see Ch. 3 above). It is
possible for aesthetic standards, like moral standards, to be both subjective
and uniform. An individual critical opinion which runs counter to the
general uniformity of sentiment is likely to be the consequence of some
failure on the part of the critic. The 'true judge in the finer arts' is a rare
being: 'Strong sense, united to delicate sentiment, improved by practice,
perfected by comparison, and cleared of all prejudice, can alone entitle critics
to this valuable character; and the joint verdict of such, wherever they are to
be found, is the true standard of taste and beauty.'[27]

Hume thus shifts the problem from that of defining the standard of taste

to that of recognizing a true critic. At this point he concludes his main
argument, but at the end of the essay he reopens the possibility of relativism
in taste by admitting

> two sources of variation, which are not sufficient indeed to
> confound all the boundaries of beauty and deformity, but will
> often serve to produce a difference in the degrees of our
> approbation or blame. The one is the different humours of
> particular men; the other, the particular manners and opinions
> of our age and country.

Thus a young man whose passions are warm will take great delight in Ovid,
but at forty he will have graduated to Horace, and at fifty to Tacitus; 'We
choose our favourite author as we do our friends, from a conformity of
humour and disposition'; sympathy is the vital factor. It is on account of
sympathy, too, that we find pleasure in 'pictures and characters that resemble objects which are found in our own age and country'.[28] Conversely,
Hume claims, we dislike the barbarous and the exotic. Evidently he will
have no truck with the increasingly fashionable primitivism of the
eighteenth century, any more than he will accept the conventional wisdom
of his age that art flourishes only in free societies.

In his *History of England* (1754–61) Hume returns to a consideration of the
effect that difference of manners may have upon the appreciation of art and
literature. He observes that Homer 'remains still the favourite of every
reader of taste and judgement' because he 'copied true natural manners,
which, however rough and uncultivated, will always form an agreeable and
interesting picture'. Manners have changed far less since Elizabethan times,
but Spenser is now less admired than Homer because he drew 'the
affectations, and conceits, and fopperies of chivalry'[29] and employed a
tedious allegory. Elsewhere, in the essay 'Of Simplicity and Refinement in
Writing' (1742), Hume declares that 'productions which are merely surprising, without being natural, can never give any lasting entertainment to the
mind. To draw chimeras, is not, properly speaking, to copy or imitate.'[30] So
much for the new, the uncommon, and the fairy way of writing.

Trailing his coat in the *History of England*, Hume suggests that the genius
of Shakespeare is overrated 'in the same manner as bodies often appear more
gigantic, on account of their being disproportioned and misshapen'.[31] The
general misfortune of all the Elizabethan and Jacobean writers, in Hume's
view, was their absolute want of taste. Hume does not doubt that there is a
standard of taste and that Shakespeare and his contemporaries do not come
up to standard. Though Voltaire had expressed broadly similar views two
decades earlier, Hume's criticisms of English authors appeared to English
readers of the 1750s to be almost as vexingly sceptical as his philosophy.
What is perhaps more noteworthy than his hostile account of Elizabethan
writers is his complete silence concerning pre-Elizabethan English literature
in the later-published volumes of the *History*, when in the earlier-published
volumes (covering a later period of history) he had made a special point of
reviewing the learning and literature of every reign. In all his writings upon

aesthetics he reveals indeed a strikingly confident belief in the universality of his own standard of taste.

Hume's refusal to notice medieval literature contrasts with Addison's well-known praise, fifty years earlier, of the heroic spirit of 'Chevy Chase' (*Spectator*, nos 70 and 74) and his more remarkable commendation of the natural simplicity of 'The Two Children in the Wood' (*Spectator*, no. 85). Medieval Scottish songs and ballads were published and praised by Hume's countryman Allan Ramsay in *The Ever-Green* (1724). Dryden and Pope shared an admiration for Chaucer. Before the end of the seventeenth century romantic literature was beginning to attract a little of the respect traditionally given to the greatest of secular primitive authors, Homer. Sir William Temple (1628–99), whose interest in exotic cultures extended literally from China to Peru and whose republication of an Old Icelandic fragment was highly influential, praised Sidney in 1690 as the greatest poet in any modern language by virtue of his *Arcadia*, which, being a romance, belonged according to Temple to the true vein of ancient poetry.[32] Steele in 1710 compared the copiousness of invention in Sir John Mandeville's *Travels* with that in the *Odyssey* and the *Faerie Queene*: 'All is enchanted ground and fairy-land' (*Tatler*, no. 254). According to Pope, in the Preface to his translation of *Homer*, invention is 'the Characteristic of Poetry itself' and Homer's greatest strength is his amazing invention, so that 'the Reader is hurry'd out of himself by the Force of the Poet's Imagination'. Everyone agreed, of course, that the greatest poetry of all was to be found in the Old Testament, especially the Book of Job, but eighteenth-century critics and scholars sought for, and found, admirable examples of ancient or primitive poetry in every age and culture. Simultaneously, Gray, Collins, Smart, Percy, Macpherson, Chatterton, Beattie, and other poets, sought, however implausibly, to revive the character of the bard, the prophet, the druid, or the minstrel. This is the primitivism which Johnson mocks in his verses beginning

> Wheresoe'er I turn my View,
> All is strange, yet nothing new.

Johnson's specific target here is the verse of Thomas Warton the younger (1728–90), the man whose critical writings may well have provided the timely occasion for Hume's attack on Spenser's displeasing strangeness. In his *Observations on the Faerie Queene of Spenser* (1754) Warton asserts that we receive pleasure from Spenser precisely because he is 'a romantic poet' whose work is 'tinctur'd by . . . appearances, which are utterly different from those with which we are at present surrounded'. The *Faerie Queene* is a work of the creative imagination: 'if there be any poem whose graces please, because they are situated beyond the reach of art, and where the faculties of creative imagination delight us, because they are unassisted and unrestrained by those of deliberate judgement, it is this'. The judicious critics who, according to Hume, set the standard of taste may be at fault, for though when we read Spenser's poem 'we are not satisfied as critics, yet we are transported as readers'.[33]

Also in contradiction to Hume, Richard Hurd (1720–1808) observes, in his *Letters on Chivalry and Romance* (1762), that 'the greatest geniuses', such as Ariosto, Tasso, Spenser, and Milton, were 'charmed by the Gothic Romances'. He then asks rhetorically, 'Was this caprice and absurdity in them? Or, may there not be something in the *Gothic* Romance peculiarly suited to the views of genius, and to the ends of poetry?' He maintains that the fairy tales of Tasso 'do him more honour than what are called the more natural, that is, the classical parts of his poem'; these classical parts 'are faint and cold, and almost insipid, when compared with his *Gothic* fictions. We make a shift to run over the passages he has copied from VIRGIL. We are all on fire amidst the magical feats of ISMEN, and the enchantments of ARMIDA.' In 1762, this is a remarkably early appearance in England of the conscious, deliberate critical debate between classical and romantic; significantly, the outcome of the debate is determined by the emotional response of the critic: 'We are all on fire.' Hurd accepts the usual opinion that Homer is superior to Virgil, not least because of the 'felicity' of the earlier poet's age 'for poetical manners'; nevertheless Hurd argues that if Homer had been fortunate enough to live in the medieval period and had known 'the improved gallantry of the Gothic knights; and the superior solemnity of their superstitions' he would have been a better poet. He explains why medieval romance could be revived so successfully by Spenser, and then shows how the rationalism which accompanied the seventeenth-century scientific revolution put to flight 'the portentous spectres of the imagination'. He concludes: 'What we have gotten by this revolution, you will say, is a great deal of good sense. What we have lost, is a world of fine fabling; the illusion of which is so grateful to the *charmed Spirit*, that, in spite of philosophy and fashion, *Fairy* SPENSER still ranks highest among the poets.'[34]

Both Warton and Hurd insist that the literature of societies unfamiliar to us itself creates the taste by which it is to be enjoyed; there is no uniform standard of taste. Other mid-century critics make the same point. Robert Lowth (1710–87), Professor of Poetry at Oxford in the 1740s, gave lectures on the Sacred Poetry of the Hebrews; these lectures were much influenced by Longinus, and in their turn, when published in Latin in 1753, were influential in Europe. Lowth believes that, difficult as it may be to grasp the original texture of Hebrew poetry, we must make the effort to read it 'as the Hebrews would have read it'; so 'it is the first business of a critic to remark . . . the situation and habits of the author, the natural history of his country and the scene of the poem'; it is his business also to note that 'each language possesses a peculiar genius and character, on which depends the principles of its versification and in a great measure the style and colour of the poetic diction'.[35]

Thomas Blackwell (1701–57) made these things his business in the *Enquiry into the Life and Writings of Homer* (1735), where he conjecturally reconstructs the life of a bard who mingled with kings and beggars, who saw all conditions of life in war and peace, who travelled widely, and who found the language in its 'simple, unconfined, and free' state. Blackwell takes the view that Homer was particularly fortunate to live in a society between barbarism and civilization, whereas such writers as Congreve and Pope had the misfortune to live in an over-refined society. Homer's poetry is energetic, natural, and passionate: 'For so unaffected and simple were the Manners of those Times, that the Folds and Windings of the human Breast lay open to the Eye; nor were People ashamed to avow Passions and Inclinations, which were entirely void of Art and Design. This was *Homer*'s Happiness.' Just as Hurd concludes that we have lost a world of fine fabling, so Blackwell accepts that epic can no longer be successfully attempted; he believes that the best hope for serious poetry in his own age is in the form of extended descriptions of landscape 'nobly executed', as in Thomson's *Seasons*.[36]

Blackwell, like Hume, takes the old view that poetry is imitative, but there was a growing tendency in the eighteenth century to regard poetry as expressive. Such a view emerges in the wholesale attack on the notion of imitation in Edward Young's *Conjectures on Original Composition* (1759). Anticipating by half a century Coleridge's distinction between mechanical making and organic growth, Young asserts that 'An *Original* may be said to be of a *vegetable* nature; it rises spontaneously from the vital root of Genius; it *grows*, it is not *made*: *Imitations* are often a sort of Manufacture wrought by those *Mechanics*, *Art*, and *Labour*, out of pre-existent materials not their own.' Young develops Addison's distinction, in *Spectator*, no. 160, between natural genius and genius acquired by learning, but does so with a degree of contempt for learning ('Many a genius, probably, there has been, which could neither write, nor read') and with a far greater emphasis upon the mysterious process by which works of art come into being. He notes that most authors of distinction have been startled by 'the first beamings of their yet unsuspected genius on their hitherto dark Composition: The writer starts at it, as at a lucid meteor in the night; is much surprized; can scarce believe it true.' A man does not know the dimensions of his own mind; there is 'a stranger within'. Developing Addison's remarks, in the *Spectator*, no. 419, on the fairy way of writing, Young again runs to the extreme of what would much later be called a romantic aesthetic:

> In the Fairyland of Fancy, Genius may wander wild; there it has
> creative power, and may reign arbitrarily over its own empire
> of Chimeras. . . . Moreover, so boundless are the bold
> excursions of the human mind, that in the vast void beyond real
> existence, it can call forth shadowy beings, and unknown
> worlds, as numerous, as bright, and, perhaps, as lasting, as the
> stars; such quite-original beauties we may call Paradisaical.[37]

Like Shaftesbury's writings, Young's treatise became well known in Germany; consequently, like those, it enjoyed renewed influence in England when its ideas were reimported by Coleridge.

Young writes upon a rising tide of belief in genius as against learning and in the validity of new-created imaginative fiction as against imitation of nature as ordinarily understood. Hurd is hardly less extreme than Young when he asserts that it is only a bad critic who believes that poets should follow nature, if 'by nature we are to suppose can only be meant the known and experienced course of affairs in this world. Whereas the poet has a world of his own, where experience has less to do, than consistent imagination.'[38] What we look for first in poetry is not philosophical or historical truth, but 'poetical truth', the truth of the creative imagination.

Young's and Hurd's statements about the creativity of the imagination go much further than anything claimed by Burke in the most famous aesthetic treatise of the eighteenth century, *A Philosophical Enquiry into the Origin of our Ideas of the Sublime and the Beautiful* (1757). The 'sort of creative power' which the mind possesses according to Burke is hardly creative at all in Young's or Warton's or Hurd's sense, for it is capable only of recombining sense impressions:

> The mind of man possesses a sort of creative power of its own;
> either in representing at pleasure the images of things in the order
> and manner in which they were received by the senses, or in
> combining those images in a new manner, and according to a
> different order. This power is called Imagination; and to this
> belongs whatever is called wit, fancy, invention, and the like.[39]

This passage comes from the 'Introduction of Taste' added to the second edition of the *Enquiry* in 1759, in which Burke, apparently unmoved by the tendency of current historicism and primitivism to support the view that taste is relative, declared that 'it is probable that the standard both of reason and of Taste is the same in all human creatures'. Burke sets out upon the same endeavour as Hume, but whereas Hume concludes that the standard of taste can only be deduced from agreement between the few good critics far separated in time, Burke believes that the standard can be established on a basis of 'philosophical solidity', that is, it can be proved scientifically. Not unexpectedly, the starting-point for this proof is in Locke's epistemology: 'as the senses are the great originals of all our ideas, and consequently of all our pleasures, if they are not uncertain and arbitrary, the whole ground-work of Taste is common to all'.[40] As the imagination is only the representative of the senses there will be as much correspondence between the imaginative impressions of different normal human beings as between their sense impressions.

In the main body of his *Enquiry* Burke establishes the grounds of distinction between the sublime and the beautiful (deliberately refusing to treat novelty, Addison's third source of the pleasures of imagination, as a distinct category). His method is empirical, inductive, and subjective, for he claims to draw his conclusions from

> a diligent examination of our passions in our own breasts; from a
> careful survey of the properties of things which we find by
> experience to influence those passions; and from a sober and
> attentive investigation of the laws of nature, by which those
> properties are capable of affecting the body, and thus of exciting
> our passions.[41]

His aesthetic, like Hume's, makes use of ordinary human faculties; it has no need of the special internal senses postulated by Shaftesbury and Hutcheson.

Burke distinguishes two classes of agreeable sensations: one is positive pleasure, the other, which he calls 'delight', is that pleasure which arises from the ideas of pain and danger when we are not in actual pain and danger; the first pleasure is a social passion and is our emotional response to the beautiful, the second is a selfish passion (arising from our instinct for self-preservation) and is our response to the sublime.

Sympathy is as central to Burke's system as it is to Hume's. According to Burke it is a complicated social passion; it 'must be considered as a sort of substitution, by which we are put into the place of another man' and are made to feel in some respects as he feels, 'so that this passion may either partake of the nature of those which regard self-preservation, and turning upon pain may be a source of the sublime; or it may turn upon ideas of pleasure', in which case it is a source of the beautiful. It is by sympathy and substitution 'that poetry, painting, and other affecting arts, transfuse their passions from one breast to another, and are often capable of grafting a delight on wretchedness, misery, and death itself'.[42] Thus Burke accounts for our pleasure in tragedy, though he proceeds then to argue, in opposition to most theorists of tragedy, that we are more delighted by real distress (in others) than by its simulation in the theatre, as evidence of which he points out that a state execution is a far more popular spectacle than the very finest stage tragedy.

The strongest aesthetic emotion which the mind is capable of feeling, an emotion strong enough to deprive the mind of power to act or reason, is distanced or modified terror: immediate pain or danger 'are incapable of giving any delight, and are simply terrible; but at certain distances, and with certain modifications, they may be, and they are delightful'. The ideas which excite this species of terror are the source of the sublime, and they can be classified under certain headings. Obscurity is sublime because darkness and uncertainty arouse fear. In support, Burke quotes Milton's descriptions of Death, where 'all is dark, uncertain, confused, terrible, and sublime to the last degree', and of Satan, where the mind 'is hurried out of itself, by a croud of great and confused images; which affect because they are crouded and confused'; he concludes: 'A clear idea is therefore another name for a little idea.'[43] So Burke continues through his other headings: power, where the idea of superior force excites fear; privations, such as vacuity, darkness, solitude (a foretaste of death), and silence; vastness of length, height, and depth, the last being the most frightening of the three, and so a particularly powerful source of the sublime; infinity, and such artificial forms of infinity as succession and uniformity (as in a colonnade) where imagination carries the mind beyond the actual limits of the object. So the list of headings continues down to 'bitters and stenches', which, admittedly, have a very tiny potential for sublimity.

The sublime is always founded, however distantly, upon the ideas of pain and terror, and so must always be fundamentally different from the beautiful, which is founded upon the ideas of love and pleasure. The experience of beauty is as immediate as that of the sublime: 'beauty demands no assistance from our reasoning; even the will is unconcerned; the appearance of beauty as effectually causes some degree of love in us, as the application of ice or fire produces the ideas of heat or cold'.[44] Burke dismisses whimsical notions, such as those of Shaftesbury and Hutcheson, which have arisen from the old habit of attaching the quality of beauty to virtue or to proportion, because such notions make beauty rely on reason and the will, rather than on immediate sense. For the same reason he rejects the notion of use or fitness advanced by Hume, Hogarth, and many others.

Burke concludes that if beauty does not depend upon proportion, fitness, or virtue, it must reside in certain qualities which act mechanically upon the senses. These qualities include, for instance, smoothness, smallness, delicacy of texture, and that gradual variety of line which Hogarth called the 'line of beauty' (see p.127 below); they are summed up in an analogy which became famous:

> Most people must have observed the sort of sense they have
> had, on being swiftly drawn in an easy coach, on a smooth turf,
> with gradual ascents and declivities. This will give a better idea
> of the beautiful, and point out its probable cause better than
> almost anything else.

This analogy is not a mere flight of fancy: Burke seeks to identify aesthetic feelings with physical sensations and to establish a mechanical theory of aesthetics in accordance with current notions of physiology. It was commonly believed that sensation is caused by vibration of the nerves or by vibration of minute particles along the nerves (see Ch. 1 and 3 above). It was also believed that one sense could cause others to react sympathetically, and this belief had already been incorporated into aesthetic theory with Addison's observation in *Spectator*, no. 412 that the ideas of different senses 'recommend each other'. Burke claims 'There is a chain in al our sensations', so that what is 'beautiful in *Feeling* . . . corresponds wonderfully with what causes the same species of pleasure to the sight'.[45] Hence the coach analogy can stand as a literal account of a sensation of the beautiful.

Dealing with the apparently more difficult case of the sublime, Burke observes that pain and fear alike produce in the body 'an unnatural tension and certain violent emotions of the nerves'.[46] It follows, he argues, that any idea which produces the same physical tension and violent motions will produce a feeling akin to terror. To explain why such a feeling can be delightful, he claims that exercise refreshes and strengthens the nerves and 'finer organs' just as it does the limbs and larger, coarser organs of the body. Burke thus accounts for aesthetic responses in wholly physiological terms: we feel the sublime and the beautiful in the same way as we feel heat and cold. This is perhaps the eighteenth century's boldest attempt to bring aesthetics into line with the physical sciences.

The fifth and last part of Burke's *Enquiry* deals with the production of beauty and sublimity by means of words, and is directed against the common notion that words affect the mind by raising in it images of the objects for which they stand. Words in poetry and oratory may affect us more strongly than the things they represent because they carry a strong, impassioned expression:

> We yield to sympathy, what we refuse to description. The truth
> is, all verbal description, merely as naked description, though
> never so exact, conveys so poor and insufficient an idea of the
> thing described, that it could scarcely have the smallest effect, if
> the speaker did not call in to his aid those modes of speech that
> mark a strong and lively feeling in himself. Then, by the
> contagion of our passions, we catch a fire already kindled in
> another, which probably might never have been struck out by
> the object described.[47]

Naked descriptions convey clear ideas, which, as we have seen, Burke
believes to be little ideas.

Burke's views did not directly affect *An Essay on Taste* by Alexander
Gerard (1728–95), first published in 1759, but written before the publication
of Burke's *Enquiry*; but Gerard, too, finds reasons for aesthetic delight in the
terrific and fearful: 'objects exciting terror . . . are in general sublime; for
terror always implies astonishment, occupies the whole soul, and suspends
all its motions'. He still holds, however, to the Hutchesonian internal senses,
of which he distinguishes seven (the first three of which accord with
Addison's three categories of objects which please the imagination): 'the
senses of novelty, of sublimity, of beauty, of imitation, of harmony, of
ridicule, and of virtue'. All these senses are, in Gerard's system, modes of the
imagination; for Gerard, imagination, acting under the power of sympathy,
is the central faculty of mind. The imagination is not a mere receptor, for it
has a kind of power, like a magnet:

> As the magnet selects from a quantity of matter the ferruginous
> particles, which happen to be scattered through it, without
> making an impression on other substances; so imagination, by a
> similar sympathy, equally inexplicable, draws out from the
> whole compass of nature such ideas as we have occasion for,
> without attending to any others.[48]

An active power comparable with that of a magnet is hardly the kind of
creativity that Young and Hurd attributed to the imagination, but when
Gerard turns from examination of the reader to examination of the writer, in
his *Essay on Genius* (1774), he finds a less mechanical analogy for the
imagination's activity. Genius, he says, 'bears a greater resemblance to *nature*
in its operations, than to the less perfect energies of *art*'. He continues with a
parallel described by M. H. Abrams as 'pregnant with implications for
literary psychology', a parallel similar to Young's characterization of
original works as vegetable growths from the root of genius, but developed
with scientific precision:

> When a vegetable draws in moisture from the earth, nature, by
> the same action by which it draws it in, and at the same time,
> converts it to the nourishment of the plant: it at once circulates
> through its vessels, and is assimilated to its several parts. In like

manner, genius arranges its ideas by the same operation, and almost at the same time, that it collects them.[49]

By that infallible principle of selection and organization known as sympathy the imagination summons up both the parts and the whole of an artistic design in a single act of conjuration.

If such notions, and such a botanical analogy, point forward to Coleridge's theory of the secondary imagination, Gerard's notions about consciousness point forward to Coleridge's theory of the primary imagination. Gerard believes that self-consciousness is innate and is not the result of experience acting upon the Lockeian *tabula rasa*: consciousness is a prerequisite to perception; every man is able 'without any information from experience, by a natural and inexplicable principle, to infer the existence of himself as the percipient and agent'.[50]

Gerard is one of several Scottish thinkers who in the 1760s and 1770s investigated the act of imagination which underlies ordinary perception and related it to those special acts of imagination of which only original genius is capable. William Duff (1732–1815) argues in his *Essay on Original Genius* (1767) that the imagination (evidently something like Coleridge's primary imagination) accounts for differences between two persons' perception of the same objects, and that such differences in perception help to account for differences of character between people. 'The outward organ, by which these sensations are conveyed, is supposed to be equally perfect in both [persons]; but the internal feeling is extremely different. This difference must certainly proceed from the transforming power of Imagination, whose rays illuminate the objects we contemplate.' Duff anticipates Coleridge's distinction between the (secondary) imagination and the fancy. He characterizes fancy as a rambling and sportive form of association and memory; its function is merely to collect the materials of composition; in its ability to yoke disparate ideas together it is the parent of wit and humour. Imagination, which is the essence of genius, is inventive and plastic, and can discover truths that were formerly unknown. 'By the vigorous efforts of the creative Imagination [the poet] calls shadowy substances and unreal objects into existence. They are present to his view, and glide, like spectres, in silent, sullen majesty, before his astonished and intranced sight.'[51]

According to Duff, original genius is the gift of only a few exalted minds; upon these minds depends the whole of society's advancement in art, science, and philosophy, even though the disposition and character of the man of genius set him apart from society and make him incapable of forming 'those bonds of attachment which render men necessary and agreeable to each other'. Genius does not flourish in, say, a Parisian salon, but it 'spreads forth in all its luxuriance in the peaceful vale of rural tranquillity'.[52] One hardly needs to add that Duff's notions about genius and imagination are coloured by the fashionable primitivism of the mid-eighteenth century. Duff believes that poetry of men far removed in time or place from the sophistications of civilization, 'being the effusion of a glowing fancy and an impassioned heart', is natural and original; the poetic genius of 'the uncultivated ages of the world' acknowledges no law 'excepting its own spontaneous impulse, which it obeys without control'.[53]

It was this primitive genius that believers, particularly Scottish believers, thought they could find abundantly in the Ossianic poems, partly translation but mostly fabrication, which James Macpherson published between 1760 and 1763. Duff believed that Ossian was one of only three 'complete geniuses' to have appeared in the world up to his day, the others being Homer and Shakespeare; but Hugh Blair (1718–1800) was the Scotsman who championed both the genius and the authenticity of the Ossianic with the most zeal and the least discretion. In his *Critical Dissertation on the Poems of Ossian* (1763) Blair praises the seriousness of an epical-romantic poetry which 'moves perpetually in the high region of the grand and the pathetic'; its 'wild and romantic' scenery, 'the extended heath by the sea-shore; the mountain shaded with mist; the torrent rushing through a solitary valley; the scattered oaks, and the tombs of warriors overgrown with moss; all produce a solemn attention in the mind'. Ossian is superior even to Homer in his union of the tender and the sublime: 'It is not enough to admire. Admiration is a cold feeling, in comparison of that deep interest which the heart takes in tender and pathetic scenes; where, by a mysterious attachment to the objects of compassion, we are pleased and delighted, even whilst we mourn.'[54] As always, the prime motive is sympathy.

Ossian appears among the poets praised for their sublimity in a much more substantial treatise, the *Elements of Criticism* (1762) by Henry Home, Lord Kames, (1696–1782); but despite such admiration for the romantic Gael, Kames is a somewhat conservative aesthetician for the 1760s. He insists that there is a close relationship between aesthetics and ethics, and believes that there are providential ends in all our aesthetic pleasures; thus our liking for order, uniformity, and regularity contributes to readiness of apprehension, our liking for change, variety, and motion serves to make us industrious, our liking for novelty helps to make us alert to avoid danger, our liking for tragedy exercises our sympathy, and so on. A taste in the fine arts 'goes hand in hand with the moral sense, to which indeed it is nearly allied: both of them discover what is right and what is wrong . . . neither of them are arbitrary or local; being rooted in human nature, and governed by principles common to all men'.[55] By the 1760s, though, the 'moral sense' was becoming unfashionable in aesthetics.

Like most critics of his period, Kames argues (against Burke's championship of obscurity and Johnson's of 'the grandeur of generality') that the chief virtue of poetry lies in its particularity; he advises poets, particularly those who aspire to the sublime, to 'avoid as much as possible abstract and general terms . . . images, which are the life of poetry, cannot be raised in any perfection but by introducing particular objects'. Kames has, however, a somewhat old-fashioned notion of the imagination; he regards it as a faculty which, in 'fabricating images of things that have no existence', is limited to dividing and recombining the 'ideas of sight'.[56] It is the great merit of Homer and Shaespeare, not to mention Ossian, that they employ particulars and avoid abstractions.

Kames is the first critic to place gardening alongside the other fine arts in a general treatise on aesthetics. It is in the nature of the fine arts to raise pleasurable emotions. Gardening can raise emotions of beauty from regularity, order, proportion, colour, and utility; it can raise emotions of grandeur, of sweetness, of gaiety, of melancholy, of wildness, and even of surprise and wonder. It is thus capable of a wider range of aesthetic effects than architecture, which can raise equivalent or greater emotions of beauty from regularity, order, proportion, and utility (but perhaps not colour) and can raise a greater sense of grandeur, but cannot compare with gardening to raise the other emotions. The emotional range of gardening, however, is less than that of painting or of sculpture, and much less than poetry, which can reach nearly every emotion of human nature. Much of the *Elements of Criticism* is taken up by a systematic examination of these emotions, with copious detailed analysis of the poetry that has succeeded, or not succeeded, in raising them. Despite his limited conception of the imagination, Kames has no doubt that poetry is expressive, not imitative.

Though Kames's treatise is longer and more inclusive than most eighteenth-century works on aesthetics, it is, like most of the others, primarily concerned with poetry. As we have seen, writers on aesthetics tended as the century advanced to address themselves more and more to the psychology of aesthetic experience and to the nature and powers of the imagination; correspondingly they tended to give less attention to the formal aspects of art. Painters, for obvious reasons, were among the more conspicuous exceptions to this general rule; so form is the prime consideration in William Hogarth's *Analysis of Beauty, written with a View of fixing the fluctuating Idea of Taste* (1753).

Hogarth's declared aim is to determine by what principles in nature and art we are required to call certain things beautiful. Adopting an appropriately analytical method, he points out that solids and shapes, when visualised, reduce themselves to lines; so to analyse beauty all that is necessary is to consider, 'more minutely than has hitherto been done, the nature of those lines, and their different combinations, which serve to raise in the mind the ideas of all the variety of forms imaginable'. On analysis it is found that six characteristics co-operate to produce linear beauty, 'mutually correcting and restraining each other occasionally'; these are 'fitness, variety, uniformity, simplicity, intricacy, and quantity'.[57]

'Fitness' is an unexpectedly non-formal characteristic to be attributed to a line, but Hogarth requires such a characteristic because he believes that it defines the species of beauty before any other factors come into play; for instance, 'in ship-building the dimensions of every part are confin'd and regulated by fitness for sailing. When a vessel sails well, the sailors always call her a beauty; the two ideas have such a connexion!' Fitness is of course the primary criterion of beauty for Hume, who also adduces the example of the sailing-ship. At the beginning of the *Analysis* fitness is so prominent a part of Hogarth's scheme that it seems sometimes to absorb his other criteria: for instance, the chapter on 'uniformity' ends: 'How pleasingly is the idea of firmness in standing convey'd to the eye by the three elegant claws of a table, the three feet of a tea-lamp, or the celebrated tripod of the ancients! Thus you see regularity, uniformity, or symmetry please only as they serve to give the idea of fitness.'[58]

Later in his discussion, however, it appears that variety and intricacy are the most important: 'those lines which have most variety in themselves contribute most towards the production of beauty'; 'the art of composing well is the art of varying well'. The eye takes a pleasure in following intricate, waving, or serpentine lines: 'Intricacy in form, therefore, I shall define to be that peculiarity in the lines, which compose it, that *leads the eye a wanton kind of chace*, and from the pleasure that gives the mind, intitles it to the name of beautiful.' The pleasure provided for the mind by the eye's wanton chase is like the pleasure of other mental pursuits, such as the solving of problems, riddles, and allegories, or the following of 'the well-connected thread of a play, or novel'; for 'the active mind is ever bent to be employ'd', and the 'love of pursuit, merely as pursuit, is implanted in our natures'.

Here, as of course more obviously in his discussion of fitness (a principle which depends wholly upon association of ideas), Hogarth displays the usual eighteenth-century predilection for analysing mental processes, but his analysis is finally directed towards the identification of beautiful forms; his final concern is with object, not subject. So the product of his theorizing is the construction of the 'line of beauty', a waving line or shallow 'S', composed of two contracted curves moving in opposite directions, neither bulging so much as to become 'gross and clumsy' or so little as to become 'mean and poor'. This line is excelled only by its three-dimensional counterpart, the flame-like line of grace, which is such a line as would be formed by a fine wire twisted in a single sweeping curve around a cone from base to vertex. According to Hogarth, the lines of beauty and of grace account for our pleasure in the forms of a great variety of objects: an iris, a bell, the stays of a corset, chairlegs, serpents, and horses, to name but a few.[59]

Hogarth's *Analysis of Beauty* is perhaps excessively schematic: the other notable aesthetic treatise by an eighteenth-century English painter, by the very circumstances of its composition and publication, could hardly be schematic at all, because it consists of the fifteen *Discourses on Art* delivered by Sir Joshua Reynolds to members and students of the Royal Academy over more than twenty years, from 1769 to 1790. Contradictions between statements in different discourses may be accounted for by this time element, but can be explained equally well by the fact that Reynolds's audience included students of very different ages and degrees of advancement in painting. We are aware that he is addressing different sections of his audience when on the one hand he recommends rules and imitation of the old masters, and on the other hand he acknowledges that taste and genius are not to be acquired by rules and that when an artist imitates other artists he falls far below them. So, in his first *Discourse* (1769) he insists that 'there are some rules, whose absolute authority, like that of our nurses, continues no longer than while we are in a state of childhood'. His considered view appears in his summary of the tendency of his eighth *Discourse* as 'not so much to place the Artist above rules, as to teach him their reason', and to clear his thoughts 'by directing his attention to an intimate acquaintance with the passions and affections of the mind, from which all rules arise, and to which they are all referable. Art effects its purpose by their means; an accurate knowledge therefore of those passions and dispositions of the mind is necessary to him who desires to affect them upon sure and solid principles.'[60] Reynolds brings his discussion back to that prime interest of the eighteenth century, the quest for knowledge of the human mind.

Like his contemporaries, he investigates the nature of genius and taste, but his views run counter to the contemporary tendency to see genius as mysterious. He curtly observes in the seventh *Discourse* (1776): 'It is supposed that their powers are intuitive, that under the name of genius great works are produced, and under the name of taste an exact judgment is given, without our knowing why, and without our being under the least obligation to reason, precept, or experience. One can scarcely state these opinions without exposing their absurdity.' Reynolds himself intends to speak of genius and taste as connected with reason and common sense, despite the possibility that this procedure will expose him, 'in the opinion of some towering talkers', as a man who 'was never warmed by that Promethean fire, which animates the canvas and vivifies the marble'. He will have nothing to do with faddish current enthusiasm for the inexplicable creativity of wild, untrammelled genius. Art is addressed to the imagination and the passions, of course, but the principles of these may be known and reasoned upon 'by an appeal to common sense deciding upon the common feelings of mankind'. Such an appeal implies that there is a general uniformity in human nature.

> The internal fabrick of our minds, as well as the external form
> of our bodies, being nearly uniform; it seems then to follow of
> course, that as the imagination is incapable of producing any
> thing originally of itself, and can only vary and combine those
> ideas with which it is furnished by means of the senses, there
> will be necessarily an agreement in the imaginations as in the
> senses of men.

It follows that the standard of taste 'is fixed and established in the nature of things; . . . that there are certain and regular causes by which the imagination and passions of men are affected'.[61]

In his very conservative notions of the imagination and his belief in a fixed standard of taste Reynolds appears to resemble Burke, but his concept of beauty is very different from Burke's: whereas Burke accounts for beauty in wholly physiological terms, Reynolds does so in wholly intellectual terms. In his ninth *Discourse*, he declares:

> The art which we profess has beauty for its object; this it is our
> business to discover and to express; but the beauty of which we
> are in quest is general and intellectual; it is an idea that subsists
> only in the mind; the sight never beheld it: it is an idea residing
> in the breast of the artist, which he is always labouring to
> impart, and which he dies at last without imparting; but which
> he is yet so far able to communicate, as to raise the thoughts,
> and extend the views of the spectator. . . .

Such a notion of ideal beauty goes back to Plato; like Plato, Reynolds links beauty with virtue, for the sentence from which I have just quoted ends by describing the purpose of art as 'disentangling the mind from appetite, and conducting the thoughts through successive stages of excellence, till that contemplation of universal rectitude and harmony which began by Taste, may, as it is exalted and refined, conclude in Virtue'[62]; but his idealism has nothing of the transcendental. 'This great ideal perfection and beauty are not to be sought in the heavens, but upon the earth. They are about us, and upon every side of us.' This is not to say that ideal beauty is plain to see in the objects of nature, for all such objects 'will be found to have their blemishes and defects'.[63]

The ideal is an abstraction or generalization; it is the specific form, every deviation from which is regarded as a deformity, and it is described by means of a revealing analogy in an essay contributed by Reynolds to Johnson's *Idler* (no. 82, 1759): 'It may be compared to pendulums vibrating in different directions over one central point; and as they all cross the center, though only one passes through any other point, so it will be found that perfect beauty is oftener produced by nature than deformity; I do not mean than deformity in general, but than any one kind of deformity.' In this same essay the painter is likened to the philosophic naturalist who determines the general form of a species from the minute examination of many specimens, no two of which are exactly alike: some such parallel between art and the natural sciences in their power to abstract and generalize is implicit throughout the *Discourses*. Though there are no precise, invariable rules for the exercise or acquisition of taste and genius, 'yet we may truly say that they always operate in proportion to our attention in observing the works of nature, to our skill in selecting, and to our care in digesting, methodising, and comparing our observations'. The artist of genius 'will permit the lower painter, like the florist or collector of shells, to exhibit the minute discriminations, which distinguish one object of the same species from another; while he, like the philosopher, will consider nature in the abstract, and represent in every one of his figures the character of its species'.[64] The business of the artist is thus remarkably similar to the business of the poet as it is ambitiously described by Imlac at the beginning of Chapter 10 of Johnson's *Rasselas*.

This conception of general nature and ideal beauty accounts for Reynolds's consistent hostility to the Dutch masters. Rembrandt introduces into his historical pictures 'exact representations of individual objects with all their imperfections', but we are mistaken if we assert that thereby he imitates nature more faithfully than the idealizing Raphael does: 'a very little reflection will serve to shew us' that Rembrandt's 'particularities cannot be nature: for how can that be the nature of man, in which no two individuals are the same?' Rubens sometimes transgresses by making his landscapes 'a representation of an individual spot', whereas Claude Lorrain is rightly convinced that 'taking nature as he found it seldom produced beauty'.[65] The painter who takes nature as he finds it is no better than the prose historian. The painter of ideal landscapes who freely exercises the power to select his materials and elevate his style is 'like the Poet', for 'he makes the elements sympathize with his subject: whether the clouds roll in volumes like those of Titian or Salvator Rosa, – or, like those of Claude, are gilded with the setting sun'. Such an inventive and poetical painter varies and disposes all the materials of his composition to correspond with the general idea of his work: 'a landskip thus conducted, under the influence of a poetical mind, will have the same superiority over the more ordinary and common views, as Milton's *Allegro* and *Penseroso* have over a cold prosaick narration or description'.[66]

It seems that Reynolds came only gradually to realize that the highest power of the painter is the same as the poet's, and that his study of Michaelangelo contributed greatly to this realization. In the fifth *Discourse* (1772) he makes a distinction between imagination and fancy, a distinction admittedly less tendentious than the one made earlier by Duff (see p.124 above) and later by Coleridge, but nevertheless significant:

> Raffaelle had more Taste and Fancy, Michael Angelo more
> Genius and Imagination. The one excelled in beauty, the other
> in energy. Michael Angelo has more of the Poetical Inspiration;
> his ideas are vast and sublime . . . Raffaelle's imagination is not
> so elevated . . . Michael Angelo's works . . . seem to proceed
> from his own mind entirely . . . Raffaelle's materials are
> generally borrowed, though the noble structure is his own.

Raphael 'possessed a greater combination of the higher qualities of art than any other man', but Michaelangelo was the world's greatest master of the sublime, that is, of 'the highest excellence that human composition can attain to'. Raphael is not belittled beside Michaelangelo, but some measure of qualitative difference between imagination and fancy is certainly implied. In the fifteenth and last *Discourse* (1790) Michaelangelo is given far higher praise than Raphael or any other artist: he possessed 'the poetical part of our art in a most eminent degree', and he is to be ranked with Homer and Shakespeare in 'the daring spirit' which urged him 'to explore the unknown regions of the imagination'.[67] The need to accommodate Michaelangelo seems to have liberated Reynolds's criticism, much as the need to accommodate Shakespeare liberated Dryden's about a century earlier.

For Reynolds the true test of a painting or a poem is not whether it is a true copy of nature, but whether it achieves 'the great end' of the arts, which is 'to make an impression on the imagination and the feeling'; for 'the imagination is here the residence of truth'. It is, of course, the residence of truth for the artist as well as for his audience. Reynolds concludes his thirteenth *Discourse* (1786): 'Upon the whole, it seems to me, that the object and intention of all the Arts is to supply the natural imperfection of things, and often to gratify the mind by realizing and embodying what never existed but in the imagination.' Though facts and events may bind the historian, they 'have no dominion over the Poet or the Painter', whose arts 'in their highest province, are not addressed to the gross senses, but to the desires of the mind, to that spark of divinity which we have within'.[68]

Notes

1. *An Essay concerning Human Understanding*, edited by Peter H. Nidditch (Oxford, 1975), pp. 508, 164; Book III, Chapter x, Section 34; II, xii, 2.

2. Ibid., p. 156; II, xi, 2.

3. *Essay on the Genius and Writings of Pope*, II, (1782), 271–72.

4. *Answer to Davenant* (1650), in *Critical Essays of the Seventeenth Century*, edited by J. E. Spingarn (Oxford, 1908), II, 59.

5. *Characteristicks of Men, Manners, Opinions, Times*, second edition (1714), II, 399, 405, 388–95.

6. Ibid., II, 404.

7. Coleridge nowhere acknowledges a debt to Shaftesbury. General and particular resemblances between the ideas of the two men are perhaps accounted for by a common source in Plato and the Cambridge Platonists, and by the fact that Coleridge took from late-eighteenth-century German philosophers what they had taken and adapted from Shaftesbury.

8. *Characteristicks* (1714), I, 207, II, 201, 203.

9. Ibid., I, 207, III, 274.

10. 'On Poesy or Art', in *Biographia Literaria*, edited by J. T. Shawcross (Oxford, 1907), II, 257.

11. *Second Characters*, edited by B. Rand (Cambridge, 1914); the phrase quoted above is on p. 106.

12. *Essay on Man*, III, 1733 21–23.

13. R. Hinton Thomas, *The Classical Ideal in German Literature, 1755–1805* (Cambridge, 1939).

14. Thomas Burnet, *Theory of the Earth* (1684), I, 188–89.

15. *Critical Works of John Dennis*, edited by E. H. Hooker, I, (Baltimore, 1943), 381.

16. *Essays Moral, Political, and Literary*, edited by T. H. Green and T. H. Grose (1875), II, 5.

17. Translation of Bellori in *A Parallel of Poetry and Painting* (1695), in *Essays of John Dryden*, edited by W. P. Ker (Oxford, 1900), II, 118.

18. *Works of Spenser*, edited by J. Hughes (1715), I, xxxiv, xxix.

19. G. H. Hartman, *Beyond Formalism* (New Haven, 1970), p. 204.

20. Line-references are to the final version of this much-revised poem, though the text is of the dates given.

21. *Inquiry into the Original of our Ideas of Beauty and Virtue* (1725), pp. 7, 9: Treatise I, Section i, para. 9; I, i, 11.

22. Ibid., pp. 7, 17, 76: I, i, 9, ii, 3, vi, 5.

23. *A Treatise of Human Nature*, edited by L. A. Selby-Bigge, second edition, revised by P. H. Nidditch (Oxford, 1978), pp. 299, 576–67, 586–87: Book II, Part i, Section 8; III, iii, 1.

24. Ibid., pp. 432–44: II, iii, 8.

25. *Essays, Moral, Political, and Literary* (Oxford, 1963), pp. 221, 227, 225. The essays 'Of Tragedy' and 'Of the Standard of Taste' were first published in Hume's *Four Dissertations* (1757).

26. Ibid., pp. 234–35.

27. Ibid., pp. 236, 238–39, 247.

28. Ibid., pp. 249, 250, 251.

29. 'Appendix to the Reign of Elizabeth', in *History of England* (Oxford, 1826), v, 433.

30. *Essays, Moral, Political, and Literary* (Oxford, 1963), p. 197.

31. 'Appendix to the Reign of James I', in *History of England*, VI, 168.

32. Essays 'Of Heroic Virtue' and 'Of Poetry', in *Five Miscellaneous Essays*, edited by S. H. Monk (Ann Arbor, 1963), pp. 143, 188.

33. *Observations on the Faerie Queene* (1754), pp. 217, 12–13.

34. *Works of Richard Hurd* (1811), IV, 239, 329, 281, 348, 350; Letters iv, x, and xii.

35. *Lectures on the Sacred Poetry of the Hebrews*, translated by G. Gregory (1787), pp. 59, 63.

36. *Enquiry into the Life and Writings of Homer* (1735), pp. 34, 35.

37. *Conjectures on Original Composition*, edited by Edith Morley (1918), pp. 7, 17, 23, 24, 18, 31.

38. *Works* (1811), IV, 324; Letter x.

39. 'Introduction on Taste', in *Philosophical Enquiry into the Sublime and Beautiful*, edited by J. T. Boulton (1958), pp. 16.

40. Ibid., pp. 11, 23.

41. Ibid., p. 1; Preface to the First Edition.

42. Ibid., p. 44; Part I, Section xiii.

43. Ibid., pp. 40, 59, 62, 63; I, vii; II, iii, iv.

44. Ibid., p. 92; III, ii.

45. Ibid., pp. 155, 120; IV, xxiii; III, xxiv.

46. Ibid., p. 134; IV, vii.

47. Ibid., pp. 175–76; v, vii.

48. *An Essay on Taste* (1767), pp. 19, 2, 173–74.

49. *Essay on Genius* (1774), pp. 60, 64; see M. H. Abrams, *The Mirror and the Lamp* (New York, 1958), p. 167.

50. *Essay on Genius*, p. 284.

51. *Essay on Original Genius* (1767), pp. 66–67, 177.

52. *Critical Observations on the Writings of the most celebrated Original Geniuses in Poetry* (1770), p. 340.

53. *Essay on Original Genius*, pp. 270, 282–84.

54. *Poems of Ossian*, translated by James Macpherson (1790), II, 291, 426.

55. *Elements of Criticism* (1762), I, xi.

56. Ibid., I, 294, 404.

57. *Analysis of Beauty*, edited by J. Burke (Oxford, 1955), pp. 21, 31.

58. Ibid., pp. 33, 38.

59. Ibid., pp. 56, 57, 41, 42.

60. *Discourses on Art*, edited by R. R. Wark (New Haven, 1975), pp. 17, 154, 162.

61. Ibid., pp. 120–21, 119, 131, 132, 134.

62. Ibid., p. 171.

63. Ibid., p. 44; third *Discourse* (1770).

64. Ibid. pp. 44, 50.

65. *Discourses on Art*, pp. 124, 69–70; seventh *Discourse* (1776) and fourth *Discourse* (1771).

66. *Discourses on Art*, pp. 237, 238: thirteenth *Discourse* (1786).

67. *Discourses on Art*, pp. 83–84, 272.

68. Ibid., pp. 241, 230, 244.

Chapter 6
Visual Arts

In drawing parallels between poetry and painting, Reynolds followed a critical practice which extended back to Plato. Despite the protests of Lessing, in his *Laokoön* (1766), that the unalterable differences between the two arts are far more significant than their similarities, because, simply, the medium of one is time, of the other, space, Reynolds's contemporaries continued to draw these parallels. They could hardly avoid doing so, in view of their strongly visual conception of the imagination; so it became a commonplace of literary criticism to interpret poems in terms of pictures, while the high reputation of Spenser's allegories and the enormous popularity of Thomson's *Seasons* testified to the general admiration for poetical pictorialism. Indeed, readers of poetry at that time seem to have possessed a remarkable ability really to *see* imaginary pictures in what they read. Whereas a modern reader might find only vague generalization in Thomson's

> softley-swelling Hills!
> On which the Power of Cultivation lies,
> And joys to see the Wonders of his Toil
> (*Summer* ll. 1435–37),

a critic of the 1750s, possibly Goldsmith, observed

> We cannot conceive a more beautiful image than that of the
> Genius of Agriculture, distinguished by the implements of his
> art, imbrowned with labour, glowing with health, crowned
> with a garland of foliage, flowers, and fruit, lying stretched at
> his ease on the brow of a gently swelling hill, and
> contemplating with pleasure the happy effects of his own
> industry.

On this comment Donald Davie has rightly remarked that the writer 'probably contributes nothing that was not in Thomson's intention. For Thomson could count on finding in his readers a ready allegorical imagination, such as seems lost to us today. The loss is certainly ours.'[1] What the mental eye of the eighteenth-century reader sees in this rather commonplace snatch of verse is an allegorical ideal form; Thomson, for all his reputation as a 'descriptive poet' is no more a straight copyist of external nature than any of the painters or other poets admired by Reynolds.

It was, of course, not only painting and poetry which appealed to the visualizing and idealizing power of the imagination, and so became natural subjects for the study of parallelism between the arts. Reynolds's thirteenth *Discourse*, from which were taken most of the remarks on poetical painting quoted at the end of my last chapter, is concerned with parallels between poetry, drama, and the four principal visual arts, architecture, sculpture, painting, and gardening: these are the arts which 'address themselves primarily and principally to the imagination', and they are the subject of the present chapter. Architecture comes first, not because Reynolds believed that, of all the visual arts, it came closest to poetry (as an art which applies itself 'directly to the imagination, without the invervention of any kind of imitation'[2]), but because, among the visual arts, it is the earliest in the eighteenth century to be able to boast of a triumphant English school of native-born artists.

Architecture

In the opening years of the eighteenth century English architecture was dominated by a triumvirate consisting of Sir Christopher Wren (1632–1723) and his close associates, Nicholas Hawksmoor (1661–1736) and Sir John Vanbrugh (1664–1726). Most of Wren's work belongs to the previous century, although St Paul's Cathedral, begun 1675, was not completed until 1711, and his second greatest work, Greenwich Hospital, on which both Hawksmoor and Vanbrugh also worked, was not begun until 1696. The two younger men, particularly Vanbrugh, are far more than mere disciples of Wren; they freely and inventively develop his vigorous, expansive, Anglicized-baroque style, with great insistence upon movement, drama, and display, and nowhere is this development seen more strikingly than at Castle Howard in Yorkshire. In the house (begun 1699) Vanbrugh's great stone hall under a painted dome flamboyantly applies the grand manner of Wren's St Paul's to what may only nominally be termed domestic purposes; in the park, Hawksmoor's severe Roman mausoleum (1729–38, see Plate 2) broods over the landscape like a sentry – a tall, dark domed drum set within a colonnade, described by Sir John Summerson as 'close and tense, a grim palisade', the interior 'a great tower of light, which pours in from clerestory windows above a rich Corinthian order'.[3]

The building by Vanbrugh which attracted most widespread contemporary attention, not least from satirists, is Blenheim Palace (begun 1704, see Plate 3). Money, albeit not enough money, for the building of Blenheim was granted by Queen and Parliament in gratitude for the Duke of Marlborough's generalship; Vanbrugh therefore, despite the objections of the Duchess, who would have preferred a private habitation, determined to create 'a Royall and National Monument'.[4] and Blenheim duly expresses the ideas of military heroism and of national power. Though undeniably baroque in style, its great pinnacled and trophied masses re-create something of the rugged strength of medieval castle architecture, what Vanbrugh himself in another connection called 'the Castle Air'. Vanbrugh wished to preserve existing medieval ruins in the landscape at Blenheim, and, in 'Vanbrugh Castle' (1717–26) at Greenwich built for himself a little picturesque sham castle, claimed by Sir Nikolaus Pevsner to be 'the first private house ever designed consciously to arouse associations with the Middle Ages'.[5] But there is a more profound Gothic feeling in the great façades of Blenheim and Castle Howard. When Reynolds, in his thirteenth *Discourse* (1786), praises Vanbrugh as a supreme poet among architects it is to draw attention to his use of the principles of Gothic architecture, by which it is evident that Reynolds means the handling of masses, and certainly not the ordinary, widespread 'carpenter's Gothic' of that century, which involves no more than the application of ornament.

The Gothic manner sometimes adopted by Hawksmoor, best exemplified in the spires and crockets of his new quadrangle at All Souls College, Oxford (1700–34), certainly does not lack vigour, but it is light and airy in comparison with Vanbrugh's; more typical of Hawksmoor is the noble, restrained, and learned classicism of his rebuilding of neighbouring Queen's College between the same dates; but the best of Hawksmoor, apart from the sublime mausoleum at Castle Howard, is in his City of London churches built under 'Queen Anne's Act' of 1711. The Act was intended to supply fifty new churches as a supplement to Wren's wholesale church rebuildings after the Great Fire, both as a monument to the Queen's piety and grandeur and as a Tory administration's timely reminder to Dissenters that the Anglican Church was by law established. In the event, twelve 'Queen Anne' churches were built, of which Hawksmoor designed six. The Act required 'Towers or Steeples' to each church; it is in those features that Hawksmoor most clearly reveals his characteristic propensity 'to obtain medieval effects with components as nearly as possible antique',[6] nowhere more so than in the steeple of his St George's, Bloomsbury (1720–30), which is composed of a tall pyramid of steps in imitation of Pliny's description of the Mausoleum at Halicarnassus, one of the ancient Seven Wonders of the World. Hawksmoor's version is crowned by a statue of George I and was once adorned by a lion and a unicorn: it is prominent in the background of Hogarth's *Gin Lane* (see Plate 11).

Something of the Wren–Hawksmoor–Vanbrugh tradition persists to the middle of the century in the designs of James Gibbs (1682–1754). His Radcliffe Camera (1737–49) at Oxford realizes the same geometrical conception (two concentric cylinders) as Hawksmoor's mausoleum at Castle Howard, but is both more massive and more intricate. His best-known and most influential building is St Martin-in-the-Fields (1722–26, see Plate 4), where he stresses the union between medieval ecclesiological tradition and neo-classicism by placing the steeple and the temple portico upon the same axis. Architectural purists were pained by this combination, because no ancient Greek or Roman building had a steeple, and the very notion of a vertical element over a portico was unclassical, but Gibbs's innovation creates a brilliant harmony. Set on its severe square base, perfectly proportioned to the pediment below, and rising, through lighter and lighter orders, to the delicate concave-sided obelisk spire, this steeple perfectly satisfies the aesthetic criterion of 'order in variety' and finely expresses the early eighteenth-century Anglican ideal of reasonable spirituality.

The moderate compromises and inventiveness of Gibbs at St Martin-in-the-Fields and the flamboyant eclecticism of Hawksmoor at St George's, Bloomsbury, were not to the taste of the school of neo-Palladian architects, whose prestige and influence rose rapidly after the accession of George I. This new school, like the one it supplanted, was headed by a triumvirate: Richard Boyle, Earl of Burlington (1694–1753), Colen Campbell (d. 1729), and William Kent (1685–1748). Campbell was the pioneer of this group in both practice and precept; his design for Wanstead House in Essex and the first volume of his *Vitruvius Britannicus*, a collection of engravings of buildings, mostly British, of the previous 100 years, both belong to 1715; but Burlington, by virtue of some ability as a practising architect as well as his undoubted superiority of rank, wealth, and taste, soon became the group's leader as well as its patron; it was Burlington, on one of his architectural study-tours of Italy, who recruited the decorative painter William Kent and turned him into an architect. Horace Walpole, in *Anecdotes of Painting* (1762–71), describes Burlington as 'the Apollo of arts', and William Kent as his 'proper priest'.[7]

The guides and masters of the neo-Palladians were also three: Vitruvius, the Roman architect and military engineer of Augustus's time and author of the only ancient treatise on architecture to have survived, who laid down rules of proportion and taught the 'correct' use of the classical orders; Andrea Palladio (1518–70) of Vicenza, whose treatise *I Quattro libri dell'architettura* (1570), based upon Vitruvius and upon a study of the archaeological evidence of classical buildings then available in Italy, propounded the laws of architecture in a neo-Platonic system of simple, mathematical-harmonic proportions, and whose designs were a practical demonstration of the manner in which an ancient Roman style could be incorporated into modern buildings; and finally Inigo Jones (1573–1652), who modelled his own architectural style upon Palladio but considerably extended the resources of Palladianism, particularly in the treatment of certain features, for instance ceilings and fireplaces, on which Palladio had given little or no guidance. When Campbell, in the preface to the first volume of *Vitruvius Britannicus*, couples the names of Palladio and Jones, and praises Jones's Banqueting House in Whitehall for its union of 'Strength with Politeness, Ornament with Simplicity, Beauty with Majesty'[8], he is implicitly condemning the baroque style (Italian baroque, admittedly, rather than English); it was the aim of the neo-Palladians to take up English architecture from the point to which Jones had brought it before the Civil War and the subsequent baroque interruption, and so their numerous publications constantly insist upon the continuity of a pure and correct Roman style from Vitruvius to themselves.

Most of these publications were associated with Burlington. He sponsored the second and third volumes of Campbell's *Vitruvius Britannicus* (1717, 1725), and notable editions of Palladio's *Four Books of Architecture* by Giacomo Leoni in 1715–16 and by Isaac Ware in 1738, both of whom were practising architects like Campbell, designing correct and derivative neo-Palladian houses in town and country. What would become one of the classic works on neo-Palladian interiors, William Kent's *Designs of Inigo Jones* (1727), which included additional designs by Kent and Burlington, was sponsored by Burlington, who sponsored also Robert Castell's *The Villas of the Ancients Illustrated* (1728), an archaeology of Palladianism which was particularly important for its attempt to re-create the garden settings of ancient Roman country houses. Burlington published reproductions from his own collection of drawings by Palladio and Jones, and encouraged other architects, such as Isaac Ware and John Vardy, to draw on his collection in their own publications. Whether or not it was the most immediately effective, the best-remembered piece of neo-Palladian propaganda is of course Pope's *Epistle to Burlington* (1731).

The most distinctive architectural form adopted by the neo-Palladians from Palladio is the villa, the type of building that urbanely expresses in a noble, learned, and classical idiom the appealing idea of rural retirement, and the most obviously derivative English Palladian villa is Mereworth in Kent, designed by Colen Campbell in 1723 on the model of Palladio's Villa Rotonda, near Vicenza. The plan of both villas embodies a Vitruvian ideal of perfect geometrical relationship, a circle within a square; the elevation of both is a circular Roman temple behind four matching colonnaded temple porticos: 'From the outside it looks as if two long rectangular or Parthenon-type temples had been driven through a square block enclosing a miniature Pantheon.'[9] In adapting the design to English conditions, Campbell was compelled to make his dome much steeper than Palladio's in order to accommodate the chimney flues essential in an English residence. A more famous, less closely derivative version of Palladio's Rotonda is the small villa (Plate 1) designed by Burlington in 1725, and attached by a short wing to his Jacobean great house at Chiswick. Because the villa is symmetrical about only one axis, not about two, as in the original Villa Rotonda, Burlington is able to produce a variety of room shapes, despite the overall stern effect of symmetry; for his octagonal central hall he goes back beyond his Palladian model to the great baths of ancient Rome. Never intended as a dwelling- place, as Mereworth was, it has more of the character of a belvedere, summer-house, or ornamental and antiquarian temple of taste; Burlington's modelling of the ground about it ensures that his villa belongs as much to the history of landscape gardening as to that of architecture.

Many Palladian country houses could be described as villas only in the sense that Timon's dwelling, in Pope's *Epistle to Burlington*, is a villa. For instance, the façade of Wentworth Woodhouse in Yorkshire, built *c.* 1740 by Henry, 'Burlington Harry', Flitcroft (1697–1769) is 606 feet long: that is, nearly as long as Castle Howard, albeit well short of the 850 feet of Blenheim. The design for Wentworth Woodhouse, derived almost wholly from models in *Vitruvius Britannicus*, runs true to the Palladian-house type as

Sir John Summerson describes it: 'the great blockish mansion . . . with a portico but otherwise sparingly adorned with elements drawn from a very limited and frigid vocabulary of ornament. It was not a particularly original invention, only a rather tepid abstraction from Palladio and Jones.'[10] Like Houghton Hall (1722–35), designed by Colen Campbell for Sir Robert Walpole and thought by some modern critics to be the Timon's villa of Pope,[11] and like many other of the scores of Palladian houses built in that century, Wentworth Woodhouse was a rural palace whose foursquare pride suggested anything but rural retirement. The masterwork among these rural palaces is perhaps Holkham Hall (1734–64) by William Kent. Its museum-like entrance hall, one of the most magnificent rooms in England, theatrically realizes Vitruvius's description of a Roman basilica, while the Hall's exterior achieves 'order in variety' by the balance between a great, severe, palatial, nobly-porticoed central block and four less pretentious villa-like wings, which are almost rural in character, seeming to add a notion of utility to the undoubted pomp of the interior.

In the greatest literary document of the neo-Palladian movement, the *Epistle to Burlington*, Pope moves naturally from the pompous utility of Roman architecture (ll.23–24) to the old English patriarchal ideal of rural landownership (ll.181–86), and then, in the remaining verses to the end of the poem, just as naturally to an expansive vision of healthy national cultural renewal expressed in great and noble civic building. In the event, no great programme of neo-Palladian public works was carried out. Westminster Bridge, the plans for which are referred to in Pope's own long note to the concluding lines of the *Epistle to Burlington*, was opened in 1750; its promoter was the neo-Palladian architect Henry Herbert (1693–1751), Earl of Pembroke, called by Horace Walpole 'a second Inigo Jones'; it was built nobly in stone, not in wood, as Pope, Thomson, and other satirists had once feared; its completion, after great technical difficulties, gave a great impetus to bridge-building all over Britain in the second half of the century; but it was not Palladian in style. The 'Palladian Bridge' inseparably associated with Pembroke's name, though perhaps equally attributable to his unennobled partner, Roger Morris (d. 1749), is a scaled-down version of Palladio's unexecuted idea of a triumphal bridge; it was erected in 1737 as a garden ornament near the Inigo Jones front of Wilton House, and copied in the gardens of Prior Park, Hagley, and Stowe: see Plate 20. The most perfect neo-Palladian civic building is probably Burlington's Assembly Rooms in York (1731–32), closely modelled upon the so-called 'Egyptian Hall' described in Vitruvius and illustrated in Palladio; the best-known must be the Horse Guards (1750–60) in Whitehall, where William Kent's design, a design which recaptured the ordered variety and movement of his great façades at Holkham, was carried out by John Vardy (d. 1765).

Vardy, like the previously-mentioned Flitcroft and Ware, and like Sir Robert Taylor (1714–88) and James Paine (1716–89), went to school on the numerous published designs of the neo-Palladians. It was said that in the 1760s Taylor and Paine nearly divided the practice of architecture between them: Taylor designed the biggest civic buildings in London, and Paine many of the greatest country houses. To these could be added a host of other neo-Palladian architects all over Britain and wherever British artistic influence extended overseas. In 1753 William Hogarth remarked impatiently, 'were a modern architect to build a palace in Lapland, or the West-Indies, Palladio must be his guide, nor would he dare to stir a step without his book'.[12]

The persistence of Palladianism is strikingly demonstrated by Sir Nikolaus Pevsner in his *The Englishness of English Art* when he places side by side illustrations of the remarkably similar façades of Campbell's Wanstead House, begun in 1715, and John Nash's Cumberland Terrace, London, begun in 1826. This juxtaposition also illustrates the fruitful application of neo-Palladianism to town planning, an application first made when John Wood the elder (1704–54) designed Queen Square, Bath, in such a way that his three great unified terraces of town houses, when viewed from the fourth side of the square, created 'the Appearance of a Palace of five hundred Feet in Extent'.[13] The neo-Palladian terraces that Wood and his son John (d. 1782) went on to build in Bath, notably the Circus (begun 1754), described by Matthew Bramble in *Humphry Clinker* as Vespasian's Colosseum 'turned outside in', and the Royal Crescent (1767–75), constituted the noblest town planning of that period, and the Woods conception of rows of town houses as palatial or monumental unities was adopted by architects in many other towns and cities.

The British neo-Palladian style was founded upon the study of Roman temples and a small number of other Roman public monuments, all in Italy; but by the second half of the eighteenth century architects had access to a considerable amount of new archaeological evidence about Roman domestic buildings and about a wide range of Roman, and increasingly of Greek, buildings outside Italy. New styles were disseminated by collections of engravings, the most notable of which were *The Ruins of Palmyra* (1753) and *The Ruins of Baalbec* (1757), both by Robert Wood (1716–71), *The Antiquities of Athens* (first volume, 1762), by James, 'Athenian', Stuart (1713–88) and Nicholas Revett (1720–1804), *Ionian Antiquities* (first volume, 1769), by Revett and others, and *The Ruins of the Palace of the Emperor Diocletian at Spalato in Dalmatia* (1764), by Robert Adam (1728–92), known as 'Bob the Roman'. The archaeological findings of Stuart and Revett immediately prompted some minor buildings copied from the Greek, for instance the garden buildings designed by Stuart himself at Shugborough and Hagley from 1758; their findings also gave support to the growing belief that the Romans were, in all cultural matters, inferior copyists of the Greeks, and thereby gave impetus to the Greek revival in general taste; but a Greek revival did not develop in the mainstream of British architecture until after 1789.

The failure of the Greek revival to make any earlier headway against the Roman style is largely attributable to the predominating influence of Sir William Chambers (1723–96) and Robert Adam. Chambers was an implacable opponent of the Grecian style; his numerous house-designs are Palladian in general plan, but more refined and eclectic in detail than the work of the Burlington circle, thanks to the much wider range of Roman models available to him after the researches of Wood, Adam, and others. His main achievement is Somerset House (1776–86), a great public shrine of learning, art, science, and bureaucracy, since its function was to accommodate government offices, the Royal Society, the Royal Academy, and the Society of Antiquaries. Chambers' design is a dignified amalgam of ancient Roman, Renaissance Italian, and modern French, lightened a little by what are effectively Pembroke-style Palladian bridges to break up the vast length of the building's river frontage. A very different aspect of Chambers's art and imagination is revealed by his work in the Chinese style, notably his pagoda at Kew (see Plate 16), but this belongs properly to the history of landscape gardening.

Though Chambers enjoyed royal favour and was widely regarded in the 1770s and 1780s as being at the head of his profession, his fame was somewhat overshadowed by that of Robert Adam and James Adam (1732–94), the brothers who gave their name to a style which was adapted almost as widely for the interiors of great houses as, in the same period, Capability Brown's style was adapted for the landscapes outside. For their interior designs the Adam brothers reject the gravity of Palladianism in favour of soft colouring, soft curves, light mouldings, and delicate enrichment; many of their new, elegant, decorative themes are drawn from recent archaeological study of Roman houses at Pompeii and Herculaneum, that is, from far less severely monumental sources than Palladio's. Though they are meticulously correct in every detail copied from the antique, the Adam brothers strive for novelty, variety, and ingenuity in their highly individual blend of Greek, Roman, Hellenistic, and English-neo-Palladian styles. In their exteriors they use Palladian components with a Vanbrugian sense of movement, a principle which Robert explains in the preface to the first volume of the *Works in Architecture of Robert and James Adam* (1773): 'Movement is meant to express, the rise and fall, the advance and recess, with other diversity of form, in the different parts of a building, so as to add greatly to the Picturesque of the composition.' Movement in architecture has the same effect as movement in a landscape: both 'serve to produce an agreeable and diversified contour, that groups and contrasts like a picture, which gives great spirit, beauty, and effect'.

'The Picturesque of the composition' could be found equally in the Gothic style, as Vanbrugh, whom the Adam brothers greatly admired, and Hawksmoor had already demonstrated. Although the various successive styles derived, whether distantly or closely, from classical models undoubtedly dominated seventeenth-century and eighteenth-century architecture, the native Gothic tradition never died out; Oxford, especially, continued to breathe the last enchantments of the Middle Ages, so that there was hardly a hiccup between the last building in an authentic, unselfconscious Gothic manner and the 'Gothic-revival' work of such men as Hawksmoor. Some of the neo-Palladians dabbled a little in Gothic: for instance Kent designed a choir screen at Gloucester Cathedral (1742), and was responsible for that much-satirized folly, Merlin's Cave (1735), built at Queen Caroline's orders in Richmond Gardens for the accommodation of Stephen Duck, the 'Thresher Poet', and a collection of patriotic busts and waxworks. As the example of Merlin's cave might suggest, neo-Gothic was at this period regarded as far less monumental, indeed far less serious, than any neo-classical style; some notion of the Gothic style's area of application may be derived from the full title of an early treatise on theory and practice, *Gothic Architecture, improved by Rules and Proportions, in many Grand Designs of Columns, Doors, Windows, Chimney-pieces, Arcades, Colonnades, Porticos, Umbrellos, Temples, and Pavillions, etc.* (1742) by Batty Langley (1696–1751). Though Langley was a useful carpenter and landscape gardener, he did not practise architecture; in the field of theory, his notion that there were five orders of Gothic, analogous to the classical orders, was, to say the least, misguided.

The most notable Gothic-revival architects before James Wyatt, whose work lies outside our period, are two amateurs. The first is the Warwickshire squire Sanderson Miller (1717–80), who built sham castles in the 1740s at the battlefield of Edgehill and in Hagley Park (the latter stained, according to Horace Walpole, with 'the true trust of the Barons' Wars'[14]), and, in a style only marginally more substantial and less unserious, designed a Gothic hall at Lacock Abbey (1753–55). The second is of course Horace Walpole himself, who, with professional assistance and the advice of a small committee of friends, designed his three-dimensional capriccio, Strawberry Hill (1748–77), the towered, battlemented exterior of which is deliberately and picturesquely irregular in plan and elevation, and the interior of which takes motifs from Westminster Abbey and Canterbury Cathedral, thus tempering the overall prettiness and gaiety with a little archaeology: see Plate 5. Walpole's little castle is a romantic literary conception. In the preface to his *Description of Strawberry Hill* he calls the house 'a very proper habitation of, as it was the scene that inspired, the author of the *Castle of Otranto*'; house and novel relate to one another in a kind of imaginative symbiosis.

Sculpture

At the end of the seventeenth century Wren justifiably complained about the uninventiveness and uncorrectness of English sculptors, but it was not until the end of the following century that a successful native school was established, with the work of John Flaxman (1755–1826) and his associates; in our period the history of sculpture in England is dominated by three immigrants, Peter Scheemakers (1691–1781) and Michael Rysbrack (1694–1770), both born in Antwerp and working in London from about 1720, and Louis François Roubiliac (1704–62), born in Lyons and working in London from the 1730s. All three can be fairly judged by their work in Westminster Abbey, the place which became, in the course of the eighteenth century, the most highly esteemed gallery of contemporary English sculpture. There are six monuments by Roubiliac there, ten by Scheemakers, and sixteen by Rysbrack, the greatest total by any sculptor.

The moral and cultural significance of funeral monuments in the Abbey is nicely brought out in Addison's *Spectator*, no. 26, which, in referring also to 'the poetical Quarter' made Englishmen for the first time aware of 'Poets' Corner'.

The work for which Scheemakers was best known in his day is the monument to Shakespeare in Poets' Corner (see Plate 7); it was carved in 1741 to a design by William Kent which adapts, to a somewhat more informal style, a famous pose (itself based upon an antique Greek original) used by yet another immigrant sculptor, Giovanni Baptista Guelfi, for the monument to James Craggs (1727), also in Westminster Abbey. Shakespeare leans with his right elbow on a pedestal bearing a pile of books and decorated by the heads of Queen Elizabeth, Henry V, and Richard III, his left hand pointing to a scroll which carries a misquotation of some of his most famous lines[15]; his legs are negligently crossed, the bent one resting on its toes. The easy informality of the Shakespeare monument caught the imagination of artists, so that some variant or other of this cross-legged pose was employed by every fashionable portrait painter and sculptor in the second half of the century.

Though it was a committee consisting of Burlington, Pope, and Dr Mead who commissioned Scheemakers to carve this monument, the favourite sculptor of the Burlington circle was the more correctly classical Rysbrack. Three of his finest monuments were, like Scheemakers' best-known work, to the designs of Kent; these are the monuments to Sir Isaac Newton (1731, see Plate 8) and its companion piece to the Earl of Stanhope (1733), both in Westminster Abbey, and the monument to the Duke of Marlborough (1732) in the chapel at Blenheim Palace. All three employ as background the pyramid, symbolizing eternity. Newton and Stanhope alike recline in Roman drapery upon a sarcophagus, in a pose derived ultimately from the figure of the Nile God in the Vatican. Stanhope is surrounded by military trophies; Newton leans upon a pile of books and points to a diagram of the solar system held up by two boys; above him is a globe depicting the path of the 1681 comet, and on this globe sits the figure of Astronomy, weeping. The Marlborough is a very large monument in a fairly small building. Its background pyramid rises clear through the cornice of the chapel, as if Marlborough's spirit is too large to be confined. Fame and History, with wings fluttering as if they have just alighted, guard a great sarcophagus, under which the ugly, writhing figure of Envy is trapped. On the plinth above imperiously stands the Duke, laurel-crowned and dressed as a Roman general; he is accompanied by his Duchess and their two sons. Flanking the pyramid, on the walls of the chapel, hang sculpted trophies and medals. All three monuments decorously combine portrait and allegory in solemn, heroic statement.

Among Rysbrack's free-standing statues are figures of George I (1739) at Cambridge, George II (1735) at Greenwich, both portrayed as Roman emperors, and the fine bronze equestrian statue of William III, also in Roman costume (1735), at Bristol, a figure based upon the famous second-century statue of Marcus Aurelius at Rome. For his admirable more-than-lifesize Hercules (1756) in the Pantheon at Stourhead, Rysbrack varied the well-known traditional pose, portrayed in the Farnese Hercules, by crossing the legs according to the model of a recently-discovered antique figure of Apollo. Following the classical principle soon to be restated by Reynolds, his figure is an imitation not of one model, but is an amalgam of the most perfect features of several. Horace Walpole writes:

> This athletic statue, for which he borrowed the head of the Farnesian god, was compiled from various parts and limbs of seven or eight of the strongest and best made men in London, chiefly the bruisers and boxers of the then flourishing amphitheatre for boxing, the sculptor selecting the parts which were the most truly formed in each. The arms were Broughton's, the breast a celebrated coachman's, a bruiser, and the legs were those of Ellis the painter, a great frequenter of that gymnasium.[16]

Rysbrack's work is Roman in spirit, its style severe, its manner restrained; the work of his greatest rival, Louis François Roubiliac, is altogether freer and more inventive. For all the major eighteenth-century London sculptors Westminster was a gallery where they competed with one another, but for Roubiliac it was something more: it was a theatre for allegorical and human drama. In his earliest great work there, the monument to the Duke of Argyll (1749), some of the main devices of Rysbrack's Newton reappear, but, instead of the noble repose of Rysbrack's work, all is movement. The Duke, wearing classical armour, reclines on his sarcophagus, half supporting himself on the lap of Clio, the Muse of History, who is caught in mid-word as she inscribes his name on the pyramid of eternity. Flanking the sarcophagus below him are the figures Eloquence and Minerva, Eloquence leaning forward in the act of speaking, with arm outstretched to involve the spectator in the action. Whereas the four figures on Rysbrack's Newton are tightly contained within the pyramid outline, Roubiliac's four figures flow asymmetrically inside and outside the pyramid.

In Roubiliac's monument to General Hargrave (1757) in Westminster Abbey the figures combine to even more theatrical effect. Upon a heap of massive, broken, leaning masonry perches a boy angel blowing the Last Trump. At its sound (imagined by the spectator) the general struggles free from his shroud and rises from his tomb, beside which the figure of Time, with bedraggled, drooping wings, breaks his scythe; below him, Death, a shrouded skeleton, his crown slipping from his skull, falls into the abyss. The most dramatic of all Roubiliac's monuments in Westminster Abbey, though, is the one to Lady Elizabeth Nightingale (1761, see Plate 6). Here the horrified bereaved husband supports his agonized wife and tries in vain to fend off a spear aimed at her by Death, again represented as a draped skeleton, who is stealing out from the open iron doors of the vault below. These two monuments express to the full the emotional excitement inspired by the great ideas of death and judgement. It is not surprising that John Wesley admired them and believed that they were the only two Christian monuments in all the mass of, in his view, otherwise unmeaning stone that cluttered up the Abbey; they are visual counterparts to a great body of immensely popular fervid, evangelical imaginative literature on death and judgement, which included such works as Young's *Night Thoughts* (1742–46), Robert Blair's *The Grave* (1743), and James Hervey's 'poetic prose' *Meditations among the Tombs* (1746, twenty-five editions to 1791).

In the same year as the Nightingale monument, Roubiliac completed his Westminster Abbey monument to Handel, in which the composer is caught in the act of taking down the notes of 'I know that my Redeemer liveth' as they are played by an angel seated upon clouds; it seems a solemn and grandoise work when compared with Roubiliac's first statue of Handel, which was set up in Vauxhall Gardens in 1738. In this earlier work Handel is seated, his elbow resting on bound volumes of his own scores as he plays a lyre; he listens intently to the music while a naked boy at his feet transcribes the notes. Though Handel's Apollonian lyre, decorated by a sun-burst, hints at sublimity, his pose is almost negligent, and the costume is contemporary and casual, including as it does nightcap, open-necked shirt, and slippers; all elements combine to express both genius and humanity. The two Handel statues, like the Hargrave monument, depend in part for their effect upon imagined, frozen sound.

Scheemakers, Rysbrack, and Roubiliac were all prolific makers of portrait busts at a time, between Kneller and Reynolds, when English portrait painting was not at its best. Historical as well as contemporary busts were much in demand: Scheemakers provided a head of Dryden and Rysbrack a head of Milton for Poets' Corner; Pope owned busts of Spenser, Shakespeare, Milton, and Dryden by Scheemakers. Rysbrack's most charac-teristic portrait busts of contemporary public figures generally follow the style of late-Republican Rome, showing their sitters with hair close-cropped and eyes unincised; the general effect is of gravity and severe virtue, con-veying the impression that these men are the heirs of the heroic senators and citizens of pre-Augustan Rome. Roubiliac generally employs a far less restrained style; he often shows his sitters in unbuttoned contemporary dress, with nightcap; though more constricted in this form than in the funeral monument, he still strives for emotional expressiveness and even the effect of arrested motion. In a remarkably sensitive bust of Pope (four versions, 1738–41), for instance, he catches a contraction of the skin above the eyebrows, the sign of a headache.

Pope sat also to Rysbrack, and his own interest in sculpture is reflected in his poetry by, for instance, the imaginary statues in the *Temple of Fame*, the personifications of the Thames in *Windsor Forest*, of Melancholy in *Eloisa to Abelard*, and of Dulness surrounded by 'Guardian Virtues' in the *Dunciad*, where he also makes an unjustly dismissive reference to the work of Cibber's sculptor father Caius Gabriel Cibber (1630–1700). Sculpture was important for Thomson too. In *Liberty* (1736), IV. 134–206, he reviews the beauties of antique sculpture; in the *Seasons* he makes much of the old notion of sculpture as arrested movement and the old conceit of people 'struck to marble' (*Summer*, ll 1217–22, 1344–49, *Winter*, 930–35); his Niobe-like mourner, 'for ever silent and for ever sad' (*Summer*, ll. 1222), gave a fruitful hint to Keats. That eighteenth-century poetical pictorialism mentioned in the opening paragraph of this chapter was indebted almost as much to sculpture as to painting: the 'picturesque', so often remarked upon by critics, was also the 'statuesque'.

Painting

Horace Walpole complains in the Preface to his *Anecdotes of Painting* (1762) that there is no history of English painting, then he admits that the greatest English painters and sculptors have all been born abroad. As we have seen, this was the case in sculpture; at the beginning of the eighteenth century it appeared to be the case in painting too. Certainly, as the century opened, the dominant presence in English painting was the portraitist Sir Godfrey Kneller (d. 1723), a German by birth, who had studied in Rome and had worked in England since the 1670s. A court artist under two dynasties, the first painter ever to be made a baronet (by George I in 1715), his praises sung by Dryden, Prior, Addison, Steele, and Pope, he was the maker of grand state portraits of monarchs and similarly aloof and formal portraits of the nobility. His best-known work is the series of forty-two portraits, painted between 1702 and 1717, of members of the Whig dining society known as the Kit-Cat Club. Of this series the finest is perhaps the portrait of the bookseller Jacob Tonson, which is more easy and informal than is usual with Kneller, and more concerned with the character than with the dignity of its subject. Kneller's only serious rival was the Swedish-born Michael Dahl (1659–1743), in whom the seventeenth-century style of Sir Peter Lely and Kneller lingered until it was supplanted in the 1730s and 1740s by a more human, informal, domestic style of portraiture.

After Kneller's death the leading court painter was Sir James Thornhill (1675–1734), not a portraitist, but the sole English heir of an ambitious school of Continental decorative painters settled in England in the seventeenth century. By 1700 the leaders of this school were the Italian Antonio Verrio (1639–1707) and the Frenchman Louis Laguerre (1663–1721), a couple well known to literary students through Pope's *Epistle to Burlington*:

> On painted Ceilings you devoutly stare,
> Where sprawl the Saints of Verrio or Laguerre,
> On gilded clouds in fair expansion lie,
> And bring all Paradise before your eye.
>   (ll. 145–48)

Thornhill, who gradually ousted Laguerre at Blenheim and succeeded Verrio at Hampton Court and Windsor, maintains the seventeenth-century grand manner, originally intended to serve absolutism and now adapted to glorify constitutional monarchy. In 1718 his status as national artist was recognized by his appointment as 'History Painter to his Majesty'. His finest work is in the Painted Hall at Greenwich Hospital (1707–26), where his subjects include *The Landing of William III* and *The Landing of George I*. It is on a sketch of the latter work that he made a list of objections to the realistic representation of such a subject, coming to the conclusion that it is better to show the scene 'as it should have been rather than as it was'; it is better to be unhistorical than 'ugly'.[17] This is what any history painter of the day would have decided; what distinguishes Thornhill from foreign predecessors in his field is that he considers realism as a serious possibility.

Although Thornhill's famous son-in-law William Hogarth (1697–1764), the epitome of realism in eighteenth-century graphic art, scorned the 'pother' made by connoisseurs about 'the grand style of history painting',[18] he cherished the ambition of succeeding to Thornhill's established position as history painter; to this end he adorned the staircase of St Bartholomew's Hospital with huge paintings of *The Pool of Bethesda* and *The Good Samaritan* (1735–36), both full of reminiscences of the old masters. Although he fabricated other paintings of this solemn, elevated, derivative kind later in his career, such work went against the grain. Hogarth never went to Italy and was impatient with the excessive respect displayed towards all things Italian by English artists and connoisseurs; his inclination is as much to ridicule as to follow the grand style.

Unlike most contemporary artists, Hogarth did not make his living from formal portraiture, though he was justifiably proud of his portrait (1740) of the philanthropist Captain Coram, which he believed would arouse the envy of 'the whole nest of Phizmongers'.[19] *Captain Coram* is life-size and full-length, and, for all the ordinary humanity and honesty expressed in face and figure, there is something of the grand manner in the pose and in such accessories as pillar, curtain, charter, and symbolic terrestrial globe. A type of portraiture more characteristic of Hogarth is the 'conversation piece', the small-scale group portrait of people apparently engaged in some ordinary activity and not formally posed for the benefit of painter or viewer; it is an art form at the furthest imaginable remove in scale and spirit from that apotheosis of the sitter which occurs in Thornhill's decorative paintings. The conversation piece is potentially dramatic: significantly, Hogarth's best-known paintings in this kind are his popular *Scene from the Beggar's Opera* (1728–29), painted in several versions, and his vivacious and tender representation of amateur dramatics, *Children playing The Indian Emperor before an Audience* (1731–32); but when Reynolds credits Hogarth with having 'invented a new species of dramatick painting',[20] he is of course referring to his paintings and engravings of 'modern moral subjects', where the painter not only depicts a scene but invents an action.

The first work of this new species was *The Harlot's Progress* (1731), consisting of six paintings, now lost, and the engravings from them, which Hogarth compared to the scenes from a play, describing himself not as 'artist' but as 'author'. In these successive scenes the story is told of a country girl's corruption on her arrival in London, and her decline into misery, imprisonment, and death. *The Rake's Progress* (1735) and *Marriage à la Mode* (1745), the first in eight, the second in six scenes, tell similar stories of corruption and decline in a higher social setting; each 'reads' like a dark comedy of manners, enlivened by allusive wit in the poses, grouping, and accessories. In later series, *Industry and Idleness* (1747) in twelve scenes, *The Four Stages of Cruelty* (1751), and *An Election* (1754), each in four scenes, and the companion pieces of *Beer Street* and *Gin Lane* (1751) the attack on corruption is extended more widely, and Hogarth's social-reforming impulse emerges even more strongly than before.

The last is probably the best known of these (see Plate 11); in it there is a wealth of reading matter. 'Gin Lane' is a scene of corruption, cruelty, decay, misery, and death, set recognizably in a disreputable quarter of St Giles. The pawnbroker's is the only prosperous house in view; its sign mockingly appears to take the place of a cross directly over the statue of George I on Hawksmoor's steeple; at the door, the carpenter pledges his tools and the housewife her pots and pans, in order to buy gin. Over the hellish entrance to the cellar is the inscription 'Drunk for a Penny, Dead drunk for two pence, Clean Straw for Nothing'. Horrors abound: a barber, ruined by gin, has hanged himself; a drunken woman lets her baby fall headlong from her breast; and a ballad-seller, with a sinister upturned glass, is so emaciated that he is almost the image of death itself. On publication, this engraving was partnered by *Beer Street*, where Hogarth glorifies the English national drink, showing a scene where the only building not in good repair is the pawnbroker's, and all the people in view are well-fed, prosperous, and happy. The pair of contrasting prints makes an indignant condemnation of the then-prevalent social evil of cheap gin, an evil attacked also in *An Enquiry into the Causes of the later Increase in Robbers* (1751) by Hogarth's friend Henry Fielding. Many of his contemporaries accused Hogarth of caricature, but Fielding justly defended him in the Preface to *Joseph Andrews* (1742) as 'a Comic History-Painter' who provides 'the exactest Copy of Nature': 'It has been thought a vast Commendation of a Painter, to say that his Figures *seem to breathe*; but surely, it is a much greater and nobler Applause, *that they appear to think.*'

There is nothing to compare with Hogarth's wit, drama, and intelligence in the conversation pieces of his contemporaries, such as the specialist in this form, Arthur Devis (1711–87), whose paintings convey a haunting sense of time arrested; or Joseph Highmore (1692–1780), whose work in this kind was good enough to be mistaken for Hogarth's and who excited much attention with his twelve paintings (1744) illustrating Richardson's *Pamela*; or Francis Hayman (1708–76), one-time scene painter at Drury Lane and illustrator of Shakespeare, Milton, Pope, and others. Hayman painted many of the large scenic pictures which adorned the boxes in the pleasure gardens of Vauxhall from the 1740s onwards; some of his scenes were modern historical subjects from the Seven Years War, but the best were on charming, simple, rural subjects such as *The Dance of the Milkmaids on Mayday*, *The Country Dancers round the Maypole*, *Bird-nesting*, and *The Play at Cricket*.[21] They are a visual equivalent to that important literary tradition of 'naturalized pastoral' to which Gay's *Shepherd's Week* and Goldsmith's *Deserted Village* belong.

In Hayman's rustic scenes, and more so in Devis's representations of country gentlemen and their families at proprietorial ease in spacious parks, the conversation piece is assimilated into the nascent English tradition of landscape painting. Topographical art flourished in seventeenth-century England, but it was only with George Lambert (1700–65), scene painter for John Rich at Lincoln's Inn Fields and Covent Garden, and with John Wootton (c. 1682–1764), the successful painter of horses and sporting subjects, that English painters began properly to exploit the pictorial possibilities of view-making and the unifying effects of light and atmosphere. Landscape was low in the hierarchy of kinds. Jonathan Richardson (1665–1745), a friend of Pope and the most influential English art theorist before Reynolds, observed that landscapes are inferior to history paintings because 'they cannot Improve the Mind, they excite no Noble Sentiments'[22]; Reynolds believed that a landscape painter could satisfy the principle of 'perfect form' to which the historical painter aspired only by rejecting 'common nature' and creating ideal landscapes, as Claude Lorrain had done. In Lambert's *Hilly Landscape with a Cornfield* (1733) 'common nature', the ordinary, workaday, open-air English countryside, is perhaps for the first time the subject of an ambitious oil-painting, but Lambert and Wootton, generally speaking, share Claude's opinion, as summarized by Reynolds, 'that taking nature as he found it seldom produced beauty'.

What English artists and collectors regarded as the pantheon of landscape art is briefly alluded to in Thomson's famous lines describing the paintings which hung in his Castle of Indolence:

> whate'er *Lorrain* light-touch'd with softening Hue,
> Or savage *Rosa* dash'd, or learned *Poussin* drew.

Whichever Poussin is meant, Nicholas or Gaspard, these are the painters who inspired Richard Wilson (1714–82), the Welshman who was widely recognized as the founder of the English landscape school. Following a fruitful inconographic tradition begun by Nicholas Poussin, Wilson painted his version of the shepherd's tomb in a timeless Arcadian landscape, *Ego fui in Arcadia* (1755); emulating Salvator Rosa in his most melodramatic vein, he painted *Landscape with Banditti: the Murder* (1752); taking suggestions from the dramatic stormy landscapes of Gaspard Poussin, he created his masterpiece in the grand style, *The Destruction of the Children of Niobe* (1760); but he was so far more heavily indebted to 'whate'er *Lorrain* light-touch'd with softening Hue' that he became known quite early in his career as 'the English Claude'. 'Wilson at his best understood the two chief lessons of Claude, that the centre of a landscape is an area of light and that everything must be subordinated to a single mood'[23]; he regularly adopts the typically Claudian compositional scheme, with its large trees against the light as a framing device, its clearly demarcated foreground with figures, mythological, heroic, or rustic, its land mass and architectural feature, such as tower or bridge, to establish the middle ground, and its view beyond into the infinite, luminous distance.

Wilson's are heroic landscapes. In his *Landscape Capriccio with the Tomb of the Horatii and the Villa of Maecenas at Tivoli* (1754), for instance, the eye is drawn through the landscape from one ruin to another, and simultaneously the reflective mind follows the decline of Rome from glorious republic to corrupt and luxurious empire. Even without such direct allusions, the Claudian manner bestows dignity upon nature wherever it is found. This point is illustrated in two Wilson landscapes painted in 1762, five years after the painter's return from Italy: one is *Holt Bridge on the River Dee*, the other is a *River Scene on the Arno*; they differ in topographical detail, but are remarkably alike in composition and in their idyllic, lyrical, yet lofty mood of nostalgia, a mixture of regret and delight. The heroic equation between Italy and Britain is even more striking in another capriccio, *The Lake of Nemi or Speculum Dianae with Dolbadarn Castle* (1764). This is one of four versions by Wilson of an ideal landscape with Diana and Callisto; all of them have Lake Nemi (Diana's mirror) in the middle distance, but this one introduces into the background two of the painter's favourite picturesque Welsh subjects, Dolbadarn Castle and Snowdon. It is with his Welsh castles and mountains nevertheless that Wilson moves furthest away from Claude; nowhere more so than in *Cader Idris: Llyn-y-Cau* (*c.* 1774, see Plate 9), which is a completely treeless scene, a raw, uncompromising mass of earth and rock and brooding lake, viewed not from some safe, low vantage point in the valley but at close range. This landscape is as undramatic, truthful, and mysterious as any lonely upland scene evoked by Wordsworth's poetry.

Wilson's younger contemporary, Thomas Gainsborough (1727–88), writing in 1764 to decline a commission to paint a particular view for an aristocratic patron, forthrightly rejects the merely topographical. He declares that 'with respect to real views from Nature in this county he has never seen any place that affords a subject equal to the poorest imitations of Gaspar [Poussin] or Claude', and that if the patron will have anything of Gainsborough's the subject must be of the artist's own brain.[24] This is true of his first important landscape, *Cornard Wood* or *Gainsborough's Forest* (1748), in which, unusually for that period, the compositional conventions of seventeenth-century Dutch landscape are employed, and is even more true of the works known as 'fancy pictures', that is, conversation pieces with low-life subjects refined by pastoral sentiment. A typical early Gainsborough fancy picture is *The Woodcutter courting a Milkmaid* (1755, see Plate 10), in which the two foreground figures named in the title have the calm, beautiful features and graceful attitudes of characters in some contemporary French rococo pastoral scene, but are complemented in the background by a donkey and an old peasant couple (with the man's shirt hanging out through a hole in the seat of his breeches) who belong to the Dutch comic-realistic genre tradition. The composition is drawn together by a picturesque, knotted, decaying tree, which shares the romance of one pair of figures and the realism of the other. In other fancy pictures an element of grandeur is sometimes introduced, for instance in *The Harvest Wagon* (*c.* 1767), where the energetic handling of a pyramidal figure-group is based upon Rubens's *Deposition from the Cross*; but the later tendency is towards more and more pastoral idealism and sentiment, culminating in the 1780s in a series of paintings of remarkably beautiful, sweet, and winsome beggar boys and cottage girls.

In Gainsborough's latest, most highly idealized treatment of rustic sub-jects we can perhaps detect the fruits of his experience as a successful fashionable portrait painter, the reviver of Van Dyck elegance, unequalled in his lyrical evocation of feminine grace. The later landscapes, including the landscape backgrounds featured in his portraits, were painted in the studio from scenic models made of 'pieces of looking-glass, broken stones, cork, coal, sand, clay, mosses, lichen, dried weeds, and that most rococo of green vegetables, broccoli',[25] to create an effect closer to impressionism than to topography; but what is perhaps Gainsborough's most evocative landscape, the background to his early conversation piece *Mr and Mrs Andrews* (*c.* 1749), conveys a distinct sense of place. This representation of a relaxed, almost dandified, squire and his elegant, doll-like wife, beside their rich harvest field, surrounded by their well-stocked pastures and pleasant woods, perfectly conveys an impression of civilized proprietorship, and portrays a whole way of life.

Gainsborough, like Hogarth and Blake, never studied in Italy. His great rival Sir Joshua Reynolds (1723–92) went to Italy at the same time as Wilson and was no less enriched by the experience; what Wilson found in Claude to lend dignity, meaning, and emotion to English landscape, Reynolds found in Raphael, Michaelangelo, and the antique sculptors to lend the same qualities to English portraiture; and as Wilson had been partly anticipated by Lambert, so Reynolds was partly anticipated by Allan Ramsay (1713–84), another Italian-trained painter. Ramsay's full-length portrait of Norman Macleod (1748) no doubt prompted Reynolds's choice of the classical Apollo Belvedere pose for his portrait of Captain Keppel (1753), but Reynolds's storm-tossed seascape in the background introduces a fresh, unclassical emotionalism and sense of drama that is quite foreign to Ramsay. This same Apollo Belvedere attitude serves to classicize the exotic in Reynolds's portrait of Omai (1776, see Plate 12), the famous Tahitian who was brought to England from Captain Cook's second voyage and fêted as the very epitome of the noble savage.

In his *Discourses on Art* Reynolds accepts the conventional view that portraiture is a lower form of art than history painting because it ordinarily does not deal with general ideas. However, in the fourth *Discourse* (1771), he points to means by which the portrait artist might approach the grandeur of generality, and raise and improve his subject by such devices as ennobling a sitter's countenance or changing the dress from a temporary fashion to one more permanent. Such change of dress is perhaps easiest to make in portraits of women, as in *Lady Sarah Bunbury sacrificing to the Graces* (1765), where the graceful pose is adapted from a classical relief, or in the more striking *Sarah Siddons as the Tragic Muse* (1784), where there is some novel and expressive visual quotation from Michaelangelo's sublimely heroic prophets in the Sistine Chapel. Visual quotation to a very different effect is found in *Garrick between Comedy and Tragedy* (1760), a witty modern parody of the old theme of Hercules between Virtue and Pleasure, in which Reynolds personifies Comedy in the style of Correggio and that of Tragedy in the style of Guido Reni, but reveals Garrick wholly, naturally, informally, and inimitably in a speaking likeness. Wit and tenderness are combined in a child portrait,

Master Crewe as Henry VIII (1776), which is a parody of Holbein, and, naturally enough, tenderness predominates in Reynolds's many intimate pictures of mother and small child. Two paintings of this type of subject, *Countess Spencer and her Daughter* (1761) and *The Duchess of Devonshire and her Daughter* (1786), make a nice pair because the mother in the later painting is in fact the child in the earlier: both are full of tender feeling, but 'the serenity of the earlier picture, which owes allegiance to the Italian masters of the High Renaissance, has given way to a lively and dramatic style akin to Rubens' baroque'.[26] Reynolds's eclectic use of the old masters always illuminates the characters of his subjects. For all the idealizing tendency of his art, his portraits are as various as his sitters, and when he adopts the grand manner he never deserts natural truth; so, for instance, the portrait of Lord Heathfield (1788), showing him holding a great key and standing as firm as the Rock of Gibraltar which he defended so resolutely, portrays a powerfully individualized character, while at the same time it conveys the great general idea of imperial strength.

The leading portraitist after Reynolds and Gainsborough was George Romney (1734–1802). Like Reynolds, he grafted the antique manner on to the fashionable portrait, as in *Mrs. Yates as the Tragic Muse* (1771); but his most expressive work is in his fifty or so pictures of the fascinating Emma Hart, later Lady Hamilton, in the 1780s. She is painted in a great variety of roles, as Circe, Calypso, Cassandra, St Cecilia, Mary Magdalene, Joan of Arc, a Bacchante, Contemplation, to name but a few, so that the entire series could almost be a visual enactment of Pope's *Epistle to a Lady*.

In the hierarchy of kinds, portraiture was ranked below history painting; so was 'genre', that is, the realistic representation of scenes of common life, what Reynolds called 'low and confined subjects' and 'the various shades of passion, as they are exhibited by vulgar minds, (such as we see in the work of Hogarth).'[27] Reynolds made it his life's work to raise portraiture to the expression of great and general ideas, and thereby in some sense unite it with history painting; something comparable was done for genre painting by Joseph Wright (1734–97), the first important English painter to pursue a career in the provinces, for which peculiarity he is known as 'Wright of Derby'. Concerning him David Piper writes:

> In his work there comes something of the hard-headed,
> practical yet romantic excitement of the dawn of the Industrial
> Revolution. He saw the world in a forced and sharpening light –
> sometimes artificial, the mill-windows brilliant in the night,
> faces caught in the circle of the lamp, or the red glow of an iron
> forge, casting monstrous shadows. This was an old trick –
> deriving from Caravaggio and the Dutch candlelight painters –
> but with it Wright brought out a sense of exploration and
> exploitation – scientific, intellectual, and commercial, the spirit
> of the Midlands of his time.[28]

Wright painted moonlit Derbyshire landscapes, Italian grottoes, the eruption of Vesuvius, and a great variety of subjects from romantic and sentimental literature, but his most strikingly original subjects are drawn from science, as in *A Philosopher giving a Lecture on the Orrery* (1766, see Plate 13) and *An Experiment on a Bird in the Air Pump* (1768), or from industry, as in *A Blacksmith's Shop* (1771), where heroic figures reminiscent of old master representations of Hercules and Vulcan are posed in a classical ruin, or as in *The Forge* (1772), where the setting is realistic but the figures are no less heroic.

Like Wright, George Stubbs (1724–1806) raised the dignity of one of the 'lower' kinds of painting (in his case animal painting); like Wright, he was strongly influenced by the scientific advances of the century; but, additionally, he contributed directly to these advances by his studies of anatomy. Having devised an elaborate apparatus to suspend the decaying carcasses of horses while he gradually stripped them, he recorded every stage of dissection in precise yet haunting drawings which were published in *The Anatomy of the Horse* (1766), a work equally of science and of art. It was said by a fellow painter that when Stubbs travelled to Italy in 1754 he did so only 'to convince himself that nature was and always is superior to Art, whether Greek or Roman, and having received this conviction he immediately resolved upon returning home'.[29] Nevertheless, such a painting as his famous *Brood Mares and Foals* (1762) has the mysterious repose of a Greek frieze, and his even more famous paintings in the 1760s and 1770s of a lion attacking a horse are rehandlings of a favourite subject for sculpture in late antiquity.

When the great improvement in the social status of British painters was confirmed by the incorporation of the Royal Academy in 1768, the high standing of Reynolds was at the same time duly confirmed by his election as first President. The *Discourses* which he read to his colleagues and students at the Academy every year or every second year from 1769 to 1790 were effectively a statement of the Academy's policy, and they make it clear that one of the primary educational aims of the Academy was the training of a national school of history painters. Hogarth, Reynolds, Wilson, Wright, and Stubbs all testify, directly or indirectly, in their very different kinds of painting, to the continuing prestige of history; but the regular history painters among their younger contemporaries make a relatively poor showing. History painting was partly reanimated by the archaeological discoveries which also influenced architecture in the second half of the century. *Dawkins and Wood discovering the Ruins of Palmyra* (1758) by Gavin Hamilton (1723–98), a Scotsman settled in Rome, is effectively a manifesto of archaeologically-inspired neo-classicism; it was followed in the 1760s by Hamilton's noble illustrations of the *Iliad* and of Roman legendary subjects, such as *The Oath of Brutus* (1764), which anticipate the work of Jacques Louis David.

English history painting at this period was, however, directed also towards modern subjects as a result of patriotic feelings generated by the Seven Years War. *The Death of Wolfe* (1771) by Benjamin West (1738–1820) achieved enormous success on exhibition and as an engraving; so did *The Death of Chatham* (1780) by John Singleton Copley (1738–1815). In both paintings a modern scene is imbued with the heroic grandeur normally reserved for an antique hero or a Christian saint, so that what is created by poses, expression, and lighting is an ideal beyond the mere historical fact. These two painters, both of them Americans working in London, went on to paint many huge battle pieces in a similarly grand manner. A more ambitious history painter in this period was the Irishman James Barry (1741–1806), whose most representative work is the cycle of huge allegorical pictures, *The Progress of Human Culture* (1777–83), with which he decorated the walls of the Great Hall of the Royal Society of Arts in their new building by Robert Adam in the Adelphi. Barry's cycle traces the rise and progress of arts in ancient Greece and then in England, the natural heir of Greece. The painting that attracted most attention is *Commerce, or the Triumph of the Thames*, which shows the river god in his chariot, supported or pushed by Captain Cook, Sir Walter Raleigh, Sir Francis Drake, and (inexplicably) the musicologist Charles Burney; the god and his attendant nereids distribute the manufactures of the industrial Midlands, while personifications of the four continents offer their typical produce, grapes and wine, silks and cottons, furs, slaves; in the background a vast lighthouse is lifted up by a partly submerged giant, his hand alone as huge as a full-rigged ship. Such a daring and absurd combination of allegory and history with private megalomaniac fantasy points forward to the work of Barry's admirer and greatest disciple, William Blake.

Although the much-desired triumph in history painting never came, the eighteenth century saw the foundation of a distinctive and flourishing English school of portraiture and an increasingly important school of landscape. Before the end of our period, the work of such unambitious masters as Alexander Cozens (1717–86) and his son John Robert (1752–97), and of Paul Sandby (1730–1809) and Francis Towne (1740–1816) was beginning to give respectability to water-colour as a medium in its own right, and was helping to introduce a new freedom, impressionism, and sense of atmosphere into landscape painting: the common English scene and the ever-changing common sky were now fully recognized as fit subjects for the painter. In the long run, the work of these water-colourists was of more significance than all the schematically illustrated theorizing about 'the picturesque' by William Gilpin (1740–1804), whose famous volumes of *Observations* 'relative to picturesque beauty' in various parts of the British Isles began to appear from the press in 1782. The greatest triumphs of landscape painting were to come with Turner and Constable after 1789: for all the considerable achievement of Wilson and Gainsborough, the garden made a greater contribution to landscape art in our period than the studio. In an international context the landscape garden was, indeed, eighteenth-century England's most notable contribution to the visual arts.

Landscape gardening

At the opening of the century, English gardens were generally laid out in a formal, symmetrical manner, following Italian, Dutch, or French models.

The part of the garden closest to the house was handled architecturally, 'like one of the rooms out of which you step into another',[30] so that it consisted of a regular series of geometrical compartments formed by closely clipped shrubs and trees, and straight gravel walks, stone paths, terraces, steps, and balustrades. Such compartments might be *parterres de broderie*, carpeted with dwarf evergreens, bedded flowers, and coloured earths, brick dust, coal dust, white and yellow sand, and so on, in regular patterns, or *parterres anglaises*, carpeted only with grass; some would contain basins and perhaps fountains. In the largest gardens the principles of geometry were imposed, if possible, as far as the eye could see: garden walks were extended by great vistas along canals and vast radiating avenues of trees; within this larger framework were basins and fountains, statues, green cabinets of *salles vertes*, mazes, and small woods, all organized symmetrically about an axis.

The masterwork in this grand style was Versailles, as laid out for Louis XIV by André le Nôtre (1613–1700), which became a model for magnificent princely gardens all over Europe, including the one laid out for William III in front of Wren's new east front of Hampton Court Palace. Henry Wise (1653–1738), one of the gardeners at Hampton Court, also worked for James Brydges, Duke of Chandos, on the elaborate, expensive garden at Cannons, Middlesex, thought by Pope's contemporaries to be the original of Timon's villa in the *Epistle to Burlington* (1731). In the loco-descriptive poem *Cannons* (1728), by Samuel Humphreys, a writer inexplicably overlooked by Pope when he came to write the *Dunciad*, Chandos's estate is hailed as a 'Grand Versailles' where the house

> Swells o'er the landskip and commands the plains:
> His pomp the prospect all around refines,
> And every object with his lustre shines.
>
> (ll. 78–80)

These verses express the spirit of a magnificent and autocratic style of gardening by which palatial grandeur is radiated outwards far from the palace itself.

The irregular landscape garden which gradually evolved in eighteenth-century England was seen by many as a reaction against the symmetry, ostentation, and tyranny of the French style, but it was also in some respects a natural development from the French. One should not forget that Pope, perhaps the most influential publicist of the new English style, linked Inigo Jones and Le Nôtre in terms of highest praise in his *Epistle to Burlington*, ll. 43–46. By creating a means of imposing a unified aesthetic conception upon a huge area of ground, the French gave an example to English gardeners. Not all seventeenth-century French gardens were laid upon terrain as flat as Versailles: some of them, like some of the finest gardens of Renaissance Italy, obtained effects of startling beauty from irregularities in the ground, and similar effects were achieved in England, when, for instance, in the 1690s the French gardener Grillet, a pupil of Le Nôtre, designed the great cascade on a steep hillside at Chatsworth, Derbyshire, in the style of those at St Cloud and at Marly, the last and favourite of Louis XIV's gardens. It was in a French treatise, A. J. Dézallier d'Argenville's *La théorie et la pratique du jardinage* (1709), well known in its English translation of 1712 by John James (1672–1746), that English gardeners found the first published reference to the 'ha-ha' or dry moat, which, serving as a substitute for a wall, hedge, or fence, kept the cattle out of the garden proper and admitted a view of the park or countryside beyond; but whereas Dézallier's theory and practice separated garden and countryside aesthetically, the English tended to use the ha-ha to make it appear 'as if the adjacent Country were all a Garden'.[31]

That last phrase is quoted from Stephen Switzer (1682–1745), who propounded in his *Nobleman, Gentleman, and Gardener's Recreation* (1715), enlarged as *Ichnographia Rustica* (1718), a system of 'Extensive or Rural and Forest Gardening', where the timber and pasture parkland is united with formal garden features, such as basins and terraces, to make a single design. In this system nature is methodized to some degree according to the geometrical principles of the French grand manner which Switzer admired, but is also 'by a kind of fortuitous Conduct persued through all her most intricate Mazes, and taught even to exceed herself in the *Natura-Linear*',[32] by which Switzer means the use of serpentine lines for paths and watercourses. There is an anticipation of Hogarth's 'line of beauty' here, but Switzer, in the classical tradition, advocates a union of the beautiful with the useful by including productive land in his ornamental layouts. His Latin motto for *Ichnographia Rustica*, cobbled together from two Horatian tags,[33] is translated as

He that the beautiful and useful blends,
Simplicity with greatness, gains all ends.

In the Preface to his treatise Switzer declares that he first began to write on gardening in order to introduce a less expensive style than the one hitherto practised; in this he is evidently responding to a general movement.

Economy, not to speak of the problem posed by the growth of planted materials in highly formal layouts, gradually encouraged a less elaborate manner of large-scale gardening than the one modelled upon Versailles. The chief objection to the gardens at Cannons was the expense of maintaining them. The Duke of Chandos laid them out with the rich profits of his years as Paymaster-General to the Forces in the War of the Spanish Succession, but he lost money in the South Sea scheme and had to economize almost as soon as the gardens were completed. It is known that in May 1721 the parterre alone engaged the attention of sixteen men and two women, carrying flowerpots back and forth, and weeding and clipping.[34] This could not last; the close-clipped hedges grew ragged, and it may be that this slowly-apparent reversion to nature added point to the triumphant and prophetic conclusion of Pope's attack upon Timon's garden in the *Epistle to Burlington*:

Another Age shall see the golden Ear
Imbrown the Slope, and nod on the Parterre,
Deep Harvests bury all his pride had plann'd,
And laughing Ceres re-assume the land.
(ll.. 73–76)

Even royal gardens were not exempt from economies: shortly after her accession, Queen Anne ordered Henry Wise to reduce by two-thirds the cost of keeping up the royal gardens, and in 1704 the box *broderie* at Hampton Court was replaced by turf in what Switzer proudly calls 'the plain but noble English manner'.[35] Addison asked in the *Spectator*, no. 414 (1712) 'why may not a whole Estate be thrown into a kind of Garden by frequent Plantations, that may turn as much to the Profit as the Pleasure of the Owner?' One of the strongest arguments for 'extensive or forest gardening' was the eventual profit from timber. John Evelyn's concern in *Sylva* (1664), for over a century the standard work on trees, was to make good the depredations of the Civil War in the nation's forests and to ensure future supplies of timber for the Royal Navy, as well to advise on the ornamental value of woodlands. Nearly 200 years later Surtees wrote in *Hawbuck Grange* (1847), Chapter 12, 'We remember when the wise ones used to counsel a man to stick trees in his fences at every yard and used to calculate to a fraction what they would be worth at the end of the world.' Bathurst's vast landscape garden at Cirencester, laid out with the help of Pope's advice, produced a valuable timber crop, and some of the spare capital of his literary friends, including Pope, was invested in plantations which would 'future Navies grow'. In the spring of 1725 Pope was asking Bathurst to send sheep to crop the springing lawns at Marble Hill, where the two friends, with Charles Bridgeman, had taken a hand the previous autumn in laying out the Countess of Suffolk's garden. A prominent feature in George Lyttelton's garden at Hagley later in the century was a great hill laid out as a sheep-walk, with an obelisk on its summit and James, 'Athenian', Stuart's celebrated Doric temple on its lower slope. Writers of topographical poetry expressed gratification whenever they found a great house that was, 'tho' Palladian, yet a farm'[36]; handbooks and histories of gardening, and even the staidly scientific *Annals of Agriculture*, analysed the beauties and the economics of the *ferme ornée*; and Pope perfectly expresses the spirit of useful and ornamental rural improvement in the *Epistle to Burlington*, ll. 177–90.

The blend of use and beauty was no mean object, but landscape gardeners also pursued the more exalted aim of creating ideal nature out of the forms of common nature, of teaching nature, in Switzer's words, 'even to exceed herself', and indeed re-creating nature as it might have appeared fresh from God's hand. As Switzer's Horatian tags reveal, the sister-art of poetry was an important influence upon gardening. Such influence appeared in the celebrations of rural life by Virgil and Horace, in the sweet pastoral landscapes of Theocritus, Virgil, and their countless successors, all celebrating harmony between man and the gentler appearances of external nature, and in literary earthly paradises, the most notable of which was, of course, Milton's in *Paradise Lost*, Book IV, whose brooks ran 'With mazie error under pendant shades', and fed

> Flours worthy of Paradise which not nice Art
> In Beds and curious Knots, but Nature boon
> Powrd forth profuse on Hill and Dale and Plaine,
> Both where the morning Sun first warmly smote

The open field, and where the unpierc't shade
Imbround the noontide Bowrs: Thus was this place,
A happy rural seat of various view.
(ll.241–47)

Joseph Spence, about 1752, said that Milton's paradise is 'chiefly like the new natural taste' in gardening, and some twenty years later Horace Walpole elaborated upon what he called Milton's prophetic eye of taste: 'The description of Eden is a warmer and more just picture of the present style than Claude Lorrain could have painted from Hagley or Stourhead.'[37]

Milton's description of ideal nature, as one must conceive paradise to have been, is far less like the geometrical formality of Versailles than it is like that common nature over which Shaftesbury enthused in his celebrated and influential dialogue *The Moralists* (1709). In this philosophical rhapsody the Platonist Theocles undertakes a great imaginative journey through the natural world, showing that 'the Wildness pleases' (see Ch. 5 above), and provokes this response from Philocles, the *quondam* sceptic:

> Your *Genius*, the *Genius* of the Place, and the GREAT GENIUS
> have at last prevail'd. I shall no longer resist the Passion
> growing in me for Things of a *natural* kind; where neither *Art*,
> nor the *Conceit* or *Caprice* of Man has spoil'd their *genuine Order*,
> by breaking in upon that *primitive State*. Even the rude Rocks,
> the mossy *Caverns*, the irregular unwrought *Grottos*, and
> broken *Falls* of Waters, with all the horrid Graces of the
> *Wilderness* it-self, as representing NATURE more, will be the
> more engaging and appear with a Magnificence beyond the
> formal Mockery of princely Gardens. [38]

Though his subject is wild nature (the art of the divine genius), Shaftesbury inspired gardeners to 'consult the genius of the place', a vital spirit which is expressed in living growth and in given, natural contours.

Addison has already been mentioned for his suggestion that a whole estate might be thrown into a kind of garden; in the same number of the *Spectator* (414) he praises large seventeenth-century French and Italian gardens because their sheer extent gives an exalted pleasure to the imagination; but about the time he was writing, English gardens were being laid out to provide unconfined prospects, particularly where Vanbrugh had a hand in siting the house, as he did in 1713 at Duncombe Park, Yorkshire, and in 1715 at Claremont, Surrey. The 'genius of the place' was surely consulted by the designer (probably Vanbrugh) of the great grass terrace at Duncombe, which runs on a serpentine ha-ha above the lip of an escarpment commanding immense views. Charles Bridgeman (1680–1738), who succeeded Wise as royal gardener, designed a geometrical, formal garden for the gentle, even slopes at Eastbury in Dorset, but at about the same date, c.1716, he produced a much freer, irregular layout for the abrupt contours at Claremont, which enjoyed what Colen Campbell called a 'singularly Romantick' site. The existence in 1718 of Wray Wood on its low hill and the curving line of what had once been a village street in front dictated, or inspired, a certain informality in the garden layout at Castle Howard in Yorkshire, which Switzer adduces, along with Lord Rochester's garden at Petersham, near Twickenham, as the earliest examples of the new, freer style of gardening. Similarly, the retention of an old lane's oblique line gave the first asymmetrical bias to the famous garden at Stowe, Buckinghamshire, as it developed under Bridgeman's hand from 1713. In this garden which survives even under the later work of William Kent and 'Capability' Brown as his masterpiece, Bridgeman gained his effects by the interplay of formal avenues, lakes, lawns, and parterres, with irregular woodland walks and the use of the ha-ha to break the barrier between garden proper and park.

For the historian, Bridgeman stands midway between Le Nôtre and Brown; so does Pope who, as we have seen, praises Le Nôtre and, as it happens, prophetically damns the style of Brown in the figure of Villario, who, 'Tir'd of the scene Parterres and Fountains yield/ . . . finds at last he better likes a field' (*Epistle to Burlington*, ll. 87–88). Pope makes it clear in this same poem that 'Nature' is to be consulted as much in rearing the column, bending the arch, swelling the terrace, and sinking the grotto, as in the planting and contouring of the ground itself; his notion of the relationship between nature and art is nicely revealed in a not altogether playful suggestion for natural architecture:

> I have sometimes had an idea of planting an old Gothic
> cathedral, or rather some old Roman temple, in trees. Good
> large poplars, with their white stems, cleared of boughs to a
> proper height, would serve very well for the columns, and
> might form the different aisles, or peristiliums, by their
> different distances and heights. These would look very well
> near, and the dome, rising all in proper tuft in the middle,
> would look as well at a distance.

Pope thought that Bathurst should have 'considered the genius of the place' and raised two or three artificial mounts at Richings Park, his garden in Buckinghamshire, 'because his situation is all a plain, and nothing can please without variety'.[39] All beauties were comprehended in variety, and if variety of contour and cover were not provided by the original site then it should be supplied by the artist.

Variety was one of the painterly qualities that Pope saw in the new style: 'All gardening is landscape-painting. . . . Just like a landscape hung up.'[40] In 1712 Addison said 'a Man might make a pretty Landskip of his own Possessions' (*Spectator*, no. 414); Vanbrugh had pleaded and plotted as early as 1709 for the retention in Blenheim Park of the picturesque medieval remains of Woodstock Manor, which, suitably planted about, 'wou'd make One of the Most Agreeable Objects that the best of Landskip Painters can invent'[41]; in the 1720s landscape gardening was taken up by William Kent, who was, in Walpole's words, 'painter enough to taste the charms of landscape, bold and opinionative enough to dare and to dictate, and born with a genius to strike out a great system from the twilight of imperfect essays'.[42] The most notable early garden laid out in the painterly manner was Rousham in Oxfordshire, where Bridgeman in the 1720s prepared the main lines for Kent's famous work in the 1730s. In 1728 Pope found it 'the prettiest place for water-falls, jets, ponds inclosed with beautiful scenes of green and hanging wood'[43]; ('scenes' here has the sense of painted stage-hangings, as in Pope's *Epistle to Augustus*, l. 315, 'Back fly the scenes'). William Kent's own drawing of Venus' Vale at Rousham (Plate 17) perfectly conveys the theatrical and painterly effects of his design. In the second half of the century Horace Walpole claimed to have found several English gardens resembling the admired paintings of Albano, Poussin, or Claude: for instance, at Hagley there was 'a pretty well under a wood, like the Samaritan woman's in a picture of Nicolo Poussin'; at Stanstead in Sussex, 'When you stand in the portico of the temple and survey the landscape that wastes itself in rivers of broken sea, the very extensive lawns, richly enclosed by venerable beech woods, recall such exact pictures of Claude Lorrain that it is difficult to conceive that he did not paint them from this very spot.'[44] Pope never compares a garden landscape with the work of any named painter; nevertheless it is possible that the system of retiring and assembling shades that he worked out in his own garden may owe something to the contrast of deep and shallow spaces in a background that one finds in Titian, Nicholas Poussin, and other seventeenth-century painters.

Pope was a presiding genius of the gardening revolution in the 1720s and 1730s, less by the example of his own five-acre garden at Twickenham than by his writings and his advice to wealthier friends as they laid out their estates. So, for instance, we find him with Lord Digby at Sherborne in Dorset, advising on the way in which the ruined Norman castle on the estate could be brought into a series of picturesque garden compositions, and itself be used as a place 'to enjoy those views, which are more romantick than Imagination can form them'. Where there was no genuine romantic structure, Pope might advise a sham ruin, such as King Alfred's Hall (see plate 18), built in Cirencester Park in the 1720s to celebrate the monarch who supposedly inaugurated trial by jury, confirmed the old Saxon institution of Parliament, and founded the Royal Navy and Oxford University, and was therefore venerated by Englishmen as the great guardian of English liberty, learning, and power. King Alfred's Hall lay in what Pope called 'Lord Bathurst's enchanted forest'. Pope wrote: 'I look upon myself as the Magician appropriated to the place, without whom no mortal can penetrate into the recesses of those sacred shades. I could pass whole days, in only describing the . . . visionary beauties, that are to rise in those scenes.' This is whimsical up to a point, but does nevertheless reveal the mood in which the creator of the garden responds to his creation; landscape gardening is an act of the imagination. Pope's letters often refer to his delight in visionary dream: as he himself explains, 'The more I examine my own mind, the more romantick I find myself . . . let them say I am romantick.'[45]

In Pope's own little suburban garden (see Plate 15) the bounds were concealed by dense thickets, to create a secret, enclosed space within which Bridgeman's principle of a relatively formal straight central axis with flanking areas treated irregularly was applied in a freer way and upon a smaller scale than was usual in Bridgeman's work. It was the tranquil and graceful setting for a Horatian way of life, but it also had something of the feeling of a classical sacred landscape focused upon certain associative monuments. At the eastern, more open, sunny end, the main feature was the shell temple, a rococo pleasure dome; at the western end the landscape was elegiacally darkened with solemn evergreens to focus on an obelisk commemorating the poet's dead mother.

From this garden a passage ran beneath the main road and into the basement of Pope's house, where he created his famous grotto. The further entrance of the grotto looked out over a lawn to the River Thames and the countryside beyond: when its doors were closed the grotto became a camera obscura,

> on the Walls of which all the objects of the River, Hills, Woods,
> and Boats, are forming a moving Picture in their visible
> Radiations: And when you have a mind to light it up, it affords
> you a very different Scene: it is finished with Shells interspersed
> with Pieces of Looking-glass in angular forms; and in the
> Ceiling is a Star of the same Material, at which when a Lamp (of
> an orbicular Figure of thin Alabaster) is hung in the Middle, a
> thousand pointed Rays glitter and are reflected over the Place.[46]

A visitor wrote of the great variety of sparkling stones in the grotto, and the falling water and hidden mirrors there, which, when the lamp was lit, presented 'an undistinguishable Mixture of Realities and Imagery'.[47] It would not be too much to claim that Pope's grotto is a concrete metaphor of that cave of dreams, the poet's mind: the 'cell of Fancy, my internal sight', as Adam called it in *Paradise Lost* (VIII. 460–61), when describing his dream of the creation of Eve. From antiquity the analogue of the human mind has been alternatively mirror or lamp (Plato, Plotinus): Pope's grotto could be a camera obscura, Locke's image of the mind (see Ch. 3 above), reflecting images of the outside world, yet it possessed a lamp of its own which shone upon the undistinguishable mixture of realities and imagery. From the mental security of his garden Pope discharged satires against the court and the city whose traffic rumbled above his grotto; he took his moral stand as the hermit of Twickenham in a self-created landscape which was the reflection of his own imaginings.

With the possible exception of Stourhead, no well-known eighteenth-century English landscape garden was so charged with private meaning and personal feeling as Pope's was. The greater gardens were generally associative in a far more public fashion, none more so than Cobham's celebrated 400-acre garden at Stowe, worked over through sixty years by a regular apostolic succession of gardeners (Bridgeman, Vanbrugh, Kent, and Brown), and likened by a visitor in the 1760s to 'one of those places celebrated in antiquity, which were devoted to the purposes of religion, and filled with sacred groves, hallowed fountains, and temples dedicated to several deities; the resort of different nations; and the object of veneration to half the heathen world'.[48] Stowe is a shrine of public virtue which announces a tendentious programme of opposition–Whig political ideas in the style and siting of its many temples. Such a programme is particularly insistent in the area of the garden known as the Elysian Fields. High on one side of a little valley, standing like the Temple of the Sibyl at Tivoli, was the Temple of Ancient Virtue, designed by Kent *c.* 1734 to contain more-than-life-size statues of Homer, Lycurgus, Socrates, and Epaminondas. Facing it from lower ground on the far side of a little stream called the River Styx was the Shrine of British Worthies, an open-air gallery, also designed by Kent, to display portrait busts of sixteen national heroes, including men of contemplation from Shakespeare to Locke, Newton, and Pope, and men of action from Alfred the Great to Sir John Barnard (1685–1764), the merchant and parliamentarian. These British worthies literally looked up to the building which housed images of the worthiest poet, lawgiver, moral philosopher, and soldier of the ancient world. For a while there was a third building close by, a Temple of Modern Virtue, built in the form of a ruin, as a concrete satire against Sir Robert Walpole.

Cobham's political views were also made explicit in the Temple of Liberty designed by Gibbs in 1741, appropriately, in view of its dedicatory purpose, in the Gothic style. Such Gothic-revival structures with such a purpose were by no means novel. Before 1718 James Tyrrell the historian, a student of the Gothic constitution, who, like his friend Locke, wrote against Filmer's *Patriarcha* (see Ch. 4 above), built in his garden at Shotover Park, near Oxford, a Gothic temple as a memorial to Anglo-Saxon political liberties. Among many landscape ornaments at Hagley Park, Worcestershire, laid out in the 1740s and 1750s by Cobham's political ally George Lyttleton, was that sham-ruined castle thought by Horace Walpole to have 'the true rust of the Barons' Wars'. Walpole no doubt is pointing here to a political association, for, according to Whig history, it was in the Barons' Wars between Simon de Montfort and Henry III that Parliament first gained its independent powers; but the castle at Hagley was not primarily a political statement. On its wooded hilltop it made a very dramatic eyecatcher in an eminently picturesque landscape composition; its one full-sized and three ruined towers served usefully to house one of Lyttelton's gamekeepers, his cow, his hens, and his coal, while its irregular curtain walls enclosed a farmyard. The kind of associative programme that such a building represents is well summarized by Switzer as early as 1715: 'the Erection of all Lodges, Granges, and other Buildings, that Gentlemen are oblig'd to build for Conveniency' should take the form of 'some antiquated Place, which will be more beautiful than the most curious Architecture', for 'there seems to be a much more inexpressible Entertainment to a Virtuous and Thoughtful Mind in desolate Prospects, cool murmuring Streams and Grottos . . . than in what many of our modern Designers have recommended'.[49] The pleasure of ruins, denied when Woodstock Manor was cleared away at Blenheim, was allowed free indulgence in many eighteenth-century gardens laid out in such a way as to incorporate views of ancient castles, as at Sherborne, or abbeys, as at Studley Royal in Yorkshire, where ornamental waters lead the eye to Fountains Abbey, or as on the great terrace walk between two neat classical temples at Duncombe Park in the same county, where gaps in the plantations give a succession of picturesque views of Rievaulx Abbey.

12   Sir Joshua Reynolds, *Omai*.

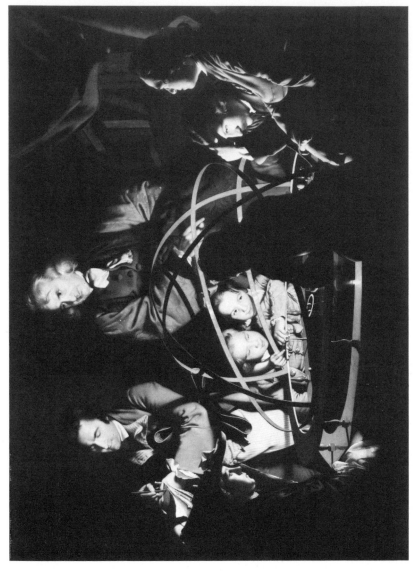

13 Joseph Wright, *A Philosopher giving a Lecture on the Orrery*.

14 Johann Zoffany, *The Death of Cook.*

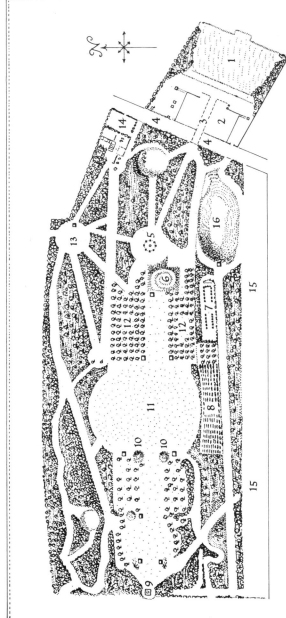

1 *Grass plot between the house and the River Thames*   2 *The house*   3 *Grotto and underground passage*
4 *Road from Hampton Court to London*   5 *Shell temple*   6 *Large mount*   7 *Stoves (i.e. hothouses)*
8 *Vineyard*   9 *Obelisk in memory of Pope's mother*   10 *Small mounts*   11 *Bowling green*
12 *Grove*   13 *Orangery*   14 *Garden house*   15 *Kitchen garden*   16 *Amphitheatre (?)*
□ *Square marks indicate urns and statues*

15   Plan of Alexander Pope's garden.

The Mosque

16 Pagoda and Mosque at Kew.

17 William Kent, *Venus' Vale at Rousham.*

18 King Alfred's Hall in Cirencester Park.

19 Lake and Pantheon at Stourhead.

20 Palladian Bridge at Wilton.

A garden with as much classical grandeur as Stowe, but far more private feeling, is Stourhead in Wiltshire, laid out in the 1740s by Henry Hoare the banker, just after the deaths in rapid succession of two of his children and his wife had left him with one heir, a son aged thirteen. Near the house a few streams ran on the bare downland; and so, consulting the genius of the place 'that tells the waters to rise or fall', he built a dam and raised a lake, which he planted about with trees and buildings to form pictures: see Plate 15. The garden is experienced as a series of views over the lake from a serpentine path near the water's edge, but at one point the path descends into a grotto built over the headspring of the River Stour. The river bursts from the urn of the god, 'The stream, like time shall hasten from my urn', and flows beneath and around the sleeping nymph. One recalls Eve awaking in Paradise to the murmuring sound of waters that issued from a cave and spread into a liquid plain. The grotto is a place for solitary reverie and reverence. The genius of the place is a haunting presence, a something hinted in the play of light and shadow on the ripples of his hidden river.

Beyond the grotto is the Pantheon: the most important visual component in the garden, it is a copy by 'Burlington Harry' Flitcroft of the Pantheon in Rome, which appears on a celebrated Claude painting, once at Stourhead, now in the National Gallery; the painting is a view of Delos, showing the priest of Delos, Anchises, Aeneas, Ascanius (three generations of the founding family of Rome). It was in the temple at Delos that Aeneas prayed for a home of his own (*Aeneid*, III); when he comes to Latium, it is the river god (of Tiber) who tells him that this is his home (*Aeneid*, VIII); Aeneas then cries: 'Nymphs, whose birth is of the rivers, and Father Tiber, you, and your hallowed stream, receive me. Whatever spring may fill the pools which are your home, and wherever you yourself emerge in grandeur from the soil, always shall you be celebrated by me'; later that day Aeneas joins in the sacrifice to Hercules. Appropriately, Henry Hoare's Pantheon houses Rysbrack's fine statue of Hercules. Virgilian allusions in the inscriptions, statuary, buildings, and even in the layout of the garden, seem to indicate that the Stourhead landscape celebrates the fact that Henry Hoare, like Aeneas, was establishing a family in a place.[50] Among surviving landscape gardens (for Pope's garden has now virtually disappeared) Stourhead has a unique quality, given by the intimate connection between a particular place and the feelings of one highly imaginative individual person. Such a distinctive projection of the human psyche into the physical forms of landscape is not to be found in the surviving work of the professional eighteenth-century gardeners, for all their success in embodying the age's general notions of 'nature', 'liberty', 'beauty', and so on. Henry Hoare's garden, as a highly individual composition of symbolic forms which crystallize the ideas and emotions of its creator, is in some extended sense a poem.

William Shenstone's famous 'ornamented farm', 'The Leasowes', which has now almost disappeared, had a comparable private, poetic quality, heightened by the fact that it was dotted about, not with expensive buildings, but with seats and urns designed to carry inscriptions, those forms of ornament that speak most directly to the garden visitor. An inscription projects its author's feeling upon the object or landscape it points to, and so becomes a means of uniting spectator with landscape in an act of imagination, most typically one charged with elegiac feeling. The rural inscription, along with the epitaph, became a regular minor verse-form of the eighteenth century; practitioners of it included Shenstone, Thomas Warton the younger, Southey, Wordsworth, and, most notable of all, Akenside, whose rural inscriptions are closest to the original models of this kind of writing, the votive epigrams of the *Greek Anthology*. Shenstone's belief that the main object of the landscape gardener is to involve the mind and literary imagination of the spectator emerges clearly in his practical handbook, *Unconnected Thoughts on Gardening*, in his *Works* (1764).

As we have seen, eighteenth-century garden ornaments were generally either classical or Gothic in style, but as the century wore on, oriental styles were increasingly employed. In the garden laid out by Charles Hamilton in the 1740s at Painshill, Surrey, dense plantations of cedar, larch, fir, and pine on the poorer soil gave the impression of a wild forest, within which, appropriately, were to be found a hermitage and a Gothic tower; descending from this area, the visitor came to Elysian glades dressed and clumped with flowering shrubs and blossoming trees, where he found not only a Grecian temple but a Turkish tent. At Shugborough Park in Staffordshire, in addition to the historically significant Greek-revival buildings mentioned above (p. 140), there was a Chinese fretted bridge leading to a Chinese house, said to be a true copy of a building sketched at Canton in 1743 by one of Commodore Anson's officers during their heroic circumnavigation of the world.

Though hardly anything was known in England concerning Chinese architecture and gardening, China was present in the thoughts of gardeners from the very beginning of the landscape movement; so much so, that when the French adopted the English style in the second half of the eighteenth century they insisted on calling it 'le jardin anglo-chinois'. Sir William Temple, writing in 1685 'Upon the Gardens of Epicurus', raised, but then dropped, the possibility of laying out English gardens in what he conceived to be the Chinese manner of 'sharawadgi' or pleasing wildness; his suggestion was revived by Addison in the *Spectator*, no. 414 (1712). Even Burlington's disciple in Palladianism, Robert Castell, whose reconstruction of Pliny's garden in his *Villas of the Ancients Illustrated* (1728) made it look like the work of Bridgeman, digresses to praise the style of Chinese gardening, which 'may not improperly be said to be an artful confusion, where there is no appearance of that skill which is made use of, their Rocks, Cascades, and Trees, bearing their natural forms'.[51]

The Chinese House at Shugborough and the House of Confucius in Kew Gardens belong to the 1740s; in the next decade many such brightly painted little pavilions, pagodas, and kiosks were erected, and many Chinese bridges too, including one across the Thames at Hampton Court. In 1759 the Duke of Cumberland created a Chinese landscape at Virginia Water, which he completed by having a replica of a Chinese junk to sail on the lake. By this date French descriptions of the Imperial Gardens at Peking had been published in English (one translation, in 1752, being the work of Pope's friend Joseph Spence); also the architect Sir William Chambers, who as a young man had travelled to Canton, had published his *Designs of Chinese Buildings, Furniture, Dresses, etc.* (1757). At Kew Gardens Chambers designed, in addition to the famous pagoda which still stands, an aviary and a bridge in the Chinese style, and a Moorish-cum-Gothic mosque.

Chambers's insistence, both in his *Designs of Chinese Buildings* and his *Dissertation on Oriental Gardening* (1772), that landscapes should agitate the mind by a great variety of passions is a calculated reaction against the exclusion of artifice and association in the landscapes of Lancelot, 'Capability', Brown (1716–83), who was far and away the most prolific designer of gardens in the second half of the eighteenth century. In Brown's hands landscape is a visual composition, not a series of associative statements; his art depends upon the contrast and relation of curves, seeming to embody the idea of the beautiful elaborated by Burke (see Ch. 5 above). Burke found beauty to consist in qualities of softness, delicacy of form, smoothness, and gradual variation. Brown creates a placid, reposeful naturalism by the use of simple means: a vast sweep of turf is punctuated by trees used singly or in irregular clumps or wavy belts, the contours of the land dip to reveal glimpses of a great, smooth, winding lake, and rise beyond to the encircling woodland. All formality disappears, no art is apparent. At Blenheim, for instance, he swept away the great parterre laid out by Henry Wise, with the walks and Vanbrugian bastions which gave it an appropriately military air; in their place he brought lawns up to the walls of the house, beside which he placed a few dark-foliaged trees to provide frames for the natural-seeming scenes to be viewed from the house windows. At Petworth in Sussex his lawns allowed deer to graze up to the windows of the principal reception rooms. Chambers complained that Brown's gardens 'differ very little from common fields, so closely is common nature copied in most of them'.[52] An obituarist wrote of Brown 'that when he was the happiest man, he will be least remembered; so closely did he copy nature that his works will be mistaken'.[53]

Brown once described his system of planting and landscaping in terms that might conceivably be thought of as literary, when he remarked to Hannah More, '*there* I make a comma, and there, where a more decided turn is proper, I make a colon',[54] but his gardens lack both the specific literary allusions of a Stowe or a Hagley, and the expressive and self-exploratory character of Stourhead or of Pope's little garden at Twickenham. Mid-century landscape gardeners used to the full devices of all the visual arts which, according to Reynolds, 'address themselves primarily and principally to the imagination', for they made very considerable use of buildings and sculptures, and they observed Pope's cardinal rule that 'all gardening is landscape-painting'. Temples and castles in gardens and in Wilson's land-scape paintings, like the satiric particulars in Hogarth's moral scenes, or the poses and costumes in Reynolds's portraits, or the roman-republican severity of Rysbrack's busts, are visual quotations which furnish the mind with literary, artistic, moral, historical, or political associations. The variety of such associations in all the visual arts testifies to an eclecticism which, as I shall show in the next chapter, is a striking feature of eighteenth-century culture.

Notes

1. *Purity of Diction in English Verse* (1952), p. 40.

2. *Discourse on Art*, edited by R. R. Wark (New Haven, 1975), pp. 229, 241.

3. J. Summerson *Architecture in Britain, 1530 to 1830*, revised edition (Harmondsworth, 1955), p. 168.

4. *Complete Works of Sir John Vanbrugh*, edited by B. Dobrée and G. Webb (1927), IV, 44.

5. *The Buildings of England*, Volume VI, *London except the Cities of London and Westminster* (1952), pp. 156–57.

6. Summerson, p. 176.

7. Quoted in J. Burke, *English Art, 1714–1800* (Oxford, 1976), p. 14.

8. Ibid., p. 8.

9. Ibid., p. 24.

10. Summerson, p. 191.

11. See M. Mack, *The Garden and the City* (1969), pp. 122–23, 272–78, and works cited. There is probably a reference to the expense of building Houghton Hall in Johnson's *London* (1738), l. 57.

12. *The Analysis of Beauty*, edited by J. Burke (Oxford, 1955), p. 62.

13. John Wood, *Description of Bath* (1742–43), II, 14, quoted in Burke, p. 12.

14. *Horace Walpole's Correspondence*, edited by W. S. Lewis, XXXV, (1973) 148; letter to Richard Bentley, September 1753.

15. See David Piper, *The Image of the Poet* (Oxford, 1982), pp. 79–82, and 'Monumental Mistakes' in *Times Literary Supplement*, 23 September and 4 November, 1965, pp. 832, 988.

16. *Anecdotes of Painting*, edited by R. N. Wornum (1876), III, 36.

17. E. Wind, 'The Revolution of History Painting', *Journal of the Warburg and Courtauld Institutes*, 2 (1938–39), 116–27.

18. 'Autobiographical Notes' in *Analysis of Beauty*, p. 202.

19. Ibid., p. 218.

20. *Discourses*, p. 254; fourteenth *Discourse* (1788).

21. See L. Gowring, 'Hogarth, Hayman, and the Vauxhall Decorations', *Burlington Magazine*, 95 (1953), 10.

22. *The Connoisseur* (1719), p. 45.

23. K. Clark, *Landscape into Art* (1949), p. 70.

24. E. Waterhouse, *Gainsborough* (1958), p. 15.

25. Burke, p. 220.

26. E. Waterhouse, *Painting in Britain, 1530 to 1790* (Harmondsworth, 1953), p. 170.

27. *Discourses*, p. 51; third *Discourse* (1770).

28. D. Piper, *Painting in England, 1500–1880* (Harmondsworth, 1965), p. 57.

29. B. Taylor, *Animal Painting in England* (1955), p. 30.

30. Sir William Temple, 'Upon the Gardens of Epicurus' (written 1685), in *Five Miscellaneous Essays*, edited by S. H. Monk (Ann Arbor, 1963), p. 24.

31. Stephen Switzer, *The Nobleman, Gentleman, and Gardener's Recreation* (1715), p. xxviii.

32. *Ichnographia Rustica* (1718), I, 87.

33. 'Omne tulit punctum, qui miscuit utile dulci' (*Ars. Poet.*, 343), 'Simplex munditiis' (*Carmina* I. v. 5).

34. M. Hadfield, *A History of British Gardening* (1969), pp. 165–66.

35. *Ichnographia Rustica*, I, 83.

36. John Dalton, describing Claremont in *Epistle to the Countess of Hertford, at Percy Lodge* (1744).

37. Joseph Spence, *Observations, Anecdotes, and Characters of Books and Men*, edited by J. M. Osborn (Oxford, 1966), I, 421; I. W. U. Chase, *Horace Walpole, Gardenist* (Princeton, NJ, 1943), pp. 14–16.

38. *Characteristicks of Men, Manners, Opinions, Times*, second edition (1714), II, 393–94.

39. Spence, I, 253, 251, 256–57.

40. Ibid., I, 252.

41. *Complete Works of Sir John Vanburgh*, IV, 30.

42. Chase, p. 26.

43. *Correspondence of Alexander Pope*, edited by G. Sherburn (Oxford, 1956), II, 513.

44. *Horace Walpole's Correspondence*, XXV, 148–49; Chase, p. 30.

45. *Correspondence*, II, 238–39, 115, I, 367.

46. Ibid., II, 296–97.

47. A description of 1747, quoted in Maynard Mack, *The Garden and the City* (1969), p. 239. My interpretation of the grotto follows Mack.

48. Thomas Whately, *Observations on Modern Gardening* (1770), p. 226.

49. *Noblemen, Gentlemen, and Gardener's Recreation* (1715), p. 239.

50. See K. Woodbridge, *Landscape and Antiquity: Aspects of English Culture at Stourhead, 1718 to 1838* (Oxford, 1970).

51. *Villas of the Ancients Illustrated* (1728), p. 117.

52. *Dissertation on Oriental Gardening* (1772), p. v.

53. Quoted in D. Stroud, *Capability Brown* (1950), p. 200.

54. Ibid., p. 198.

Chapter 7
Models

Hume, Burke, and others tried unavailingly to fix the standard of taste as a reaction against the great variety of tastes which they saw about them in the middle years of the century. 'There is at present', said Hogarth in 1753, 'a thirst after variety'[1]; variety of taste was the reflection of a multiplicity of models. Cultural horizons were widening rapidly, as global exploration was undertaken more and more with the primary intention of seeking knowledge, rather than merely trade or power; Burke wrote of these widening horizons in a letter of 1777 to the historian William Robertson:

> Now the Great Map of Mankind is unrolld at once; and there is
> no state or Gradation of barbarism, and no mode of refinement
> which we have not at the same instant under our View. The
> very different Civility of Europe and of China; The barbarism
> of Persia and Abyssinia. The erratick manners of Tartary, and
> of arabia. The Savage State of North America, and of New
> Zealand.[2]

As an example of Burke's own excited response to widening horizons we may turn to his praise of the enterprising New England whalers, quoted above (p.91). We find a similarly romantic sense of distance in, for instance, the conclusion of Pope's *Windsor Forest*, in the great geographical flights of the *Seasons*, and in Thomson's inspiration for such imaginary aerial voyages, Shaftesbury's *Moralists*.

Elsewhere, in *Advice to an Author*, Shaftesbury somewhat uncharacteristically inveighs against the contemporary flood of travel books, with their '*Barbarian* Customs, *Savage* Manners, *Indian* Wars, and Wonders of the *Terra Incognita*'.[3] Locke, by contrast, thought such narratives important enough for him to act as adviser to the booksellers John and Awnsham Churchill when in 1704 they began publication of a great collection of voyages and travels, the first large-scale work of its kind since Hakluyt and Purchas. Eighteenth-century voyagers brought home a vast quantity of new information; they revealed societies hitherto little known or even unknown to Western Europe, and they made possible what philosophers liked to call 'a natural history of man'. The historical record was fragmentary, but observation of the present condition of primitive peoples in other parts of the world could throw light upon the early history of all men, and a study of exotic civilizations could illuminate the natural laws by which all societies grew and decayed. Travel was in a sense time-travel into the past.

As early as 1692, in his influential essay *Of Heroic Virtue*, Sir William Temple complains that the outlying parts of the civilized world have been neglected by historians; he then duly offers his own survey of four exotic cultures far beyond the spatial and temporal bounds of the classical world, that is China, Peru, the Gothic North, and Islam. All of these societies, and many others, were closely or cursorily examined by eighteenth-century Englishmen in search of moral, political and artistic lessons. The attentions of satirists (most notably the Scriblerans, in particular Swift, when, for instance, he puts several of Temple's observations on the Chinese into Gulliver's mouth) failed to restrain the vigorous growth of an increasingly exotic cultural eclecticism. Nevertheless, the primary cultural model for England in 1700 was the familiar civilization of classical Rome.

Roman

By the beginning of the eighteenth century an idea of Augustan Rome had maintained a strong presence in English cultural life for over a century: Jonson praised James I, Waller praised Cromwell, and Dryden praised Charles II, under the name of Augustus; but after 1688 the hostile, Tacitean attitude to Augustus is more evident in England. The message is the same, whether it comes from the Whig Commonwealthmen in *Cato's Letters* or the Tory Bolingbroke in the *Craftsman*, whether from Swift the controversialist or Gibbon the judicious historian, that Augustus was an infamous, cruel, and artful tyrant, and his destruction of the Roman constitution marked the beginning of Rome's irreversible decline (see Ch. 4 above). More than this, he was lewd and profligate. When Bolingbroke presents his idea of a patriot king and meditates upon the importance of the moral character of a ruler, he recalls the colourful period 'when *Rome* was ransacked by the pandars of *Augustus*, and matrons and virgins were stripped and searched, like slaves in a market, to chuse the fittest to satisfy his lust'. Bolingbroke adds: 'we must not wonder that the people, who bore the *tyrants*, bore the *libertines*; nor that indulgence was shewn to the vices of the great, in a city where universal corruption and profligacy of manners were established'.[4]

Augustus's complicity in the murder of Cicero, his banishment of Ovid, and his notorious institution of royal censorship of the arts showed him to be no consistent friend of literature; nevertheless liberty-loving Englishmen had to come to terms with his patronage of Virgil and Horace, and with their willing acceptance of this patronage. It was commonplace that the *Aeneid* was written in order to reconcile the subjected Romans to Augustan absolutism; Augustus is the object of flattery in Virgil's *Eclogues* and *Georgics*, as well as in many of Horace's poems. As Christopher Pitt observed, 'we should have entertained a far different Notion of *Augustus*, who was in reality no better than the Enslaver of his Country . . . if *Virgil* and *Horace* had not so highly celebrated him'.[5] One reaction was simply to condemn the servility of these court poets, as Dryden does when he compares Horace with Juvenal and describes the former as 'a temporizing poet, a well-mannered Court slave', or as Joseph Warton does, over 100 years later, when he observes that 'the integrity of *Lucan* and *Juvenal*, though not their genius, was superior to that of Horace and Virgil; and that the Death of one and the Exile of the other, confers on them more real honour, than all the favours lavished on the other *two* great *Court Poets*'.[6] Alternatively, it was possible to point out that Virgil and Horace were not Augustan poets at all, because their minds were formed under the republic. Shaftesbury, for instance, notes in *Advice to an Author* (1710) that it was the fate of Rome 'to have scarce an intermediate Age, a single Period of Time, between the Rise of Arts and Fall of liberty'. He claims that Virgil and Horace 'were plainly such as had seen the Days of Liberty, and felt the sad Effects of its Departure'; though Augustus was 'a Prince naturally cruel and barbarous', his two great court poets taught him how to charm mankind: 'They were more to him than his Arms or military Virtue; and, more than *Fortune* herself, assisted him in his Greatness, and made his usurp'd Dominion so inchanting to the World, that it cou'd see without regret its Chains of Bondage firmly riveted.'[7]

The complexity of eighteenth-century attitudes to the Roman Augustan age are nicely illustrated by Pope. He was aware of the paradox that the two noblest Roman poets were also, morally speaking, slaves; of Virgil's *Georgics* he remarked to Spence that it opens with 'the grossest flattery to Augustus that could be invented. The turn of mind in it is as mean as the poetry in it is noble'[8]; his *Epitaph on one who would not be buried in Westminster Abbey* (1738) proudly asserts his own moral superiority over the Augustan court poets:

> Heroes and Kings! your distance keep:
> In peace let one poor Poet Sleep,
> Who never flatter'd Folks like you:
> Let Horace blush, and Virgil too.

Nevertheless, Pope chose the mask of Horace for the most personal and most outspoken of his mature poems in the 1730s, and in doing so made much of the contrast between Horace's situation as a court favourite and his own as an opposition writer. The ironies of the *Epistle to Augustus* comprehend the belief that George II is somewhat similar to the Roman Augustus politically and morally, while at the same time being totally unlike him in that he is not a patron of the modern Horace (i.e. Pope); also that Pope is like Horace in his poetic art, but unlike him in not wanting patronage from Augustus: 'Pope parodies flattery of a monarch, with Horace's own flattery of Caesar as Pope's satiric butt. The praise that sits so grotesquely on the narrow shoulders of George II copies praise almost equally unfitting for Augustus, a successful tyrant and subverter of poetry.'[9] This paradox of being and yet not being a modern Horace is explored more openly in the First Dialogue of the *Epilogue to the Satires*. Pope's 'Friend' opens the dialogue by chiding the poet for not being so delicate as Horace, the poet who 'lack'd no sort of *Vice*', but cleverly flattered the great:

> His sly, polite, insinuating stile
> Could please at Court, and make *Augustus* smile:
> An artful Manager, that crept between
> His Friend and Shame, and was a kind of *Screen*.
>
> (ll. 19–22)

The Friend concludes that Pope's proud declarations of independence will be attributed merely to the fact that the 'Great Man' (Walpole) 'never offer'd you a groat'; Horace, who took the groat, and Augustus, who gave it, are just as much under attack as Walpole and George Augustus. It might be argued that the epithets 'sly' and 'insinuating' suggest the possibility that the original Horace's praise of the original Augustus is ironic (Shaftesbury, indeed, had raised this very possibility[10]), but the weight of evidence is that Pope believed that Horace's praise of the Roman Augustus was sincere. What is certain is that there were enough ironies in Pope's imitations of Horace's Augustan verse to cause confusion among his literary enemies: generally he was attacked for not being true to the spirit of Horace, but sometimes for being too true to his model; Lord Hervey, for instance, represents Horace, the professed lover of virtuous retirement, as being in reality a devotee of luxury, a flatterer of courtiers, and a worshipper of absolutism, and he then argues that Pope is no less of a hypocrite than Horace.[11]

Enough has been said to indicate that the idea of Augustan Rome aroused complicated and conflicting reactions in eighteenth-century England. Response to the idea of the Roman republic was simple by comparison; the English, for the most part, venerated Cato of Utica, Cicero, and Marcus Brutus, the men who sought vainly to defend the republic against Caesarism. In the third voyage of *Gulliver's Travels*, when Caesar and Brutus are summoned from the dead, Gulliver is immediately 'struck with a profound veneration at the sight of Brutus, and could easily discover the most consummate virtue, the greatest intrepidity and firmness of mind, the truest love of his country, and general benevolence for mankind, in every lineament of his countenance'. In *Rome* (1735), the third part of *Liberty*, Thomson reviews the lives and virtues of great Romans from the beginning of the republic down to Cato, Cicero, and 'The last of Romans, matchless Brutus' (l.482). These three are again the crown and culmination of a long line of Roman heroes reviewed in the 1744 version of the *Seasons* (*Winter*, ll.498–529). Adam Ferguson notes in his *Essay on Civil Society* (1762) that the love of liberty displayed by Cato and Brutus 'has thrown a lustre on human nature'.[12]

Cicero was the Roman most admired by Bolingbroke, and so is the object of frequent praise in the *Craftsman*: 'No Man of Antiquity is handed down to us in a more amiable Light than *Marcus Tullius Cicero*' (*Craftsman*, no. 42, 1727). There is a palpable hit at the modern Caesarism of George Augustus and Walpole in the *Craftsman*, no. 221 (1730), where Demosthenes and

Cicero are praised as honest, beneficial 'incendiaries', and are linked with those later incendiaries who facilitated the Glorious Revolution of 1688 by exasperating the people against the mischiefs of tyranny in Church and State. The eighteenth-century general reader's sympathetic understanding of Cicero was greatly enlarged by the elegant and much-admired *History of the Life of Marcus Tullius Cicero* (1741) by Conyers Middleton (1683–1750). This work directed Gibbon to the complete writings of Cicero, as he acknowledges in his *Memoirs*: 'I tasted the beauties of language, I breathed the spirit of freedom, and I imbibed from his precepts and examples the public and private sense of a man.'[13] Although in the *Decline and Fall* Gibbon applauds the prosperity of the Antonine era, he takes Cicero's republicanism as a measure against which even the most glorious decades of the Empire fall short.

Cicero was widely applauded as a martyr for liberty, but his reputation was to some degree tarnished by his occasional timidity and his compromising with the tyrants. Cato's republican virtue was altogether sterner and purer. Despite the conventional Christian objections to his suicide, advanced for instance in Steele's *Christian Hero* (1701), Cato was greatly admired throughout the eighteenth century. In the *Tatler*, no. 81 (1709) Swift scans the works of ancient writers to find arguments for the relative placings of Alexander, Caesar, Socrates, Cicero, Hannibal, Cato, and Augustus in an allegorical *Palace of Immortality*, and, following Lucan, he sets Cato in first place. Lucan's own heroic characterization of Cato was given renewed vitality for eighteenth-century English readers in Nicholas Rowe's spirited and widely-known translation of the *Pharsalia* (1718). In the *Spectator*, no. 237, Addison approvingly quotes Seneca's praise of 'Cato, amidst the ruins of his country, preserving his integrity', and dying in a manner of which the Gods could approve. Seneca's words also provided a motto for Addison's *Cato* (1713), certainly the most influential English presentation of its subejct, and possibly the most admired of all eighteenth-century English tragedies. The liberty-loving Roman provided the pen-name for the opposition Whigs who wrote the periodical *Cato's Letters* in the 1720s. Thomson, in *Summer* (1727), represents liberty herself withdrawing from 'stooping *Rome*,/And guilty Caesar' to follow Cato to his noble death in North Africa. Similar representations are found later in the century: in Lyttelton's *Dialogues of the Dead* (1760), where Cato denounces Augustus as the destroyer of Roman liberties, for instance; or in Ferguson's *Essay on Civil Society* (1767):

> This illustrious personage stood distinguished in his age like a
> man among children, and was raised above his opponents, as
> much by the justness of his understanding, and the extent of his
> penetration, as he was by the manly fortitude and
> disinterestedness with which he strove to baffle the designs of a
> vain and childish ambition, that was operating to the ruin of
> mankind.[14]

The 'vain and childish ambition' is, of course, that of Julius Caesar, making his way 'to usurpation and tyranny'. Ferguson repeats these notions in his

Roman Republic (1782), where he also conjectures that different forms of philosophical education may have influenced the course of history; on a hint from Sallust, he notes that Cato was a Stoic who acknowledged no good other than public good, whereas Caesar was an Epicurean who identified good and evil with pleasure and pain. The constant references to Roman history in English parliamentary debate, the cultural importance of the study of history in a century when, arguably, the greatest literary achievements were great works of philosophical history, the predominance of the Roman style in architecture through the Palladian movement and its extension in the work of Chambers, the general practice among sculptors of representing their sitters in Roman dress, all tended to fix in the imagination an idea of Roman civic virtue.

Though ancient Rome bequeathed important and very influential models of civic and martial virtue and of literary excellence, the Roman ideas and values that penetrated more deeply and widely into the consciousness of educated eighteenth-century Englishmen were those associated with rural life and labour. Such values were set forth in what was thought in the eighteenth century to be the oldest surviving Latin prose work, the *De Agri Cultura* of Cato the Censor, born of peasant stock, great-grandfather of Cato of Utica, and stern denouncer not only of Carthage itself but of the whole commercial spirit embodied in Carthage. Cato's book is a practical treatise on agriculture, but it also proclaims that the countryside is the home of health and honesty, that farming is the most needful and noble of employments, and is undertaken by the best of men. The Romans particularly admired the small farmer; in the imperial period Varro and Columella, among others, represented early republican Rome as enjoying a kind of golden age when it was a nation of small, hardy, independent, busy, virtuous, patriotic, landowning farmers.

The most admired classical celebrations of the virtuous rural life were probably those of Horace and Virgil. Horace's second epode, 'Beatus ille', was much imitated by English poets, most of whom tactfully omitted the cynical postscript in which Horace reveals that this idyllic account of the farmer's joys is uttered by a usurer who intends to return to his covetous commercial life. Horace's own retired life on his 'Sabine Farm', as described in his satires and epistles, became a model for Pope and even for Bolingbroke, as well as for countless other eighteenth-century gentlemen. A more complete, because more public, imaginative statement of the Roman rural ideal was to be found in Virgil's *Georgics*. In some quarters this great poem was even accepted as a textbook of husbandry: as late as 1733, in his *Practical Husbandman and Planter*, the landscape gardener Stephen Switzer furiously defended the practical usefulness of the *Georgics* against the strictures of Jethro Tull, that pioneer of the Agricultural Revolution; there were attempts to combine Virgil and modern science in, for instance, Richard Bradley's *A Survey of the Ancient Husbandry and Gardening, collected from Cato, Varro, Columella, Virgil, and others . . . the whole rendered familiar to our Climate, with Variety of new Experiments* (1725), the title of which speaks volumes for eighteenth-century eclecticism. When it was not in practical use, Virgil's *Georgics* provided tags for nearly every eighteenth century

English writer on rural subjects; the passage in praise of the husbandman's life beginning with verse 458 of the second book, 'O fortunatos nimium, sua si bona norint/agricolas', was paraphrased time and time again. The whole poem was of course a prime model for a succession of poets who eagerly adapted Virgil's precepts about ancient Roman husbandry, his idealization of rural life, his love of the earth, and his patriotism to modern England.

The idealized happy husbandman of Virgil and Columella, in so far as he corresponded to reality at all, was a peasant, not a large-scale commercial farmer. Eighteenth-century English writers upon political economy never tired of pointing out that one of the effects of luxury in the ancient Roman world was to collect land into fewer and fewer hands, and to reduce the number of hardy landowning patriots; needless to say, it was feared that England would go the way of Rome. Wordsworth's famous letter to Charles James Fox about the need to protect and preserve small landowners, such as the hero of *Michael*, is only one late contribution to a controversy about rural depopulation that had raged for over half a century; *The Deserted Village* is another of the literary bequests of that controversy. From time to time the ancient Romans had sought to impose an agrarian law which would set severe restrictions upon the size of any man's estate; as it was believed that such laws were essential to the balance of the much-admired Roman republican constitution, they were much discussed in the eighteenth century. According to Walter Moyle in 1699, the Roman agrarian law 'established the great Ballance of the Commonwealth, and would have render'd it immortal'[15] had it been effectively put into execution. In *Cato's Letters*, no. 35 (1721), it is claimed that, had the agrarian law been properly enforced, 'one Man would never have been set above all the rest, and have established, as *Caesar* did at last, a Tyranny in that great and glorious State'. During the second half of the century Tories such as Goldsmith and Radicals such as Richard Price advocated an English agrarian law similar to that of ancient Rome.

The Roman example exercised a powerful influence upon the eighteenth-century imagination in the fear of national decline. It seemed that in the histories of all ancient nations there was an inevitable cycle: poverty–courage–conquest–prosperity–luxury–decline. Rome was the best-known case of this cycle, and the most awe-inspiring in the extent of its conquests, the height of its prosperity, and the completeness of its fall. Swift repeatedly makes analogies between Roman and English history; Bolingbroke, much in Swift's vein, consistently equates Elizabethan England with the best period of the Roman republic in the second and third centuries B.C., and his own days with the Augustan tyranny, from which must begin an irreversible decline.

The fallen state of Rome was an ever-present idea for educated men and was also a vivid visual memory for many who made the Grand Tour and found they could not help but contrast the degenerate modern Romans with their heroic ancestors. Successive generations of eighteenth-century writers were inspired by the sight of the ruins of ancient Rome dwarfing the achievements of modern Romans: Addison reflected upon this in his *Letters from Italy* (1703) and Dyer in his *Ruins of Rome* (1740); Thomson's *Liberty*

(1735–36) begins and ends amid these ruins, 'the Tomb of Empire'; and a greater imaginative artist than any of those three conceived his *Decline and Fall of the Roman Empire* 'at Rome, on the 15th October, 1764, as I sat musing amidst the ruins of the Capitol, while the bare-footed fryars were singing vespers in the Temple of Jupiter'.[16]

Grecian

Addison, Dyer, Thomson, and Gibbon all saw Rome, but never set foot in Athens. Greece and the ancient Greek cities of the eastern Mediterranean were under Turkish domination throughout nearly all of the century, and travel there was somewhat unsafe, so they received far fewer English visitors than did Italy; by no means all the English Grand Tourists went beyond Rome to explore southern Italy and Sicily, the area known as Magna Graecia in the ancient world; nevertheless it does not follow that the idea of Greece was fainter than the idea of Rome in the consciousness of educated eighteenth-century Englishmen. In the mind's eye there was a vivid and ever-present image of the ancient Greek world, in particular of

> Athens, the eye of Greece, Mother of Arts
> And Eloquence, native to famous wits
> Or hospitable . . . (Milton, *Paradise Regain'd*,
> (iv. 240–42)

Eighteenth-century study of both natural philosophy and moral philosophy tended to confirm that the Greeks were far ahead of the Romans in almost every field of intellectual endeavour. Though the Roman republican period was rich in models of public virtue, the longer history of the various Greek states was even richer: for instance, in all versions of his catalogue of public-spirited heroes in *Winter*, Thomson devotes twice as much space to Greece as to Rome, and his whole conception of civic virtue rests heavily on Plutarch; all four heroes commemorated in the Temple of Ancient Virtue in the garden at Stowe are Greeks (i.e. Homer, Lycurgus, Socrates, and Epaminondas); there are many more references to Greek philosophy and literature than to Roman in the pages of the *Tatler* and the *Spectator*.

Homer was the first writer of epic and Theocritus the originator of pastoral poetry; Virgil was their greatest classical successor in both fields. From the beginning of the eighteenth century Homer, 'the prince of poets', was generally preferred to Virgil as the more simple, impassioned poet, the man of more natural genius; from the middle of the century onwards Theocritus was generally preferred to Virgil too, and on roughly the same grounds. When Lady Mary Wortley Montagu, on the banks of the Hebrus in Thrace, observed the same customs as those described by Theocritus, or when Robert Wood found that the values of Arab chieftains differed little from those of Homeric society, they attested to these poets' truth to nature.[17] Despite the inadequacy of editions and translations before the second half of the century, Greek tragedy was always more highly regarded than Roman; it provided a beacon towards which many high-minded playwrights set their course, though none came near their goal. In criticism, Longinus was more to eighteenth-century taste than Horace. Pindar was the prime model for Gray and Collins in their great revival of the English lyric. Socrates, hailed by Thomson as 'Wisest of Mankind' (*Winter*, ll. 445), was the most celebrated exponent of the leading principle of eighteenth-century thought, 'know thyself;' his death was seen as the price exacted from enlightened philosophy by superstition. For the eighteenth century he was to a large extent the character portrayed by Xenophon, but Plato's writings were certainly not disregarded: Gray, for instance, was a discerning reader of Plato; though Coleridge thought that Gray had misconceived that divine philosopher, he observes that 'the poet Plato, the orator Plato, Plato the exquisite dramatist of conversation, the seer and the painter of character, Plato the high bred, highly educated, aristocratic republican, the man and the gentleman of quality stands full before us from behind the curtain as Gray has drawn it back'.[18] In the eighteenth, as in earlier centuries, it was recognized that Plato was 'animated with all the ardour and enthusiasm of Imagination which distinguishes the Poet'.[19] The main stream of English philosophy from Locke to Hume owed nothing to him, but his doctrine of ideal forms was a strong influence on aesthetics from Shaftesbury to Reynolds.

Shaftesbury is perhaps the most outspoken advocate in the age of Queen Anne of the Grecian, as against the Roman taste. Aware of claims made on behalf of 'Eastern' writers, whether Egyptian, Hebrew, or more distant, he roundly asserts that the arts and sciences were formed in Greece: 'Whatever flourish'd, or was rais'd to any degree of Correctness, or real Perfection in the kind, was by means of GREECE alone, and in the hand of that sole, polite, most civiliz'd, and accomplish'd Nation.' Shaftesbury routinely praises Homer, as 'the Father and Prince of Poets', and, less routinely, Euripides. Tragedy and 'the higher Style' were brought to perfection by Euripides: 'And now in all the principal Works of *Ingenuity* and *Art*, SIMPLICITY and NATURE began chiefly to be sought: And this was the TASTE which lasted thro' so many Ages, till the Ruin of all things, under a Universal Monarchy.' This monarchy is of course the 'specious Machine of Arbitrary and Universal Power' established by Augustus; for Shaftesbury insists that there was only the shortest interval between the refining of Roman art on Grecian models and the establishment of tyranny, with a rapid consequent decline of arts. Despite the contemporary example of France under Louis XIV, Shaftesbury, like many of his countrymen, took it as an article of faith that the arts could flourish only in free societies:

> Hence it is that those *Arts* have been deliver'd to us in such
> perfection, by *Free Nations*; who from the Nature of their
> Government, as from a proper Soil, produc'd the generous
> Plants: whilst the mightiest Bodys and vastest Empires,

govern'd by *Force* and a *Despotick Power*, cou'd, after Ages of
Peace and Leisure, produce no other than what was deform'd
and barbarous of the kind.

The implication is that arbitrary government is politically barbarous and can
produce only a barbarous art. The Greek poets were nourished by political
freedom; so they survive for the admiration of a free, and therefore polite,
society: 'The more the Age is enlighten'd, the more they shine.'[20]
    The idea of Greece was asssociated above all with the idea of freedom.
Long before Byron, Englishmen had acquired the habit of musing upon the
spectacle, actual or imagined, of 'Fair Greece, sad relic of departed worth',
the nurse of liberty prostrate beneath Turkish domination, its spirit as
completely ruined as its buildings. A visitor to Delos in the 1740s felt his
'heart pierced with real concern to see the devastations which had been made
among such glorious edifices, and which I considered as the ruins of some
friend's habitation', and was reduced to a 'sullen pensiveness'; at the Temple
of Apollo he recalled to mind 'those animated statues, and breathing
pictures, that decorated this hallowed spot', and cursed the fact 'that they
were afterwards exposed to the blind zeal and superstitious fury which
prevailed in the first ages of Christianity, and afterwards totally ruined by
the avarice and barbarity of Turkish conquerors'.[21] Other travellers to
Athens told of a mosque in the Parthenon and of the Tower of the Winds
being used for worship by dancing dervishes. Gibbon never saw Athens, but
he used travellers' descriptions of that city as effectively as he used his own
first-hand knowledge of Rome:

it would not be easy, in the country of Plato and Demosthenes,
to find a reader, or a copy, of their works. The Athenians walk
with supine indifference among the glorious ruins of antiquity;
and such is the debasement of their character, that they are
incapable of admiring the genius of their predecessors.[22]

Associated as they were with intellectual degradation, the ruins of Greece
were thus more sad even than those of Rome.
    The notion of Greece as the birthplace of political freedom runs through
Johnson's *Irene* (1749), through a crop of mid-century Pindaric odes of
which Collins's (1746) and Gray's (1757) are the most distinguished, and
through such long didactic poems as Thomson's *Liberty* (1735–36) and
Falconer's *Shipwreck* (1762). Thomson, Collins (in *Ode to Liberty* and *Ode to
Simplicity*), and Gray (in *The Progress of Poesy*) follow the first flight of
freedom from Greece at the time of Philip of Macedon and trace it through
various migrations to its settlement in Britain, associating it at every step
with the migration or progress of the arts. Such a theme is not itself new in
poetry for in *A Presage of the Ruin of the Turkish Empire* (1684) Waller
describes Greece conventionally enough as

That source of Art and cultivated Thought,
Which they to *Rome*, and *Romans* hither brought;

but what is new in the mid-eighteenth century is the self-consciousness with which English poets seek to return to this source by reintroducing what they take to be Grecian subjects and recapturing what they take to be Grecian style: in Akenside's words, to 'tune to Attic themes the British lyre' (*Pleasures of Imagination*, I. 604), or in Collins's to 'Revive the just Designs of Greece' (*The Passions*, l. 116).

Akenside's principal Grecian theme, one that owes almost as much to Shaftesbury as to Shaftesbury's master Plato, is that 'Truth and Good are one/And beauty dwells in them' (*Pleasures of Imagination*, I. 374). Collins pictures the allegorical subject of his *Ode on Simplicity* as 'a decent Maid/In Attic Robe array'd (ll. 10–11); for, as the Grecian spirit was identified with freedom, the Grecian style was identified with simplicity. Pope, in defining simplicity as 'the Mean between Ostentation and Rusticity', set an aesthetic ideal that many other poets aspired to as well as himself. Though his translation of Homer was condemned by Cowper, Joseph Warton, and many others because it had over-refined its original, Pope himself greatly admired that 'pure and noble Simplicity' which was found in its greatest perfection, he claimed, only in Homer and the Bible.

Pope is responsive most of all to Homer's powerful and copious creative imagination, which quite overwhelms the reader: 'It is to the strength of this amazing Invention we are to attribute that unequal'd Fire and Rapture, which is so forcible in *Homer*, that no Man of a true Poetical Spirit is Master of himself while he reads him.' Such imagination is most strong and fruitful in what the eighteenth century looked upon as the most challenging area of invention, allegory: 'How fertile will that Imagination appear, which was able to cloath all the Properties of Elements, the Qualifications of the Mind, the Virtues and Vices, in Forms and Persons; and to introduce them into Actions agreeable to the Nature of the Things they shadow'd? This is a Field in which no succeeding Poets could dispute with *Homer*.'[23]

It was largely through a widespread admiration for Homer that the eighteenth century came to study and to arrive at a fuller understanding of the nature of myth. Thomas Blackwell observes in his *Enquiry into the Life and Writings of Homer* (1735) that '*Homer's Mythology* is little understood; or to express it better, is *little felt*' by his readers; for 'there are but few who look upon the *Divine Persons* he employs, otherwise than so many *groundless Fictions*, which he made at Pleasure, and might employ indifferently'. The truth, however, is that 'His *Gods*, are all *natural Feelings of the severall Powers of the Universe. . . . *They are not a bundle of extravagant Stories; but the most delicate, and, at the same time, the most *majestick Method* of expressing the Effects of those natural Powers, which have the greatest Influence upon our *Bodies* and *Minds*.'[24] Blackwell's study of Homer's mythology is extended by Robert Wood, who suggests, in his *Essay on the Original genius of Homer* (1767), that the development of myth may have been shaped to some extent by a love of picturesque landscape shared by ancient Greek and modern Englishmen alike:

> When the sun goes down behind the cloud-capped mountains
> of Macedonia and Thessaly, there is a picturesque wildness in

the appearance, under certain points of view, which naturally
calls to mind the old fable of the rebel giants bidding defiance to
Jupiter, and scaling the heavens, as the fanciful suggestion of
this rugged perspective. And we find this striking face of nature
adapted to so bold a fiction with the fitness and propriety,
which its extravagance would forbid us to expect.[25]

However irrational they may be, the Greek myths are felt to convey our
sense of mystery and divinity in nature more forcefully and perhaps more
truthfully than the physico-theological argument from design could do.
Myths are a natural imaginative bridge between human nature and external
nature; they represent, as Akenside declared in 1746, 'the mutual agreement
or opposition of the corporeal and moral powers of the world; which hath
been accounted the very highest office of poetry' (*Hymn to the Naiads*, note
MM, to l. 327). Such speculations opened the way to the romantic recreation of myth in the early nineteenth century.

   Greek literature and philosophy were living presences in English intellectual life from the beginning of the eighteenth century, but the systematic study of Greek antiquities began only after the foundation of the Society
of Dilettanti in 1732. This society originated as a mere Grand-Tourist dining
club, for membership of which, as Horace Walpole sourly observed, 'the
nominal qualification was having been to Italy, and the real one being
drunk'[26]; but, quite early, its members began to sponsor and supervise the
excavation, collection, and study of archaeological remains in the Greek
world. It was the Society of Dilettanti which sent James Stuart and Nicholas
Revett to Athens to carry out what was, in effect, a cultural rescue. In the
Proposals (1751) for their *Antiquities of Athens* (1762) the two men complain
that, though there is accurate documentation of Roman antiquities,

> Athens, the mother of Elegance and Politeness, whose
> magnificence scarce yielded to that of Rome, and who for the
> beauties of a correct style must be allowed to surpass her, as
> much as an original excels a copy, has been almost entirely
> neglected, and unless exact drawings from them be speedily
> made, all her beautious Fabricks, her Temples, her Theatres,
> her Palaces will drop into oblivion, and Posterity will have to
> reproach us, that we have not left them a tolerable idea of what
> is so excellent, and so much deserves our attention.

The *Antiquities of Athens* and other similar works in the 1750s and 1760s (see
Ch. 6, Architecture, above), in most of which the Society of Dilettanti was
involved, were designed as much to improve the taste of practising architects as to provide an archaeological record for scholars. Greece was to be
revived and, so to speak, acquired. Thanks to the work of Stuart and Revett,
the great Athenian monuments became as familiar to educated Englishmen
as the Roman long had been; and in the fullness of time Greek-revival
architects dispossessed the Palladians, despite the long rearguard action by
Sir William Chambers.

Something of the imaginative excitement aroused by these archaeological expeditions is conveyed in the painting of the *Discovery of Palmyra by Wood and Dawkins* (1758), by Gavin Hamilton (see Ch. 6, Painting, above), who was himself something of an archaeologist. Evidently the rediscovery of Greek, or in this case lateish Graeco-Roman, remains could be as satisfying to romantic sentiment as to refined taste. Palmyra was a remote and legendary object in the depths of the Syrian desert; it was thought to be that Tadmor which King Solomon built in the desert; it had remained virtually unbuilt-over since its destruction in the third century. Robert Wood thus describes the first sight of the place in his *Ruins of Palmyra* (1753):

> The hills opening discovered to us, all at once, the greatest
> quantity of ruins we had ever seen, all of white marble, and
> beyond them to the Euphrates a flat waste, as far as the eye
> could reach. . . . It is scarce possible to imagine anything more
> striking than this view. So great a number of Corinthian
> columns, mixed with so little wall or solid building, afforded a
> most romantic variety of prospect.[27]

Palmyra was associated with the accomplished, beautiful, and courageous warrior-queen Zenobia: in Gibbon's words, 'perhaps the only female whose superior genius broke through the servile indolence imposed on her sex by the climate and manners of Asia'.[28] Under her reign the city became briefly the rival of Rome; so the completeness of its present ruin made it in some respects more full of melancholy romantic associations than even Rome itself. Volney's grand and solemn dissertation on time and change, *Les Ruines, ou Méditations sur les Révolutions des Empires* (1792), was conceived there, in much the same fashion as Gibbon's great work was conceived at Rome.

The newly discovered glories of Greek art aroused as much admiration in the 1760s as Greek literature and thought already enjoyed, but there was as yet no attempt in England to form some overall view of the whole of Greek culture. This task was first undertaken by Johann Joachim Winckelmann (1717–68), one of several influential German thinkers who had themselves been influenced by Shaftesbury. In our period Winckelmann was known in England mostly by his earliest treatise, translated by the painter Henry Fuseli, and published in 1765 under the title *Reflections on the Painting and Sculpture of the Greeks: with Instructions for the Connoisseur, and an Essay on Grace in Works of Art*. Here Winckelmann reasserts Shaftesbury's notions concerning ideal beauty and the moral value of good taste, but offers a far more detailed case than Shaftesbury does for the supremacy of the Greeks. He claims that the only path to artistic greatness is by imitation of the Greeks, that among the moderns this was sufficiently recognized only by Raphael, Michaelangelo, and Poussin, and that the excellence of ancient Greek art was due to free political institutions, a happy climate, and the physical beauty of the ancient Greeks themselves, whose bodies were developed by exercise and gymnastics. He found the coherence and unity of Greek art in noble simplicity and calm grandeur, as he indicates in the most

•

famous simile in the *Reflections*: 'The last and most eminent characteristic of the Greek works is a noble simplicity and sedate grandeur in Gesture and Expression. As the bottom of the sea lies peaceful beneath a foaming surface, a great soul lies sedate beneath the strife of passions in Greek figures.'[29] It was under Winckelmann's guidance that Flaxman, Barry, Fuseli, and probably Blake, approached Greek art; Blake's case is particularly interesting and important, if only because most critics have tended to underestimate the Greek element in his work[30]; but the story of Winckelmann's influence in England lies for the most part outside our period.

Gothic

Blake once wrote: 'the purpose for which alone I live' is 'to renew the lost Art of the Greeks'; a modern critic has observed that 'the earliest, formative influences on Blake's imagination were Grecian, and, however much they would be masked by later Gothic influences, they remained dominant'.[31] Though Blake's is a highly peculiar composite art, he is far from being the only artist or man of letters to combine the Grecian and the Gothic tastes. Thomas Warton devoted his considerable scholarly abilities to the study of both Greek and northern poetry; the artistic ideal proclaimed (but not very impressively embodied) in his own poetry is the combination of Gothic spirit and Grecian grace. This combination is implicit in the greater lyric poets who sought to effect a thorough reformation of English poetry in the 1740s and 1750s by attaching themselves to far more primitive and sublime literary traditions than the Roman. In *The Bard* (1757) Gray attempts 'directly to embody, rather than merely to describe, the true sources of poetry identified by the age in the prophetic, the medieval, the Celtic, the visionary, and the natural sublime, and to dramatize the connection of poetry and political liberty'[32]; this poem, which surpassed even the *Elegy* in popularity and influence during our period, is of course a Pindaric ode, drawing its rhetorical sublimity and its idea of liberty from the Greek tradition too. The climax of Collins's *Ode to Liberty* (1746) is the allegorical vision of a Druid temple of freedom in the green woodland depths of Britain:

> In Gothic pride it seems to rise,
> Yet Graecia's graceful orders join
> Majestic through the mixed design.

His ostensible and well-worn subject is the progress of liberty from ancient Greece to Britain, but his implicit theme is the renewal of English poetry.

The forms of Gothic and Greek art could hardly be more different from one another; nevertheless the Goths and the Greeks were closely linked together in the English mind by the concept of political liberty. Educated

Englishmen believed that the principle of liberty was embodied in certain institutions originating among ancient German tribes and developing in England to become the balanced 'Gothic constitution' confirmed in 1688: we have seen (Ch. 4 above) that this was the belief of Addison, Swift, and Bolingbroke, among others, and that it played a large part in eighteenth-century English political debate. The Gothic temples erected in so many landscape gardens were as often intended to provide a political statement as an aesthetic object, and though the full-scale Gothic revival in great public architecture, like the Greek revival, had to wait until the nineteenth century, some of the eighteenth-century opposition to Palladianism was inspired by sentiments associated with the idea of Gothic liberty. There is a revealing essay in the opposition journal *Common Sense*, no. 150 (15 December 1739), which denounces the contemporary luxurious mania for building, and regrets that so many old-fashioned English houses have been pulled down to make way for gimcrack imitations of Italian villas:

> Methinks there was something respectable in those old
> hospitable *Gothick* Halls, hung round with the Helmets,
> Breast-Plates, and Swords of our Ancestors; I entered them
> with a Constitutional Sort of Reverence, and look'd upon those
> Arms with Gratitude, as the Terror of former Ministers, and
> the Check of Kings. Nay, I even imagin'd that I here saw some
> of those good Swords, that had procur'd the Confirmation of
> *Magna Carta*, and humbled *Spencers* and *Gavestons*. And when I
> see these thrown by, to make Way for some tawdry Gilding and
> Carving, I can't help considering such an Alteration as ominous
> even to our Constitution. Our old *Gothick* Constitution had a
> noble Strength and Simplicity in it, which was well enough
> represented by the bold Arches, and the solid Pillars of the
> Edifices of those Days. And I have not observed that the
> modern Refinements in either have in the least added to their
> Strength and Solidity.

As the most enlightened early upholder of the Gothic constituion, with its equal balance of power between king, lords, and commons, and as a model of patriotism, courage, wisdom, learning, and humanity, Alfred the Great was the object of universal admiration in eighteenth-century England. There were monuments to him in many great gardens; he is the hero of several plays, in one of which, the masque *Alfred* (1740), Thomson's patriotic hymn 'Rule, Britannia!' was sung for the first time. Even Johnson, a writer not given to cant on political or other matters, furthered the legend of 'Alfred's golden Reign' (*London* 1738), l. 248). The general eighteenth-century opinion was summed up by Thomas Davies in a work for which there is evidence of Johnson's hand: 'I scarce know of any character in history so truly sublime and venerable as that of Alfred; and we may defy all the writers from his days to our own to furnish one equal in every princely virtue to this renowned king.'[33]

The cult of the North may have had its origins in political discussions concerning constitutional liberties thought to be derived from the Anglo-Saxon period, but there was a very different, altogether wilder, kind of Gothic liberty which appealed far more directly to the eighteenth-century imagination. Discussing the circumstances most favourable to the composition of epic poetry, Thomas Blackwell observes that it is in periods of danger and disorder that heroic characters appear: 'the Times of such Struggles have a kind of *Liberty* peculiar to themselves: They raise a free and active spirit, which overspreads the Country: Every Man finds himself on such Occasions his own Master'.[34] Blackwell is investigating the background of Homer's work, but his generalization about the conditions which give rise to martial heroism was readily applicable to northern history. In such works as Temple's celebrated essay *Of Heroic Virtue* (1692), eighteenth-century readers found an overview of the whole northern region, from Norway to Siberia, in its heroic age, when its fierce swarms of warriors overcame virtually every one of the old civilizations. Particularly striking was Temple's account of the hardy, fearless Northmen who believed that if they died in battle they would go to an after-life of perpetual feasting in Odin's hall. The most colourful feature of this description concerned the warriors 'carousing every man in bowls made of the skulls of their enemies they had slain'[35]; it was based on a mistranslation of a piece of Old Icelandic poetry, and in due course it did much to colour the impression of the North popularized by the generation of Gray, Thomas Warton, and Percy. Not all that generation of course: Hume, always armed in proof against enthusiasm, and on this occasion (in his *History of England*) bent on refuting the whole notion of 'Gothic liberties', recounts somewhat dryly the story about drinking from skulls and adds: 'We know little of the other theological tenets of the Saxons.'[36]

Even less was known about the theological tenets of our other northern ancestors, the British Druids, so there was, if anything, even more speculation. The Druids were known from classical sources such as Caesar, Strabo, Lucan, and Pliny; they were already 'famous' when Milton introduced them into *Lycidas* (l. 53), but they became far more so in the eighteenth century. Out of rediscovered fragments of Welsh, Gaelic, and Erse poetry, and out of a vast deal of philological, ethnological, and archaeological guesswork on such recondite matters as the kinship of Welsh and Hebrew, the common origin of all mythologies, and the purpose of Stonehenge, generations of poets, scholars, and cranks created the Druids as those imaginative presences who haunt the poetry of, for instance, Blake and Wordsworth. Blake, like Toland (see Ch. 2 above), often stresses the evil and obscurantist nature of the Druids as priests, and Wordsworth allows the 'giant wicker' and the 'baleful rite' of Druidic human sacrifice to intrude sensationally into his *Prelude*, but these two poets are not indifferent to the nobler characteristics which preoccupied most earlier eighteenth-century writers upon Druids.

In the eighteenth century Druids were generally idealized as the original patriots, the poet-priests who stand up for liberty in the face of Roman or other oppressions, as in Thomson's *Liberty*, Collins's *Ode to Liberty*, Gray's *The Bard*, or Cowper's *Boadicea* (1782). It is evident from Pope's sketches for his unwritten epic *Brutus* that virtuous, patriotic Druids would have found a place in his account of the very beginning of Britain. In Thomson's *Castle of Indolence* (1748) and in several poems by the Warton brothers Druids are given a more peaceable image as enlightened religious or nature poets; it is this view of the Druidic character which impels Collins to call Thomson a Druid in his haunting memorial verses on that poet (1748). All students believed that the Druids had links with Pythagoras. In the *Areopagitica* Milton suggests that both Persian philosophy and the school of Pythagoras had their beginnings in Druidic wisdom; in the *History of the Druids* (1726) Toland asserts his belief that it was a delegation of Druids, coming from the Outer Hebrides to Delos, who first brought the doctrine of the immortality of the soul into Greek philosophy. For William Stukeley, in *Stonehenge: a Temple restored to the British Druids* (1740), Pythagoras was 'the Arch-Druid'; but Stukeley was more concerned to show that the Druids shared the religious beliefs of the Old Testament patriarchs, as well as that, contrary to Inigo Jones's belief, they had enough mathematical and engineering skill to enable them to build Stonehenge. John Cleland, perhaps better known as the author of *Fanny Hill*, also wrote a differently curious treatise, *The Way to Things by Words, and to Words by Things* (1766), in which he suggests that Celtic is the parent of all other languages, and claims to be able to demonstrate that Greek mythology is the invention of the Druids. Speculations such as these all feed Blake's imaginative conviction that Britain was the primitive seat of the patriarchal religion, the original Holy Land, and that 'All things Begin and End in Albion's Ancient Druid Rocky Shore' (*Milton*, I. 6; see also *Jerusalem*, 27. 9).[37]

Blake's own style owes more than a little to the bardic manner of James Macpherson, whose Ossianic prose poems of the 1760s are the century's most ambitious effort to restore an ancient Celtic imaginative world, or, in this case, largely to fabricate such a world, tailor-made to suit contemporary notions of the sublime, the natural, the primitive, and the romantic. The heroic actions of the poems of 'Ossian' are set in a northern landscape of barren hills, adorned only with aged trees, mossy stones, and the cairns which mark the graves of warriors; the emotional atmosphere is established by the howling of the wind among the mountains and the shrieking of the torrent down the rocks. In Ossian, as in Dennis, Addison, and Shaftesbury (see Ch. 5 above), and in Gray's famous description of the Grande Chartreuse,[38] the wildness certainly pleases, but here it is a specifically Celtic wildness. The imaginative appeal of the Celtic Fringe is intimately associated with the relatively new romantic taste for wild scenery, a taste being fulfilled at this period by tourism as well as by literature.

One of the earliest romantic tourists into the Celtic fastnesses of North Wales was George Lyttelton, whose *Account of a Journey into Wales* was written in 1756, though not printed until 1774. He employs the term 'romantick' very frequently, more often applying it to pleasingly fertile valleys than to the many ruined medieval castles which so delighted him, but he is moved more deeply by the sublime. Here, for instance, he describes in Addisonian terms, his reaction to the view from Festiniog:

The grandeur of the ocean, corresponding with that of the
mountain, formed a majestick and solemn scene; ideas of
immensity swelled and exalted our minds at the sight; all lesser
objects appeared mean and trifling, so that we could hardly do
justice to the ruins of an old castle, situated upon the top of a
conical hill, the foot of which is washed by the sea, and which
has every feature that can give a romantick appearance.

When Snowdon was seen on the following day, 'covered with darkness and
thick clouds' it brought to mind 'Mount Sinai, with the laws delivered from
it, and filled my mind with religious awe'.[39] The Celtic and the Old
Testament Hebrew worlds are naturally associated with one another.

In 1765 Gray went to Scotland in order to look upon romantic and
sublime scenes similar to those which had astonished him in the Alps more
than a quarter of a century earlier; after his Scottish tour he noted that 'the
Mountains are extatic, and ought to be visited in pilgrimage once a year'.[40]
In 1772 Joseph Banks, fresh from his voyage to the Pacific with Cook, went
to Iceland; he visited Staffa *en route* and, thanks partly to a mistranslation or
mistake of his guide, and more to his own enthusiasm for Ossian, bestowed
the romantic name of Ossian's hero Fingal upon the now famous basalt
sea-cave there. Johnson made his tour of the Highlands and Western Isles in
the following year. As we might expect, he had nothing but scorn for
Ossian and the whole bardic tradition, true or false, but he found to his
surprise that there was something to admire in mountains and stormy seas.
Of an anxious journey after dark in the almost pathless wilds of Skye he
wrote:

> The fictions of the Gothick romances were not so remote from
> credibility as they are now thought. In the full prevalence of the
> feudal institution, when violence desolated the world, and
> every baron lived in a fortress, forests and castles were regularly
> succeeded by each other, and the adventurer might very
> suddenly pass from the gloom of woods, or the ruggedness of
> moors to seats of plenty, gaiety, and magnificence. Whatever is
> imaged in the wildest tale, if giants, dragons, and enchantments
> be excepted, would be felt by him, who, wandering in the
> mountains without a guide, or upon the sea without a pilot,
> should be carried amidst his terror and uncertainty, to the
> hospitality and elegance of Raasay or Dunvegan.[41]

The imaginative leap which Johnson makes in the wild surroundings of
Skye is one made in their studies by Richard Hurd, Thomas Warton, and
those other mid-century scholar-critics whose work gave rise to a new concept
of the imagination. These are the men who tread 'the Mazes of enchanted
Ground',[42] in order to explore the medieval romantic tradition from which,
in their opinion, the greatest English poets, Spenser, Shakespeare, and
Milton, drew nourishment; in order, that is, to find the northern literary
origins of what Dryden and Addison called 'the fairy way of writing'. The

most influential of such explorations was Thomas Percy's famous *Reliques of Ancient English Poetry* (1765), though Thomas Warton's great *History of English Poetry* (1774–89), for which over seven hundred manuscripts of medieval verse were unearthed, is immeasurably more thorough. Percy, Warton, Hurd, and their fellows believed that 'the world of fine fabling' embodied in 'Gothic romance' was especially suited to the ends of true imaginative poetry. Thomas Warton wrote of the romances: 'such are their Terrible Graces of magic and enchantment, so magnificently marvellous are their fictions and fablings, that they contribute, in a wonderful degree, to rouse and invigorate all the powers of imagination; to store the fancy with those sublime and alarming images, which true poetry best delights to display'.[43] Wordsworth thought that English poetry was 'absolutely redeemed' by Percy's *Reliques*, though perhaps it can hardly be claimed that this redemption came about in that first romantic revival associated with the names of Gray, Chatterton, Macpherson, Percy, Beattie, and the ubiquitous Wartons.

In Gothic, as in the Grecian revival, tastes in literature and in architecture tended to feed one another. John Hughes defended the structure of Spenser's *Faerie Queene* in his edition of 1715 by declaring that it resembles a Gothic, rather than a Grecian building. Shortly afterwards, Pope likened Shakespeare's work to a great peice of Gothic architecture. Thomas Warton, gathering material for his *Observations on the Faerie Queene*, found that, in order to complete a scholarly examination of medieval romance, it was necessary to write a dissertation upon Gothic architecture; he notes in passing that Milton's literary imagination probably received strong impressions from the 'awful solemnity of a Gothic chruch' when he was a schoolboy at St Paul's.[44] A modern critic suggests, in similar vein, that Chatterton's 'notion of the Midle Ages was derived primarily from St Mary Redcliffe [Bristol], in whose shadow his youth was spent. It is a church which in size and splendour is calculated to create awe and delight.'[45]

Thomas Warton believed that the wild exuberance of Gothic architecture could be explained only by the theory that this style originated among the Arabs; by the same token he argued that romantic fiction also originated in the Near East. According to theories widely held in his day, marvellous tales, hyperbolic descritpions, and such extravagant inventions as dragons, giants, dwarfs, fairies, and enchanters, were the products of a 'warm' imagination, which in its turn was the product of a warm climate. Warton therefore proposes, in his *History of English Poetry*, the theory that there was a migration of peoples from the shores of the Black Sea to Scandinavia after the defeat of the Persian King Mithridates by Pompey in the first century B.C., and that subsequently, after the general collapse of Roman power, the Scandinavian scalds, or minstrels, brought their romantic tales to the courts of all the Western world. According to Warton's theory there was also a further influx of oriental romance to the West when the Crusaders returned home.

Oriental

Though Blake and a few others gave absolute primacy to the Druids in their cultural chronologies, Warton's theories are in accord with the generally-held belief that the most ancient poetry, wisdom, and religion came from the Near East. Thomas Blackwell utters a commonplace when he declares that Thales, founder of the first school of Greek philosophy, and Homer both studied in Egypt at a time when Greece had scarcely emerged from barbarism and when the Egyptians 'were living in Peace and Splendour, flourishing in all the *Arts* they chose to encourage, reverenced for their Wisdom, and renowned in Arms'.[46] Like Pope, in the Preface to his trans-lation of the *Iliad*, Blackwell goes on to speculate on what Homer might have learned from the religion of the Egyptians. It was widely accepted that the Hebrew patriarchs, too, learned their religion in Egypt, and learned a very ugly lesson, if Shaftesbury is to be believed when he makes Theocles, in *The Moralists* (1709), proclaim that the 'spiritual Plague, dire *Superstition*', is native to the soil of Egypt, 'where first Religion grew unsociable, and among different Worshippers bred mutual Hatred and Abhorrence of each others Temples'.[47] The eighteenth-century freethinkers of course made much of the elements of Egyptian superstition thought to be preserved in Judaeo-Christian religion.

By virtue of the Egyptian connection, Homer and the writers of the Old Testament could be placed side by side as primitive, 'eastern' authors: Pope, for instance, remarks in the Preface to his translation of the *Iliad* that Homer's poem is very much in the language of Scripture and in 'the Spirit of the Orientals'. Much is heard in the eighteenth century of this spirit: Addison notes in the *Spectator*, no. 160 that poets from warm climates, among them the Old Testament prophets, had most heat and life in their imaginations; Montesquieu lays it down as a well-known axiom, in *L'Esprit des Lois* (1748), that hot climates discourage reasoning but encourage a quick and fertile imagination. Joseph Spence, in *An Essay on Pope's Odyssey* (1726), coins the new word 'orientalism' with reference to Homer's most sublime and spirited passages, where he most nearly approaches the manner of the Old Testament prophets. Sir William Temple speculates, in his essay *Of Poetry* (1692), that the Book of Job was written before the time of Moses, being a translation from the Chaldean or Arabic; Edward Young duly claims in the *Guardian*, no. 86 (1713) that this work is 'the most ancient poem in the world', and that it possesses much greater 'spirit in thought' and 'energy in style' than the epics of Homer and Virgil.

The whole Bible had always been regarded as a divinely-inspired guide to moral conduct, but just at the time when freethinkers were beginning to undermine its authority in that field, particularly as regards the Old Testament, it came to be recognized as the world's finest work of literature. As early as 1663, in *Some Considerations touching the Style of the Holy Scriptures* (1663), the great chemist Robert Boyle had made claims for the literary superiority of the Bible over Greek and Roman literature; Addison, Young, and others repeated these claims, but it was only when scholars were able to distinguish Old Testament poetry from prose that informed criticism of the literary qualities of Hebrew poetry became possible. The pioneer work in this field was by Robert Lowth (1710–87), whose lectures on *The Sacred Poetry of the Hebrews* were delivered in Oxford in the 1740s, published in their original Latin in 1753, and translated into English in 1787. Lowth demonstrates that Hebrew poetry is based metrically upon parallelism, and he points to the marked difference between prose and poetry in the Hebrew Scriptures: the prose gives a 'correct, chaste, and temperate' effect by its attention to regular word order; in the poetry, by contrast,

> The free spirit is hurried along, and has neither leisure nor
> inclination to descend to those minute and rigid attentions.
> Frequently, instead of disguising the secret feelings of the
> author, it lays them quite open to public view; and the veil
> being as it were suddenly removed, all the affections and
> emotions of the soul, its sudden impulses, its hasty sallies and
> irregularities, are conspicuously displayed.[48]

Lowth points out, for instance, that the difference between 'the historical proem' of the Book of Job and Job's speeches is at least as great as that between Herodotus and Homer.

   Christopher Smart learned the principles of parallelism from Lowth, and contrived in his own religious verse to catch the movement and excitement of Hebrew poetry; Macpherson reproduced the Hebrew cadences analysed by Lowth effectively enough for his defenders to take them as evidence for the great antiquity of the Ossianic poems; Blake's visionary, prophetic style was modelled directly upon the Bible as well as upon Ossian. After Lowth, eighteenth-century hymn writers were more prepared than ever before to allow themselves the same personal expressiveness and passion as the Psalmist. At the same time, critics newly attentive to the literary as distinct from the theological value of the Old Testament, were less inclined than earlier readers to accept allegorical meanings. The new attitude is seen in, for instance, Thomas Percy's preface to his translation of the *Song of Songs* (1764), when he describes his original as 'one of the most beautiful pastorals in the world', an oriental love-song which has been unnecessarily obscured by those 'busily employed in opening and unfolding its allegorical meaning'. Warm-spirited 'orientalism' was not limited to Hebrew poetry. The life and fire of the Book of Job was attributable as much to its supposed Arabian original as to its present Hebrew form. It is the view of Robert Wood, the archaeologist, that the oriental qualities of Homer's poetry and the manners of his heroes can best be understood by reference to the Arabs: 'The modern Arab, in whom I have seen the characters of prince, shepherd, and poet united, retains, in his [poetry] the wildness, irregularity, and indelicacy of his forefathers, with a considerable share of the same original glowing imagination.'[49] The pastoral idea of the Near East, rather than the epical, provides the inspiration, such as it is, for Collins's *Persian Eclogues* (1742). This idea is associated with the image of Arabia Felix, 'esteemed the loveliest and sweetest region of the world', as Temple affirms in his essay *Of Heroic Virtue*.[50]

A very different oriental idea, but one no less fascinating, was provided by the *Arabian Nights' Entertainments*, which became a European sensation when translated into French by Antoine Galland at the beginning of the eighteenth century. Its English version was sufficiently popular for a chapbook version to be advertised as early as 1708, though it was not until 1788 that one of its stories ('Aladdin and his Wonderful Lamp') achieved the most permanent form of popular success in the form of a pantomime. The *Arabian Nights* was imitated in such works as James Ridley's lively *Tales of the Genii* (1764), and in collections of *Mogul Tales, Chinese Tales, Tartarian Tales, Peruvian Tales*, and the rest; even Pope considered writing some Turkish tales. Periodical essayists from Steele to Johnson retell or fabricate oriental tales for moral instruction as well as for romantic excitement. The variety of ways in which orientalism could be employed is well indicated by the difference between Johnson's fable on the vanity of human wishes, the *History of Rasselas, Prince of Abisinnia* (1759), and William Beckford's exotic, erotic, sultry, and decadent *History of the Caliph Vathek* (1786).

Oriental taste, like Gothic, could be expressed in scholarship as well as in sensationalism: for instance, oriental learning was one of the many glories of seventeenth-century Oxford, where the two successive occupants of the Laudian Chair of Arabic from its foundation in 1636 down to the early years of the eighteenth century were the greatest oriental scholars in Europe. The scholarly tradition established by these men, Edward Pococke and Thomas Hyde, remained vigorous, so that, despite what Gibbon says of the dull potations of his elders, it was Oxford that greatly improved the historian's knowledge of the Arabs, Persians, Tartars, and Turks. In Gibbon's later years the greatest oriental scholar was Sir William Jones (1746–94), a poet-critic who was as much concerned to extend the resources of English poetry as those of philology. His *Persian Grammar* (1771) concludes with a widely-admired translation of *A Persian Song of Hafiz*, which foreshadows some of the lush and colourful work in this exotic vein by Southey, Byron, Moore, and Shelley, to name but a few.

Jones's work in India after his appointment as judge of the High Court of Calcutta in 1783 is more significant. His mastery of Sanskrit and his realization of the kinship of Indo-European languages enabled him to make the all-important first step in modern comparative philology, his codifying of local Islamic and Hindu laws brought a measure of enlightenment to British rule in India, but his original *Hymns*, based on Hindu mythology, are perhaps of more importance to the literary student on account of their direct influence upon Wordsworth and Shelley. The colourful history of the Islamic dynasties who ruled northern India fascinated English writers from the time of Dryden's *Aurungzebe* (1676) to that of Moore's *Lallah Rookh* (1816), but Hindu culture began to make an impression in England only with the work of Jones and of a fellow Sanskrit scholar Sir Charles Wilkins, whose translation of *The Bhagvat-Geeta, or Dialogues of Kreeshna and Arjoon*, with an Introductory Letter by Warren Hastings (1785), was sufficiently important to Blake for him to dedicate no. 10 of his *Descriptive Sketches* to it.

Blake responds to the mythic force of Hindu religion, Wilkins to its intellectual distinction: somewhat after the fashion of the early-eighteenth-
century freethinkers, he distinguishes between the polytheistic superstition
of the masses and the enlightenment of their priests, whom he evidently
regards as his own intellectual kindred, for he notes, 'The most learned
Brahmans of the present time are unitarians. They believe but in one God,
an universal spirit.'[51]

Some such distinction was commonly made in Western references to
Chinese religion too. Temple, for instance, notes in his essay *Of Heroic
Virtue* that though the common people in China are idolatrous, as common
people everywhere tend to be, the educated differ very little from European
freethinkers: 'the learned adore the spirit of the world, which they hold to be
eternal; and this without temples, idols, or priests'. These learned Chinese
are the true followers of Confucius, the apostle of reason, ranked by Temple
alongside Solomon and Socrates as a man 'of very extraordinary genius, of
mighty learning, admirable virtue, excellent nature, a true patriot of his
country, and lover of mankind'.[52] Confucius and Socrates are bracketed
again in Addison's *Spectator*, no. 166, and Pope adds his tribute in *The
Temple of Fame*, where, on the eastern front,

> Superior and alone *Confucius* stood
> Who taught that useful Science, to be *good*
>
> (ll. 107–08)

The greatest Western Sinophile was Voltaire, who dramatized Confucian
moral philosophy in his *Orphelin de la Chine* (1755), and repeatedly found
room in his historical writings to contrast the rational religious principles of
the Chinese with the superstition and cruel fanaticism of the Christian
Church.

In the light of such opinions of China it is not surprising that Chinese
stories figured prominently among the oriental fables invented by periodical
essayists from Addison onwards. A wise Chinaman provides the satiric
viewpoint in Horace Walpole's much-admired squib, *A Letter from Xo Ho, a
Chinese Philosopher at London, to his friend Lien Chi at Peking* (1757), and in
Goldsmith's far more substantial *Citizen of the World* (1762), both works of
the same kind as the *Lettres Persanes* (1721) of Montesquieu and the *Letters
from a Persian in England* (1735) of Lyttelton. The exotic, romantic appeal of
China appears, together with its morally normative function, in Thomas
Percy's translation of a Chinese play, *Hau Kiou Choaan* (1761); but China
had been pressed into the service of a factitious exoticism much earlier, in,
for instance, poor Elkanah Settle's dismal tragedy *The Conquest of China*
(1675) and the transformation scene set in a Chinese garden which he
provided for Purcell's opera *The Fairy Queen* (1692), a work modelled,
surprisingly, upon Shakespeare's *A Midsummer Night's Dream*.

Settle no doubt hoped that his oriental pantomime would be congenial to
the developing Chinese taste in the decorative arts at this time. Literary
students do not need to be reminded that references to porcelain imported
from China figure largely in Wycherley's *Country Wife* (1675) and Pope's

Rape of the Lock (1712). Chinese textiles, lacquer work, wallpaper, 'Indian screens', and other household objects were first imported, and later, like 'china' itself, were copied by European craftsmen and designers; Chinese garden buildings began to appear in the 1750s at the same time that Chippendale was designing furniture in the Chinese taste; Voltaire's studies at Cirey and Ferney were decorated, as one might expect, in the Chinese style; Chinese designs were still very popular when the willow pattern made its first appearance in England about 1780.

Though the idea of China still exercised its influence over the decorative arts at the end of the eighteenth century, it had begun to lose its respectability among philosophers and historians. In 1692 Temple, drawing on idealized French accounts, could write: 'the kingdom of China seems to be framed and policed with the utmost force and reach of human wisdom, reason, and contrivance; and in practice to excel the very speculations of other men, and all those imaginary schemes of the European wits, the institutions of Xenophon, the republic of Plato, the Utopias, or Oceans of our modern writers'[53]; but as first-hand knowledge became more generally available in England the view of China darkened: the author of Commodore George Anson's *Voyage round the World* (1748), for instance, gave a very hostile eye-witness account of the Chinese. In the light of such new knowledge, and under the influence of a new English admiration for progress, it came to be seen that China, like many other Asian states, was an obstinately stagnant society. Both Hume and Adam Smith were puzzled and disappointed that China, despite its possession of great wealth and its very early development of arts, sciences, and manufactures, had made so little progress in recent years.

Of the societies discussed so far, only China was completely unknown to the classical world of Greece and Rome; once discovered, it took its place with other ancient civilizations in the 'Old World'. By the time, though, that Burke made his observation on the unrolling of 'the Great Map of Mankind', many regions beyond the Eurasian landmass had been brought under view. The New World which Europeans began to explore and colonize in the sixteenth and seventeenth centuries revealed old Aztec and Inca civilizations, the second of which was dignified by a place in Temple's essay *Of Heroic Virtue*, but it was perhaps more important in the European imagination as the home of the noble savage.

Savage

As early as the sixteenth century, with Montaigne's essay *Of Cannibals*, men had mourned the loss of an innocent world which was America before the first arrival of Europeans. A similar note of pastoral regret is heard in the eighteenth century, even from men who had actually visited the Americas: the sea captain George Shevlocke, for instance, writing in 1721 in that famous journal which gave Coleridge his albatross, observes that the Indians of California 'are endowed with all the humanity imaginable, and they make some nations (who would give these poor people the epithet of savages or barbarians) blush to think that they deserve that appelation more than they.' Shevlocke notes that they are free from luxury, pride, and covetousness: 'In a word they seem to pass their lives in the purest simplicity of the earliest ages of the world, before discord and contention were heard amongst men.'[54]

The arts duly absorbed the New-World noble savage. The earliest English novel on the noble savage theme, Aphra Behn's *The Royal Slave* (1678), is set in South America, with a Negro slave as hero; dramatized by Thomas Southerne as *Oroonoko* (1695), it held the stage throughout the eighteenth century; an Indian princess sold into slavery by her ungrateful English lover is the heroine of the sentimental tale of Inkle and Yarico, popularized by Steele in the *Spectator*, no. 11 (1711), and retold in many versions in several European languages later in the century. There is an idealized representation of South American Indians in Prévost's novel *Cleveland* (1732–39); a clear-sighted and right-judging innocent educated among the Huron (i.e. Iroquois) Indians is the hero of Voltaire's satirical romance *L'Ingénu* (1767); a philosophical Cherokee makes his appearance in Benjamin West's painting of *The Death of Wolfe* (1771); Joseph Wright's *The Indian Widow* (1783) is a figure of noble sentiment and romantic pathos.

Europeans in the early eighteenth century obtained their most detailed knowledge of American Indians, as they obtained their most detailed knowledge of the Chinese, from accounts by Jesuit missionaries. It was the Jesuits who showed that Confucius had much in common with the most enlightened philosophers of ancient Greece, and it was also the Jesuits who indicated that a study of the characters and manners of the Red Indians could illuminate ancient history. After living among the Iroquois, the French Jesuit Joseph François Lafitau wrote his *Mœurs des sauvages ameriquains comparées aux mœurs des premiers temps* (1724), in which he claims that the religious practices of the Red Indians resemble ancient accounts of Bacchic rites and the mysteries of Isis and Osiris, that Indian social and military organizations are very like those of the Greeks in their heroic age, and even that their dances and songs throw light on the ancient origins of epic, ode, and tragedy in Greece.

Such comparisons were intended as much to discredit the ancient pagans as to honour the modern, and they belong as much to the tradition of the ignoble savage as to that of the noble savage. The darker tradition was marked, for instance, by accounts of Red Indian atrocities going back to the earliest period of European settlement, or by Hobbes's depiction, in *Leviathan* (1651), of the brutish misery of ungoverned men in a 'state of nature' for which he takes the North American Indian as his model, or by Locke's demonstration that a day-labourer is fed, clothed, and housed better than a Red Indian king (see p. 71 above). The authoritative eighteenth-century view is William Robertson's in his *History of America* (1777), where he stresses, in somewhat Lockeian terms, the emptiness of that continent and the backwardness of its inhabitants before the arrival of Europeans:

A naked savage cowering over the fire in his miserable cabin, or stretched under a few branches which afford him a temporary shelter, has as little inclination as capacity for useless speculation. His thoughts extend not beyond what relates to animal life; and when they are not directed towards some of its concerns, his mind is totally inactive.[55]

By the time of Robertson, another model of the noble (or, if it was preferred, ignoble) savage and another new world were under close examination. The eighteenth century witnessed an extensive exploration of the Pacific Ocean and the publication of many popular accounts of voyages, not without an effect upon the literary imagination. William Dampier's voyages were sufficiently famous for Lemuel Gulliver (also a bringer-back of strange tales from the Pacific) to claim Dampier as his cousin; Alexander Selkirk, the prototype of Robinson Crusoe, was marooned on the uninhabited Pacific island of Juan Fernandez in 1704 from a ship in one of Dampier's privateering squadrons and was rescued over four years later by another. It so happens that it was in the year that *Robinson Crusoe* was published (1719) that an officer on Captain Shevlocke's ship, rounding Cape Horn, shot the Coleridgean albatross. Anson's *Voyage round the World*, which ran into fifteen editions between 1748 and 1776, supplied the idyllic earthly paradise of Tinian for Rousseau's *Nouvelle Héloïse* and provided a dreadful image of despair for Cowper's *Castaway*. Other descriptions of voyages satisfied their readers' appetite for the romantic and the sublime. Andrew Kippis, for instance, writes enthusiastically about the 'very romantic appearance' of the great icebergs seen on Cook's second voyage: 'The foaming and dashing of the waves into the curious holes and caverns which were formed in many of them, greatly heightened the scene; and the whole exhibited a view that at once filled the mind with admiration and horror.'[56]

Perhaps the most imaginatively significant European discovery in the Pacific was Tahiti, visited by Samuel Wallis in 1767, Louis Antoine de Bougainville in 1768, and James Cook in 1769. Bougainville described Tahiti as if it were the Garden of Eden, a place of lush beauty, whose inhabitants enjoyed the fruits of the earth without labour and the delights of the flesh without guilt. He named the island La Nouvelle Cythère and spoke alluringly in his journal of a naked young Tahitian girl appearing on the deck of his ship 'as Venus . . . herself to the Phrygian shepherd, having . . . the celestial form of that goddess'; according to Bougainville, men, too, had the shape of Greek gods: 'I never saw men better made, and whose limbs were more proportionate: in order to paint a Hercules or a Mars, one could nowhere find such beautiful models.'[57]

With a nice irony, in view of Bougainville's name for the island, Cook was sent to Tahiti to observe the transit of Venus (see Ch. 1 above); he spent four months there, compared with the nine days spent by Bougainville. It is perhaps because of his opportunity for longer observation that his account is more sober than the Frenchman's, as too are those of his scientist shipmates, Joseph Banks and Daniel Solander; but when their journals were collated by John Hawkesworth to make *An Account of the Voyage for making Discoveries in the Southern Hemisphere* (1773) they were idealized and sentimentalized in keeping with received notions about the noble savage. Hawkesworth refers accurately enough to the easy subsistence of the Tahitians and observes that 'they seem to be exempted from the first general curse "that man should eat his bread in the sweat of his brow"', but he also declares that they 'are brave, open, candid, without suspicion or treachery, cruelty or revenge. They have a knowledge of right and wrong from the mere dictates of natural conscience.'[58] In short, the Tahitians supplied Hawkesworth with good freethinking argument against revealed Christianity. Hawkesworth was outdone by Diderot in his revolutionary *Supplément au Voyage du Bougainville*, where Tahiti is represented as a happily promiscuous and fortunately atheistical society, free from crime for the very reason that it has no laws. Though the *Supplément* was written in 1772, it was not published until 1796; however, Diderot was able to publish views on the virtues of savagery through his contribution to the large-scale collective work known as Abbé Raynal's *Histoire Philosophique des Européens dans les deux Indes* (1770), which provided the eighteenth century's most voluminous documentation of the idea of the noble savage, and suffered the not-uncommon fate of being ordered to be burned by the common hangman of Paris. With the Pacific voyages being discussed everywhere, it is not surprising that Rousseau's Scottish disciple, James Boswell, should want to go and live for three years in Tahiti or New Zealand, 'in order to obtain a full acquaintance with people, so totally different from all that we have ever known, and be satisfied what pure nature can do for man'; nor is it surprising that Johnson should declare that nothing could be learned from such people, and that, on another occasion when Boswell praised the Tahitians, he should retort: 'Don't cant in defence of Savages.'[59]

Stay-at-homes were able to judge Pacific islanders for themselves when Omai was brought from Tahiti in 1774, to become the most famous as well as the most noble of a succession of savage visitors to eighteenth-century London, a succession which included four Iroquois chiefs in 1710, three Cherokee chiefs in 1762, and five Eskimos in 1772. Omai mingled with the highest English society, behaving with a natural patrician grace that was much admired: his character was used by many satirists of the 1770s to attack the corruptions of civilization; he was portrayed as the 'gentlest savage' in Cowper's *Task*, i. 631–72; Fanny Burney said that his manners shamed education; even Johnson was impressed, though he was sure that Omai had learned his good manners from Europeans. The full-length portrait of Omai painted by Reynolds (see Plate 12) is all nobility and no savagery: the pose of the figure is an adaptation of the Belvedere Apollo, the costume is the robe and turban of an Arabian prince; the landscape background, despite its exotic vegetation, is Claudian in feeling. Reynolds, like Bougainville, assimilates his Polynesian to the classical idea, and so, even more strikingly, does Johann Zoffany in his painting of *The Death of Cook* (begun 1789, see Plate 14), where the leading assassin is represented in the pose of the *Discobolus* and his victim in the pose of the *Dying Gaul*, or *Dying Gladiator*. In the artist's eclectic imagination both the noble savages of Hawaii and the dying hero of scientific discovery and maritime empire take on the noble simplicity and sedate grandeur of the Greek ideal. The savages are seen to be not brutal murderers, but instruments of Fate in a grand tragic drama. Though the painting itself is not a masterpiece, it is a thoroughly representative work in its expression of patriotism, public virtue, exoticism, and noble savagery, in a style that is both romantic and classical.

Notes

1. *Analysis of Beauty*, edited by J. Burke (Oxford, 1955), p. 62.

2. *Correspondence of Edmund Burke*, III edited by G. H. Guttridge (Cambridge, 1961), 35l. Some of the cultural effects of this exploration are discussed in P. J. Marshall and G. Williams, *The Great Map of Mankind* (1982).

3. *Characteristicks of Men, Manners, Opinions, Times*, second edition (1714), I, 344.

4. *Letters on the Spirit of Patriotism and on the Idea of a Patriot King*, edited by A. Hassall (Oxford, 1917), pp. 129–30.

5. *Works of Virgil*, edited by J. Warton (1753), I, 19.

6. Dryden, *Discourse concerning Satire*, in *Essays*, edited by W. P. Ker (Oxford, 1900), II, 87; *Works of Pope* edited by J. Warton (1797), VIII, 226.

7. *Characteristicks*, I, 219–20.

8. Quoted in H. D. Weinbrot, *Augustus Caesar in 'Augustan' England* (Princeton, NJ, 1978), p. 127. See Weinbrot's book for a thorough study of Pope's 'Augustanism'; for an alternative view see H. Erskine-Hill, *The Augustan Idea in English Literature* (1983).

9. E. Rothstein, *Restoration and Eighteenth-Century Poetry, 1660–1780* (1981), pp. 97–98.

10. *Characteristicks*, I, 269–70; III, 249–50.

11. *The Difference between Verbal and Practical Virtue* (1742), Augustan Reprint Society (1967).

12. *Essay on Civil Society*, edited by D. Forbes (Edinburgh, 1966), p. 135; Part III, Section ii.

13. *Memoirs*, edited by G. B. Hill (1900), p. 92.

14. *Essay on Civil Society* p. 134; III, ii.

15. *Essay upon the Constitution of the Roman Government*, in *Works* (1726), I, 98.

16. *Memoirs*, p. 167.

17. *Complete Letters of Lady Mary Wortley Montagu*, edited by R. Halsband (Oxford, 1965–67) I, 332, 406; Robert Wood, *Essay on the Original Genius of Homer* (1767).

18. *Coleridge's Miscellaneous Criticism*, edited by T. N. Raysor (1936), p. 308.

19. William Duff, *Essay on Original Genius* (1767), p. 104.

20. *Characteristicks*, III, 138 196, III, 141, I, 220, 239, 264.

21. Alexander Drummond, *Travels . . . as far as the Banks of the Euphrates* (1754), quoted in B. H. Stern, *The Rise of Romantic Hellenism in English Literature, 1732–1786* (Menasha, Wis., 1940), pp. 32–33.

22. *Decline and Fall of the Roman Empire*, edited by J. B. Bury, revised edition, (1926–29), VI, 486.

23. *Preface to the Iliad* in the *Twickenham Edition of the Poems of Alexander Pope*, VII edited by M. Mack (1967), 18, 4, 6.

24. *Enquiry* (1735), p. 142.

25. Quoted in T. Webb, *English Romantic Hellenism, 1700–1824* (Manchester, 1982), p. 145.

26. Letter of 14 April 1743, in *Horace Walpole's Correspondence*, edited by W. S. Lewis XVIII (New Haven, 1955), 211.

27. Quoted in Rose Macaulay, *The Pleasure of Ruins* (1966), p. 72.

28. *Decline and Fall*, I, 302.

29. *Reflections on the Painting and Sculpture of the Greeks*, translated by Henry Fuseli (1765), p. 30.

30. A distinguished exception is John Buxton, in *The Grecian Taste* (1978), pp. 85–104.

31. Ibid., pp. 85, 86.

32. Gray and Collins, *Poetical Works*, edited by Roger Lonsdale (1977), p. xv.

33. Thomas Davies, *Life of David Garrick* (1780), II, 38.

34. *Enquiry into the Life and Writings of Homer* (1735), p. 64.

35. *Five Miscellaneous Essays*, edited by S. H. Monk (Ann Arbor, 1963), p. 142.

36. *History of England* (Oxford, 1826), I, 23.

37. See A. L. Owen, *The Famous Druids* (Oxford, 1962), especially pp. 224–36.

38. Thomas Gray, *Correspondence*, edited by P. Toynbee and L. Whibley (Oxford, 1935), I, 71, 74; letters of 13 October, 16 November 1739.

39. *Works of Lyttelton*, second edition (1775), pp. 719, 720.

40. *Correspondence*, II, 415; letter of 8 November 1765.

41. *A Journey to the Western Islands of Scotland*, edited by Mary Lascelles (New Haven, 1971), p. 77.

42. James Thomson, *Summer*, l. 1575; first published 1744; see *The Seasons*, edited by James Sambrook (Oxford, 1981), p. 132.

43. *Observations on the Faerie Queene of Spenser*, second edition (1762), II, 268.

44. Ibid., II, 135.

45. John Butt, in *The Mid-Eighteenth Century*, by John Butt and Geoffrey Carnall, *Oxford History of English Literature* VIII, (1979), 112.

46. *Enquiry into the Life and Writings of Homer* (1735), p. 141.

47. *Characteristicks*, second edition (1714), II, 387–88.

48. *Sacred Poetry of the Hebrews*, translated by G. Gregory (1787), lecture XIV.

49. *Essay on the original Genius and Writings of Homer* (1775), p. 173.

50. *Five Miscellaneous Essays*, p. 151.

51. Quoted in P. J. Marshall, *The British Discovery of Hinduism in the Eighteenth Century* (Cambridge, 1970), p. 194.

52. *Five Miscellaneous Essays*, pp. 123, 115.

53. Ibid., p. 121.

54. *A Voyage round the World by George Shevlocke*, edited by W. G. Perrin (1928), p. 224.

55. *History of America* (1977), ii, 94.

56. 'Cook', in *Biographia Britannica*, second edition iv, (1789), 158.

57. *Voyage round the World*, translated by J. R. Forster (1772), pp. 219, 249.

58. *Account of the Voyages* (1773), ii, 186, 101.

59. *Boswell's Life of Johnson*, edited by G. B. Hill, revised by L. F. Powell (Oxford, 1934), iii, 49; iv, 308–9.

Chapter 8
Conclusion

Exploration, empiricism, and evolution

The death of Captain Cook 'struck a note of high emotional tragedy which was hardly to recur in England until the loss of Nelson at Trafalgar twenty-five years later'.[1] Cook was a man whom the English people could regard with special affection and complacency, as a peculiarly English sort of national hero, both in his character and his achievements. He was a man of low birth who had risen to greatness by his own efforts; he was plain in appearance and unassuming in manner; he was patient, humane, practical, courageous, dependable, and full of intellectual curiosity. His great voyages were undertaken not to plunder and destroy, but in order to spread the benefits of civilization, whatever those benefits may be, and to enlarge the store of human knowledge: in Charles Darwin's phrase, he added a hemisphere to the civilized world. Sailing as much under the banner of science as under the British flag, Captain Cook is an epitome of the pragmatic and empirical spirit in which new worlds, both material and intellectual, were accurately charted in the eighteenth century.

Cook's first biographer, summarizing his subject's genius, observed: 'By genius I do not here understand imagination merely, or that power of culling the flowers of fancy which poetry delights in; but an inventive mind; a mind full of resources; and which, by its own native vigour, can suggest noble objects of pursuit, and the most effectual methods of attaining them.'[2] Nevertheless, Cook's useful career of practical seamanship provided flowers of the fancy for others to cull, and served to widen the horizons of imagination along with those of science: his descriptions of luminous protozoa in slimy seas and of polar fogs and icebergs fed Coleridge's visual imagination no less generously than Newton's untwisting of the rainbow had fed Pope's and Thomson's and Smart's and many another poetic imagination earlier in the century. Few poets before Blake and Keats were prepared to accept that all charms fly at the mere touch of cold natural philosophy; many believed that the experimental scientist and the poet were allies: Addison, for instance, claimed that, after the poets themselves, 'there are none who more gratify and enlarge the Imagination, than the Authors of the new Philosophy' (*Spectator*, no. 420); Thomson's *Seasons*, Pope's *Essay on Man*, and Young's *Night Thoughts* are only the best known of a great crop of didactic poems which testify to the immensity, variety, and beautiful fitness of the universe newly revealed by scientists.

Though the pace of scientific discovery, or at least scientific speculation, continued to accelerate during the eighteenth century, what was perhaps more significant was the wide extent to which new ideas, born of the seventeenth-century and eighteenth-century scientific revolution, spread and settled into general public consciousness. Addison speaks, as usual, for his generation when he says: 'I shall be ambitious to have it said of me, that I have brought Philosophy out of Closets and Libraries, Schools and Colleges, to dwell in Clubs and Assemblies, at Tea-Tables, and in Coffee-Houses' (*Spectator*, no. 10). It was in his lifetime that, despite sporadic Scriblerian sniping at the *virtuosi*, science began to enjoy a wide prestige that has continued constantly to increase down to the present day. The successes of science, particularly those associated with the heroic name of Newton, inspired thinkers in other fields to employ the inductive, experimental method in a search for 'natural laws'. Locke's *Essay concerning Human Understanding* follows the Baconian and Newtonian empirical way, and sets the course for the main stream of British philosophy in the eighteenth century. Bishop Butler defends Christianity by the methods of empirical philosophy in his *Analogy of Religion*. The methods of empirical science are adapted to the fine arts when Reynolds argues, in his *Discourses*, that the artist must, like the natural historian, abstract the general form of a species from his minute examination of many individual specimens, all of which differ from one another and none of which itself possesses the ideal form. Hume announces on the title-page that his *Treatise of Human Nature* is an attempt to introduce the experimental method of reasoning into moral subjects, and claims in the body of his treatise that association of ideas is a force as effective in the mental world as gravitation in the physical.

The subject of Newton's great treatise is the *mathematical* principles of natural philosophy. Locke, like Descartes, Spinoza, and Leibniz, among others, thought it would be possible to devise a science of morals as exact as mathematics; even Shaftesbury referred to his own doctrine of the good heart as 'moral arithmetic'.[3] George Cheyne begins his *Philosophical Principles of Religion* (1715) with definitions and axioms and then proceeds, by way of theorems and corollories deduced from his axioms, to elaborate a complete theological system. Hutcheson devised mathematical formulae for natural laws governing beauty and good: he claimed that the quality of beauty is a compound ratio between variety and uniformity in the object, and, similarly, that the quality of public good is a compound ratio between benevolence and ability in the moral agent. Just as Halley's astronomical calculations were useful to the practical art of navigation, so Hutcheson's moral algebra served useful ends, by definition, when it was developed by Bentham into the 'felicific calculus' upon which he erected his utilitarian system of philosophy.

As Newton's discoveries served to justify an empirical and mathematical approach in all avenues of intellectual enquiry, so the Newtonian system gave authority to the old conception of the universe as a great machine, the handiwork of an intelligent creator. Eighteenth-century theologians, down to Paley's time, never tire of the clock-and-divine-clock-maker analogy; many writers on politics before Burke regard the English constitution as a finely contrived, well-balanced machine; some see the whole of society as a moral machine, in which, according to Adam Smith, virtue is 'the fine polish to the wheels', and vice 'the vile rust, which makes them jar and grate upon one another'.[4] Man's body is regarded as a particularly elaborate and delicate clock, which, according to the physiologist George Cheyne, is kept in motion by an internal spring made out of 'spiritual substance',[5] and, according to Bishop Butler, is contrived for the purpose of virtue, just as a watch is made to measure time. None of those theologians and moralists was a materialist, neither was Newton; but the idea of the universe or the individual man being a machine obviously could have materialistic implications, as La Mettrie was to demonstrate with Gallic logic, in *L'homme machine* (1748).

The notion of the universal machine was always countered by organic images: Shaftesbury ridicules the philosophers who limit their studies to physiology, because they are not considering 'the real operation or Energy' of man, or even the real man, as human agent, but only 'as a *Watch* or common *Machine*'[6]; expanding his view, Shaftesbury declares that all things in this world are united as the branch is united with the tree; Hume's Philo demonstrates that the world resembles more an animal or a vegetable, than a watch or knitting loom. We may suspect a trace of sceptical irony in Hume, but in the case of Shaftesbury such an organic image is consonant with his seriously-held neo-Platonic belief in a universal plastic nature, which, subordinate to God, forms and organizes all matter; such a plastic power does not operate upon matter externally and mechanically, as gravitation might be thought to, but works from within, vitally as a soul, to animate all thought and all objects of thought.

In Shaftesbury, a Platonic and metaphysical world-view is united with a freethinking religion of nature which is anti-metaphysical in its exclusion of supernatural revelation, particularly miracles. One of the most far-reaching effects of the spread of scientific knowledge was to dispel a belief in miracles and prodigies. Natural religion made headway against revealed religion, of course; but even the stoutest English Protestant defenders of biblical revelation were sceptical of modern miracles if such miracles involved the suspension of some natural law by which the movements of the universal machine were regulated. There were signs of the times when Royalty and Parliament (institutions not traditionally associated with innovation) demonstrated their disbelief in modern miracles: on his accession in 1714, George I abolished the ritual of the monarch touching children to cure scrofula, or the 'King's Evil'; in 1736 Parliament repealed the old English statutes against witchcraft. Eventually, it appeared that the only certain, acceptable modern miracle was the continuing miracle of individual personal faith: each man feels the truth of religion by the testimony of the spirit, an inward impression of the soul; this truth is generated by his hopes and fears, for, like the rest of his knowledge and experience, it is provided by the imagination. Hume's proof of such a miracle of faith may have been intended to be ironic, but, in the event, he pointed out the best refuge for

Christianity, as the expansion of scientific knowledge appeared to make, first the argument from revelation, and later the argument from design, increasingly untenable.

Viewed in one aspect, the effect of science upon religion was to force supernaturalism back from external nature into the imagination; viewed in another, it was to liberate human intelligence from that biblical system of time and space in which earlier men had placed unquestioning faith. It thus became yet another front of the general intellectual expansion of the eighteenth century, another part of the unrolling of the great map of mankind. At the same time, navigation, under the banner of science, brought under view a great variety of hitherto unknown or little-known societies, and thus widened the knowledge of human nature. Modern Europeans believed that they could see their own ancestors in the primitive societies of their own day: the Homeric Greek warrior lived on in the contemporary Red Indian or the Arab tribesman. The scope of history was greatly enlarged; its triumphs almost rivalled those of science; indeed, it became, in Vico's words, the 'new science' (*Scienza Nuovo*).

The new science regarded history, not as a parade of events, not necessarily as a providential chronicle of God's dealings with mankind, not even as philosophy teaching political wisdom by examples, but as the great process by which whole societies pass through their life-cycles. This process is governed in its first stages by circumstances of geography, climate, and natural resources, and in its later stages by gradually evolving institutions, customs, laws, religions, commerce, and other social activities, which interact to bring about further evolution. Gibbon's is the greatest English example of the new, philosophical history in our period: despite its subject, 'the triumph of barbarism and religion', and its author's sceptical temper, the *Decline and Fall of the Roman Empire* affirms the idea of progress; Gibbon is happy 'to acquiesce in the pleasing conclusion, that every age of the world has increased, and still increases, the real wealth, the happiness, the knowledge, and perhaps the virtue, of the human race'.[7]

Study of cultural evolution was paralleled by the rise of evolutionary theories in the natural sciences. Before the end of the seventeenth century, scientists were beginning to realize that fossil evidence proved that, during the passage of geological time, some whole species of creatures had become extinct and others had come into existence. Leibniz therefore argued that the great chain of being was still in the process of completion, as the ever-living monads regrouped themselves again and again according to a programme predetermined by God; thus the universe was in perpetual progress. On a more mundane level, La Mettrie argued that if an orang-outang were educated by means of the deaf-and-dumb alphabet he would rapidly acquire the understanding and sensibilities of *Homo sapiens*; by that acquisition he would have progressed up the great chain of being. Hartley saw the mental and moral life of each man in terms of progress; in his view, the gentle, moulding power of the association of ideas directed every mind towards virtue and happiness: 'Association . . . has a Tendency to reduce the State of those who have eaten of the Tree of the Knowledge of Good and Evil, back to a paradisiacal one.' If this state were not enough, 'the dim Spaces of Futurity' provided, according to Thomson, an arena

> where the Mind,
> In endless Growth and infinite Ascent,
> Rises from State to State, and World to World.[8]

Thomson is developing the belief expressed in *Paradise Lost*, v. 469–500, and Addison's *Spectator*, no. 111; this same doctrine of spiritual progress, that all created life moves upwards towards God, is reasserted by Young, in *Night Thoughts*, and Akenside, in *Pleasures of the Imagination*, using terms which draw on nascent scientific theories of evolution. As the eighteenth century advanced, it became easier to think about external nature, society, and human nature in terms of a process than in terms of a state; the idea of perfectibility was born, and, as applied to human nature, this idea was interpreted by some as meaning that it was possible for man to reach a state of felicity by his own powers.

Perception and imagination

The fully formed doctrine of the moral perfectibility, that is, of the indefinite improvement of man upon earth, proclaimed by Helvétius and Priestley for example, was regarded as a corollary of Locke's notion of the *tabula rasa*. If the mind was a sheet of white paper upon which sensory experience impressed characters, then there was real hope of transforming human nature through a reshaping of the environment. Not only the idea of perfectibility, but political radicalism, scepticism (religious and philosophical), and even the 'romantic' doctrine of the primary imagination have their origins partly in Locke's thought. As Newton established a point of departure for eighteenth-century exploration of the world of external nature, so Locke established one for exploration of the strangest region of the great map of mankind, the mind itself. Though his findings were more often rejected, or, at least, heavily qualified, by eighteenth-century thinkers than Newton's discoveries were, he laid down the main lines upon which men sought to investigate identity, perception, understanding, and imagination, and attempted to deal with the vexing problem of the relationship betwen mind and matter.

Locke's theory that all ideas are derived ultimately from sense impressions, and that perception is brought about by the action of physical objects on the mind through the senses and the brain, seemed to receive support from Newton's experimental work in optics and from contemporary attempts by others to carry out a systematic anatomical study of the nervous system. According to various mechanical theories, visual perception was caused by the vibration of corpuscles of light or the flow of light-waves in the ethereal medium between the object and the eye, followed by vibration of the optic nerves themselves or of minute particles through the nerves, or by the passage of electrical impulses or flow of animal spirits along the nerves to the brain. Comparable mechanical systems were postulated to account for the impressions of senses other than sight. To describe the activity of perception after the point at which impulses reach the brain even the most clinical of physiologists were obliged to fall back on metaphor: George Cheyne likens 'the intelligent Principle, or *Soul*', which 'resides somewhere in the Brain', to an organist, the keys of whose 'finely fram'd and well-'tun'd organ' are the nerves; Locke says that the senses and nerves are like conduits which convey ideas 'from without to their Audience in the Brain, the Mind's Presence-room'.[9] Mechanical theories of perception were elaborated by Hartley, and were extended even into aesthetics when Burke attempted to prove that the ideas of beauty and sublimity are certain qualities in objects which act mechanically upon the senses, brain, and mind to produce specific emotional responses, just as the application of ice or fire produces the sense impressions of cold or heat.

Locke's distinction between primary qualities, which would exist if no one perceived them, and secondary qualities, which depend upon perception for their existence, was denied by Berkeley and Hume, but not before Addison had made it an important feature of his highly influential writings upon the imagination. According to Addison, the discovery of Locke and Newton, 'that Light and Colours, as apprehended by the Imagination, are only Ideas in the Mind, and not Qualities that have any Existence in Matter (*Spectator*, no. 13), means that, in our ordinary perception of the external world, we are like the enchanted hero of a romance, who sees pleasing apparitions, imaginary glories, and visionary beauty. The enchantment which so delights the hero is not explained further than that it is a way in which God communicates with man; there is no consideration of possible subjectivist implications in the ordinary perceiver being an enchanted hero, and the ordinary world the pleasing delusion of his imagination.

Shaftesbury's version of Platonism postulated a wholly non-mechanical process by which the external world is related to the internal and by which man is related to God, that is, to the 'great genius', 'original soul', or diffusive vital spirit of natural religion. The key for Shaftesbury is in the unLockeian internal 'moral sense', which is also the sense of beauty: this sense, at its most highly developed, links the whole man to external nature in an immediate, delightful intuition that the beautiful, the good, and the true are all one. In the rhapsodic climax of *The Moralists*, when both interlocutors find themslves, like other lovers, 'deep in the romantic way', man's genius, 'the genius of the place', and 'the great genius' meet in an act of imagination which is also a feeling of love; man sees into the true life and 'genuine order' of things because his mind itself is part of a divine universal harmony.[10]

The fashion in which English poets responded to Locke and Shaftesbury and reconciled their systems, is nicely illustrated in a passage from Thomson's *Spring* (1728):

> 'Tis *Harmony*, that World-embracing Power,
> By which all Beings are adjusted, each
> To all around, impelling and impell'd

In endless Circulation, that inspires
This universal Smile. Thus the glad Skies,
The wide-rejoycing Earth, the Woods, the Streams,
With every *Life* they hold, down to the Flower
That paints the lowly Vale, or Insect-Wing
Wav'd o'er the Shepherd's Slumber, touch the Mind
To Nature tun'd, with a light-flying Hand,
Invisible; quick-urging, thro' the Nerves,
The glittering Spirits, in a Flood of Day.

(ll. 165–76)

The external world 'touches' the mind as a result of the motion of animal spirits along the optic nerves, but what floods into the mind is a sudden awareness of the universal harmony of mind and matter, where all is charged with joy.

Berkeley and Hume did not directly influence eighteenth-century imaginative literature as much as Locke and Shaftesbury did, but they contributed no less to a developing awareness of the central importance of the imagination in the act of perception. Berkeley develops Locke's theories about ideas far more systematically than Addison, and rejects some of Locke's main premises, in his proof that the 'external world', if not a delusion, is wholly mind-dependent: it exists only as it is perceived, and it has continuity only by virtue of its being an idea in the mind of God. Hume takes the thinking of Locke and Berkeley to a sceptical conclusion. After his destructive analysis of our rational beliefs, including the belief in human identity itself, we are left only with the imagination, which unites a succession of distinct impressions into the appearance of continued reality; the only world that we have any knowledge of is, in Hume's words, 'the universe of the imagination'. Though Hume tempered his subjectivism with an ironic reflection that we do not live our ordinary social lives according to speculative philosophy, it appeared that he had reduced (or raised) man to the state of Addison's enchanted hero in a romance; Thomas Reid, the philosopher of common sense, protests, indeed, that Hume made of the mind 'an enchanted castle', within which we are 'imposed upon by spectres and apparitions.'[12]

Hume himself would have readily agreed that the truths of religion are spectres and apparitions of the imagination; in his view, men are led to a belief in a god or gods, not by reason, but by the passions of hope and fear playing upon the idea of futurity. His demolition of the external 'evidences' of natural and of revealed religion was, no doubt, intended to discompose the orthodox, but his argument that religious belief rests upon the subjective basis of man's imagination places him very unexpectedly in the company of the saintly William Law, who asserts that our desires and imaginations 'are the greatest reality we have, and are the true *Formers* and *Raisers* of all that is real and solid in us'. According to Law, 'our own Will and desirous Imagination . . . resemble in some Degree the Creating Power of God, which makes things out of itself or its own working Desire'.[13] Here, as early as 1740, we find, in all its creative fullness, the Coleridgean primary imagination, where perceived images of the external world are united with the desires and passions of the perceiver. Law, like Coleridge, conceives of the imagination in religious terms; so, in their various ways, do Shaftesbury, Addison, and Berkeley; only Hume gives a wholly secular theory.

If perception of the ordinary world is an act of the imagination, so, too, must be perception of works of art. In the course of the eighteenth century, critics came to recognize more and more fully that a work of art is not to be apprehended by the reason, but by the passions and the imagination. Dennis, Shaftesbury, Addison, and Hume, all in their very different ways, explore the pleasurable effect upon the reader's and the viewer's mind of those strong emotions aroused by the sublime and the tragic. It is found that a kind of wildness pleases and a kind of terror delights the imagination; the reader becomes accustomed to being 'hurried out of himself,' to being 'transported', or 'charmed'. The principle of sympathy, so central to the moral thought of the eighteenth century, is invoked in aesthetics to explain how poetry and painting, and what Burke calls the 'other affecting arts',[14] transfuse passions from artist to audience: art achieves its effects by a strong contagion of feeling. Towards the end of our period, Reynolds sums up the great end of art as 'to make an impression on the imagination and the feeling'; he claims that poetry and painting are addressed 'to the desires of the mind', and he declares roundly that 'the imagination is here the residence of truth'.[15] In 1786, few men would have contested these assertions.

Imagination is the residence of truth for the audience because it is the residence of truth for the artist too. The eighteenth century was no less ready than earlier centuries to recognize and applaud that creative faculty which Coleridge called the secondary imagination, and to regard the artist as a second maker under God. For Shaftesbury, writing in the first decade of the century, the poet is 'a just Prometheus under Jove'; he is the human genius who animates and shapes his material into a unity, just as the 'Great Genius', or universal, organic 'plastic'[16] principle animates and shapes nature itself. Fifty and sixty years later than Shaftesbury, Edward Young and Alexander Gerard develop a more original organic analogy for the process of artistic creation, when they liken it to the growth of a vegetable. Duff writes of 'the vigorous efforts of the creative Imagination', by which the poet 'calls shadowy substances and unreal objects into existence. They are present to his view, and glide, like spectres, in silent, sullen majesty, before his astonished and intranced sight.'[17] Such spectres glide through English writing on the creative imagination from the beginning of the century, critical interest in them being prompted initially by the general admiration and delight aroused by Spenser's fairy world, whose inhabitants so obviously are apparitions generated by the magical power of the imagination. Addison takes up and greatly develops Dryden's discussion of 'the fairy way of writing'; Hurd, like Duff, is awed by 'the portentous spectres of the imagination'.[18] The poetic (secondary) imagination is regarded as a kind of fairyland, a self-sufficient mental region, free from all ordinary constraints of space, time, and matter, where, as Edward Young observes, genius has creative power 'and may reign arbitrarily over its own empire of Chimeras'.[19]

Whether the imagination was being considered as the creative power peculiar to the artist or as the prime agent of all ordinary human perception, it was closely associated with sympathy, that affective power happily described in Hume's metaphor of the human violins: 'As in strings equally wound up, the motion of one communicates itself to the rest; so all the affections readily pass from one person to another, and beget correspondent movements in every human creature.' Johnson, in *Rambler*, no. 60, recognizes the beneficial power of imaginative sympathy: 'All joy or sorrow for the happiness or calamities of others is produced by an act of the imagination, that realizes the event . . . by placing us, for a time, in the condition of him whose fortune we contemplate; so that we feel . . . whatever emotions would be excited by the same good or evil happening to ourselves.' Sympathy, as defined by Adam Smith, is 'our fellow-feeling with any passion whatsoever'; it is an activity solely of the imagination, because only the imagination can 'carry us beyond our own person'[20] to bridge the gap between subject and object.

'Age of Reason' and other clichés

The theory of imagination developed in the eighteenth century represents for students of literature probably the most important result of a general reduction of the authority of reason during that period, in religion, morals, politics, and aesthetics, indeed, in all areas of human thought other than the natural sciences. By 1740, Hume was able to show that 'reason is, and ought only to be the slave of the passions, and can never pretend to any other office than to serve and obey them'.[21] Poetic eyes are said to be quicker than philosophic ones: in his *Essay on Man*, the philosophy of which is very far from innovatory, Pope had described man as 'reas'ning but to err' and had seen the clue to human behaviour in the 'ruling passion'. It was therefore odd of Matthew Arnold to refer to Pope as a 'high priest of an age of prose and reason'. The phrase 'age of reason' unfortunately stuck to literary history; it was adopted as a handy label by several generations of the men who packaged English literature for school and college, and it is still sometimes attached to the eighteenth century by historians of thought and literature, despite the strenuous efforts of critics (mostly American) over the past thirty years, to unstick it. J. W. Johnson reasonably observes: 'When applied to the conceptual bases of most Restoration and eighteenth-century prose', the term 'Age of Reason' is 'grossly inappropriate. Dryden, Swift, Pope, Addison, Steele, Johnson, Goldsmith were all cautious in their reliance on the ratiocinative faculties of the human mind as the agency of truth.'[22] Donald Greene rightly points out that the label was first popularized by Tom Paine's *The Age of Reason*, which was published in 1794, after the end of our period. Greene notes:

Its thesis seems to be that the priest-ridden eighteenth century then ending is anything *but* the age of reason; that presumably is to come in the more enlightened future. To symbolize this, the French Revolutionaries about the same time converted Notre Dame into the Temple of Reason and installed an actress as its Goddess of Reason. How the thought of Pope, Swift, and Johnson could be assimilated to these antics it is hard to say.[23]

That 'these antics' could just about be assimilated to the anticlerical spirit of some mid-eighteenth-century French philosophers who were part of the European intellectual movement later called 'the Enlightenment' is perhaps a sufficient indication that 'the Age of the Enlightenment' is no more a suitable label for eighteenth-century English literature and thought than 'the Age of Reason' is. There is no doubt that eighteenth-century Englishmen were aware of being enlightened by rapid advances in knowledge: Pope's famous epigram upon Newton tells us that 'all was Light', and Addison reminds us that 'the fairy way of writing' flourished in the Elizabethan period, before 'the World was enlightened by Learning and Philosophy' (*Spectator*, no. 419). Perhaps we need not suspect Addison of irony, but Berkeley's reference to atheists as 'select spirits of this enlightened age', in *Alciphron* (1732) is undoubtedly ironic.[24] Though it is true that Locke, Newton, Shaftesbury, and the English freethinkers nourished the thinking of mid-century Continental philosophers, the Enlightenment remains a label most clearly understood when it is attached only to the writings of a specific group of French *philosophes* in the middle and later years of the eighteenth century and their associates and fellow spirits in other countries, notably Hume and Gibbon in Britain. Hume and Gibbon are, of course, untypical English writers of this period, inasmuch as they were not professing Christians.

Oddly, the somewhat constricting designation of eighteenth-century English literature and thought as 'the Age of the Enlightenment' has never been as popular among twentieth-century English critics and historians as the much narrower (and positively misleading) label, 'the Augustan Age'. This modern use of 'Augustan' to define the artistic and intellectual character of all or part of the eighteenth century, or all of the period from 1660 to 1820, rests upon the assumption that Augustus was the object of admiration during the period referred to, but, as Howard Weinbrot demonstrates in *Augustus Caesar in 'Augustan' England* (1978), such an assumption is ill-founded. With a wealth of detailed reference which scarcely begins to exhaust the available evidence, Weinbrot shows that 'to call the eighteenth century an "Augustan age" with any pretence to serious meaning, is to misrepresent British history and much of what that century said and thought of itself'; he concludes that it is best to 'avoid the curious practice of saddling those 140 years, or significant parts of them, with the name of a man who would have been as welcome there as hemlock to a philosopher'.[25]

Though 'the Augustan Age' is an inadequate and misleading label for the period, it does not follow that Roman models were unimportant in the eighteenth century: the Roman rural ideal and the Roman republican ideal of civic virtue each had a positive value greater than either the positive or the negative values of the Augustan example. Nevertheless, for the greater part of the century, Greek literature and art were valued more highly than Roman; it was agreed that much of what was most valuable in Roman culture had been borrowed from Greece, the liberty-loving land where the arts and sciences were first formed and brought to perfection. Furthermore, the idea of classical culture was not derived only from Greece and Rome: Byzantium, the Christian Fathers, and the Renaissance Humanists all added their contributions. Christopher Dawson, in an essay on Edward Gibbon, one of the eighteenth century's most complete classicists, points out that Gibbon's culture was 'the tradition of the classical world transmitted through medieval Christendom and reinforced by the Humanism of the Italian Renaissance and the classicism of the seventeenth and eighteenth centuries'; Dawson, incidentally, notes Gibbon's responsiveness to the 'exotic appeal' of Arabic and Persian writers, and the 'romantic allure' of Petrarch and Rienzi.[26]

The terms 'neo-classical' and 'classical' undoubtedly cover vastly more of the thought and culture of the eighteenth century than 'Augustan' does, but they also cover rather more than our period. Of the many European eighteenth-century 'classical revivals', from the cult of Cato onwards, the most broadly based and most self-conscious one is perhaps that movement in the visual arts which is associated with the Adam brothers, Flaxman, David, Ingres, and Winckelmann; but this movement reached its full strength and maturity in the French Revolutionary period (when Tom Paine was proclaiming the dawn of the Age of Reason) and in the first two or three decades of the nineteenth century. Donald Greene observes: 'What use the student of literature can make of this knowledge is hard to say, except perhaps to suggest . . . that it would make more sense to call the "Romantic period" the "Classical period".'[27] The far more important point, as Greene makes abundantly clear, is that writers and thinkers in the eighteenth century were no more and no less awed by, or dependent upon, classical models than were writers in the sixteenth, seventeenth, and nineteenth centuries: for instance there is quite as much of the Greek and Roman classics in Spenser, Johnson, Milton, Shelley, Tennyson, Arnold, and Morris as in any eighteenth-century poet. Thomas Warton was a more alert historian of English poetry than most of his nineteenth-century and twentieth-century successors when he referred to the Earl of Surrey (d. 1547) as 'our first English classical poet'.[28]

No doubt it would be absurd to match Greene's exasperated, half-humorous suggestion, that it would make more sense to call the 'Romantic period' the 'Classical period', with the complementary suggestion that it would make more sense to call the 'Classical period' the 'Romantic period'. Nevertheless, we should not forget that Spenser's reputation in the early eighteenth century stood as high as if not higher than, it did at any other time, and that he was, like Shakespeare, idolized and imitated as a 'romantic', not a 'classical' writer. Milton, the third dominating English presence in poetry and criticism at that period, contributed much to Gothic taste with his widely influential *Il Penseroso*; features of *Paradise Lost* were rightly admired by Addison as 'romantic'. Addison himself, the author of *Cato*, the interpreter of Milton, the apostle of Newton and Locke, the lover of medieval ballads, the admirer of 'the fairy way of writing', and the theorist of the creative imagination, is discussed by F. W. Bateson in terms of his 'classical prose' and his 'incipient Romanticism'.[29] R. L. Brett says of Shaftesbury 'that, though his own taste in art was classical, his philosophy contained the seeds of romanticism'; Basil Willey implicitly agrees when he entitles his radio talk on Shaftesbury 'A romantic Augustan' (despite the fact that Shaftesbury's thought probably owes rather more to Greece than to Rome and that his few references to Augustus are conventionally hostile).[30] This is to limit ourselves to the reign of Queen Anne: it need hardly be argued that there are many more signs of 'seminal' or 'incipient Romanticism' under the first two Georges, however one cares to define that maddeningly opaque term 'romantic'.

The notion of 'incipient Romanticism' and the older, now discredited, notion of 'pre-Romanticism' rest, of course, upon the implicit belief that in the eighteenth and early nineteenth centuries there was a definable 'Classical' age followed by a sort of cultural change of government, which instituted a definable 'Romantic' age; this is essentially a Private-Willis-eye view of cultural history, a view not materially altered when critics introduce a third party called the 'Age of Sensibility', into a supposed chronological gap between the 'Classical' age and the 'Romantic' age. Such views are nicely parodied by Northrop Frye, when he writes of the way that many modern undergraduates learn about English poetry from Pope to Wordsworth: 'Our students are thus graduated with a vague notion that the age of sensibility was the time when poetry moved from a reptilian Classicism, all cold and dry reason, to a mammalian Romanticism, all warm and wet feelings.'[31] The truth is that, on any reasonable definition of these two epithets, both 'romantic' and 'classical' features may be found early and late in the eighteenth century, just as they may be found early and late in the nineteenth century. It is high time that we took notice of what David Nichol Smith wrote nearly fifty years ago: 'I sometimes doubt if we shall ever understand the poetry of [the eighteenth] century till we get rid of the terms "classical" and "romantic" in one and all of their forms. Johnson, Coleridge, and Hazlitt – perhaps our three greatest critics – did not find the need of them; nor should we.'[32]

This chapter began with a suggestion that the genius of Captain Cook is somehow typical of the eighteenth century. Cook's lifetime (1728–79), spanned much of the working lives of Burke, Goldsmith, Hogarth, Hume, William Law, Johnson, William Pitt, Priestley, Reynolds, Thomson, Horace Walpole, and John Wesley, every one of whom could with equal or greater justice be regarded as typical of this age. Of the last man on my list, Donald Greene writes: 'it is hard to think of Wesley as a "Pre-romantic", and still harder as a "Neoclassical" figure or a representative of the "Age of Reason". Surely there must be some inadequacy in all these labels if none of them can find room for a figure so powerful, so influential, so genuinely characteristic of the eighteenth century as Wesley.' Though one or other of the tendentious labels discarded by Greene might just fit some of the other men in my list, none of the labels is remotely suitable for all of them. Greene does more justice to the spirit of the eighteenth century than most critics when he characterizes it as a combination of Augustinianism and empiricism, or, in another context, calls this period 'the Age of Exuberance',[33] but there is no sign that other literary historians are following his example. Perhaps we should not worry too much on this account; perhaps there is no need to suppose that this period has to be 'the Age of' any one, or even any two, qualities in particular. We might better avoid prejudgement of the complicated, varied, and eclectic literary and intellectual life of the eighteenth century if we habitually referred to the period as just that – the eighteenth century.

Notes

1. Alan Moorehead, *The Fatal Impact: An Account of the Invasion of the South Pacific 1767–1840* (Harmondsworth, 1968), p. 9.

2. 'Cook', in *Biographia Britannica*, second edition (1789), IV, 236.

3. *Characteristicks of Men, Manners, Opinions, Times*, second edition (1714), II, 173.

4. *Theory of Moral Sentiments*, edited by D. D. Raphael and A. L. Macfie (Oxford 1976), p. 316.

5. *Essay on Regimen* (1740), pp. 122–24.

6. *Characteristicks*, second edition (1714), I, 293.

7. *Decline and Fall of the Roman Empire*, edited by J. B. Bury, revised edition (1926–29), IV, 169.

8. *Oberservation on Man, His Frame, His Duty, and His Expectations* (Liverpool, 1967), I, 83; *Winter*, ll. 606–08 (first printed in *The Seasons*, 1730).

9. George Cheyne, *The English Malady, or, A Treatise of Nervous Diseases of all Kinds* (1733), pp. 4–5, quoted in John A. Dussinger, 'The Sensorium in the World of a "Sentimental Journey"', *Ariel*, 13 (1982), 6; *An Essay concerning Human Understanding*, edited by Peter H. Nidditch (Oxford, 1975), p. 121; Book II, Chapter iii, Section 1.

10. *Characteristicks*, second edition (1714), II, 395.

11. *The Seasons*, edited by James Sambrook (Oxford, 1981), pp. 47–49.

12. *A Treatise of Human Nature*, edited by L. A. Selby-Biggs, second edition, text revised by P. H. Nidditch (Oxford, 1978), pp. 67–68; Book I, Part ii, Section 6; *An Inquiry into the Human Mind*, edited by T. Duggan (Chicago, 1970), p. x, quoting Reid's *Essays on the Intellectual Powers* (1785).

13. *An Appeal to all that Doubt or Disbelieve the truths of the Gospel, whether they be Deists, Arians, Socinians, or Nominal Christians . . . to which are added. Some Animadversions upon Dr. Trapp's Late Reply* (1740), in *Works* (1762, reprinted 1892–93), VI, 72.

14. *Philosophical Enquiry into the Sublime and the Beautiful*, edited by J. T. Boulton (1958), p. 44.

15. *Discourses on Art*, edited by R. R. Wark (New Haven, 1975), pp. 241, 230, 244; thirteenth *Discourse* (1786).

16. *Characteristicks*, second edition (1714), I, 207.

17. *Essay on Original Genius* (1767), p. 177.

18. Works of Richard Hurd (1811), IV, 348.

19. *Conjectures on Original Composition*, edited by Edith Marley (1918), p. 31.

20. *Treatise of Human Nature*, pp. 575–76; III, ii, 1; *Theory of Moral Sentiments*, edited by D. D. Raphael and A. L. Macfie, (Oxford, 1976), p. 9.

21. *Treatise of Human Nature*, p. 415, II, iii, 3.

22. J. W. Johnson, *The Formation of English Neo-Classical Thought*(Princeton, 1967), p. 4.

23. Donald Greene, 'Augustanism and Empiricism' in *Eighteenth-Century Studies*, I (1967–8), 38.

24. *Works of George Berkeley*, ed. A. A. Luce and T. E. Jessop, vol. III (1950), p. 45.

25. *Augustus Caesar in 'Augustan' England* ('Princeton, 1978), pp. 52, 241.

26. 'Edward Gibbon', in *Proceedings of the British Academy*, xx (1934), 180.

27. 'Augustanism and Empiricism', in *Eighteenth-Century Studies*, I (1967–8), 34.

28 .*History of English Poetry* (1824), III. 312.

29. 'Addison, Steele and the Periodical Essay', in *Dryden to Johnson*, edited by Roger Lonsdale (1971), pp. 145–54.

30. R. L. Brett, *The Third Earl of Shaftesbury* (1951), p. 199; Basil Willey, 'A Romantic Augustan', in *The Listener* (27 March 1952) pp. 518–19.

31. 'Towards defining an Age of Sensibility', in *ELH*, 23 (1956), 144.

32. *Some Observations on Eighteenth Century Poetry* (Toronto, 1964), p. 56.

33. 'Eighteenth-Century Miscellanies', in *Eighteenth-Century Studies*, 3 (1969–70), 423; also see note 23 above, and Bibliography, Section (i), 'Greene', below.

Chronology

DATE	VERSE, DRAMA, FICTION	OTHER WORKS	HISTORICAL/CULTURAL EVENTS
1700	Congreve *Way of the World* Dryden *Fables* Prior *Carmen Seculare*	Locke *Essay concerning Human Understanding* (4th edn)	Dryden (b. 1631) died Le Nôtre (b. 1613) died Thomson (d. 1748) born
1701	Defoe *True-born Englishman* John Philips *Splendid Shilling* Rowe *Tamerlane*	Dennis *Advancement and Reformation of Poetry* Norris *Ideal and Intelligible World* (−1704) Steele *Christian Hero* Swift *Contests in Athens and Rome*	James II (b. 1633) died Act of Settlement Society for the Propagation of The Gospel
1702		Clarendon *History of the Great Rebellion* (−1704) Defoe *Shortest Way with Dissenters* King *De Origine Mali*	Doddridge (d. 1751) born William III (b. 1650) died, succeeded by Anne War of Spanish Succession (−1713)

DATE	VERSE, DRAMA, FICTION	OTHER WORKS	HISTORICAL/CULTURAL EVENTS
1703	Addison *Letter From Italy* Defoe *Hymn to the Pillory* Rowe *Fair Penitent*	Dampier *Voyage to New Holland* (−1709) Hickes *Thesaurus of the Ancient Northern Languages* (−1705)	Pepys (b. 1633) died John Wesley (d. 1791) born Great Storm
1704	Cibber *Careless Husband* Psalmanazar *Description of Formosa* Swift *Tale of Tub* *Battle of the Books*	Churchill *Collection of Voyages* (−1732) Defoe *Review* (−1713) Dennis *Grounds of Criticism in Poetry* Newton *Opticks*	Locke (b. 1632) died Roubiliac (d. 1762) born Battle of Blenheim Capture of Gibraltar
1705	Addison *Campaign* Mandeville *Grumbling Hive* Steele *Tender Husband*	Addison *Remarks on Italy* Halley *Astronomiae Cometicae*	Hartley (d. 1757) born Ray (b. 1627) died Newcomen's steam-engine
1706	Defoe *Jure Divino* Farquhar *Recruiting Officer* Watts *Horae Lyricae*	Newton *Opticks*, Latin trans. by Clarke (with additional queries)	Evelyn (b. 1620) died Franklin (d. 1790) born Battle of Ramillies
1707	Farquhar *Beaux Stratagem* Watts *Hymns and Spiritual Songs*	Echard *History of England*	Buffon (d. 1788) born Farquhar (b.1678) died Fielding (d. 1754) born Linnaeus (d. 1778) born Charles Wesley (d. 1788) born Act of Union with Scotland

DATE	VERSE, DRAMA, FICTION	OTHER WORKS	HISTORICAL/CULTURAL EVENTS
1708	John Philips *Cyder* Swift *Predictions for 1708*	Shaftesbury *Letter concerning Enthusiasm* Swift *Argument against abolishing Christianity*	Hayman (d. 1776) born Battle of Oudenarde
1709	*Poetical Miscellanies* (inc. *Pastorals* of Pope and Ambrose Philips) Rowe's edition of Shakespeare	Berkeley *New Theory of Vision* Hearne's edn. of Spelman's *Life of Alfred* Shaftesbury *Essay on Wit and Humour Moralists* Steele *et al.* *The Tatler* (–1711)	Johnson (d. 1784) born La Mettrie (d. 1751) born Battle of Malplaquet First Copyright Act
1710		Berkeley *Principles of Human Knowledge* Leibniz *Théodicée* Shaftesbury *Advice to an Author* Swift *et al.* *The Examiner* (–1711)	Arne (d. 1778) born Lowth (d. 1787) born Reid (d. 1796) born Trial of Dr Sacheverell
1711	Pope *Essay on Criticism*	Addison, Steele *et al.* *The Spectator* (–1714) Shaftesbury *Characteristicks* Swift *Conduct of the Allies* Whiston *Primitive Christianity Revived* (–1712)	Devis (d. 1787) born Hume (d. 1776) born Norris (b. 1657) died

DATE	VERSE, DRAMA, FICTION	OTHER WORKS	HISTORICAL/CULTURAL EVENTS
1712	Arbuthnot *History of John Bull* Blackmore *Creation* Pope *Rape of the Locke* (two cantos)	Addison *Pleasures of Imagination* (in the *Spectator*) Clarke *Scripture Doctrine of the Trinity* Swift *Proposals for correcting the English Tongue*	Rousseau (d. 1778) born Handel settles in England Last witch convicted in England
1713	Addison *Cato* Gay *Rural Sports* Pope *Windsor Forest* Lady Winchilsea *Miscellany Poems*	Berkeley *Dialogues between Hylas and Philonous* Collins *Discourse of Freethinking* Derham *Physico-Theology* Newton *Principia* 2nd edn (with *General Scholium*) Steele *Guardian* (−1714)	Diderot (d. 1784) born Shaftesbury (b. 1671) died Sterne (d. 1768) born James Stuart (d. 1788) born Treaty of Utrecht
1714	Gay *Shepherd's Week* Pope *Rape of the Locke* (five cantos) Rowe *Jane Shore*	Leibniz *Monadologie* Mandeville *Fable of the Bees* (−1729) Shaftesbury *Miscellaneous Reflections* (in *Characteristicks*, 2nd edn) Steele *Englishman* Swift *Public Spirit of the Whigs*	Queen Anne (b. 1665) died, succeeded by George I Monboddo (d. 1799) born Shenstone (d. 1763) born Whitefield (d. 1770) born Wilson (d. 1782) born

DATE	VERSE, DRAMA, FICTION	OTHER WORKS	HISTORICAL/CULTURAL EVENTS
1715	Hughes's edn of Spenser Pope, trans., *Iliad* (–1720); *Temple of Fame* Watts *Divine Songs for the use of Children*	Campbell *Vitruvius Britannicus* (–1725) Defoe *Family Instructor* (–1718) Derham *Astro-Theology* Leoni's edition of Palladio (–1716) Switzer *Nobleman's Recreation*	Capability Brown (d. 1783) born Dampier (b. 1652) died Jacobite Rebellion
1716	Gay *Trivia*	Addison *Freeholder*	Thomas Gray (d. 1771) born Leibniz (b. 1646) died James Paine (d. 1789) born Robert Wood (d. 1771) born Wycherley (b. 1640) died Septennial Act
1717	Pope *Collected Works* (inc. *Unfortunate Lady* and *Eloisa to Abelard*)	Bangorian Controversy (–1720) Penn *Religion professed by Quakers*	Garrick (d. 1779) born Sanderson Miller (d. 1780) born Horace Walpole (d. 1797) born
1718	Prior *Poems* (inc. *Alma* and *Solomon*) Rowe, trans., Lucan's *Pharsalia*	Newton *Opticks,* new edn (with additional queries) Switzer *Ichnographia Rustica*	Hugh Blair (d. 1800) born Parnell (b. 1679) died Penn (b. 1644) died Rowe (b. 1674) died
1719	Defoe *Robinson Crusoe* Watts *Psalms of David*		Addison (b. 1672) died

DATE	VERSE, DRAMA, FICTION	OTHER WORKS	HISTORICAL/CULTURAL EVENTS
1720	Defoe *Captain Singleton* Gay *Collected Poems*	*Cato's Letters* (−1723) Mandeville *Free Thoughts on Religion*	Hurd (d. 1808) born Revett (d. 1804) born Gilbert White (d. 1793) born South Sea Bubble War with Spain (−1729)
1721	Urry's edn of Chaucer	Montesquieu *Lettres persanes* Swift *Letter to a young Gentleman*	Akenside (d. 1770) born William Collins (d. 1759) born Laguerre (b. 1663) died Prior (b. 1664) died Robertson (d. 1793) born Smollett (d. 1771) born First inoculations against smallpox
1722	Defoe *Colonel Jack* *Plague Year* *Moll Flanders* Steele *Conscious Lovers*	Wollaston *Religion of Nature Delineated*	Marlborough (b. 1650) died Smart (d. 1771) born Toland (b. 1670) died Joseph Warton (d. 1800) born
1723	Mallet *William and Margaret*	Law *Remarks on Fable of the Bees* Mandeville *Essay on Charity* and *Search into the Nature of Society* (in *Fable of the Bees*, 2nd edn)	Blackstone (d. 1780) born Chambers (d. 1796) born Adam Ferguson (d. 1816) born Gavin Hamilton (d. 1798) born Kneller died Richard Price (d. 1791) born Reynolds (d. 1792) born Adam Smith (d. 1790) born Wren (b. 1632) died

DATE	VERSE, DRAMA, FICTION	OTHER WORKS	HISTORICAL/CULTURAL EVENTS
1724	Defoe *Roxana* Ramsay *Ever-Green* *Tea-Table Miscellany* (–1727)	Defoe *Tour thro' Great Britain* (–1726) Charles Johnson *History of Pirates* Lafitau *Mœurs des sauvages amériquains* Swift *Drapier's Letters*	Gilpin (d. 1804) born Kant (d. 1804) born Stubbs (d. 1806) born
1725	Pope, trans., *Odyssey* (–1726); edn of Shakespeare Ramsay *Gentle Shepherd*	Hutcheson *Inquiry into Beauty and Virtue* N. Tindal, trans., *Rapin's History of England* (–1731) Vico *Scienza Nuova* (–1730) Watts *Logic*	John Newton (d. 1807) born

1726	Dyer
	Grongar Hill (rev. 1727)
	
	Swift
	Cadenus and Vanessa
	Gulliver's Travels
	
	Thomson
	Winter
		Bolingbroke,
		  Chesterfield, *et al.*
		  The Craftsman (–1750)
		
		Joseph Butler
		Fifteen Sermons
		
		Law
		Christian Perfection
		Unlawfulness of Stage Entertainments
		
		Newton
		Principia, 3rd (definitive) edn
		
		Shevlocke
		Voyage round the World
		
		Spence
		Essay on Pope's Odyssey
			Charles Burney (d. 1814) born
			Collier (b. 1650) died
			Vanbrugh (b. 1664) died
			Voltaire in England
			(–1729)

DATE	VERSE, DRAMA, FICTION	OTHER WORKS	HISTORICAL/CULTURAL EVENTS
1727	Gay *Fables* (–1750) Pope, Swift, Arbuthnot *Miscellanies* (–1735) Thomson *To the Memory of Newton* *Summer*	Defoe *History of Apparitions* Hales *Vegetable Staticks* Kent *Designs of Inigo Jones* Newton *Principia* trans. into English	Gainsborough (d. 1788) born George I (b. 1660) died, succeeded by George II Newton (b. 1642) died Wilkes (d. 1797) born
1728	Defoe *Captain Carleton* Gay *Beggar's Opera* Pope *Dunciad* (three books) Thomson *Spring* Voltaire *Henriade*	Castell *Villas of the Ancients* Chambers *Cyclopaedia* (–1729) Hutcheson *Nature and Conduct of the Passions and Affections* Pemberton *View of Newton's Philosophy*	Robert Adam (d. 1792) born Boulton (d. 1809) born Joseph Black (d. 1799) born Gerard (d. 1795) born Thomas Warton (d. 1790) born
1729	Pope *Dunciad Variorum* Savage *Wanderer* Swift *Modest Proposal* Thomson *Britannia*	Law *Serious Call* Oldmixon *History of England* (–1739)	Blackmore (b. 1650) died Burke (d. 1797) born Colen Campbell died Samuel Clarke (b. 1675) died Congreve (b. 1670) died Lessing (d. 1781) born Thomas Percy (d. 1811) born Steele (b. 1672) died Treaty of Seville

DATE	VERSE, DRAMA, FICTION	OTHER WORKS	HISTORICAL/CULTURAL EVENTS
1730	Duck *Poems* Fielding *Tom Thumb* Thomson *The Seasons* (inc. *Autumn* and *Hymn*)	Bolingbroke *Remarks upon History* (in *Craftsman*) Newton *Opticks,* 4th (definitive) edn Tindal *Christianity as old as the Creation* Watts *Catechisms*	Goldsmith (d. 1774) born Methodist society formed in Oxford
1731	Lillo *George Barnwell* Marivaux *Marianne* (–1741) Pope *Epistle to Burlington*	*Gentleman's Magazine* (–1907) Law *Case of Reason* Tull *Horse-hoeing Husbandry* Voltaire *Histoire de Charles XII*	Cavendish (d. 1810) born Cowper (d. 1800) born Defoe (b. 1660) died
1732	Fielding *Covent Garden Tragedy* Pope *Epistle to Bathurst* Voltaire *Zaire*	Berkeley *Alciphron* Boerhaave *Elements Chymia* Franklin *Poor Richard's Almanac* (–1757) Watts *Scripture History*	James Adam (d. 1794) born Charles Churchill (d. 1764) born Duff (d. 1815) born Falconer (d. 1769) born Gay (b. 1685) died

DATE	VERSE, DRAMA, FICTION	OTHER WORKS	HISTORICAL/CULTURAL EVENTS
1733	Pope *Essay on Man* (–1734) *Horace's Satire, II.i* Prévost *Manon Lescaut*	Bolingbroke *Dissertation upon Parties* (in *Craftsman*) Cheyne *English Malady* Switzer *Practical Husbandmen* Voltaire *Letters on the English Nation*	Mandeville (b. 1670) died Priestley (d. 1804) born Matthew Tindal (b. 1653) died Georgia founded Kay's flying shuttle Walpole's Excise Bill withdrawn
1734	Pope *Horace's Satire, II.ii*	Montesquieu *Grandeur et décadence des Romains*	Dennis (b. 1657) died Romney (d. 1802) born Thornhill (b. 1675) died Joseph Wright (d. 1797) born
1735	Pope *Epistle to Arbuthnot* *Epistle to a Lady* Somerville *The Chace* Thomson *Liberty* (–1736)	Berkeley *Querist* (–1737) Blackwell *Life and Writings of Homer* de Halde *Description de l'Empire de la Chine* Linnaeus *Systema Natura* Lyttleton *Letters from a Persian* Wesley *Journal* (–1790)	Arbuthnot (b. 1667) died Beattie (d. 1803) born Abraham Darby smelts iron from coke
1736	Fielding *Pasquin*	Joseph Butler *Analogy of Religion* Newton *Method of Fluxions* Voltaire *Éléments de la philosophie de Newton*	Hawksmoor (b. 1661) died Macpherson (d. 1796) born James Watt (d. 1819) born Gin Act Statutes against witchcraft repealed

DATE	VERSE, DRAMA, FICTION	OTHER WORKS	HISTORICAL/CULTURAL EVENTS
1737	Fielding *Historical Register for 1736* Pope *Horace's Epistles, I. i., vi; II. i, ii* Shenstone *Poems* (inc. *Schoolmistress*) John Wesley, ed. *Psalms and Hymns*	Algarotti *Il Newtonianismo per le Dame* Cruden *Biblical Concordance* Warburton *Divine Legation of Moses* (–1741)	Gibbon (d. 1794) born Tom Paine (d. 1809) born Theatre Licensing Act
1738	Johnson *London* Pope *Epilogue to Satires*	Maupertius *Figure de la terre* Ware's edition of Palladio Watt *World to Come*	Boerhaave (b. 1668) died Bridgeman died Copley (d. 1815) born Derham (b. 1657) died Herschel (d. 1822) born Benjamin West (d. 1820) born Henry Wise (b. 1653) died Herculaneum excavated
1739	Swift *Verses on the Death of Swift* J. and C. Wesley *Hymns and Sacred Poems* (–1749)	Hume *Treatise of Human Nature* (–1740)	Jervas (b. 1675) died Lillo (b. 1693) died War with Spain; capture of Porto Bello
1740	Dyer *Ruins of Rome* Garrick *Lethe* Richardson *Pamela* (–1742) Thomson and Mallet *Alfred* (inc. 'Rule, Britannia!')	Cibber *Apology* Stukeley *Stonehenge* Whitefield *Short Account of God's dealings with George Whitefield*	Boswell (d. 1795) born John Cartwright (d. 1824) born Anson's circumnavigation (–1744) War of Austrian Succession (–1748)

DATE	VERSE, DRAMA, FICTION	OTHER WORKS	HISTORICAL/CULTURAL EVENTS
1741	Arbuthnot *et al.* *Memoirs of Scriblerus* Fielding *Shamela*	Hume *Essays, Moral and Political* (−1742) Middleton *Life of Cicero* Watts *Improvement of the Mind*	James Barry (d. 1806) born Arthur Young (d. 1820) born
1742	Collins *Persian Eclogues* Fielding *Joseph Andrews* Pope *New Dunciad* (i.e. Book IV) Young *Night Thoughts* (−1745)	John Campbell *Lives of the Admirals* Langley *Gothic Architecture Improved* John Wesley *Character of a Methodist*	Bentley (b. 1662) died Halley (b. 1656) died Somerville (b. 1675) died Walpole resigns
1743	Blair *The Grave* Fielding *Miscellanies* Pope *Dunciad* (four books)	Pococke *Description of the East* (−1745)	Banks (d. 1820) born Cheyne (b. 1671) died Dahl (b. 1659) died Paley (d. 1805) born Battle of Dettingen
1744	Akenside *Pleasures of Imagination* Armstrong *Art of preserving Health* Thomson *The Seasons* (rev.) Joseph Warton *The Enthusiast*	Berkeley *Reflections on Tar-Water* (i.e. *Siris*) Johnson *Life of Savage* Voltaire *Nouvelle considérations*	Pope (b. 1688) died Vico (b. 1668) died First Methodist Conference

DATE	VERSE, DRAMA, FICTION	OTHER WORKS	HISTORICAL/CULTURAL EVENTS
1745	Akenside *Odes*	Doddridge *Rise and Progress of Religion in the Soul* La Mettrie *Histoire naturelle de l'âme* Swift *Directions to Servants*	Swift (b. 1667) died Robert Walpole (b. 1676) died Battle of Fontenoy Jacobite Rebellion (–1746)
1746	Collins *Odes* Joseph Warton *Odes*	Diderot *Pensées philosophiques* James Hervey *Meditations and Contemplations* John Wesley *'Standard' Sermons* (–1760)	William Jones (d. 1794) born Battle of Culloden
1747	Gray *Ode on Eton College* Richardson *Clarissa* (–1748) Thomas Warton *Pleasures of Melancholy* Voltaire *Zadig*	Kippis *et al.* *Biographia Britannica* (–1766) Needham *Observations microscopiques* Joseph Spence *Polymetis* Whitefield *Full Account of God's Dealings with George Whitefield* *Further Account*	Hutcheson (b. 1694) died
1748	Dodsley (ed.) *Collection of Poems* (–1758) Smollett *Roderick Random* Thomson *Castle of Indolence*	Anson *Voyage round the World* Hume *Philosophical Essays concerning Human Understanding* *Three Essays* La Mettrie *L'homme machine* Maclaurin *Newton's Philosophy* Montesquieu *De l'esprit des lois*	Bentham (d. 1832) born Kent (b. 1685) died Thomson (b. 1700) died Strawberry Hill begun Isaac Watts (b. 1674) died Ruins of Pompei discovered Treaty of Aix-la-Chapelle

DATE	VERSE, DRAMA, FICTION	OTHER WORKS	HISTORICAL/CULTURAL EVENTS
1749	Fielding *Tom Jones* Johnson *Irene* *Vanity of Human Wishes* West, Trans., Pindar's *Odes*	Bolingbroke *Idea of a Patriot King* Buffon *Histoire naturelle* (–1804) Diderot *Letre sur les aveugles* Hartley *Observations on Man* Law *Spirit of Prayer* Swedenborg *Arcana celesta* (–1756)	Goethe (d. 1832) born Laplace (d. 1827) born Roger Morris died Ambrose Philips (b. 1675) died
1750		Johnson *Rambler* (–1752) Rousseau *Discours sur les sciences et les arts*	
1751	Gray *Elegy* Smollett *Peregrine Pickle*	D'Alembert, Diderot, *et al* *Encyclopédie* (–1766) Fielding *Late Increase of Robbers* Hume *Enquiry concerning Principles of Morals* Kames *Principles of Morality and Natural Religion* Voltaire *Siècle de Louis XIV*	Bolingbroke (b. 1678) died Doddridge (b. 1702) died Frederick, Prince of Wales (b. 1707) died Clive at Arcot

DATE	VERSE, DRAMA, FICTION	OTHER WORKS	HISTORICAL/CULTURAL EVENTS
1752	Fielding *Amelia* Smart *Poems* Voltaire *Micromégas*	Bolingbroke *Study and Use of History* Hume *Essays, Moral, Political and Literary* *Political Discourses* Law *Way to Divine Knowledge*	Joseph Butler (b. 1692) died Chatterton (d. 1770) born Gregorian calendar adopted in Britain
1753	Richardson *Sir Charles Grandison* (–1754) Smollett *Ferdinand Count Fathom* J. and C. Wesley *Hymns and Spiritual Songs*	Hogarth *Analysis of Beauty* Linnaeus *Species Plantarum* Lowth *De Sacra Poesi Hebraeorum* Voltaire *Essai sur les mœurs* Robert Wood *Ruins of Palmyra*	Berkeley (b. 1685) died Burlington (b. 1694) died Sheridan (d. 1816) born
1754		Condillac *Traité des sensations* Diderot *De l'interpretation de la nature* Hume *History of Great Britain* (–1761) Newton *Two Notable Corruptions of Scripture* Thomas Warton *Observations on the Faerie Queene*	Crabbe (d. 1832) born Gibbs (b. 1682) died Fielding (b. 1707) died John Wood, the elder, (b. 1704) died

DATE	VERSE, DRAMA, FICTION	OTHER WORKS	HISTORICAL/CULTURAL EVENTS
1755	Doddridge *Hymns* Smollett, trans., *Don Quixote* Voltaire *Orpheline de la Chine*	Ellis *Natural History of Corallines* Fielding *Voyage to Lisbon* Hutcheson *System of Moral Philosophy* Johnson *Dictionary* Kant *Allgemeine Naturgeschichte und Theorie des Himmels* Rousseau *Discours sur l'inegalité*	Flaxman (d. 1826) born Montesquieu (b. 1689) died Lisbon earthquake
1756	Voltaire *Désastre de Lisbonne*	Burke *Vindication of Natural Society* Alban Butler *Lives of the Saints* (–1759) Joseph Warton *Essay on Pope* (–1782)	Godwin (d. 1836) born Seven Years War (–1763)
1757	Dyer *The Fleece* Gray *Odes* Home *Douglas*	Burke *Enquiry into the Sublime and the Beautiful* Chambers *Designs of Chinese Buildings* Haller *Elementa Physiologiae* Hume *Four Dissertations* (inc. *Natural History of Religion*) Wood *Ruins of Baalbec*	Blackwell (b. 1701) died Blake (d. 1827) born Cibber (b. 1671) died Hartley (b. 1705) died Battle of Plassey Warrington Academy founded (–1786)

DATE	VERSE, DRAMA, FICTION	OTHER WORKS	HISTORICAL/CULTURAL EVENTS
1758		Helvétius *De l'esprit* Hume *Enquiry concerning Human Understanding* Johnson *Idler* (–1760)	Dyer (b. 1700) died Halley's comet returns Nelson (d. 1805) born Allan Ramsay, the elder, (b. 1686) died
1759	Johnson *Rasselas* Voltaire *Candide*	Gerard *Essay on Taste* Goldsmith *Present State of Polite Learning* Robertson *History of Scotland* Smith *Theory of Moral Sentiments* Edward Young *Conjectures on Original Composition*	Burns (d. 1796) born Collins (b. 1721) died Handel (b. 1685) died Schiller (d. 1805) born British Museum opened Capture of Quebec
1760	Lyttleton *Dialogues of the Dead* Macpherson *Fragments of Ancient Poetry* ('Ossian') Sterne *Tristram Shandy* (–1767) Smollett *Sir Lancelot Greaves* (–1761)		Beckford (d. 1844) born George II (b. 1683) died, succeeded by George III Capture of Montreal
1761	Churchill *Rosciad* Rousseau *Nouvelle Héloise*		William Law (b. 1686) died Samuel Richardson (b. 1689) died Bridgewater Canal cut

DATE	VERSE, DRAMA, FICTION	OTHER WORKS	HISTORICAL/CULTURAL EVENTS
1762	Churchill *The Ghost* Falconer *Shipwreck* Goldsmith *Citizen of the World* Macpherson *Fingal*	Ferguson *Essay on Civil Society* Hurd *Letters on Chivalry and Romance* Kames *Elements of Criticism* Rousseau *Émile* *Du Contrat sociel* Stuart and Revett *Antiquities of Athens* (–1814) Walpole *Anecdotes of Painting* (–1771)	Bowles (d. 1850) born Bradley (b. 1693) died Roubiliac (b. 1704) died
1763	Churchill *Prophecy of Famine* Macpherson *Temora* Smart *Song to David*	Blair *On the Poems of Ossian* Voltaire *Traité sur la tolérance*	Cobbett (d. 1835) born Rogers (d. 1855) born Shenstone (b. 1714) died Treaty of Paris Wilkes arrested
1764	Evans *Specimens of Ancient Welsh Bards* Goldsmith *The Traveller* Ridley *Tales of the Genii*	Robert Adam *Ruins of the Palace of Diocletian* Reid *Inquiry into the Human Mind* Voltaire *Dictionnaire philosophique* Winckelmann *Geschichte der Kunst des Alterhums*	Charles Churchill (b. 1732) died Hogarth (b. 1697) died Black measures latent heat Hargreaves' spinning jenny Harrison's chronometer

DATE	VERSE, DRAMA, FICTION	OTHER WORKS	HISTORICAL/CULTURAL EVENTS
1765	Johnson's edition of Shakespeare Percy *Reliques of Ancient English Poetry* Walpole *Castle of Otranto*	Blackstone *Commentaries on the Laws of England* Leibniz *Nouveaux essais* Winckelmann *Painting and Sculpture of the Greeks* (trans. Fuseli)	Lambert (b. 1700) died Edward Young (b. 1683) died Soho Works built by Boulton
1766	Goldsmith *Vicar of Wakefield*	Lessing *Laokoon* Pennant *British Zoology* (–1770) Smollett *Travels through France and Italy*	Rousseau in England (–1767)
1767	Voltaire *L'Ingénu* J. and C. Wesley *Hymns for the use of Families*	Duff *Essay on Original Cenius* Ferguson *Essay on Civil Society* Lyttelton *History of Henry II* Priestley *History of Electricity* Voltaire *Examen de Bolingbroke* Robert Wood *Essay on the Original Genius of Homer* Arthur Young *Farmer's Letters*	Royal Crescent, Bath, begun Wallis visits Tahiti

DATE	VERSE, DRAMA, FICTION	OTHER WORKS	HISTORICAL/CULTURAL EVENTS
1768	Gray *Poems* Goldsmith *Good Natur'd Man*	Boswell *Account of Corsica* *Encyclopaedia Britannica* (–1771) Sterne *Sentimental Journey* Tucker *Light of Nature pursued* (–1778)	Sterne (b. 1713) died Bougainville visits Tahiti Cook's First Voyage (–1771) Royal Academy founded
1769	Smollett *Adventures of an Atom*	Falconer *Marine Dictionary* *Letters of Junius* Revett *et al.* *Ionian Antiquities* (–1797) Reynolds *Discourses on Art* (–1790) Robertson *History of Charles V*	Falconer (b. 1732) died Flitcroft (b. 1696) died Cook at Tahiti Shakespeare Jubilee Watt's condenser patented Wilkes expelled from Commons and thrice re-elected
1770	Goldsmith *Deserted Village* Mercier *L'an 2440*	Beattie *Essay on Truth* Burke *Thoughts on Present Discontents* Holbach *Système de la Nature* Raynal *Histoire des deux Indes*	Akenside (b. 1721) died Chatterton (b. 1752) died Hegel (d. 1831) born Rysbrack (b. 1694) died Whitefield (b. 1714) died Wordsworth (d. 1850) born Cook at Botany Bay

DATE	VERSE, DRAMA, FICTION	OTHER WORKS	HISTORICAL/CULTURAL EVENTS
1771	Beattie *The Minstrel* (–1774) Mackenzie *Man of Feeling* Smollett *Humphry Clinker*	W. Jones Persian Grammer (inc. *Songs of Hafiz*) Walpole *Modern Gardening* John Wesley *Collected Prose Works* (–1774)	Thomas Gray (b. 1716) died Smart (b. 1722) died Smollett (b. 1721) died Walter Scott (d. 1833) born Robert Wood (b. 1716) died Arkwright's first spinning-mill
1772	Foote *The Nabob* W. Jones *Poems from Asiatick Languages*	Bougainville *Voyage round the World* (trans. Forster) Chambers *Dissertation on Oriental Gardening* Ferguson *Institutes of Moral Philosophy*	Coleridge (d. 1834) born Cook's Second Voyage (–1775) Warren Hastings Governor of Bengal
1773	Goldsmith *She Stoops to Conquer* Goethe *Goetz von Berlichingen* Graves *Spiritual Quixote* Mackenzie *Man of the World*	Adam *Works in Architecture* Hawkesworth *Voyages in the Southern Hemisphere* Herder *Von deutscher Art und Kunst* Monboddo *Origin and Progress of Languages* (–1792)	Chesterfield (b. 1694) died James Mill (d. 1836) born Boston Tea Party Cook in the Antarctic

DATE	VERSE, DRAMA, FICTION	OTHER WORKS	HISTORICAL/CULTURAL EVENTS
1774	Goethe *Werther* Langhorne *County Justice*	Burke *Speech on American Taxation* Chesterfield *Letters to his Son* Gerard *Essay on Genius* Goldsmith *History of the Earth and Animated Nature* Kames *Sketches of the History of Man* Walpole *Description of Strawberry Hill* Thomas Warton *History of English Poetry* (–1789)	Goldsmith (b. 1730?) died Southey (d. 1843) born Omai in London Priestley discovers oxygen
1775	Beaumarchais *Barbier de Seville* Sheridan *Rivals* *St. Patrick's Day* *Duenna* Tyrwhitt's edn of Chaucer (–1778)	Burke *Conciliation with the Colonies* Johnson *Journey to the Western Isles* Kant *Anthropologie* Priestley *Hartley's Theory of Mind* Thomas Spence *Real Rights of Man*	Jane Austen (d. 1817) born Lamb (d. 1834) born Landor (d. 1864) born Schelling (d. 1854) born War of American Independence (–1783) Watt's improved steam-engine

DATE	VERSE, DRAMA, FICTION	OTHER WORKS	HISTORICAL/CULTURAL EVENTS
1776	Toplady *Psalms and Hymns*	Bentham *Fragment on Government* Charles Burney *History of Music* (–1789) Cartwright *Take your Choice* Gibbon *Decline and Fall of the Roman Empire* (–1788) Paine *Common Sense* Price *Observations in Civil Liberty* Smith *Wealth of Nations*	Hayman (b. 1708) died Hume (b. 1711) died American Declaration of Independence Cook's Third Voyage (–1779)
1777	Chatterton 'Rowley' *Poems* Sheridan *Trip to Scarborough* *School for Scandal*	Cook *Voyage towards the South Pole in 1772–5* Priestley *Disquisitions concerning Matter and Spirit* *Doctrine of Philosophic Necessitry* Robertson *History of America*	
1778	Fanny Burney *Evelina* Foot *The Nabob*		Arne (b. 1710) died Hazlitt (d. 1830) born Linnaeus (b. 1707) died William Pitt (b. 1708) died Rousseau (b. 1712) died Voltaire (b. 1694) died

DATE	VERSE, DRAMA, FICTION	OTHER WORKS	HISTORICAL/CULTURAL EVENTS
1779	Cowper and Newton *Olney Hymns* Sheridan *The Critic*	Buffon *Époques de la Nature* Hume *Dialogues concerning Natural Religion* Johnson *Lives of the Poets* (–1781) Monboddo *Antient Metaphysics* (1799)	Cook (b. 1728) died Garrick (b. 1717) died Warburton (b. 1698) died Siege of Gibraltar Crompton's 'mule' First iron bridge
1780	J. and C. Wesley *Hymns for Methodists* Wieland *Oberon*	T. Davies *Memoirs of Garrick*	Blackstone (b. 1723) died Highmore (b. 1692) died Sanderson Miller (b. 1717) died Gordon Riots Yorkshire petition for Parliamentary reform
1781	Crabbe *The Library* Schiller *Die Raüber*	Kant *Kritik der reinen Vernunft* Watson *Chemical Essays* (–1787)	Lessing (b. 1729) died Scheemakers (b. 1691) died Cornwallis surrenders at Yorktown Uranus discovered Watt's rotary steam-engine
1782	Fanny Burney *Cecilia* Cowper *Poems* Laclos *Liaisons dangereuses*	Ferguson *Roman Republic* Gilpin *Observations on the River Wye* Priestley *Corruptions of Christianity* Rousseau *Confessions* (–1789)	Kames (b. 1696) died Allan Ramsay, the younger, (b. 1713) died Wilson (b. 1714) died John Wood, the younger, died Battle of the Saints

DATE	VERSE, DRAMA, FICTION	OTHER WORKS	HISTORICAL/CULTURAL EVENTS
1783	Blake *Poetical Sketches* Crabbe *The Village* Day *Sandford and Merton*	Beattie *Dissertations Moral and Critical* Blair *Lectures on Rhetoric and Belle Lettres*	Capability Brown (b. 1716) died Treaty of Versailles
1784	Beaumarchais *Mariage de Figaro*	Arthur Young *Annals of Agriculture* (–1809) Cook *Voyage to the Pacific Ocean in 1776–80*	Diderot (b. 1713) died Leigh Hunt (d. 1859) born Johnson (b. 1709) died India Act
1785	Cowper *The Task* Wilkins, trans., *Bhagvat-Geeta*	Boswell *Tour to the Hebrides* Johnson *Prayers and Meditations* Paley *Moral and Political Philosophy* Reid *Essays on Intellectual Powers*	De Quincey (d. 1859) born Peacock (d. 1866) born Cartwright's power-loom
1786	Beckford *Vathek* Burns *Poems in the Scottish Dialect*		Coal gas used for lighting
1787	Goethe *Egmont* Saint-Pierre *Paul et Virginie*	Hawkins *Life of Johnson*	Devis (b. 1711) died Lowth (b. 1710) died Impeachment of Warren Hastings (–1795)

DATE	VERSE, DRAMA, FICTION	OTHER WORKS	HISTORICAL/CULTURAL EVENTS
1788		Kant *Kritik der praktischen Vernunft* Reid *Essay on the Active Powers of Man*	Byron (d. 1824) born Gainsborough (b. 1727) died Schopenhauer (d. 1860) born James Stuart (b. 1713) died Charles Wesley (b. 1707) died Convict settlement at Botany Bay
1789	Blake *Songs of Innocence* Bowles *Sonnets* Darwin *Loves of Plants* Ann Radcliffe *Castles of Athlin and Dunbayne*	Bentham *Principles of Morals and Legislation* Lavoisier *Traité élémentaire de Chémie* White *Natural History of Selborne*	Fall of the Bastille Mutiny on the *Bounty*

General Bibliographies

Note: Each section is arranged alphabetically. Place of publication is London, unless otherwise stated.

(i) General Background

Bredvold, L. I.   *The Brave New World of the Enlightenment* (Ann Arbor, 1961). (Stresses the modernity of some key eighteenth-century ideas.)

Clifford, J. L.   *Man Versus Society in Eighteenth-Century Britain* (Cambridge, 1968). (A symposium, discussing the measure of self-realization possible for the artist, the composer, the writer, the churchman, and the individual man in political and economic society.)

Greene, D.   *The Age of Exuberance: Backgrounds to Eighteenth-Century English Literature* (New York, 1970). (An admirable corrective to the stale half-truths of many literary histories: it conveys better, perhaps, than any other short study a sense of the vitality and energy of eighteenth-century political and social life, and the moral intensity and bold imagination of its best art, literature, and thought.)

Hughes, P., and D. Williams, eds,   *The Varied Pattern: Studies in the Eighteenth Century* (Toronto, 1971). (Miscellaneous essays on specific topics in the history of art and aesthetics, and the general intellectual background of the period.)

Humphreys, A. R.   *The Augustan World: Life and Letters in Eighteenth-Century England* (1954). (Mostly a study of the influence of socio-historical factors upon literature.)

Moore, C. A.   *Backgrounds of English Literature, 1700–1760* (Minneapolis, 1953). (Old, but not outdated, essays on some scientific, religious, philosophical, and political sources of such literary ideas as sentimentalism, melancholy, patriotism, etc.)

Porter, R., and M. Teich,   *The Enlightenment in National Context* (Cambridge, 1981). (Two of the thirteen chapters broadly survey the 'Enlightenment' in England and in Scotland.)

Rogers, P., ed. *The Context of English Literature: The Eighteenth Century* (1978). (Unlike many such background books, this one gives due weight to psychology and medicine.)

Smith, P. *The Enlightenment, 1687–1776*: vol. II of *A History of Modern Culture* (New York, 1934, repr. with Introduction by C. Brinton, 1962). (A wide-ranging cultural history.)

Stephen, L. *English Literature and Society in the Eighteenth Century* (1903). (The elegant and lively classic survey of the spirit of that age.)

Turberville, A. C., ed. *Johnson's England*, 2 vols (1933). (A lavishly-illustrated collection of twenty-seven essays, each by a notable authority, on various aspects of social, cultural, and intellectual life.)

Wasserman, E. R., ed. *Aspects of the Eighteenth Century* (Baltimore, 1965). (Seminar papers devoted to some large and some small topics in cultural and intellectual history, with no attempt at broad 'coverage'.)

Watt, I., ed. *The Augustan Age: Approaches to its Literature, Life, and Thought* (New York, 1968). (Reprinted essays on various topics; Watt's introduction adopts a suitably cautious attitude towards the use of the term 'Augustan'.)

Williams, K., ed. *Backgrounds to Eighteenth-Century Literature* (1971). (A good selection of previously published essays, illustrating the great range and complexity of intellectual life in that period.)

(ii) Science

Armitage, A. *Edmond Halley* (1966). (A historical valuation of Halley's wide-ranging scientific researches.)

Arthos, J. *The Language of Natural Description in Eighteenth-Century Poetry* (Ann Arbor, 1949). (On the relationship between poetic and scientific language.)

Berry, A. J. *Henry Cavendish: His Life and Scientific Work* (1960). (An assessment of the work in chemistry and physics of 'one of the greatest scientific discoverers of all time'.)

Burtt, E. A.   *The Metaphysical Foundations of Modern Physical Science* (1925). (Argues that the main current of modern thought begins with Newton, 'the one Englishman whose authority and influence in modern times has rivalled that of Aristotle over the late medieval epoch'.)

Bush, D.   *Science and English Poetry: A Historical Sketch, 1590–1950* (New York, 1950). (In his chapter on 'Newtonianism, Rationalism, and Sentimentalism', Bush explores the establishment and the breakdown of a 'triangular harmony of science, religion, and poetry'.)

Butterfield, H.   *The Origins of Modern Science, 1300–1800* (1949, rev. 1967). (The tribute paid by a distinguished historian to the part played by science in transforming man's habitual mental operations.)

Cameron, H. C.   *Sir Joseph Banks, the Autocrat of the Philosophers* (1952). (Life of the first great English naturalist-explorer.)

Cohen, I. B.   *Benjamin Franklin: Scientist and Statesman* (New York, 1975). (Treats of Franklin as a distinguished theoretical scientist, as well as an inventor of gadgets.)

Donovan, A. L.   *Philosophical Chemistry in the Scottish Enlightenment: The Doctrines and Discoveries of William Cullen and Joseph Black* (Edinburgh, 1975). (Relates eighteenth-century developments in chemistry to the larger intellectual climate of Scotland and England.)

Hall, A. R.   *The Scientific Revolution, 1500–1800: The Formation of the Modern Scientific Attitude* (Cambridge, 1954, rev. 1957). (A character study of the scientific mind, rather than a mere history.)

Hall, M. B., ed.   *Nature and Nature's Laws: Documents of the Scientific Revolution* (New York, 1970). (A very useful selection of key texts from the late sixteenth to the late eighteenth century.)

Jacob, M. C.   *The Newtonians and the English Revolution, 1689–1720* (1976). (Offers a social, even political, explanation for the rapid triumph of Newtonianism.)

Jones, R. F.   *Ancients and Moderns: A Study of the Rise of the Scientific Movement in Seventeenth-Century England* (St Louis, 1936, rev. 1961). (Analyses the scientific attitudes inherited by the eighteenth century, and argues that our modern scientific utilitarianism is the offspring of Bacon begot upon Puritanism.)

Jones, W. P. *The Rhetoric of Science: A Study of Scientific Ideas and Imagery in Eighteenth-Century English Poetry* (Berkeley, 1966). (A wide-ranging study of the impact of the various sciences upon poetry.)

Koyre, A *From the Closed World to the Infinite Universe* (Baltimore, 1957). (On the mental and spiritual changes consequent upon the astronomical revolution; considers Newton, Bentley, Berkeley, and Leibniz, among others.)

Lindeboom, G. A. *Boerhaave and Great Britain: Three Lectures on Boerhaave, with Particular Reference to his Relations with Great Britain* (Leiden, 1974). (Boerhaave's reception in Britain.)

Nicholson, M. H. *Science and Imagination* (Ithaca, NY, 1956). (Essays on some of the connections between science and literature.)

Porter, R. *The Making of Geology: Earth Science in Britain, 1660–1815* (1977). (A history of the process by which study of the earth became 'scientific' and 'geological'.)

Schofield, R. E. *Mechanism and Materialism: British Natural Philosophy in an Age of Reason* (Princeton, NJ, 1970). (On eighteenth-century theories of matter.)

Singer, C. *et al.* *A History of Technology*, vol. III: *From the Renaissance to the Industrial Revolution, c. 1500–c. 1750*, and vol. IV: *The Industrial Revolution, c. 1750 to c. 1850* (Oxford, 1957, 1958). (The standard work; comprehensive and lavishly illustrated.)

Taton, R., ed. *The Beginnings of Modern Science, from 1450 to 1800* (1964). (Translated from the French: vol. II of the authoritative *Histoire générale des sciences*, 1958).

Whitehead, A. N. *Science and the Modern World* (Cambridge, 1926). (A classic essay, treating the advance of science as 'the epic of an episode in the manifestation of reason'.)

Wolf, A. *A History of Science, Technology, and Philosophy in the Eighteenth Century* (1938, 2nd edn, rev. D. McKie, 1952). (A compendious narrative; fully illustrated.)

See *Individual Authors*:   Bentley, Cheyne, Newton, Priestley.

(iii) Religious Ideas

Armstrong, A.   *The Church of England, the Methodists and Society, 1700–1850* (1973). (A lively, brief account of the social and intellectual impact of Methodism.)

Bennett, G. V.   *The Tory Crisis in Church and State, 1688–1730: The Career of Francis Atterbury, Bishop of Rochester* (Oxford, 1975). (On the changing relations between Church and State, as reflected in the life of this turbulent bishop.)

Carpenter, S.C.   *Eighteenth-Century Church and People* (1959). (A theological, ecclesiastical, and social history.)

Cragg, G.R.   *Reason and Authority in the Eighteenth Century* (Cambridge, 1964). (On reason's challenge to revelation, and scepticism's challenge to reason.)

Creed, J. M., and J. S. Boys Smith   *Religious Thought in the Eighteenth Century* (Cambridge, 1934). (A selection of key texts, with helpful introductions.)

Davie, D.   *Dissentient Voice* (1982). (Includes essays on eighteenth-century Dissent.)

A Gathered Church: The Literature of the English Dissenting Interest, 1700–1930 (1978). (Shows that English Dissent was not 'puritan' in the (culturally) pejorative sense, or philistine, and demonstrates the literary significance of Watts and Charles Wesley.)

Davies, H.   *Worship and Theology in England from Watts and Wesley to Maurice, 1690–1850* (Princeton, NJ, 1961). (Includes a discussion of church and chapel architecture, as well as liturgy and doctrine.)

Davies, R., and G. Rupp   *A History of the Methodist Church of Great Britain*, vol. I (1965). (The authoritative account.)

Downey, J.   *The Eighteenth-Century Pulpit: A Study of Sermons of Butler, Berkeley, Secker, Sterne, Whitefield, and Wesley* (Oxford, 1969). (A study of the style and substance of an interestingly varied body of eighteenth-century sermons.)

Fairchild, H. N.   *Religious Trends in English Poetry*, 6 vols (New York, 1939–68). Vol. I: *1700–1740, Protestantism and the Cult of Sentiment*. Vol. II: *1740–1780, Religious Sentimentalism in the Age of Johnson*. (An exhaustive study of theology in major and minor poetry of our period, taking note of philosophical and scientific thought where it shows, as it usually does, a religious trend.)

Gill, F. *The Romantic Movement and Methodism* (1937). (Mostly on the eighteenth century.)

Manuel, F. E. *The Eighteenth Century Confronts the Gods* (Cambridge, Mass., 1959). (Concerned with the effects upon European thought of the study of ancient pagan religions.)

Raven, C. F. *Natural Religion and Christian Theology* (Cambridge, 1953). (On the challenge to supernaturalism of eighteenth-century natural religion.)

Semmel, B. *The Methodist Revolution* (New York, 1973). (Argues that Methodism was the 'levelling revolution' in England.)

Stephen, L. see: (iv) Philosophy.

Stromberg, R. N. *Religious Liberalism in Eighteenth-Century England* (Oxford, 1954). (On the challenge to orthodoxy of rationalism, unitarianism, and deism.)

Sykes, N. *Church and State in England in the XVIIIth Century* (Cambridge, 1934). (A detailed study of ecclesiastical life, which ought to have destroyed the old myth that the Anglican Church was torpid throughout the eighteenth century.)

Watts, M. R. *The Dissenters*, vol. i: *From the Reformation to the French Revolution* (Oxford, 1978). (Well-researched social and demographic history.)

Wearmouth, J. R. *Methodism and the Common People* (1945). (Discusses Methodism in its eighteenth-century social context.)

See *Individual Authors*: Addison, Bolingbroke, Butler, Clarke, Hume, Law, Locke, Shaftesbury, Toland, Wesley.

(iv) Philosophy

Becker, C. L. *The Heavenly City of the Eighteenth-Century Philosophers* (New Haven, 1932). (Focusing on the Augustinian ideal of the heavenly city, Becker argues that the thought of the French *philosophes* and their intellectual fellows in other countries is essentially more 'medieval' than 'modern'.)

Bryson, G. *Man and Society: The Scottish Inquiry of the Eighteenth Century* (Princeton, NJ, 1945). (On the efforts of Scottish philosphers to establish an empirical basis for the study of man and society: covers Ferguson, Hume, Hutcheson, Kames, Monboddo, Reid, Smith, and Stewart.)

Bury, J.B. *The Idea of Progress: An Inquiry into Its Origin and Growth* (1920). (The standard survey of eighteenth-century optimism.)

Cassirer, E. *The Philosophy of the Enlightenment,* trans. F. C. A. Koelln and J. P. Pettegrove (Princeton, NJ, 1951). (A classic study, in which eighteenth-century thought is reduced to a unity.) *The Platonic Renaissance in England,* trans. J. P. Pettegrove (Princeton, NJ, 1953). (Important in our period for its treatment of Shaftesbury.)

Chitnis, A. C. *The Scottish Enlightenment: A Social History* (1976). (Considers the Church, the law, and the universities as the three institutions which fostered the Enlightenment in Scotland.)

Cobban, A. *In Search of Humanity: The Role of the Enlightenment in Modern History* (1960). (A history of ideas, centred upon France, but fully aware of the importance of Bacon, Newton, Locke, Hume, and Bentham in European thought.)

Fussell, P. *The Rhetorical World of Augustan Humanism: Ethics and Imagery from Swift to Burke* (Oxford, 1965). (An interpretation of some major poets and critics in the light of the classical–humanist ethical tradition.)

Gay, P. *The Enlightenment: An Interpretation,* 2 vols (1966–69). Vol. i: *The Rise of Modern Paganism.* Vol. ii: *The Science of Freedom.* (Concerned mostly with Continental thought: analyses a dialectic between paganism, Christianity, and science.)

Grave, S. A. *The Scottish Philosophy of Common Sense* (Oxford, 1960). (On Thomas Reid and his school.)

Hazard, P. *The European Mind, 1680–1715* (1953, trans. from the French edn of 1935). (A classic exploration of 'the most significant single revolution in human thought: the birth of Newtonian science and of comparative religion'.)

European Thought in the Eighteenth Century (1954, trans. from the French edn of 1946). (Sees the search for happiness as the mainspring of European thought in the period from 1715 to the 1780s.)

Lovejoy, A. O.   *Essays in the History of Ideas* (Baltimore, 1948). (Includes essays on the concept of 'Nature' as an aesthetic norm and on relationships between deism and classicism.)

The Great Chain of Being: A Study of the History of an Idea (Cambridge, Mass., 1936). (A highly influential book, which has tempted some scholars perhaps to overemphasize the importance of the 'chain-of-being' idea in eighteenth-century literature.)

Mandelbaum, M.   *Philosophy, Science, and Sense Perception: Historical and Critical Studies* (Baltimore, 1964). (A study of theories of sense perception from Locke to Hume in the context of science, particularly of atomist theory.)

Raphael, D. D.   *The Moral Sense* (Oxford, 1947). (On Hutcheson, Hume, Price, and Reid.)

Rockwood, R. O., ed.   *Carl Becker's Heavenly City Revisited* (Ithaca, NY, 1958). (A symposium to develop and criticize the thesis of Becker's book: see Becker, C. L., above.)

Rosenbaum, S. P., ed.   *English Literature and British Philosophy* (Chicago, 1971). (A collection of essays, some of them dealing with the influence of Hobbes, Locke, and Hume on literature.)

Stephen, L.   *History of English Thought in the Eighteenth Century* (1876, 3rd edn 1902, new edn with Preface by C. Brinton, 1962). (A classic survey, somewhat weighted towards the freethinkers.)

Vereker, C.   *Eighteenth-Century Optimism: A study of the Interrelations of Moral and Social Theory in English and French Thought between 1689 and 1789* (Liverpool, 1967). (An enquiry into the influence of optimistic views of human nature on ideas of moral freedom, and into successive attempts during the eighteenth century 'to frame a thorough-going substitute religion'.)

Willey, B.   *The Eighteenth Century Background: Studies on the Idea of Nature in the Thought of the Period* (1940). (Mainly on 'natural religion' and 'natural morality'.)
The English Moralists (1964). (Deals with Locke, Shaftesbury, Addison, Hume, Chesterfield, and Burke.)

*The Seventeenth Century Background: Studies in the
Thought of the Age in relation to Poetry and Religion*
(1934). (Includes chapters on Locke and Wordsworth,
as well as other material relevant to our period.)

See *Individual Authors*:   Berkeley, Butler, Hartley, Hume, Hutcheson, Locke,
Mandeville, Priestley, Reid, Shaftesbury, Smith.

(v) Politics

Ashton, T. S.   *An Economic History of England: The Eighteenth Century*
(1955). (Authoritative and readable.)

Boulton, J. T.   *The Language of Politics in the Age of Wilkes and Burke*
(1963). (On political rhetoric and ideology in the
second half of the eighteenth century.)

Brewer, J.   *Party Ideology and Popular Politics at the Accession of
George III* (Cambridge, 1976). (A study of both
parliamentary and extra-parliamentary political
opinions and activities in the Wilkes era.)

Cannon, J.   *Parliamentary Reform, 1640–1832* (Cambridge, 1973).
(Stresses the antiquity and continuity of reformist
attitudes.)

Carswell, J.   *The South Sea Bubble* (Stanford, 1960). (A detailed
narrative of this economic, social, and moral crisis,
and an assessment of its significance in the 'financial
revolution'.)

Deane, P.   *The First Industrial Revolution* (Cambridge, 1965). (An
interpretation of the eighteenth-century Industrial
Revolution in the light of modern economic theories
of growth and change.)

Dickinson, H. T.   *Liberty and Property: Political Ideology in Eighteenth-
Century Britain* (1977). (Argues that ideological
principles played a greater part in eighteenth-century
politics than many historians have allowed.)

Politics and Literature in the Eighteenth Century (1974).
(An anthology of eighteenth-century texts.)

Dickson, P. G. M.   *The Financial Revolution in England: A Study in the
Development of Public Credit, 1688–1756* (1967). (A
study of the establishment of that sound system of

government finance which underpinned Britain's international power in the eighteenth century.)

Foord, A.   *His Majesty's Opposition, 1714–1830* (Oxford, 1964). (Traces the novel development of a 'legitimate' opposition, and argues that the division between 'court' and 'country' was more significant than that between Whig and Tory.)

George, M. D.   *England in Transition: Life and Work in the Eighteenth Century* (Harmondsworth, 1953). (Lively and authoritative social history.)

Hadfield, C.   *The Canal Age* (1968). (On the contribution made by canals to social and economic change between 1760 and 1850.)

Holmes, G.   *British Politics in the Age of Anne* (1967). (A study of ideas as well as events, arguing that the terms 'Whig' and 'Tory' embodied different principles.)

Jacob, M. C.   *The Radical Enlightenment: Pantheists, Freemasons, and Republicans* (1981). (On the political implications of freethinking in Toland and others.)

Kenyon, J. P.   *Revolution Principles: The Politics of Party, 1689–1720* (Cambridge, 1977). (A history of ideas, not events, examining the ways in which Whigs and Tories absorbed the Glorious Revolution into their ideologies.

Kliger, S.   *The Goths in England* (Cambridge, Mass., 1952). (A study of the northern origins of eighteenth-century notions of political liberty.)

Mantoux, P.   *The Industrial Revolution in the Eighteenth Century: An Outline of the Beginnings of the Modern Factory System in England,* trans. M. Vernon (1928, rev. edn, with Preface by T. S. Ashton, 1961). (A classic.)

Marshall, D.   *English People in the Eighteenth Century* (1956). (An analysis of social structure before and during the early stages of the Industrial Revolution.)

Mingay, G. E.   *English Landed Society in the Eighteenth Century* (1963). (A study of landownership as the foundation of the social, economic, and political structures of eighteenth-century England.)

Namier, L.   *England in the Age of the American Revolution* (1930). *The Structure of Politics at the Accession of George III,* 2 vols (1929). (The most influential twentieth-century studies of eighteenth-century politics.)

Owen, J. B.   *The Eighteenth Century, 1714–1815* (1974). (A political history written from the 'Namierite' standpoint, according to which familial and electoral interests are seen to be more important than party ideologies.)

Parry, J. H.   *Trade and Dominion: European Overseas Empires in the Eighteenth Century* (1974). (On the politics and economics of expansion.)

Plumb, J. H.   *England in the Eighteenth Century* (Harmondsworth, 1950). (A lively and reliable short general history.)

Sir Robert Walpole, 2 vols (1956–60). (The standard life of a political colossus.)

Pocock, J. G. A.   *The Machiavellian Moment: Florentine Political Thought and the Atlantic Republican Tradition* (Princeton, NJ, 1975). (On the contribution of the ideas of classical republicanism to eighteenth-century political thought in England and America.)

Robbins, C.   *The Eighteenth-Century Commonwealthman* (Cambridge, Mass., 1959). (A study of the ideology of the 'Old Whigs' in the light of its debt to seventeenth-century republicanism and its contribution to radicalism and to the American Revolution.)

Rogers, P.   *Grub Street: Studies in a Subculture* (1972). (A social history of this important literary subculture.)

Sekora, J.   *Luxury: The Concept in Western Thought from Eden to Smollett* (Baltimore, 1977). (A study of the key idea of luxury, with particular reference to Smollett.)

Speck, W. A.   *Stability and Strife: England 1714–1760* (1977). (A detailed account of the process by which the very deep party divisions of Queen Anne's reign were replaced by a stable oligarchy in George II's last years.)

Trevelyan, G. M.   *England under Queen Anne*, 3 vols (1931–34). (A vivid large-scale history, with great literary merit.)

See *Individual Authors*:   Bolingbroke, Burke, Ferguson, Gibbon, Hume, Locke, Mandeville, Price, Priestley, Smith.

(vi) Aesthetics

Abrams, M. H. *The Mirror and the Lamp: Romantic Theory and the Critical Tradition* (New York, 1953). (A widely admired study of the 'Romantic' theory of poetry as both a reaffirmation of and a reaction against eighteenth-century aesthetic theories.)

Anderson, H., and J. S. Shea, eds, *Studies in Criticism and Aesthetics, 1660–1800: Essays in Honor of Samuel Holt Monk* (Minneapolis, 1967). (Mostly essays on particular poets, critics, and artists.)

Battestin, M. C. *The Providence of Wit: Aspects of Form in Augustan Literature and the Arts* (Oxford, 1974). (On the reflection of a religious concept of order in literature, art, architecture, and music.)

Draper, J. W. *Eighteenth Century Aesthetics* (Heidelberg, 1931). (Still a useful guide to primary texts.)

Elledge, S., ed. *Eighteenth-Century Critical Essays*, 2 vols (Ithaca, NY, 1961). (Well-annotated collection of essays in criticism and aesthetics.)

Engell, J. *The Creative Imagination, Enlightenment to Romanticism* (Cambridge, Mass., 1981). (Shows how the 'Coleridgean' ideas of the primary and the secondary imagination were formulated in the literature, aesthetics, epistemology, religion, and science of the eighteenth century.)

Hagstrum, J. H. *The Sister Arts: The Tradition of Literary Pictorialism and English Poetry from Dryden to Gray* (Chicago, 1958). (Traces the history of the critical precept 'ut pictura poesis', and examines the pictorialism of Dryden, Pope, Thomson, Collins, and Gray.)

Hepworth, B. *The Rise of Romanticism: Essential Texts* (Manchester, 1978). (A selection of texts from 1684 to 1817 which illustrate a changing conceptualization of time and space.)

Hipple, W. J. *The Beautiful, the Sublime, and the Picturesque in Eighteenth-Century British Aesthetic Theory* (Carbondale, 1957). (Deals in turn with every major critic, from Addison to Dugald Stewart, who developed a theory on one or more of those three categories of aesthetic experience.)

Hussey, C.   *The Picturesque: Studies in a Point of View* (1927). (On
the critical formulation of this aesthetic idea, and its
reflection in painting, gardening, architecture, and
literature.)

Kallich, M.   *The Association of Ideas and Critical Theory in
Eighteenth-Century England: A History of a Psychological
Method in English Criticism* (The Hague, 1970). (A
thorough coverage of its subject, from Hobbes and
Locke to Wordsworth.)

Lee, R.   *Ut Pictura Poesis: the Humanistic Theory of Painting*
(New York, 1967). (On the classical theory that
painting, like poetry, is the ideal imitation of human
action.)

Lipking, L.   *The Ordering of the Arts in Eighteenth-Century England*
(Princeton, NJ, 1970). (On the ways in which their
early historians comprehended the arts of music,
painting, and literature.)

Monk, S. H.   *The Sublime: A Study of Critical Theories in
Eighteenth-Century England* (1935). (Traces the
development of this aesthetic concept, noting its change
from the 'rhetorical sublime' to the 'natural sublime'.)

Morris, D. B.   *The Religious Sublime: Christian Poetry and Critical
Tradition in Eighteenth-Century England* (Lexington,
Kentucky, 1972). (On the way poets employ the
sublime for the purposes of devotion.)

Malek, J. S.   *The Arts Compared: An Aspect of Eighteenth-Century
British Aesthetics* (Detroit, 1974). (On the sisterhood of
the arts.)

Nicholson, M. H.   *Mountain Gloom and Mountain Glory: The Development
of the Aesthetics of the Infinite* (Ithaca, NY, 1959). (On
the scientific, religious, and philosophical background
to that change in taste which made mountains appear
beautiful instead of hideous.)

Thacker, C.   *The Wildness Pleases: The Origins of Romanticism*
(1983). (One of the liveliest, as well as most
wide-ranging, studies of eighteenth-century
romanticism.)

Tinker, C. B.   *Nature's Simple Plan: A Phase of Radical Thought in the
Mid-Eighteenth Century* (Princeton, NJ, 1922). (On
various aspects of literary primitivism.)

Tuveson, E. L.   *The Imagination as a Means of Grace: Locke and the
Aesthetics of Romanticism* (Berkeley and Los Angeles,
1960). (On the development of a theory of creative
imagination in the eighteenth century.)

Wellek, R. *The Rise of English Literary History* (1941). (On the growth of a historical sense in literary criticism.)

See *Individual Authors*: Addison, Blair, Burke, Dennis, Duff, Gerard, Hogarth, Hume, Hurd, Hutcheson, Kames, Lowth, Reynolds, Shaftesbury, Warton, Wood, Young.

(vii) Visual Arts

A. General works

Allen, B. S. *Tides in English Taste, 1619–1800*, 2 vols (Cambridge, Mass., 1937). (A comprehensive history of taste in all the arts.)

Brownell, M. *Alexander Pope and the Arts of Georgian England* (Oxford, 1978). (Detailed account of Pope's career as a 'virtuoso'.)

Burke, J. *English Art, 1714–1800* (Oxford, 1976). (Vol. ix in the standard Oxford History of Art.)

Hook, J. *The Baroque Age in England* (1976). (A general cultural history, stressing the great differences between English and Continental baroque art, music, and literature.)

Irwin, D. *English Neo-Classical Art: Studies in Imagination and Taste* (1966). (Chiefly on painting and sculpture: includes Gavin Hamilton and Barry, but is concerned mostly with the period after 1789.)

Klingender, D. *Art and the Industrial Revolution* (1947), rev. A. Elton (1968). (Deals with the impact of industrialization upon the visual arts, especially in the work of Joseph Wright of Derby.)

Paulson, R. *Emblem and Expression: Meaning in English Art of the Eighteenth Century* (1975). (On a shift in the visual arts, during the 1750s, from meaning based primarily on explicit readable structures to meaning based primarily on spatial or formal structures.)

Pevsner, N. *The Englishness of English Art* (1956). (Includes chapters on Hogarth and Reynolds.)

Rosenblum, R. *Transformations in Late Eighteenth-Century Art* Princeton, NJ, 1967). (The best detailed study of neo-classicism.)

Steegman, J. *The Rule of Taste from George I to George IV* (1936). (A broad survey of architecture, gardening, painting, and the decorative arts.)

Whinney, M., and O. Millar *English Art, 1625–1714* (Oxford, 1957). (Vol. VIII in the standard Oxford History of Art.)

Whitley, W. T. *Artists and their Friends in England, 1700–99*, 2 vols (1928, repr. 1968). (A detailed, anecdotal account of the artists, their patrons, and their academies.)

B. Architecture

Beard, G. *The Work of Robert Adam* (Edinburgh, 1978). (Brief introductory essays and over two hundred good plates.)

Bolton, A. T. *The Architecture of Robert and James Adam (1758–1794*, 2 vols (1932). (The most detailed account.)

Campbell, C., *et al.* *Vitruvius Britannicus, or the British Architect*, 6 vols (1715–71), repr. 3 vols (New York, 1967–70), with *Guide to 'Vitruvius Britannicus'*, by P. Breman and D. Addis (New York, 1972). (The influential collection of Palladian architectural designs.)

Clark, K. *The Gothic Revival: An Essay on the History of Taste* (1928, rev. edn, Harmondsworth, 1974). (Relates architecture to literature and antiquities.)

Colvin, H. M. *A Biographical Dictionary of British Architects, 1600–1840* (1954, rev. 1978). (A model of its kind.)

Colvin, H. M., *et al.* *The History of the King's Works*, vol. V: *1660–1782* (1976). (The definitive account of royal and public building in this period.)

Crook, J. M. *The Greek Revival: Neo-Classical Attitudes in British Architecture, 1760–1870* (1972). (The origins of this great nineteenth-century revival lie in our period.)

Downes, K. *Christopher Wren* (1971). (Standard work.) *English Baroque Architecture* (1966). (The authoritative survey; splendidly illustrated.) *Hawksmoor* (1959). (Standard work.) *Hawksmoor* (1969). (Expert introduction.) *Vanbrugh* (1977). (Standard work on the architecture.)

Hussey, C. *English Country Houses, 1715–1840*, 3 vols (1955–58). (Introductory essays and detailed descriptions of selected examples.)

Ketton-Cremer, R. W. *Horace Walpole* (1940, rev. 1946). (The best biography of the builder of Strawberry Hill.)

Lees-Milne, J. *English Country Houses: Baroque (1685–1715)* (1970). (Complements Hussey's study of the period 1715–1840: see above.)

Little, B. *The Life and Work of James Gibbs, 1682–1754* (1955). (Largely biographical.)

Macaulay, J. *The Gothic Revival, 1745–1845* (1975). (Concentrates on Scotland and the north of England.)

Sitwell, S. *British Architects and Craftsmen: A Survey of Taste, Design and Style during Three Centuries, 1600–1830* (1945). (A classic: stylish, vivid, and loving.)

Stutchbury, H. E. *The Architecture of Colen Campbell* (Manchester, 1967).

Summerson, J. *Architecture in Britain, 1530 to 1830* (Harmondsworth, 1953, 5th edn 1969). (A volume in the standard Pelican History of Art.)

Georgian London (1943). (Brief architectural history.)

Whinney, M. *Christopher Wren* (1971). (Useful introduction.)

Whistler, L. *Sir John Vanbrugh: Architect and Dramatist, 1664–1726* (1938, repr. 1971).
The Imagination of Vanbrugh and his Fellow Artists (1954).
(Two lively and stylish studies.)

Whittkower, R. *Palladio and English Palladianism* (1974). (Essays on the English Palladian revival and its broad cultural effects.)

See *Individual Authors*:   Chambers, Wood.

C. Painting and sculpture

Constable, W. G. *Richard Wilson* (1953). (Standard life and *catalogue raisonné.*)

254 THE EIGHTEENTH CENTURY

Decorative Painting in England, 1537–1837, vol. II (1970). (Includes Kent, Hogarth, Hayman, the Adam brothers, etc.; contains an authoritative account of history painting in our period too.)

Esdaile, K. A.

The Life and Works of Louis François Roubiliac (1928). (Standard life.)

Gunnis, R.

Dictionary of British Sculptors, 1660–1851 (1953, 2nd edn 1968). (Standard work; less detailed than Colvin's *Architects*.)

Hardie, M.

Watercolour Painting in Britain, vol I: *The Eighteenth Century* (1966, 2nd edn. 1967). (The authoritative work.)

Hayes, J.

Gainsborough: Paintings and Drawings (1975). (Copiously illustrated and expert introduction.) *The Drawings of Thomas Gainsborough*, 2 vols (1970). (Authoritative study and *catalogue raisonné*.) *The Landscape Paintings of Thomas Gainsborough*, 2 vols (1982). (Authoritative study and *catalogue raisonné*.)

Hermann, L.

British Landscape Painting of the Eighteenth Century (1973). (Chapters cover 'The Rise of the Classical Tradition', 'The Topographical Tradition', 'The Discovery of Italy', 'The Tradition of the Netherlands', and 'The Rise of the Picturesque.)

Kerslake, J.

Early Georgian Portraits, 2. vols (1977). (Comprehensive *catalogue raisonné* of portraits in the National Portrait Gallery, covering the period 1714–60.)

Manwaring, E. W.

Italian Landscape in Eighteenth Century England: A Study chiefly on the Influence of Claude Lorrain and Salvator Rosa on English Taste, 1700–1800 (1925). (An influential study, which overstates its case.)

Nicolson, B.

Joseph Wright of Derby: Painter of Light, 2 vols (1968). (Standard biography, critical study, and *catalogue raisonné*.)

Oppé, A. P.

Alexander and John Robert Cozens (1952). (Standard account of the water-colourists, father and son.)

Paviere, S. H.

The Devis Family of Painters (1950).

Physick, J.

Designs for English Sculpture, 1680–1860 (1969). (An annotated selection.)

Pressley, W. L.   *The Life and Art of James Barry* (1981). (Standard account of his life, art, and writings; with *catalogue raisonné.*)

Solkin, D. H.   *Richard Wilson; the Landscape of Reaction* (1982). (Exhibition catalogue.)

Smart, A.   *The Life and Art of Allan Ramsay* (1952). (Standard life.)

Stewart, J. D.   *Sir Godfrey Kneller and the English Baroque Portrait* (Oxford, 1983). (Authoritative life and catalogue.)

Taylor, B., ed.   *Painting in England 1700–1850*, 2 vols (Richmond, Va., 1963). (Illustrated catalogue of the Mellon Collection.)
Stubbs (1971). (Authoritative, well-illustrated introduction.)

Tinker, C. B.   *Painter and Poet: Studies in the Literary Relations of English Painting* (Cambridge, Mass., 1938). (On the reflection of literary movements in eighteenth-century painting.)

Waterhouse, E. K.   *Gainsborough* (1958). (Catalogue now superseded by Hayes, but still an excellent general account of the painter.)
Painting in Britain, 1530 to 1790 (Harmondsworth, 1953). (A volume in the standard Pelican History of Art.)

Webb, M. I.   *Michael Rysbrack, Sculptor* (1954). (Standard life.)

Whinney, M.   *English Sculpture, 1720–1830* (1971). (Descriptions of selected works.)
Sculpture in Britain, 1530–1830 (Harmondsworth, 1964). (A volume in the standard Pelican History of Art.)

Williamson, G. C., ed.   *Bryan's Dictionary of Painters and Engravers* 5 vols (1930–34). (Revised edition of the work first published in 1816.)

See *Individual Authors*:   Hogarth, Reynolds.

D. Landscape gardening

Chase, I. W. U.   *Horace Walpole, Gardenist* (Princeton, NJ, 1943). (Includes the text of Walpole's *Essay on Modern Gardening*, 1785).

Clark, H. F. *The English Landscape Garden* (1948, repr. 1980). (A pioneering essay: well illustrated.)

Green, D. B. *Gardener to Queen Anne: Henry Wise (1653–1738) and the Formal English Garden* (1956). (Standard life of the greatest English gardener before the landscape movement.)

Hadfield, M. *A History of British Gardening* (1969). (A revision of *Gardening in Britain* (1960); its chapters on the eighteenth century are authoritative.)

Hunt, J. D. *The Figure in the Landscape: Poetry, Painting and Gardening during the Eighteenth Century* (1977). (On the interaction of these three 'graces' in their adornment of nature.)

Hunt, J. D., and P. Willis *The Genius of the Place: The English Landscape Garden, 1620–1820* (1975). (A selection of contemporary texts to illustrate the origin and development of the landscape garden.)

Hussey, C. *English Gardens and Landscapes, 1700–1750* (1967). (A well-informed essay on the origins of the landscape garden, together with detailed, copiously illustrated, studies of several surviving landscapes.)

Jacques, D. *Georgian Gardens: The Reign of Nature* (1983). (Includes a large collection of garden plans.)

Jourdain, M. *The Work of William Kent* (1948). (Standard life, dealing with Kent's work in architecture and the decorative arts, as well as his gardening.)

Mack, M. *The Garden and the City: Retirement and Politics in the Later Poetry of Pope, 1731–43* (1969). (On the moral significance of Pope's garden.)

Malins, E. *English Landscaping and Literature, 1660–1840* (1966). (On the mutual influences of landscape gardening and literature.)

Stroud, D. *Capability Brown* (1950, new edn 1975). (Standard life; covers Brown's architecture as well as his landscape design.)

Willis, P. *Charles Bridgeman and the English Landscape Garden* (1977). (Standard account of the creator of Stowe and pioneer of the landscape movement.)

Woodbridge, K. *Landscape and Antiquity: Aspects of English Culture at Stourhead, 1718 to 1838* (Oxford, 1970). (Includes an account of the making and the significance of Henry Hoare's unparalleled landscape garden.)

(viii) Models

Appleton, W. W. *The Cycle of Cathay: The Chinese Vogue in England during the Seventeenth and Eighteenth Centuries* (New York, 1951).

Beaglehole, J. C. *The Life of Captain James Cook* (1974). (Authoritative.)

Buxton, J. *The Grecian Taste: Literature in the Age of Neo-Classicism* (1978). (Includes chapters on Akenside, Collins, Goldsmith, and some later figures.)

Clarke, M. L. *Greek Studies in England, 1700–1830* (Cambridge, 1945). (Mainly on scholarship.)

Erskine-Hill, H. *The Augustan Idea in English Literature* (1983). (The most learned and detailed exposition of the traditional notion of Augustanism; but see Weinbrot, below.)

Fairchild, H. N. *The Noble Savage: A Study in romantic Naturalism* (New York, 1928). (The most complete account of the noble savage in English literature from the sixteenth century to 1830.)

Honour, H. *Chinoiserie: The Vision of Cathay* (1961). (On Chinese taste in Europe as a whole; the sections on Britain are authoritative.)

Johnson, J. W. *The Formation of English Neo-Classical Thought* (Princeton, NJ, 1967). (Surveys a very wide range of, mostly non-Roman, classical influences upon eighteenth-century English culture.)

Johnston, A. *Enchanted Ground: The Study of Medieval Romance in the Eighteenth Century* (1964). (Includes chapters on Hurd, Percy, Thomas Warton, and later figures.)

Marshall, P. J., ed. *The British Discovery of Hinduism in the Eighteenth Century* (1970). (A selection of primary documents.)

Marshall, P. J. and G. Williams *The Great Map of Mankind: British Perceptions of the World in the Age of Enlightenment* (1982). (On the ways in which growth of knowledge about, and of imperial power in, distant parts of the world changed the British view of other peoples and of themselves.)

Meek, R. L. *Social Science and the Ignoble Savage* (Cambridge, 1976). (On the effect of the study of North American Indians upon Rousseau, Ferguson and other social theorists.)

Moorehead, A.   *The Fatal Impact: An Account of the Invasion of the South Pacific, 1767–1840* (1966). (A study of the fateful moment when the natives of the South Pacific were confronted by European civilization.)

Owen, A. L.   *The Famous Druids* (Oxford, 1962). (On the figure of the Druid in the English literary imagination, mainly in the eighteenth century.)

Roston, M.   *Prophet and Poet: The Bible and the Growth of Romanticism* (1965). (Shows how study of the literary qualities of the Bible led to new developments in aesthetics and poetry.)

Smith, B.   *European Vision and the South Pacific, 1768–1850: A Study in the History of Art and Ideas* (Oxford, 1960). (Mainly on painting.)

Snyder, E. D.   *The Celtic Revival in English Literature, 1760–1800* (Cambridge, Mass., 1923). (Covers the work of Morris, Evans, Gray, Mason, and Macpherson.)

Spencer, T.   *Fair Greece, Sad Relic: Literary Philhellenism from Shakespeare to Byron* (1954). (A survey of literary contacts between England and modern Greece.)

Wasserman, E. R.   *Elizabethan Poetry in the Eighteenth Century* (Urbana, 1947). (On the admiration and imitation of the Elizabethans by eighteenth-century critics and poets.)

Webb, T.   *English Romantic Hellenism, 1700–1824* (Manchester, 1982). (This annotated selection of texts, which illustrate the influence of Greek culture upon English literature in our period, shows that what is often called 'Romantic Hellenism' began at the end of the seventeenth century.)

Weinbrot, H. D.   *Augustus Caesar in 'Augustan' England: The Decline of a Classical Norm* (Princeton, NJ, 1978). (A much-needed and amply documented demonstration of the inappropriateness of the term 'Augustan' to describe eighteenth-century English thought and literature.)

Individual Authors

Notes on biography, major works,
and suggested further reading

ADDISON, Joseph (1672–1719), eldest son of a future Dean of Lichfield, was born at his father's rectory near Amesbury. He was educated at the Charterhouse and at Queen's College and Magdalen College, Oxford, where he acquired great skill as a Latin poet and a reputation for elegant scholarship; he was a Fellow of Magdalen from 1697 to 1711. Dryden encouraged his first efforts in English poetry. By the patronage of Charles Montagu, later Earl of Halifax, he was enabled to travel in France, Italy, and Switzerland between 1699 and 1703; the literary fruits of these travels appeared in his verse *Letter from Italy* (1703), and his prose *Remarks on Several Parts of Italy* (1705). He became a member of the Kit-Cat Club of leading Whigs; his poem *The Campaign* (1705), in celebration of the victory at Blenheim, won him an under-secretaryship, from which he gradually rose in government service until the Whigs lost office in 1710; between 1708 and 1719 he was a Member of Parliament, first for Lostwithiel, then for Malmesbury. His English opera *Rosamund* (1707) was written in order to counter the contemporary taste for unintelligible Italian opera. His contributions to the *Tatler*, founded in 1709 by his former schoolmate at the Charterhouse, Richard Steele, set the tone and manner of the eighteenth-century periodical essay; he was the principal author of the *Spectator* (1711–12 and 1714), the finest and most influential example of this form of writing; his *Spectator* papers on the Pleasures of the Imagination and on *Paradise Lost* became standard works of aesthetics and criticism, and were separately reprinted. Of the five other periodicals with which he was engaged betwen 1710 and 1719, the only significant ones are the *Guardian* (1713), with Steele, and the *Freeholder, or Political Essays* (1715–16), written entirely by Addison. His tragedy *Cato* (1713), with a prologue by Pope, was enormously successful and held the stage throughout the eighteenth century; his prose comedy *The Drummer, or the Haunted House* was not a success. With the triumph of the Whigs on George I's accession in 1714, Addison returned to government and rose to the rank of Secretary of State in 1717: this elevation may have been assisted by his marrige to the Countess of Warwick in 1716. He retired on account of ill health in 1718 and died at Holland House, Kensington, on 17 June 1719.

Guthkelch, A. C., ed., *Miscellaneous Works of Joseph Addison*, 2 vols (1914). (Omits periodical essays.)

Bond, D. F., ed., *The Spectator*, 5 vols (Oxford, 1965). (Well annotated.)

Leheny, J., ed., *The Freeholder* (Oxford, 1979). (Well annotated.)

Graham, W., ed., *The Letters of Joseph Addison* (Oxford 1941).
Smithers, P., *The Life of Joseph Addison* (Oxford, 1954).

See: Macaulay, T. B., 'The Life and Writings of Addison', in *Critical and Historical Essays* (1843).
Johnson, S., 'Addison', in *Lives of the English Poets*, ed. G. B. Hill (Oxford, 1905).
Bloom, E. A. and L.D. Bloom, *Joseph Addison's Sociable Animal, in the Market Place, on the Hustings, in the Pulpit* (Providence, 1953). (On Addison's moral and political philosphy in its religious, social, and intellectual context.)
Bloom, E. A., and L. D. Bloom, *Addison and Steele: The Critical Heritage* (1980). (A selection of criticism, early and late.)

BEATTIE, James (1735–1803), born in Kincardineshire, the son of a shopkeeper, was educated at Marischal College, Aberdeen, and worked as a schoolmaster before becoming Professor of Moral Philosophy and Logic at Marischal College in 1760. He published volumes of verse in 1761, 1765, and 1766, but, of all his poetry, only *The Minstrel* (1771–74) has escaped oblivion. His *Essay on the Nature and Immutability of Truth* (1770) was thought by some to have confuted Hume; reprinted many times, it earned Beattie a doctorate of civil law from Oxford, a pension from George III, and the distinction of a place in an allegorical painting by Reynolds. His other publications included *Essays* on poetry and music, on laughter, and on classical learning (1776), *Dissertations Moral and Critical* (1783), *Evidences of the Christian Religion* (1786), and *Elements of Moral Science* (1790–93).

Walker, R. S., ed., *James Beattie's London Diary, 1773* (Aberdeen, 1946). (Beattie's work is discussed in the Preface.)

See: King, E. H., *James Beattie* (Boston, 1977). (Handy, short critical biography.)

BENTLEY, Richard (1662–1742), son of a yeoman, was born in the West Riding of Yorkshire, and educated at Wakefield Grammar School and St John's College, Cambridge. He was ordained in 1690, and owed his early advancement in the Church to the patronage of Edward Stillingfleet, Bishop of Worcester, whose son he tutored. In 1692 Bentley gave the first course of Boyle lectures, into which, after correspondence with Newton, he introduced the new ideas of the *Principia* and applied them to the proof of religion. In 1694 he was appointed Royal Librarian and elected Fellow of the Royal Society; in 1695 he became a Royal Chaplain. He inaugurated a new era in the study of classical antiquities, chronology, and philology with his formidable *Dissertation on the Letters of Phalaris* (1699), very much the weightiest product of that English debate between the Ancients and Moderns which also produced Swift's *Battle of the Books*. As Master of Trinity College, Cambridge, from 1700, he did much to raise standards, particularly in the physical sciences; he established an observatory (the only one in Cambridge) and a chemical laboratory in the college, and he furthered the careers of the disciples of his friend Newton. He continued his own work as a classical critic with editions of Horace (1711), Terence (1726), Manilius (1739), and, altogether less happily, Milton's *Paradise Lost* (1732). He presided over his college tyrannically, flouting its statutes; as a result, his Fellows made repeated efforts to eject him and the college was torn by internal feuds for most of the forty-two years of his rule. Bentley died on 14 July 1742 in Cambridge.

See: White, R. J., *Dr. Bentley, a Study in Academic Scarlet* (1965).

BERKELEY, George (1685–1753), son of a kinsman to Lord Berkeley, Lord
Lieutenant of Ireland, was born near Kilkenny, but always considered himself
an Englishman. He was educated at Kilkenny School and Trinity College,
Dublin, where he was elected Fellow and Tutor in 1707, and subsequently held
lectureships in Greek and Hebrew. After studying Locke, he expounded his
own philosophy of immaterialism in an *Essay towards a New Theory of Vision*
(1709), *A Treatise concerning the Principles of Human Knowledge* (1710), and *Three
Dialogues between Hylas and Philonous* (1713), but these works occasioned very
little immediate serious discussion. He travelled in France and Italy as chaplain
to the Earl of Peterborough (1713–14) and as tutor to a young gentleman on the
Grand Tour (1716–20); from 1728 to 1731 he was in America, attempting
unsuccessfully to carry through a long-cherished scheme to found a college on
Bermuda to educate Protestant clergy for the colonies. For most of those years
between 1713 and 1734 when he was not on his foreign travels he lived in
London, associating with, and much admired by, the leading literary figures
there. His most important later philosophical writings are *Alciphron, or the
Minute Philosopher, in Seven Dialogues* (1732), and *Siris, or a Chain of
Philosophical Reflexions and Inquiries concerning the Use of Tar-Water* (1744),
which contains both medical and metaphysical theories. His many other
writings include several works on mathematics, in Latin and English, the most
notable of which is *De Motu* (1721), and many tracts on ecclesiastical, social,
and economic subjects, including *An Essay towards preventing the Ruin of Great
Britain* (1721), which condemns luxury in the aftermath of the South Sea
Bubble, and *The Querist* (1735–37), the most wide-ranging of his
socio-economic works. After ten years as (mostly non-resident) Dean of
Down, he was consecrated as Bishop of Cloyne in 1734; he was an active
bishop and he resided in his diocese until a few months before his death in
Oxford, 14 January 1753.

> Luce, A. A., and T. E. Jessop, eds, *The Works of George Berkeley,
> Bishop of Cloyne*, 9 vols (Edinburgh, 1948–52).
> Ayers, M. R. ed., George Berkeley, *Philosophical Works, including the
> Works on Vision* (1975, rev. 1980). (Excellent selection.)
> Luce, A. A., *The Life of George Berkeley, Bishop of Cloyne* (Edinburgh,
> 1949).

See: Luce, A. A., *Berkeley's Immaterialism* (Edinburgh, 1945).
        Warnock, G. J., *Berkeley* (Harmondsworth, 1953).
        Tipton, I. C., *Berkeley: The Philosophy of Immaterialism* (1974).
        Pitcher, G., *Berkeley* (1977).

BLACKWELL, Thomas (1701–57), born and educated in Aberdeen, was Professor of
Greek at Marischal College from 1724 and Principal of the College from 1748;
he died in Edinburgh on 8 March 1757. His *Enquiry into the Life and Writings of
Homer* (1735) helped to shape the primitivist views of Macpherson and such
critics as Beattie, Duff, and Monboddo; he also wrote *Letters concerning
Mythology* (1748) and *Memoirs of the Court of Augustus* (1752–64).

BLAIR, Hugh (1718–1800), son of a merchant, was born in Edinburgh and educated
at the university there. He was ordained into the Presbyterian ministry in 1742
and served as minister of the High Church of St Giles, Edinburgh, from 1758
to his death on 27 December 1800; his *Sermons* (1777–1801) were widely
admired and often reprinted. He occupied the Chair of Rhetoric at Edinburgh

from 1760 to 1762 and a specially-created Chair of Rhetoric and *Belles-Lettres* from 1762 to 1783. He encouraged James Macpherson to print the 'Ossian' poems in 1760 and he unwisely authenticated them with *A Critical Dissertation on the Poems of Ossian*; this dissertation, like Blair's *Lectures on Rhetoric and Belle Lettres*, was often reprinted.

> Harding, H. F., ed., *Hugh Blair, Lectures on Rhetoric and Belle Lettres*, 2 vols (Carbondale, 1965).

> See: Schmitz, R. M., *Hugh Blair* (New York, 1948). (Biographical and critical.)

BOLINGBROKE, Henry St John, Viscount (1678–1751), son of a baronet and grandson of the Earl of Warwick, was born in his father's manor-house at Battersea; after attendance at Eton, be became a dissipated man-about-town. As Tory Member for the family borough of Wooton-Bassett, Wiltshire, from 1700 to 1708, and for Berkshire from 1710 to 1712, he gained a reputation as the most brilliant parliamentary orator of his day; in 1704 he became Secretary at War until the fall of the ministry in 1708. Returning with the Tories in 1710, he became Secretary of State, being created Viscount Bolingbroke in 1712 as a reward for his engineering the Peace of Utrecht, a treaty seen by the Whigs as a betrayal of Britain's war aims and her allies. For a few days in 1714 he was effectively Prime Minister, but he was utterly ruined by the death of Queen Anne. Dismissed from office by George I and threatened with impeachment, he fled to France in 1715, where he briefly entered the Pretender's service, before retiring to his country estate, La Source, to study history and philosophy. Returning to England in 1725, he lived at Dawley, near Uxbridge, where he associated with his old friend Pope, for whom he wrote the philosophical essays worked up into the *Essay on Man*. His attempts to organize and put himself at the head of an effective opposition to Walpole's government, through his polemical writings in the *Craftsman* and through extra-parliamentary intrigue, were unsuccessful, so he returned to France in 1735; he lived again in England from 1743 until his death, at Battersea, on 12 December 1751, but his direct political influence was now negligible. Some of his most important contributions to the *Craftsman* were gathered in volumes: *A Dissertation on Parties* (1735), *Remarks on the History of England* (1743). The other important works published in his lifetime were *Letters on the Spirit of Patriotism, On the Idea of a Patriot King*, and *On the State of Parties* (1749). After his death appeared *Letters on the Study and Use of History* and *Reflections concerning Innate Moral Principles* (1752). These and other writings were collected and edited by David Mallet (1754).

> Wellek, R., ed., Bolingbroke, Henry, Viscount, *Philosophical Works*, 5 vols (1976, reprint of the 1777 edn).

> Krammick, I., ed., Lord Bolingbroke, *Historical Writings* (Chicago, 1972). (Includes *Letters on the Study and Use of History* and *Remarks on the History of England*.)

> Varey, S., ed., Lord Bolingbroke, *Contributions to the Craftsman* (Oxford, 1982). (With a useful introduction.)

> Dickinson, H. T., *Bolingbroke* (1970). (Fullest modern biography.)

> See: James, D. G., *The Life of Reason: Hobbes, Locke, Bolingbroke* (1949). (A brilliant study of the writings by these three men which treat of human knowledge, imagination, and religious feeling.)

> Hart, J., *Viscount Bolingbroke: Tory Humanist* (1965). (Argues that the

clue to Bolingbroke's politics is that he believed traditional humanist values to be under attack from commerce, individualism, moral relativism, and the growth of towns.)
Krammick, I., *Bolingbroke and his Circle: The Politics of Nostalgia in the Age of Walpole* (1968). (Concerned with the grounds of the attack launched upon Walpole's 'corruption' by Bolingbroke and his literary associates.)

BURKE, Edmund (1729–97), son of a Dublin attorney, was educated at a Quaker school in Kildare and at Trinity College, Dublin. In the 1750s he was in London, reading half-heartedly for the Bar and associating with literary and theatrical figures; his satire upon Bolingbroke, *A Vindication of Natural Society* (1756), and his important aesthetic treatise, *A Philosophical Enquiry into the Origin of our Ideas of the Sublime and Beautiful* (1757), attracted wide notice; in 1759 he founded the *Annual Register*; from 1764 he was a much-admired member of Johnson's literary circle. He was a Member of the House of Commons from 1766 until his death, representing first Wendover, then Bristol, and finally Malton; in Parliament he attached himself to that section of the Whig Party led by the Marquis of Rockingham, and later became an ally of Charles James Fox. In those short periods when his party formed the government, Burke obtained nothing more than the lowly office of Paymaster-General; he was far more formidable in opposition, particularly in advocating such causes as 'economical', non-radical, reform of Parliament and government, conciliation with the American colonists, fair trade between England and Ireland, Roman Catholic emancipation, and justice and efficiency in the government of India. His pamphlets and published speeches on these subjects include *Thoughts on the Causes of the Present Discontents* (1770), *Speech on American Taxation* (1774), *Speech on Conciliation with the Colonies* (1775), *Speech on the Nabob of Arcot's Debts* (1785). He took a leading part in the impeachment of Warren Hastings, 1787–94. His immensely popular *Reflections on the Revolution in France* (1790) did much to polarize English opinion concerning the French Revolution; his continuing campaign against English supporters of the Revolution led to a breach with the Foxite Whigs, and induced Burke to reaffirm conservative Whig doctrine in *An Appeal from the New to the Old Whigs* (1791). His *Letter to a Noble Lord* (1796) is the reply to attacks made upon him for accepting a government pension. The last of his many denunciations of revolutionary principles was a succession of *Letters on a Regicide Peace* (1796–97). He died on 9 July 1797 at his country house near Beaconsfield.

> *The Works of Edmund Burke*, 6 vols (1854).
> Langford, P., et al., ed., *The Writings and Speeches of Edmund Burke*, 12 vols (Oxford, 1981–). (In progress.)
> Stanlis, P. J., ed., *Edmund Burke: Selected Writings and Speeches* (New York, 1963). (Very substantial and wide-ranging selection.)
> Boulton, J. T. ed., *A Philosophical Enquiry into the Origin of our Ideas of the Sublime and the Beautiful* (1958). (With a comprehensive introduction.)
> Cove, C. B., *Burke and the Nature of Politics*, 2 vols (Lexington, 1957–64). (Detailed biographical and historical study.)

See: Cobban, A., *Edmund Burke and the Revolt against the Eighteenth Century* (1929, 2nd edn, 1960). (Treats of Burke's influence on early nineteenth-century poetry.)
Stanlis, P. J., *Edmund Burke and the Natural Law* (Ann Arbor, 1958). (On the political philosophy.)
Cameron, D., *The Social Thought of Rousseau and Burke: A Comparative Study* (1973). (Finds much in common between these two apparently antagonistic philosophers.)

BUTLER, Joseph (1692–1752), born at Wantage, was the son of a wealthy retired draper. As a precocious youth at the Dissenting Academy in Tewkesbury, he carried on a philosophical correspondence with Samuel Clarke concerning Clarke's Boyle lectures. He studied at Oriel College, Oxford, from 1714 to 1718, was ordained into the Church of England, and thereafter obtained steady preferment on account more of his scholarship and piety than his politics. His *Fifteen Sermons* (1726) and *The Analogy of Religion, Natural and Revealed, to the Constitution and Course of Nature* (1736) were well received. He became Bishop of Bristol in 1738, Dean of St Paul's in 1740, and Bishop of Durham in 1750. He died at Bath, 16 June 1752.

> Bernard, J. H., *The Works of Joseph Butler*, 2 vols (1900).

> See: Mossner, E. C., *Bishop Butler and the Age of Reason* (1936). (On the *Analogy* as an index to the scientific, philosophical, and religious thought of its age.)
> Duncan-Jones, A., *Butler's Moral Philosophy* (Harmondsworth, 1952). (An authoritative account.)
> Babolin, A., *Joseph Butler*, 2 vols (1973). (The fullest available study.)

CHAMBERS, Sir William (1726–96), was born in Stockholm of Scottish descent; he passed most of his youth in England, but from the age of sixteen made one or more voyages to China as supercargo in a Swedish East Indiaman. He studied architecture in Italy, returning to London in 1755 to set up a prosperous practice. Using the sketches he had made on his early visits to China, he published *Designs for Chinese Buildings* (1757) and erected some buildings in that style at Kew which he illustrated in *The Gardens and Buildings at Kew* (1763). His *Treatise of Civil Architecture* (1759) was for many years a standard work; he was the first Treasurer of the Royal Academy; in 1771 he was given a Swedish knighthood and allowed by George III to use the title in England. His *Dissertation on Oriental Gardening* (1772) was the object of satire, but did not undermine his position at the head of the architectural profession. He died in London on 8 March 1796.

> See: Harris, J., *Sir William Chambers: Knight of the Polar Star* (1970). (Standard monograph, with contributions by E. Harris and J.M. Crook.)

CHEYNE, George (1671–1743), a Scotsman, was a medical student at Edinburgh. His earliest writings on medicine expounded the mathematical and mechanical theories of his teacher Archibald Pitcairne, but he combined theology with science in *Philosophical Principles of Natural Religion* (1705) and *Philosophical Principles of Revealed Religion* (1715). He was elected a Fellow of the Royal Society in 1702, after which he practised medicine with profit and celebrity, first in London and later in Bath, where he died on 13 April 1743. In a string of works, including *Observations on Gout* (1720), *An Essay of Health and Long Life* (1724), and *An Essay on Regimen* (1740), he attempted to persuade the scurvied and carnivorous upper classes to adopt a healthier diet; his *English Malady* (1733) deals with nervous diseases, such as the spleen and vapours.

> Mullett, C. F., ed., *The Letters of George Cheyne to Richardson* (1733–43) (Columbia, Mo., 1943).

CLARKE, Samuel (1675–1729), son of a prosperous alderman, was born in Norwich, educated at Norwich Free School and Caius College, Cambridge, and ordained into the Church of England. In 1704 and 1705 he delivered the Boyle lectures, which were published as *A Discourse concerning the Being and Attributes of God, the Obligations of Natural Religion, and The Truth and Certainty of the Christian Revelation* (1705–6); in these, and in later theological writings, of which *The Scripture Doctrine of the Trinity* (1712) was the most celebrated, he expressed Arian views which drew him into controversy with churchmen who thought him heterodox and with freethinkers who thought him too orthodox. He also wrote on scientific subjects, and in 1706 translated Newton's *Opticks* into Latin. In 1709 he was made a Royal Chaplain by Queen Anne; after her death he regularly attended the Princess of Wales, afterwards Queen Caroline, as a kind of court philosopher, and, at the Princess's request, engaged in a philosophical controversy with Leibniz. Clarke died on 17 May 1729.

See: Ferguson, J. P., *The Philosophy of Dr. Samuel Clarke and its Critics* (1974). (A survey of Clarke's theology and moral theory and the controversies they gave rise to.)

DENNIS, John (1657–1734), son of a prosperous London saddler, was educated at Harrow, and at Caius College and Trinity Hall, Cambridge. After travels in France and Italy, when he was much impressed by the sublimity of the Alps, he returned to London and obtained a government sinecure through the patronage of the Duke of Marlborough. He wrote patriotic poems and stage plays with very little success; Pope's ridicule of his last play, *Appius and Virginia* (1709), in his *Essay on Criticism*, led to bitter, long-running quarrel between the two men. Dennis wrote many critical works, the most important of which are *The Advancement and Reformation of Modern Poetry* (1701), *The Grounds of Criticism in Poetry* (1704), and *Three Letters on the Genius and Writings of Shakespeare* (1711); his chief critical concern was to recommend the sublime. He declined into great poverty in his later years, and died on 6 January 1734.

Hooker, E. N., ed., *The Critical Works of John Dennis*, 2 vols (Baltimore, 1939–43). (The standard edition and the best critical account of Dennis.)

DUFF, William (1732–1815), a Scotsman, was for sixty years a Presbyterian minister in various Aberdeenshire parishes; he died on 23 February 1815. He wrote *An Essay on Original Genius* (1767) and its supplement, *Critical Observations on the Writings of the Most Celebrated Geniuses in Poetry* (1770), also an 'oriental tale' *The History of Rhedi, the Hermit of Mount Ararat* (1773) and other miscellaneous works.

Mahoney, J. L., ed., *William Duff, An essay on Original Genius* (Gainesville, 1964).

FERGUSON, Adam (1723–1816), born in Perthshire, the son of a Presbyterian minister, studied for the ministry at St Andrews. Between 1745 and 1754 he served as (Gaelic-speaking) Chaplain to the Black Watch; he was present at the Battle of Fontenoy (1745), and always retained a high regard for martial courage. Abandoning the clerical profession, he was for a short while Keeper of the Advocates' Library, in succession to his friend David Hume; then, from 1759 to 1785, he occupied in turn the Chairs of Natural Philosophy and of Moral Philosophy at Edinburgh, after which he effectively retired to a sinecure Chair of Mathematics. His principal publications were *An Essay on the History of Civil Society* (1767), *Institutes of Moral Philosophy* (1769), *The History of the Progress and Termination of the Roman Republic* (1783), and *Principles of Moral and Political Science* (1792). He died at St Andrews on 22 February 1816.

266 THE EIGHTEENTH CENTURY

Forbes, D., ed., Adam Ferguson, *An Essay on the History of Civil Society* (Edinburgh, 1966).

See: Kettler, D., *The Social and Political Thought of Adam Ferguson* (Ohio, 1965). (Authoritative survey.)

GERARD, Alexander (1728–95), was born in Aberdeenshire and educated at Marischal College, Aberdeen, where he was Professor of Philosophy, 1750–60, and Professor of Divinity 1760–71; he became Professor of Divinity at King's College in 1771; he died on 22 February 1795. His prize-winning *Essay on Taste* was published in 1759, revised 1764, and his *Essay on Genius* in 1774. As a Presbyterian minister and Royal Chaplain he wrote on theological subjects and preached against the American Revolution.

Hipple, W. J., ed., Alexander Gerard, *An Essay on Taste* (Gainesville, 1963).

Fabian, B., ed., Alexander Gerard, *An Essay on Genius* (Munich, 1966).

GIBBON, Edward (1737–94), the sickly, precocious, and only surviving child of a landed, independent Tory MP, spent some time at Westminster and Magdalen College, Oxford, but was mainly self-educated. In 1753 he was converted to Roman Catholicism, whereupon his horrified father placed him under the care of a Swiss Calvinist pastor in Lausanne, by whom he was restored to Protestantism in a year and a half; he fell in love with Suzanne Curchod, later to become Mme Necker and mother of Mme de Staël, but his father would not allow him to marry her. Returning to England in 1758, he took a commission in the Hampshire Militia and completed his *Essai sur l'étude de la littérature* (1761, trans. into English, 1764). He considered several projects for a major historical work; then, at Rome on 15 October 1764, he fixed upon his topic. In 1774 he joined Johnson's literary club. As MP for Liskeard and later for Lymington (1774–83), he supported the Tory ministry throughout the American War and held minor government posts. His *History of the Decline and Fall of the Roman Empire* (1776–88) rapidly established his position as the leading English historian. He finished this great work at Lausanne, where he had settled in 1783 and where he wrote his posthumously published *Autobiography*. He returned to England in 1793 and died in London, 16 January 1794.

Bury, J. B., ed., Edward Gibbon, *History of the Decline and Fall of the Roman Empire*, 7 vols (1896–1900, rev. 1909–14).

Cradock, P. B., ed., *The English Essays of Edward Gibbon* (Oxford, 1972). (All the English writings except the autobiographical materials and the *Decline and Fall*.)

Murray, J., ed., *The Autobiographies of Edward Gibbon* (1896). (Prints the original six drafts from which Lord Sheffield compiled Gibbon's *Autobiography* in 1796.)

Bonnard, G. A., ed., Edward Gibbon, *Memoirs of my Life* (1966). (A rearrangement of the Sheffield materials.)

Low, D. M., ed., *Gibbon's Journal to January 28th 1763* (1929).

Bonnard, G. A., ed., *Gibbon's Journey from Geneva to Rome* (1961). (Edition of the 1764 Journal.)

Norton, J. E., ed., *The Letters of Edward Gibbon*, 3 vols (1956).

Low, D. M., *Edward Gibbon, 1737–1794* (1937). (Standard biography.)

Cradock, P. B., *Young Edward Gibbon: Gentleman of Letters* (Baltimore, 1982). (Authoritative account of Gibbon to the age of thirty-five.)

See: Bond, H. L., *The Literary Art of Edward Gibbon* (Oxford, 1960).
        (Sensitive and shrewd.)
        Braudy, L. B., *Narrative Form in History and Fiction: Hume, Fielding, and
        Gibbon* (Princeton, NJ, 1970). (A stimulating comparative study.)
        Parkinson, R. N., *Edward Gibbon* (New York, 1973). (An enthusiastic
        account, containing good literary criticism.)

HARTLEY, David (1705–57), son of an Anglican clergyman, was born at Halifax,
and educated at Bradford Grammar School and Jesus College, Cambridge. He
practised as a physician in London from 1735 to 1742, then moved to Bath,
where he remained until his death on 28 August 1757. In addition to his own
notable philosophical work, *Observations on Man* (1749), he wrote a few
pamphlets on medical matters.

HOGARTH, William (1697–1764), born in Smithfield, the son of an unsuccessful
schoolmaster and hack-writer, was apprenticed to an engraver, and set himself
up in this trade about 1720. His early work was engraved book-illustrations,
satirical plates, and trade items, but in the later 1720s he began painting
'conversation pieces' and other works in oils. In 1729 he eloped with and
married the daughter of Sir James Thornhill, the leading English painter of that
day, and in 1734 he inherited and revitalized his father-in-law's painting
academy. His reputation was established by sets of paintings and engravings on
'modern moral subjects', including *A Harlot's Progress* (1732), *A Rake's Progress*
(1735), *Marriage à la Mode* (1745), and *Industry and Idleness* (1747).
Unsuccessfully seeking recognition as a serious history painter, he adorned the
walls of St Bartholomew's Hospital with biblical paintings in 1736; he painted
oil portraits in the 1730s and 1740s which are much admired today, but were
not highly regarded then. His aesthetic treatise, *The Analysis of Beauty* (1753),
was generally received with indifference or ridicule. In 1757 he was appointed
Serjeant-Painter to the King, an office once held by his father-in-law. He died
on 25 October 1764 in Leicester Square, London.

        Burke, J., ed., William Hogarth, *The Analysis of Beauty, with the Rejected
        Passages from the Manuscript Drafts and Autobiographical Notes* (Oxford,
        1955).
        Paulson, R., ed., *Hogarth's Graphic Works*, 2 vols (New Haven, 1965).
        (*Catalogue raisonné* and commentary.)
        Paulson, R., *Hogarth: His Life, Art, and Times*, 2 vols (New Haven,
        1971). (Standard critical biography.)
See: Antal, F., *Hogarth and his Place in European Art* (1962). (Valuable as an
        exploration of Hogarth's connections with earlier and later artists.)
        Paulson, R., *The Art of Hogarth* (1975). (Well-illustrated introduction.)
        Burke, J., *Hogarth and Reynolds: A Contrast in English Art Theory* (1943).
        (On their antagonistic aesthetic notions.)

HUME, David (1711–76), born at Ninewells, Berwickshire, lost his father, a landed
gentleman, in infancy; he was educated at Edinburgh University, where he
developed a passion for literature and philosophy. Between 1734 and 1737 he
lived frugally in rural France and wrote his *Treatise of Human Nature*, which
aroused little notice on publication (1739–40). From 1737 to 1751 he lived in
hardly less frugal retirement at Ninewells, except for brief periods as a tutor in
an English noble family, as a civilian member of the expeditionary force sent to
attack Lorient, and as the secretary of a military embassy to Vienna and Turin.

A stream of publications gradually established his reputation as a philosopher: *Essays, Moral and Political* (1741–42), with additional essays (1748), *Philosophical Essays concerning the Human Understanding* including the notorious 'Essay on Miracles' (1748), reissued as *An Enquiry*, etc. (1758), *An Enquiry concerning the Principles of Morals* (1751), *Political Discourses* (1752), and *Four Dissertations* (1757), of which one is *A Natural History of Religion*. From 1751 he lived in Edinburgh; his reputation as a freethinker excluded him from the academic posts which he desired, but his appointment as Keeper of the Advocates' Library facilitated the writing of his *History of Great Britain* (1754–61), the work that confirmed his literary reputation and rendered him 'opulent'. While Secretary to the British Embassy in Paris from 1763 to 1766, he was fêted in literary circles; he helped to protect Rousseau from persecution and in 1766 brought him to England, but the Frenchman's unbalanced mental condition led to a famous public quarrel between the two philosophers. Hume died in Edinburgh on 25 August 1776, the calmness of his death causing offence to the pious. His freethinking *Dialogues on Natural Religion* were published in 1779, though written by 1751.

> Green, T. H., and T. H. Grose, eds, David Hume, *Philosophical Works*, 4 vols (1874–75).
> Selby-Bigge, L. A., ed., David Hume, *A Treatise of Human Nature*, 2nd edn., rev. P. H. Nidditch (Oxford, 1978).
> Selby-Bigge, L. A., ed., David Hume, *Enquiries concerning the Human Understanding and concerning the Principles of Morals*, 3rd edn., rev. P. H. Nidditch (Oxford, 1975).
> Colver, A. W., ed., *The Natural History of Religion*, and *Dialogues concerning Natural Religion*, ed. J. V. Price (Oxford, 1976).
> Greig, J. Y. T., *The Letters of David Hume*, 2 vols (Oxford, 1932).
> Klibansky, R., and E. C. Mossner, eds, *New Letters of David Hume* (Oxford, 1954).
> Mossner, E. C., *The Life of David Hume* (1954). (Standard biography.)

See:
> Kemp Smith, N., *The Philosophy of David Hume* (1941). (Authoritative.)
> Pears, D. F., ed., *David Hume: A Symposium* (1963). (Lively radio talks, each exploring a different aspect of Hume's work.)
> Price, J. V., *David Hume* (New York, 1969). (Brief, but balanced introduction to the life and work.)
> Noxon, J., *Hume's Philosophical Development: A Study of his Methods* (Oxford, 1973). (On Hume's development of a scientific method learned from Newton.)
> Forbes, D., *Hume's Philosophical Politics* (Cambridge, 1975). (Systematic study of Hume's philosophical and historical writings as they are related to the politics of his day.)
> Livingston, D., and J. T. King, eds, *Hume: a Re-evaluation* (1976). (Wide variety of papers by members of the Hume Society.)

HURD, Richard (1720–1808), son of a Staffordshire farmer, was educated at Brewood Grammar School and Emmanuel College, Cambridge; he became a Fellow of Emmanuel in 1742. His elaborately annotated editions of Horace's *Arts Poetics* (1749) and *Epistola ad Augustam* (1751) expressed admiration for, and were admired by, the formidable William Warburton, who thereafter did much to further Hurd's literary and ecclesiastical career. Hurd's *Moral and Political Dialogues* (1759–65), a series of imaginary conversations, were much admired, as too was his most important work, *Letters on Chivalry and Romance*

(1762). He was consecrated Bishop of Lichfield and Coventry in 1774 and translated to Worcester in 1781, where he remained till his death on 28 May 1808.

> Trowbridge, H., ed., Richard Hurd, *Letters on Chivalry and Romance* (Los Angeles, 1963).

HUTCHESON, Francis (1694–1746), son and grandson of Presbyterian ministers, was born in County Down, and educated at schools in Ireland and at the University of Glasgow. Returning to Ireland, he started a private academy, and published his first philosophical works, *An Inquiry into the Original of our Ideas of Beauty and Virtue* (1725) and *An Essay on the Nature and Conduct of the Passions and Affections, with Illustrations of the Moral Sense* (1728). These writings led to his unsolicited election in 1729 to the Chair of Moral Philosophy at Glasgow, which he occupied until his death, Adam Smith being one of his pupils. His *System of Moral Philosophy* was published in 1742.

> See: Blackstone, W. T., *Hutcheson and Contemporary Ethical Theory* (Atlanta, 1965).

JONES, Sir William (1746–94), son of a famous mathematician and friend of Newton, was born in Westminster, and educated at Harrow and University College, Oxford; he was elected Fellow of his college in 1766 and soon acquired the reputation of a considerable orientalist. In 1770 he translated a Persian historical work into French and published his *Traité sur la poésie orientale*; these were rapidly followed by his *Dissertation sur la littérature orientale* and *Grammar of the Persian Language* (both 1771), his *Poems* (1772), mostly translated from oriental languages, and accompanied by critical essays, and his *Poeseos Asiaticae Commentariorum Libri Sex* (1774), the work that set the seal on his reputation. He was elected a Fellow of the Royal Society in 1772. After being called to the Bar in 1774, he wrote extensively on legal matters. In 1783 he was knighted and appointed judge of the High Court in Calcutta, where he renewed and extended his oriental studies. He founded the Bengal Asiatic Society in 1784; his eleven annual discourses as President of the Society, his contributions to the Society's *Asiatick Researches* and *Asiatick Miscellany*, and his translations of Indian laws and literature mark an era in Western study of Indian society, language, literature, philosophy, and religion. He died in Calcutta on 27 April 1794.

> Cannon, G. H., ed., *The Letters of Sir William Jones*, 2 vols (Oxford, 1970).

> See: Cannon, G. H., *Oriental Jones: A Biography of Sir William Jones* (1964)

KAMES, Henry Home, Lord (1696–1782), son of a country gentleman, was born at Kames in Berwickshire. Mostly self-educated, he became an advocate at the Scottish Bar, obtained notice through his writings on legal matters, and was raised to the Bench with the title Lord Kames in 1752; despite increasing infirmities, he continued to exercise his judicial functions until his death on 27 December 1782. He wrote much on the law and on many other subjects; among his more notable publications were *Essays upon Several Subjects concerning British Antiquities* (1747), *Essays on the Principles of Morality and Natural Religion* (1751), *Elements of Criticism* (1762), and *Sketches of the History of Man* (1774); his handbook *The Gentleman Farmer* (1776) was based partly upon his own experience as an agricultural improver.

See: Lehmann, W. C., *Henry Home, Lord Kames, and the Scottish Enlightenment* (The Hague, 1971). (A study of Kames's work in its social and intellectual context.)
Ross, I. S., *Lord Kames and the Scotland of his Day* (Oxford, 1972). (Biography and critical study, vividly displaying the range of Kames's interests.)

LAW, William (1686–1761), son of a grocer, was born at King's Cliffe, near Stamford; he was educated at home by his pious parents, and at Emmanuel College, Cambridge, where he was ordained and elected Fellow in 1711. As his Jacobite conscience prevented him from taking the oath of allegiance to George I, he held no preferment in the Church of England after 1714. A vigorous controversialist, he wrote against Bishop Hoadly during the Bangorian Controversy (1717), against Mandeville's moral philosophy (1723), against Tindal's freethinking (1731), and, in *The Absolute Unlawfulness of the Stage-Entertainment Fully Demonstrated* (1726), against the theatre; but his more durable work was in manuals of devotion such as *A Practical Treatise upon Christian Perfection* (1726) and his famous *Serious Call to a Devout and Holy Life* (1728). He acted as tutor to Edward Gibbon's father and aunts; when, in 1740, he retired to King's Cliffe to follow a strictly-regulated religious life, one of these aunts became his disciple. As a result of his study of Jacob Behmen in the late 1730s, there is a deeper strain of mysticism in Law's later writings, such as *The Way to Divine Knowledge* (1752) and *The Spirit of Love* (1752–54). He died at King's Cliffe on 9 April 1761.

The Works of the Reverend William Law, 9 vols (1762, repr. 1892–93).

See: Overton, J. H., *William Law, Nonjuror and Mystic* (1881). (Standard biography.)
Rudolph, E. P., *William Law* (Boston, 1980). (Readable short account of the life and work.)

LOCKE, John (1632–1704), son of an attorney who fought on the Parliamentary side in the Civil War, was born in Somerset, and educated at Westminster and Christ Church, Oxford. After taking his degree he became a Student (i.e. Fellow) of Christ Church, held various teaching posts in the university, studied medicine, formed a lifelong friendship with the great scientist Robert Boyle, and became acquainted with other scientists who later formed the Royal Society; Locke himself was elected to the Society in 1668. By this time, he was friend, physician, and confidential secretary to Anthony Ashley Cooper, afterwards first Earl of Shaftesbury; when Shaftesbury was Lord Chancellor and President of the Board of Trade, 1672–73, Locke served him in important public business. After Shaftesbury's ruin and death in 1683, Locke retired to the Netherlands where he remained until the Glorious Revolution of 1688 made it safe for him to return to England and publish various philosophical and political writings upon which he had been working for some years; these included three *Letters concerning Toleration* (1689–90), the first of which had been published earlier in the Netherlands in a Latin version, *Two Treatises on Government* (1690), and that *Essay concerning Human Understanding* (1690), which rapidly made him the leading philosopher of his age. There followed *Some Thoughts concerning Education* (1693), and *The Reasonableness of Christianity* (1695), supplemented by two *Vindications* (1695 and 1697) in reply to hostile criticism. His writings on currency reform were the basis for legislation in 1696; from 1696 to 1700 he was the most energetic member of a newly-formed

government Council of Trade. He died at High Laver, Essex, on 28 October
1704,

The Works of John Locke, 10 vols (1823, repr. 1963).
Nidditch, P. H., ed., John Locke, An Essay concerning Human
Understanding (Oxford, 1975).
Laslett, P., ed., John Locke, Two Treatises on Government (Cambridge,
1960).
Ramsey, I. T., ed., John Locke, The Reasonableness of Christianity, with
A Discourse on Miracles, and part of A Third Letter concerning Toleration
(1958).
Laslett, P., ed., Locke on Politics, Religion and Education (New York,
1965).
Yolton, J. W., ed., The Locke Reader (1977). (Both useful selections.)
De Beer, E. S., ed., The Correspondence of John Locke, 8 vols (Oxford,
1976–   ). (In progress.)
Cranston, M., John Locke, a Biography (1957). (The standard work.)
Dewhurst, K., John Locke (1632–1704), Physician and Philosopher: A
Medical Biography (1963). (On the extent to which Locke's
epistemology was shaped by his studies of medicine and physiology.)

See: Aaron, R. I., John Locke (1937, rev. 1955). (The most authoritative
survey of Locke's philosophy; concentrates chiefly on the theory of
knowledge.)
James D. G., The Life of Reason: Hobbes, Locke, Bolingbroke (1949).
Gough, J. W., John Locke's Political Philosophy (Oxford, 1950).
Mabbott, J. D., John Locke (1973). (Good introduction to the whole of
Locke's philosophy.)
MacLean, K., John Locke and the English Literature of the Eighteenth
Century (New Haven, 1936). (Traces the influence of Locke's theories
of knowledge in literature.)

LOWTH, Robert (1710–87), born at Winchester, was educated at Winchester College
and New College, Oxford; after taking orders he held a series of comfortable
livings. He was Professor of Poetry at Oxford, 1741-50; his Praelectiones de
Sacra Poesi Hebraeorum were first published in 1753, and translated by G.
Gregory as Lectures on the Sacred Poetry of the Hebrews (1787). He also wrote a
Life of William of Wykeham (1758) and a frequently-reprinted Short Introduction
to English Grammar (1762), and he applied his sensitive understanding of
Hebrew poetry to an annotated translation of Isaiah (1778). From 1766 he was
appointed successively to the bishoprics of St David's, Oxford, and London;
he was offered the Archbishopric of Canterbury in 1783, but refused it on
account of declining health; he died in London on 3 November 1787.

See: Hepworth, B., Robert Lowth (Boston, 1978). (Handy account of life and
works.)

MANDEVILLE, Bernard (1670–1733), was born in the Netherlands, took his degree
as doctor of medicine at the University of Leyden, and practised as a physician
in London without much success; he died on 21 January 1733. His poem The
Grumbling Hive (1705) was republished in 1714, together with a longer prose
Inquiry into the Origin of Moral Virtue and a series of long notes, under the title
The Fable of the Bees; this augmented work was then revised and reissued under
the same title in 1723, with the addition of An Essay on Charity and Charity

Schools and *A Search into the Nature of Society*. Mandeville's Hobbesian system of morality was now attacked by John Dennis, Francis Hutcheson, William Law, and many others, but he continued to elaborate his system with *The Fable of the Bees, Part II* (1729). Berkeley attacked him in *Alciphron* (1732), to which Mandeville replied in *A Letter to Dion* (1732). Mandeville's other writings include medical works, such as *A Treatise of the Hypochondriack and Hysteric Passions, vulgarly call'd the Hypo in Men and Vapours in Women* (1711), and satires, such as *The Virgin Unmask'd* (1709) and *A Modest Defense of Public Stews* (1724).

> Kaye, F. B., ed., Bernard Mandeville, *The Fable of the Bees, or Private Vices, Publick Benefits*, 2 vols (Oxford, 1924). (With a full commentary, critical, historical, and explanatory.)

See: Monro, H., *The Ambivalence of Bernard Mandeville* (Oxford, 1975). (Contrasts the 'two Mandevilles': ascetic and cynic.)
Horne, T. A., *The Social Thought of Bernard Mandeville: Virtue and Commerce in Early Eighteenth-Century England* (1978). (Relates Mandeville to French moralists, to Shaftesbury, and to mercantilism.)

MONBODDO, James Burnett, Lord (1714–99), was born at Monboddo, Kincardineshire, and educated at Aberdeen and Edinburgh Universities; in 1737 he was called to the Scottish Bar and in 1767 raised to the judicial Bench as Lord Monboddo. He wrote *Of the Origin and Progress of Language* (1773–92) and *Antient Metaphysics, or the Science of Universals* (1779–99); in both works he professes deep veneration for the literature, learning, and philosophy of the ancient Greeks, whose simplicity and virtue he sought to emulate in his own way of life. He died in Edinburgh on 26 May 1799.

See   Cloyd, E. L., *James Burnett, Lord Monboddo* (Oxford, 1972). (Standard biography and analysis of Monboddo's thought.)

NEWTON, Sir Isaac (1642–1727), the posthumous son of a landed gentleman of small estate, was born at Woolsthorp, Lincolnshire, and educated at Grantham Grammar School and Trinity College, Cambridge. From early youth he was a brilliant mathematician: by 1666 he had begun his optical experiments, conceived his theories of gravitation and of colour, and had discovered the elements of differential and integral calculus. In 1667 he was elected Fellow of Trinity, in 1669 Lucasian Professor of Mathematics at Cambridge, and in 1672 Fellow of the Royal Society, shortly after which he delivered the paper describing his famous experiment with the prism; during this period he made his first reflecting telescopes. Newton's published theories on optics in 1672 and 1675–76 gave rise to a controversy with Robert Hooke which was later renewed when Hooke claimed to have anticipated Newton's work on the theory of gravitation. The discoveries by which Newton confirmed this theory and proved his general laws of motion were made at various times between 1665 (when he sat in his garden at Woolsthorp and, according to Voltaire, saw the apple drop) and 1685, but it was only under pressure from his friend Edmund Halley that he agreed to publish his *Philosophiae Naturalis Principia Mathematica* (1687), with Halley undertaking the expense and labour of seeing the work into print. New editions appeared in 1713 (edited by Roger Cotes) and in 1726 (edited by Henry Pemberton), both significantly revised by Newton; the work was translated into English by Andrew Motte in 1729. Newton, who was a Whig, began to take active part in public affairs after the 1688 Revolution: at various times between 1689 and 1705 he was Member of

Parliament for Cambridge University; in 1695 he and John Locke were
engaged by the government to draw up a scheme for currency reform, the
successful implementation of which was in great part due to Newton's energy
and efficiency as Warden (1696) and Master (1699) of the Royal Mint. He
resigned his Cambridge posts in 1701, by which time he was living mainly in
London; in 1703 he was elected President of the Royal Society, and he was
annually re-elected to this office until his death. His *Opticks*, the fruit of forty
years' work in this field, was published in 1704; revised editions followed in
1706 (translated into Latin by Samuel Clarke), and in 1718, 1721, and 1730. He
was knighted by Queen Anne in 1705. His later years, from 1705, were soured
by a disagreement with the Astronomer-Royal John Flamsteed over the
publication of Flamsteed's work, and by a far more widely-reverberant and
even less edifying quarrel with the great German philosopher Leibniz over
which of them had first invented calculus. Newton died on 20 March 1727 and
was buried in Westminster Abbey. After his death were published a few of the
theological and historical writings which had occupied much of his time for
some sixty years: these included *The Chronology of Ancient Kingdoms* (published
in 1728 to correct an imperfect version printed in France without Newton's
authority in 1725), *An Historical Account of Two Notable Corruptions of the
Scriptures* (sent to Locke in 1690, published in 1754), and *Observations upon the
Prophecies of Daniel and the Apocalypse* (1733). Newton wrote extensively upon
alchemy, apparently with no intention of publication.

> *Opticks, or a Treatise of the Reflections, Refractions, Inflections, and Colours
> of Light*, 4th edn (1704), repr. (1931).
> *Sir Isaac Newton's Mathematical Principles of Natural Philosophy and his
> System of the World*, trans. A. Motte (1729), rev. F. Cajori (Berkeley,
> 1947). (With a historical and explanatory appendix.)
> Cohen, I. B., ed., *Isaac Newton's Papers and Letters on Natural Philosophy,
> and Related Documents* (Cambridge, 1958).
> Turnbull, H. W., *et al.*, eds, *The Correspondence of Isaac Newton*, 7 vols
> (Cambridge, 1959–77).
> Voltaire, *The Elements of Sir Isaac Newton's Philosophy*, trans. J. Hanna
> (1738, repr., with index, 1967). (The French edition was the most
> famous and influential popularization of Newton; the reprinted
> English version still makes a lively introduction.)
> Westfall, R. S., *Never at Rest: A Biography of Isaac Newton* (Cambridge,
> 1980). (The definitive scientific biography.)

See: Nicholson, M. H., *Newton demands the Muse: Newton's 'Opticks' and the
      Eighteenth Century Poets* (Princeton, NJ, 1946). (On the poets'
      reception of Newton's theories of light and colour.)
      Butts, R. E., and J. W. Davis, *The Methodological Heritage of Newton*
      (Oxford, 1970). (Seminar papers on various aspects of Newton's
      influence upon some eighteenth-century philosophers.)
      Manuel, F. E., *The Religion of Isaac Newton* (Oxford, 1974). (A study of
      an aspect of Newton's thought far more highly regarded by Newton
      himself than by his modern students.)
      Dobbs, B. J. T., *The Foundations of Newton's Alchemy, or 'The Hunting of
      the Greene Lyon'* (Cambridge, 1975). (Argues that Newton was
      seriously committed to alchemy.)

PRICE, Richard (1723–91), son of a Congregationalist minister, was born in
    Glamorgan; after training in several academies for Dissenters, he practised his

ministry in various London congregations. His philosophical treatise *A Review of the Principal Questions in Morals* appeared in 1757. He was encouraged by the Earl of Shelburne, Priestley's patron, and he became a close friend of Priestley, whose unitarian opinions he partly shared; he was also a close friend of Franklin, and supported the American colonists in such publications as *Observations on Civil Liberty and the Justice and Policy of the War with America* (1776), the work that made him famous in his day. His writings on national finance are thought to have influenced William Pitt to re-establish the Sinking fund in 1786. His welcome to the French Revolution in a sermon *On the Love of our Country* (1789) began the controversy that gave rise to Burke's *Reflections*. Price died in London on 19 April 1791.

> Raphael, D. D., ed., Richard Price, *A Review of the Principal Questions in Morals* (Oxford, 1948).

> See: Thomas, D. O., *The Honest Mind: The Thought and Work of Richard Price* (Oxford, 1977). (Fully reveals Price's versatility.)

PRIESTLEY, Joseph (1733–1804), son of a cloth-dresser, was born at a farmhouse in the West Riding of Yorkshire. He was educated at Batley Grammar School and prepared for the Presbyterian ministry at the Daventry Academy. Between 1755 and 1761 he was minister at Needham Market in Suffolk and at Nantwich in Cheshire; from 1761 to 1767 he was tutor in languages and *belles-lettres* at the Warrington Academy for Dissenters; from 1767 to 1772 he was minister of Mill Hill Chapel, Leeds. During this period he gained a considerable reputation as a scientist with such works as *The History and Present State of Electricity* (1767, enlarged 1769 and 1775) and *The History and Present State of Discoveries relating to Vision, Light and Colours* (1772); he also wrote, in addition to many theological works, *A Course of Lectures on the Theory of Language and Universal Grammar* (1762), *An Essay on a Course of Liberal Education* (1765), *A Course of Lectures on Oratory and Criticism* (1777), and *An Essay on the First Principles of Government* (1768), to which Jeremy Bentham considered himself indebted for the phrase 'the greatest happiness of the greatest number'. From 1772 to 1780 Priestley acted as librarian and 'literary companion' to the Earl of Shelburne, and superintended the education of Shelburne's son. Priestley continued his scientific work, and, in his *Experiments and Observations on Different Kinds of Air* (1774–86), published his discovery of no fewer than nine new gases, including the one later called oxygen. Profoundly influenced by Hartley's *Observations on Man* (1749), which he ranked next to the Bible, he published a popular abridgement of Hartley's work (1775), and developed Hartley's system in wholly unorthodox directions with his *Disquisitions relating to Matter and Spirit* and *Doctrine of Philosophical Necessity Illustrated* (both 1777). On quitting Shelburne's service he became minister of the New Meeting in Birmingham. His increasingly unorthodox religious beliefs, as expressed in his *History of the Corruptions of Christianity* (1782) and *History of the Early Opinions concerning Jesus Christ* (1786), brought him to unitarianism. His political opinions were somewhat radical too: he vindicated the principles of the French Revolution in *Letters to Burke* (1791); in the same year his house in Birmingham was burned by a 'Church and King' mob after he had attended a public dinner to commemorate the fall of the Bastille. He moved to London and then, in 1794, to Northumberland, Pennsylvania, where he died on 6 Feburay 1804.

> Rutt, J. T., ed., *The Theological and Miscellaneous Writings of Joseph Priestley*, 25 vols (1817–32).

Passmore, J. A., ed., *Priestley's Writings on Philosophy, Science, and Politics* (1965). (Wide-ranging selection from this versatile writer.)
Schofield, R. E., ed., *A Scientific Autobiography of Joseph Priestley* (1966). (A selection from Priestley's correspondence, edited with a commentary to give an account of his scientific career.)
Lindsay, J., ed., *Autobiography of Joseph Priestley* (1970). (Priestley's *Memoir* and some other writings, with a substantial Introduction.)
Gibbs, F. W., *Joseph Priestley, Adventurer in Science and Champion of Truth* (1965). (Lively, broad survey.)
Kieft, L., and B. R. Willeford, eds, *Joseph Priestley, Scientist, Theologian and Metaphysician* (1980). (Seminar papers.)

REID, Thomas (1710–96), son of a Presbyterian minister, was born at Strachan, Kincardineshire, and was educated at Marischal College, St Andrews, where he was librarian from 1733 to 1736. He became minister of a parish near Aberdeen; then, in 1751, Professor of Philosophy at King's College, Aberdeen. The success of his *Inquiry into the Human Mind, on the Principles of Common Sense* (1764), an answer to Hume's scepticism, resulted in his appointment in the same year to succeed Adam Smith in the Chair of Moral Philosophy at Glasgow, where he remained till his death on 7 October 1796. He published his Glasgow lectures in *Essays on the Intellectual Powers of Man* (1785) and *Essays on the Active Powers of Man* (1788).

Kivey, P., ed., *Thomas Reid, Lectures on the Fine Arts* (The Hague, 1973).
Lehrer, K., and R. E. Beanblossom, *Thomas Reid's Inquiry and Essays* (Indianapolis, 1975). (A handy paperback collection, with a long and useful introduction.)

REYNOLDS, Sir Joshua (1723–92), son of an Anglican clergyman and schoolmaster, was born at Plympton in Devon, and educated at the grammar school kept by his father. From 1740 to 1744 he was apprenticed to the portrait-painter Thomas Hudson in London; from 1750 to 1752 he studied in Italy; between these periods he lived and painted in Plymouth. After setting up his first studio in London in 1752, his reputation and fees as a portrait-painter rose steadily; he moved in fashionable society and became a close friend of Goldsmith, Burke, and particularly Johnson, to whose periodical the *Idler* he contributed three papers in 1759, and for whose benefit he founded the Literary Club in 1764. He enlarged his practice and employed a number of assistants in the great studio in Leicester Square, which he occupied from 1760 to his death. His pre-eminent position in English art was recognized when, on the incorporation of the Royal Academy in 1768, he was elected its first President and s knighted shortly afterwards. His presidential *Discourses* to the Academy, delivered between 1769 and 1790, were widely admired and often reprinted. He died on 23 February at his house in Leicester Square.

Wark, R. R., ed., *Sir Joshua Reynolds, Discourses on Art* (1959, new edn, New Haven, 1975).
Hilles, F. W., ed., *The Letters of Sir Joshua Reynolds* (Cambridge, 1929).

See: Hilles, F. W., *The Literary Career of Sir Joshua Reynolds* (Cambridge, 1936). (On Reynolds's criticism and aesthetics.)
Waterhouse, E., *Reynolds* (1941). (The fullest *catalogue raisonné*.)
Burke, J., *Hogarth and Reynolds: A Contrast in English Art Theory* (1943). (On their antagonistic aesthetic notions.)
Hudson, D., *Sir Joshua Reynolds* (1958). (Readable biography.)

Waterhouse, E., *Reynolds* (1973). (A shorter, revised version of
Waterhouse's 1941 work, with better-quality illustrations.)

SHAFTESBURY, Anthony Ashley Cooper, third Earl of (1671–1713) was born at
the London house of his grandfather, the first Earl of Shaftesbury; his early
education was supervised by his grandfather's friend John Locke, and he spent
three years at Winchester College. He travelled in France, Germany, and Italy,
sat as Member for Poole in the House of Commons from 1695 to 1698, and,
after succeeding to his earldom in 1699, was as active a Member of the House
of Lords as his poor health would allow. He was always more interested in
philosophy than politics: his first publication was a *Preface* to the *Select Sermons*
(1698) of the Cambridge Platonist Benjamin Whichcote; it was followed by *A
Letter concerning Enthusiasm* (1708), *Sensus Communis: An Essay on the Freedom of
Wit and Humour, The Moralists, a Philosophical Rhapsody* (both 1709), and
Soliloquy, or Advice to an Author (1710); his *Inquiry concerning Virtue* was
published without authority by his protégé John Toland. All these works,
except the *Preface*, were gathered in *Characteristicks of Men, Manners, Opinions,
Times* (1711), a collection which also included *Miscellaneous Reflections on the
preceding Treatises, and other Critical Subjects*. Shaftesbury travelled to Naples in
1711 for the sake of his health, but died there on 15 February 1713. His last
work was the *Historical Draught or Tablature of the Judgement of Hercules* (1713);
this, together with revised versions of the texts published in 1711, was included
in the second edition of *Characteristicks* (1714).

> Rand, B., ed., Shaftesbury, *Second Characters, or the Language of Forms*
> (1914).
> Rand, B., ed., *The Life, Unpublished Letters, and Philosophical Regimen of
> Anthony, Earl of Shaftesbury* (1900).
> Robertson, J. M., ed., Shaftesbury, *Characteristicks of Men, Manners,
> Opinions, Times*, 2 vols (1900).

> See: Brett, R. L., *The Third Earl of Shaftesbury: A Study in Eighteenth-Century
> Literary Theory* (1951). (On Shaftesbury's aesthetic notions and their
> influence upon poetry and criticism down to Coleridge.)

SMITH, Adam (1723–90), son of a writer to the signet, was born at Kircaldy and
educated at Glasgow University, where Frances Hutcheson was one of his
teachers, and at Balliol College, Oxford. Between 1751 and 1764 he occupied
first the Chair of Logic and then the Chair of Moral Philosophy at Glasgow; his
Theory of Moral Sentiments was published in 1759, with a third edition in 1761
to which was added *A Dissertation on the Origin of Languages*. During this period
he became a close friend of David Hume; years later in 1777, when Smith
published a short memoir of his friend, his description of Hume's virtues and
of the peacefulness of his last illness and death caused great offence to the
orthodox. Between 1764 and 1766 Smith was in France and Switzerland as
travelling tutor to the young Duke of Buccleugh. In 1767 he was elected as
Fellow of the Royal Society, by which time he had retired to Kircaldy to work
on his *Inquiry into the Nature and Causes of the Wealth of Nations*, a treatise which
obtained great authority very soon after its first publication in 1776; it was
thought to have given hints to Lord North in his framing of legislation, and its
principles were certainly studied and put into practice by William Pitt. In 1777
Smith was appointed to the lucrative post of Commissioner of Customs in
Edinburgh, where he lived till he death on 17 July 1790. A volume of *Essays on
Philosophical Subjects*, containing also a *Life* by Dugald Stewart appeared in 1795.

Raphael, D. D., et al., eds, *The Glasgow Edition of the Works and Correspondence of Adam Smith*, 6 vols (Oxford, 1976–80).
Rae, J., *Life of Adam Smith* (1895, repr. with Introduction by J. Viner, 1965).

See: Campbell, T. D., *Adam Smith's Science of Morals* (1971).
Lindgren, J. R., *The Social Philosophy of Adam Smith* (The Hague, 1973).
Hollander, S., *The Economics of Adam Smith* (1973).
Campbell, R. H., and A. S. Skinner, *Adam Smith* (1982). (Handy biographical and critical study.)

TOLAND, John (1670–1722), an Irish convert from Roman Catholicism to Protestantism, studied in Glasgow, Edinburgh, Leyden, and Oxford between 1687 and 1695 His freethinking *Christianity not Mysterious* (1696) aroused much controversy and was ordered to be burnt by the common hangman in Dublin. Thereafter he followed a somewhat precarious literary career; he gave voice to extreme political views in editing the prose works and writing the lives of several seventeenth-century republicans, including Milton; in a flood of other miscellaneous writings he denounced churchmen, Tories, and Jacobites, challenged the authority of the Bible and the truth of revelation, and propounded his own pantheistic notions.

WARTON, Joseph (1722–1800), son of an Oxford Professor of Poetry and brother of Thomas Warton (below), was educated at Winchester College and Oriel College, Oxford. After ordination, he served as curate or rector of various parishes, published two volumes of verse (1744 and 1746), translated Virgil's *Eclogues* and *Georgics* (1753), and, at the invitation of Johnson, contributed two dozen critical essays to the *Adventurer* (1752–54). He was appointed second master at Winchester in 1755 and headmaster in 1766, whereupon he almost discontinued his literary pursuits, except for his important *Essay on the Genius and Writings of Pope* (1756–82); he was a long-standing member of Johnson's literary circle. He resigned his headship in 1793, edited Pope's *Works* (1797), and died at Wickham on 23 February 1800.

See: Pittock, J., *The Ascendancy of Taste: The Achievement of Joseph and Thomas Warton* (1973).

WARTON, Thomas (1728–90), brother of Joseph, was educated at Trinity College, Oxford, and remained an Oxford academic for the rest of his life. From 1745 onwards he wrote a considerable amount of light or lyrical verse, but he gained his literary reputation by his scholarship. His *Observations on the Faerie Queene of Spenser* (1754, enlarged 1762) marked an era in the historical criticism of English literature; he contributed, at Johnson's request, to the *Idler* (1758–59) and later joined Johnson's literary club; he wrote various biographical and topographical antiquarian works; but his most substantial piece of scholarship was his unfinished *History of English Poetry from the Close of the Eleventh to the Commencement of the Eighteenth Century* (1774–81). He became Professor of Poetry at Oxford (1757–67), as his father once had been, and Camden Professor of History (1785–90); also in 1785, he was appointed Poet Laureate, but his most important achievement in that year was the publication of his model edition of Milton's minor poems. He died at Oxford on 20 May 1790.

See: Rinaker, C., *Thomas Warton* (Urbana, 1916).
Pittock, J., *The Ascendancy of Taste: The Achievement of Joseph and Thomas Warton* (1973).

WESLEY, John (1703–91), son of the poet Samuel Wesley, was born in his father's rectory at Epworth, Lincolnshire, and was educated at the Charterhouse and Christ Church, Oxford; he was ordained in 1725 and elected Fellow of Lincoln College in 1726. After a period as curate to his father at Epworth, he returned to Lincoln College to find that his younger brother Charles and some fellow undergraduates had formed a group for religious study and strict observance, nicknamed 'Methodists'; of this group John Wesley soon became leader. With his brother, John undertook a mission to Georgia in 1735, where he associated with Moravian missionaries, whose strict piety much influenced him and where he edited and published his first collection of hymns (1737); after his return to England in 1737, John visited some Moravian communities in Germany. Following the example of George Whitefield, a former member of the Oxford 'Methodist' group, Wesley began open-air preaching in 1737, near Bristol; in this city, in the same year, he laid the foundation-stone of what would become the first Methodist chapel and received a famous reproof from Bishop Butler; at the end of 1739 the first Methodist society was formed in London. Over the next fifty years Wesley continued to preach, to organize Methodist societies, and to open chapels all over Britain, recruiting a strong band of itinerant and resident preachers as he did so; it is said that he preached altogether 40,000 sermons and travelled 250,000 miles. He published collections of his sermons in 1746, 1748, 1750, and 1760, and edited volumes of hymns, the most significant of which was the *Collection of Hymns for the People called Methodists* (1780), but he wrote with copious versatility on other subjects, providing his followers with manuals of history, civil and religious, physics, medicine, and philology, and abridgements of Young's *Night Thoughts*, Milton's *Paradise Lost*, and Henry Brooke's novel *A Fool of Quality*, not to mention more simply devotional works. The first major collection of his writings (1771–74) ran to thirty-two volumes. By his preaching and miscellaneous writing Wesley was undoubtedly the most widely-influential educator of his day. He continued to regard himself as a full member of the Church of England into which he had been ordained, but Methodism gradually grew into a distinct sect, which had separated from the Church of England by the date of Wesley's death, 2 March 1791.

Baker, F. *et al.*, eds, *The Oxford Edition of the Works of John Wesley* (Oxford, 1975–). (In progress.)
The Works of the Rev. John Wesley, 14 vols (1872), repr. 1958).
Curnock, N., ed., *The Journal of the Rev. John Wesley*, 8 vols (1909–16).
Sugden, E. H., ed., *The Standard Sermons of John Wesley*, 4 vols (1921).
Telford, J., ed., *The Letters of the Rev. John Wesley*, 8 vols (1931, repr. 1960).
Southey, R., *The Life of John Wesley*, 2 vols (1820). (A classic of English biography).

See: Green, V. H. H., *John Wesley* (1964). (Admirable short study.)
Baker, F., *John Wesley and the Church of England* (1970). A detailed study, combining biography and theology.)
Ayling, S., *John Wesley* (1979). (Shrewd and sympathetic biography from a secular viewpoint.)

WOOD, Robert (1717–71), an Irishman, travelled extensively in the Near East as a young man; he revisited the area in 1750–52, accompanied by the young and wealthy Englishman James Dawkins and the Italian architect G. B. Borra; the fruits of this journey were published in Wood's nobly-illustrated accounts of *The Ruins of Palmyra* (1753) and *The Ruins of Balbec* (1757) and in his *Essay on the Original Genius of Homer* (1767), which was enlarged by the addition of *A Comparative View of the Antient and Present State of the Troade* in a posthumous edition (1775). He became a Member of Parliament and held minor offices, in one of which he was obliged in 1763 to seize the papers of John Wilkes, who thereupon prosecuted him and secured substantial damages. Wood died at Putney on 9 September 1771.

YOUNG, Edward (1683–1765), son of a future Dean of Salisbury, was educated at Winchester College and at New College and Corpus Christi College, Oxford; in 1708 he became a Fellow of All Souls College. In the following years he attached himself to various political figures in London, where he wrote for the stage with moderate success and published a considerable amount of panegyrical, patriotic, and religious verse; his best-received poems were the satires collected as *Love of Fame: The Universal Passion* (1728). He took holy orders, became in 1728 a Royal Chaplain, and in 1730 Rector of Welwyn, Hertfordshire, where he died on 5 April 1765. At Welwyn he wrote *Night Thoughts* (1742–46), one of the most widely-influential of all English poems; in 1759 appeared his most valuable piece of criticism, *Conjectures on Original Composition*.

> Morley, E. J., ed., *Conjectures on Original Composition* (Manchester, 1918).
> Pettit, H., *The Correspondence of Edward Young* (Oxford, 1971).

See: Wicker, C. V., *Edward Young and the Fear of Death: A Study in Romantic Melancholy* (Albuquerque, 1952).
> Bliss, I. S., *Edward Young* (New York, 1969). (Handy introduction.)

Index

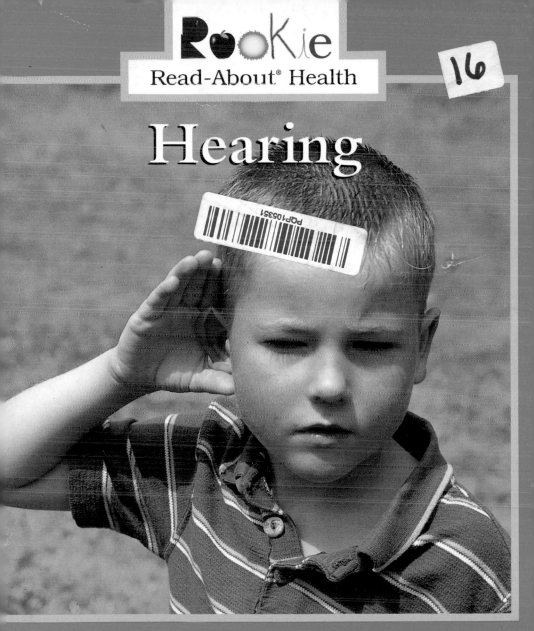

Rookie
Read-About® Health

16

Hearing

PQP105351

By Sharon Gordon

PUSEY SCHOOL